The Best of Cooking

The Best of Cooking

Arne Krüger & Annette Wolter
Photography by Christian Teubner

Larousse Co., Inc.
New York

English edition published by
Hamlyn Publishing

© Copyright Hamlyn Publishing
1977, a division of The Hamlyn
Publishing Group

First published under the title
Koch vergnügen wie noch nie
© Copyright by Gräfe und Unzer
GmbH, München

This edition published in the
United States by
Larousse and Co., Inc.
572 Fifth Avenue,
New York, N.Y. 10036

Fourth impression 1985

ISBN 0-88332-268-4

Phototypeset by Tradespools Ltd.,
Frome, Somerset
Printed in Czechoslovakia

Acknowledgements
The Publishers would like to
thank the following for their
co-operation in supplying two
photographs for pages 4 and 5
of this book:
Mazola Pure Corn Oil – top
photograph
Colman's Mustard – center
photograph

Introduction

In *The Best of Cooking*, the magnificent all-color cook book containing recipes for every occasion, we have created a comprehensive guide to good cooking and eating. In it every recipe is illustrated, to help you in deciding what to cook. The measurements are given in level cups and spoons and the recipes are clearly set out.

From the vast selection of carefully chosen and tested recipes you'll never run out of ideas for what to serve – whatever the occasion. If you are expecting guests, special demands are made on your cooking skills and imagination and this demand has been catered for in the first section which covers recipes for entertaining at home. Whether you're cooking country style and want to serve a delicious homely peasant meal, or entertaining on a grander scale, the recipes are here.

The second section contains a selection of classic gourmet recipes for special occasions, which when prepared and served at home are certainly much less expensive than eating such dishes in a restaurant.

We have to eat every day, so why not serve dishes which the family will really enjoy? In the section on cooking for every day you'll find a host of recipes which will bring variety, flavor and imagination to your daily fare.

At some time in our lives most of us have to consider our waistlines so a section has been included on recipes for healthy eating. Here we have proved that you can consider the calories and still enjoy food. To guide you, the calorie counts have been given alongside each recipe so that you can pursue your gastronomic inclinations with a degree of moderation!

Every cook wants to be able to produce delicious cakes and cookies. Whether you are looking for something sweet or savory, simple or more elaborate the section on home baking is your guide to baking for all occasions.

The final recipe section is devoted to drinks, and it caters for those who have the odd bottle in the cupboard as well as those whose shelves are more abundantly stocked. In this section recipes are given for well known cocktails as well as some for more unusual and adventurous concoctions. There are punches for cold winter evenings, cups for summer parties, aperitifs and long drinks.

In order to ensure that *The Best of Cooking* is as complete as possible we have given hints on the uses of herbs and spices in cooking, on the home freezing of dishes, which is fast becoming an accepted part of every cook's life, and on entertaining.

We hope that this cook book will bring you success and enjoyment in cooking and be one which you will use for many years to come.

Note The herbs used in the recipes are fresh unless otherwise stated.

Arne Krüger
Annette Wolter
Christian Teubner

Contents

Hawaiian Toasts

4 slices toast
2 tablespoons butter
4 slices lean cooked ham
4 canned pineapple rings
4 thin slices cheese
½ teaspoon curry powder
pinch cinnamon
pinch allspice

Spread the slices of toast with butter. Place a slice of ham, a pineapple ring and a cheese slice on each piece of toast, making sure the cheese slices are large enough to cover the pineapple. Cut each in four with a sharp knife. Place on a greased baking sheet, sprinkle with the curry powder, cinnamon and allspice and cook in a moderate oven (350° F) for 20 minutes. Serve warm.
Serves 4

Variation
Use fresh pineapple in place of the canned. It is less sweet and gives the Hawaiian toasts a delicious flavor.

Cucumber Rings

1 cucumber
3 eggs
3 tablespoons half-and-half
½ teaspoon salt
½ teaspoon white pepper
½ teaspoon paprika pepper
2 tablespoons butter
¼ cup chopped cooked ham
1 tablespoon chopped parsley
Garnish
parsley
tomato wedges

Remove the end from the cucumber and cut into ½-inch slices. Scoop out some of the cucumber with a teaspoon, leaving the shells intact. Drain the slices on paper towels and chop 3 tablespoons of the scooped-out cucumber; drain on paper towels. Lightly beat the eggs with the chopped cucumber, half-and-half, salt, pepper and paprika. Melt the butter in a saucepan and cook the egg mixture until set, stirring all the time. Stir in the ham and parsley. With a teaspoon, spoon the egg mixture into the cucumber slices. Arrange on a serving plate and garnish with parsley and tomato wedges.
Serves 4

Canapés

1 large white thinly sliced
  bread loaf
butter
toppings (see method)

Canapés are ideal to serve with pre-lunch or pre-dinner cocktails. Remove the crusts from the bread, spread with butter and cut each slice into three.

Use any of these toppings:

1 A slice of cheese and hard-cooked egg garnished with a walnut.

2 Slices of salami topped with hard-cooked egg.

3 Slices of cooked lean meat, garnished with mayonnaise and chopped pistachio nuts.

4 A slice of pâté topped with chopped green and red peppers and cocktail onions.

5 Cream cheese mixed with sour cream, topped with a lemon slice and parsley.

6 A slice of cooked pork, topped with sliced canned mushrooms and capers and garnished with red pepper.

7 Slices of salami, formed into cornucopias; garnished with hard-cooked egg and parsley.

8 Slices of smoked salmon, formed into rolls, and garnished with mayonnaise, caviar and olives.

9 Shelled shrimp and drained canned pineapple chunks, garnished with a wedge of hard-cooked egg and chopped chives.

10 A slice of cooked ham, topped with half a canned pineapple ring drained and garnished with sour cream and a candied cherry.

11 A slice of cheese, tomato and hard-cooked egg garnished with a slice of canned truffle.

12 A slice of cooked beef, topped with two slices of hard-cooked egg and garnished with sour cream and olives.

Victorian Rolls

4 rolls
½ cup liver sausage
1 sweet dill pickle
2 eggs, hard-cooked
1 tablespoon chopped parsley
2 teaspoons anchovy paste
1 tablespoon tomato paste

Cut the rolls in half and take out the soft centers. Spread with liver sausage. Chop the pickle and hard-cooked eggs and mix with the parsley, anchovy paste and tomato paste. Spoon into each half roll, put the halves back together and place on a greased baking sheet. Bake in a moderately hot oven (400° F) for about 10 minutes. To serve, cut each roll in half.
Serves 4

Variation
The filling in these rolls may be varied. In place of the liver sausage use cooked sausagemeat blended with a pinch of mixed herbs, or a smooth-textured pâté.

Cook's Tip
A speedy way of preparing chopped parsley is to cut the sprigs with a pair of scissors.

Veal Toasts

4 veal cutlets or scallops
juice of 1½ lemons
1 teaspoon salt
1 teaspoon white pepper
¼ cup oil
4 slices white bread
¼ cup mango chutney
2 large tomatoes
4 slices cheese
2 teaspoons paprika pepper
3 tablespoons chopped parsley

Pound the veal and sprinkle on both sides with lemon juice and salt and pepper. Heat the oil in a pan and fry the scallops on each side for 4 minutes. Keep warm.
Toast the bread and spread with mango chutney.
Arrange a veal scallop on each slice, then top with the tomato slices.
Finally, place a slice of cheese over the tomatoes. Place under the broiler until the cheese melts. Garnish with paprika and chopped parsley.
Serves 4

Cook's Tip
To pound the veal scallops, place them between two sheets of wax paper and beat with a meat mallet or wooden rolling pin.

Egg and Shrimp Toasts

4 eggs
pinch salt
3 tablespoons butter
4 slices bread
2 teaspoons prepared
  mustard
8 oz shelled shrimp
Garnish
4 teaspoons tomato ketchup
capers

Beat the eggs with 1 tablespoon water and pinch of salt. Melt 2 tablespoons of the butter in a pan and lightly brown the bread on one side. Place on a serving dish with the browned side uppermost. Keep warm. In the same pan melt the remaining butter and cook the egg mixture, stirring, until lightly set. Spread the fried bread with mustard then spoon on the egg mixture. Lastly top with the shrimp and serve garnished with tomato ketchup and a few capers. Serve with a celery salad.
Serves 4

Cook's Tip
Do not overcook the egg mixture as it will separate. Remove the pan from the heat just as the mixture sets – it will continue cooking in the heat from the pan.

Dutch Toasts

1 small sweet dill pickle
2 small tomatoes
1 cup chopped cooked
  chicken
1 tablespoon chopped parsley
1 tablespoon oil
2 teaspoons capers
½ cup mayonnaise
4 slices bread
½ cucumber
4 slices Gouda cheese

Finely chop the pickle. Put the tomatoes into boiling water for 30–45 seconds; peel and cut into thick slices. Mix the chicken with the pickle, parsley, oil, capers and mayonnaise. Toast the slices of bread. Cover with tomato slices and then spoon on the chicken mixture. Slice the cucumber very thinly and arrange on the chicken mixture. Cover with a slice of cheese and place under the broiler until the cheese melts.
Serves 4

Variation
In place of the cooked chicken use either flaked canned salmon or tuna. Use the oil from the can to moisten the mixture. Season the salmon or tuna with black pepper.

Hors d'oeuvre

Smoked Eel Savories

8 oz smoked eel
2 dessert apples
juice of 1 lemon
$\frac{3}{8}$ cup liver sausage
8 canned pineapple slices
pinch cayenne pepper
Garnish
parsley sprigs

Cut the smoked eel into cubes. Peel, core and slice the apples; sprinkle with lemon juice. Spread each apple slice with some liver sausage, then place a ring of pineapple on each. Sprinkle with a pinch of cayenne pepper and top with a cube of smoked eel. Cut in half and secure each savory with a wooden toothpick.

Serve garnished with parsley sprigs.
Serves 4

Variation
Smoked mackerel fillets may be used in place of the eel. Other fresh or canned fruits may be used in place of the apples and pineapple, but choose fruits which complement each other – try a combination of pears and apricots, or bananas and peaches. If using fresh fruits sprinkle the cut surfaces with lemon juice to prevent them from discoloring.

Cheese Puffs

1 cup water
6 tablespoons butter
pinch salt
$1\frac{1}{2}$ cups sifted all-purpose flour
4 eggs
Filling
$\frac{1}{2}$ cup cream cheese
$\frac{1}{2}$ teaspoon paprika pepper
pinch celery salt
1 tablespoon chopped chives
$\frac{1}{4}$ cup milk
Garnish
stuffed olives, sweet dill pickles, walnut halves, candied cherries and red pepper strips

Put the water in a small pan with the butter and a pinch of salt and bring to the boil.

Remove the pan from the heat and add the flour. Mix with a wooden spoon to form a paste. Return to the heat and beat until the mixture forms a smooth ball. Cool, then beat in the eggs, one at a time. Pipe or spoon the mixture in small balls on to greased baking sheets. Bake in a hot oven (425° F) for about 20 minutes, until well risen and golden brown.
Remove, cut in half and leave to cool on a cake rack. Mix the ingredients together for the filling and pipe some into half the cheese puffs. Top with the remaining puffs and pipe with the rest of the filling. Garnish as shown in the picture.
Serves 4

Cheese and Pepper Toasts

¼ cup butter
½ teaspoon prepared
   mustard
juice of 1 lemon
4 slices bread
4 slices Gouda cheese
1 green pepper
1 red pepper
5 tablespoons thick
   mayonnaise
paprika pepper

Cream the butter with the mustard and lemon juice. Spread on the bread slices. Lay a slice of cheese on each piece of bread. Cut the peppers with a sharp knife into slices, discarding the core and seeds. Arrange on the cheese. Garnish with a piping of mayonnaise and sprinkle with paprika.
Serves 4

Note Do not prepare these more than 1 hour in advance of serving as the cheese will become dry.

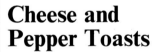

Cook's Tip
To make these hors d'oeuvre more attractive, try to buy a pepper which is both green and red, so that when it is sliced the two colors will show.

Open Sandwiches

1 cup cottage cheese
½ cup milk
1 teaspoon salt
1 onion
3 tablespoons chopped chives
3 tablespoons chopped
   parsley
2 canned peach halves
3 tablespoons butter
2 slices rye bread
2 slices brown bread
Garnish
tomato slices
cucumber slices
dill sprigs
maraschino cherries

Mix the cheese with the milk and salt, until it is smooth, then divide the mixture into three equal parts. With one-third mix the finely chopped onion; with the second third, the chopped herbs; with the final third, the cubed peach halves. Spread on the buttered bread slices, cut into halves and garnish as shown in the picture with tomato and cucumber slices, dill sprigs and cherries.
Serves 4

Variation
Instead of using bread as a base for these open sandwiches try crackers or melba toast for a change. Do not prepare them too far in advance of serving as the crackers will soften.

Sardines on Toast

2 cans sardines in oil
3 tablespoons mayonnaise
2 sprigs parsley
2 sprigs tarragon
2 sprigs dill
2 egg yolks
4 slices bread
$\frac{1}{4}$ cup grated cheese
$\frac{1}{4}$ cup butter
Garnish
parsley sprig

Mash the sardines and oil with the mayonnaise and mix until smooth. Chop the herbs finely and mix into the sardine mixture. Beat in the egg yolks. Toast the bread. Spread the sardine mixture on to the toast. Sprinkle with cheese and dot with butter. Place under the broiler until heated through and the cheese melts. Serve garnished with parsley.
Serves 4

Cook's Tip
The egg whites left from this recipe can be used to make meringues or a meringue topping for a dessert. Beat with $\frac{1}{2}$ cup sugar until stiff.

Sausage and Cheese Kebabs

1 (8-oz) can pimientos
1 green pepper
1 lb continental sausage
$\frac{1}{2}$ teaspoon white pepper
pinch dry mustard
4 oz Edam cheese
$\frac{1}{4}$ cup oil
2 tablespoons butter

Drain and slice the pimientos. Halve the green pepper and discard the core and seeds. Cut the flesh into cubes. Cut the sausage into $\frac{1}{2}$-inch cubes and sprinkle with the pepper and mustard.
Cut the cheese into cubes the same size as the sausage. On each piece of sausage place a cube of cheese, then a slice of pimiento and a slice of green pepper. Spear with a toothpick. Heat the oil and butter in a frying pan and fry the kebabs until lightly browned on all sides. Drain on paper towels and serve hot.
Serves 4

Variation
These sausage and cheese kebabs may be served cold and without being fried in the oil and butter. Arrange on a serving plate and serve garnished with parsley sprigs.

Hors d'oeuvre

Turkish Liver Toasts

12 oz calf liver
1 tablespoon all-purpose flour
1 tablespoon oil
2 tablespoons butter
1 teaspoon salt
¾ teaspoon pepper
2 teaspoons meat extract
3 tablespoons raisins
½ cup Madeira
1 clove garlic, crushed
¼ cup chopped almonds
4 slices toast
Garnish
chopped parsley

Cut the liver into strips and toss in the flour.
Heat the oil in a pan and fry the liver quickly for 2 minutes, then remove from the pan. Place the butter, salt, pepper, meat extract, raisins, Madeira and garlic in the pan, bring to the boil, stirring, and simmer for 3–4 minutes. Lower the heat, replace the liver and cook for a further 2 minutes. Add the chopped almonds. Spoon on to the slices of toast and serve garnished with chopped parsley.
Serves 4

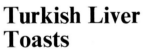

Cook's Tip
When cooking liver, never overcook it, otherwise it becomes tough.

Beef and Anchovy Savories

8 slices bread
¼ cup butter
8 oz lean ground beef
2 egg yolks
1 teaspoon dry mustard
pinch cayenne pepper
½ teaspoon salt
½ teaspoon celery salt
¼ cup grated fresh
* horseradish root*
3 tablespoons brandy
1 small can anchovy fillets
* in oil*
Garnish
tomato quarters
sweet dill pickles

Spread the bread with butter. Mix the beef with the egg yolks, mustard, cayenne pepper, salt, celery salt, horseradish and brandy. Spread the meat mixture on the bread, forming a slight dome in the center of each slice. Form a diagonal cross with 2 anchovy fillets on each savory and spoon over a little oil from the can. Place on a baking sheet and bake in a moderately hot oven (400° F) for 20 minutes. Cut into small squares and serve garnished with tomato quarters and pickles.
Serves 6–8

Danish Open Sandwiches

2 onions
4 slices brown bread
2 tablespoons butter
4 tablespoons chopped dill
8 canned sardines
2 tomatoes
1 cup chopped peeled
  cucumber
½ cup mayonnaise
  or sour cream
½ teaspoon sugar

Peel the onions and cut into thin slices. Pour over boiling water, and leave to cool. Spread the bread thinly with the butter and sprinkle over half the dill. Drain the sardines and arrange two on each piece of bread. Cut the tomatoes into thick slices. Place the drained onion and tomato slices on the sardines, and top with the cucumber mixed with the mayonnaise or sour cream, sugar and remaining dill.
Serves 4

Variation
The cucumber topping on these sandwiches may be replaced with a potato salad topping. Omit the sugar and replace the dill with chopped chives.

Roast Beef Sandwiches

1 tablespoon mayonnaise
juice of 1 lemon
1 tablespoon pickle relish
½ teaspoon sugar
4 slices wholewheat bread
4 slices roast beef
1 orange
pinch celery salt

Mix the mayonnaise with the lemon juice, pickle relish and sugar. Spread over the pieces of bread and place the roast beef on top. Peel and slice the orange and use to garnish each sandwich. Sprinkle with celery salt.
Serves 4

Variation
In place of the pickle relish, mix 1 teaspoon prepared mustard with the mayonnaise and lemon juice.
The recipe is equally good with slices of lamb or pork.

Cook's Tip
This is an excellent way of using up any meat left over from a roast.

Beef and Cheese Toasties

1 medium onion
2 egg yolks
1 tablespoon oil
1–2 tablespoons grated fresh
  horseradish root
1½ teaspoons dry mustard
1–2 teaspoons paprika
  pepper
1 teaspoon celery salt
½ teaspoon pepper
8 oz cooked ground beef
1 tablespoon cream cheese
1 tablespoon tomato ketchup
1 tablespoon mayonnaise
4 slices white bread
Garnish
parsley

Peel and chop the onion
and mix with the egg yolks,
oil, horseradish, mustard,
paprika, celery salt, pepper
and ground beef.
Beat the cheese with 4
tablespoons hot water, the
ketchup and mayonnaise
until frothy.
Lightly toast both sides of
the white bread and spread
evenly with the meat
mixture. Place on a baking
sheet and bake in a
moderately hot oven
(400° F) for 20 minutes.
Spoon over the cheese
mixture and return to the
oven for a further 5
minutes. Serve garnished
with parsley.
Serves 4

Ground Beef Squares

8 slices bread
¼ cup butter
8 oz ground beef
2 egg yolks
1 teaspoon dry mustard
pinch cayenne pepper
½ teaspoon salt
½ teaspoon celery salt
3 tablespoons brandy
3 tablespoons grated fresh
  horseradish root
1 can anchovy fillets
4 teaspoons capers

Spread the bread with
butter, and quarter each
slice. Mix the meat with the
egg yolks, mustard,
seasonings and brandy.
Spread the mixture on the
bread, piling it up in the
middle. Place a spoonful
of horseradish on the top
of each and then garnish
with a piece of anchovy
fillet and a few capers.
Serves 6–8

Cook's Tip
This is a version of
the famous steak
tartare recipe. The
beef should be
freshly ground fillet,
round or chuck.

Horseradish Dip

2 dessert apples
juice of 1 lemon
2 teaspoons grated fresh horseradish root
1 teaspoon prepared mustard
1 tablespoon cream cheese
1 teaspoon sugar
⅔ cup whipping cream

Peel and quarter the apples, removing the cores, and chop very finely, or blend in the blender with the lemon juice. Add the horseradish, mustard, cheese and sugar and blend for a further 2–3 minutes. Lightly whip the cream and fold into the apple mixture. Either serve this as a dip, or spread thickly on small crackers.
Serves 4

Variation
Sour cream may be used in place of the whipping cream. If fresh horseradish is not available, use the bottled horseradish sauce.

Cook's Tip
If serving the horse-radish mixture on crackers, do not prepare them too far ahead of time as the crackers will become soft.

Philadelphia Truffles

2 teaspoons caraway seeds
8 oz (1 cup) Philadelphia cream cheese
5 tablespoons chopped parsley
1 teaspoon paprika pepper
½ teaspoon white pepper
2 slices pumpernickel bread
Garnish
parsley

Mix the caraway seeds with the cheese, chopped parsley, paprika and pepper. Leave to chill for 30 minutes. Crumble the pumpernickel bread. Form the cheese mixture into small balls and coat in the pumpernickel crumbs. Chill for a further 30 minutes. Arrange in a dish and serve garnished with parsley.
Serves 4

Variation
Finely chopped walnuts may be used in place of the pumpernickel crumbs to coat the cheese balls. The caraway seeds may be replaced by 1 teaspoon curry paste.

Cook's Tip
These cheese balls may be frozen. Flash freeze until solid, then pack in layers with dividers, in a rigid container. Allow to thaw at room temperature.

Miniature Cheese Savories

8 slices pumpernickel
    bread
10 oz cheese
¼ cup butter
8 oz (1 cup) cream cheese
½ teaspoon paprika pepper
pinch each salt, pepper and
    celery salt
4 tablespoons port
4 tablespoons milk
½ cup chopped cooked ham
small crackers
Garnish
strips red pepper
strips cheese
stuffed olives
chopped pistachio nuts

Cut the pumpernickel
slices into rectangles
measuring 1½ inches by
3 inches. Cut the cheese into
slices the same size. Spread
two pieces of pumpernickel
with butter on one side,
and spread two pieces on
both sides. Put the cheese
slices between the pumpernickel, as shown in the
picture.
Mix together the cream
cheese, seasonings, port and
milk. Fold the ham into
the cheese mixture. Use to
sandwich the crackers
together in threes. Pipe or
spoon some of the cheese
mixture on the top cracker
and garnish with red pepper
strips, strips of cheese,
sliced stuffed olives and a
few chopped pistachio nuts.
Serves 6–8

Hungarian Rolls

1 French bread loaf
¼ cup butter
4 oz salami slices
5 tablespoons mayonnaise
½ teaspoon dry mustard
Garnish
lemon slices
paprika pepper
chopped parsley

Cut the loaf in half lengthwise and cut each half in two, making four portions in all. Spread with the butter. Form each slice of salami into a cornucopia by cutting each one from the center to the outside. Arrange some salami cornucopias on each half of bread. Mix the mayonnaise with the mustard and use to fill the salami cornucopias. Serve garnished with lemon slices, paprika and chopped parsley.
Serves 4

Variation
The salami may be replaced by slices of any continental sausage.

> **Cook's Tip**
> The easiest way to fill the salami cornucopias is to place the mayonnaise in a pastry bag fitted with a large star tube and to pipe a star of mayonnaise into each cornucopia.

Cheese-Stuffed Potatoes

8 even-sized potatoes
2 teaspoons salt
½ cup cottage cheese
3 tablespoons chopped chives
1 teaspoon white pepper
¼ cup butter
2 teaspoons coarse salt
1 teaspoon paprika pepper

Wash the potatoes and cook in their skins in boiling, salted water, until tender. Drain and cut each one in half.
Using a spoon, scoop out the insides carefully and mix with the cottage cheese, chives, pepper and butter to form a smooth mixture. Fill the potato skins with this mixture and place the two halves back together. Place on a baking sheet, sprinkle with the coarse salt and paprika. Bake in a moderate oven (350° F) for 10 minutes.
Serves 8

Variation
In place of the cottage cheese use crumbled blue cheese and omit the chopped chives.
If preferred the potatoes may be wrapped in foil and baked in the oven instead of being cooked in boiling water.

Cornish Toasts

1 orange
3 tablespoons mayonnaise
½ cup whipping cream
1 tablespoon grated fresh
  horseradish root
2 cooking apples
1 onion
¼ cup butter
4 slices roast beef
½ teaspoon pepper
½ teaspoon salt
4 large slices white bread

Squeeze the juice from the orange. Beat together the orange juice, mayonnaise cream and horseradish. Peel and quarter the apples, remove the cores and cut into very thin slices. Peel and slice the onion. Melt the butter in a pan and cook the slices of apple and onion together for 10–15 minutes, making sure they do not brown. Remove and keep warm. Sprinkle the meat with pepper and cook in the pan for 2–3 minutes on each side. Season with salt. Arrange a slice of beef on each piece of bread and spoon over the apple and onion slices. Top with the orange mayonnaise and serve at once.
Serves 4

Flemish Cabbage Rolls

1 small head white cabbage
2 teaspoons salt
1 tablespoon oil
1 onion, diced
1 cup soft breadcrumbs
1 small can tuna, drained
1 teaspoon white pepper
2 eggs
1 cup plain yogurt
1–2 teaspoons paprika
  pepper
1 teaspoon sugar

Separate the cabbage leaves and cook for 5 minutes in boiling, salted water. Drain and keep the cooking liquid. Cut away the larger stalks from the leaves. Heat the oil in a pan and fry the diced onion until softened. Stir in the breadcrumbs, tuna, pepper and eggs. Form the mixture into rolls and around each one wrap a cabbage leaf, making a secure package. Place in a pan and pour over the reserved cooking liquid. Simmer in the liquid for 5 minutes. Meanwhile, mix the yogurt with the paprika and sugar. Drain the rolls and place in a serving dish. Spoon over the yogurt sauce.
Serves 4

Variation
Sour cream may be used in place of the plain yogurt. The tuna may be replaced by a small can of sardines.

Mixed Cold Platter with Salad

8 oz sliced roast veal
8 oz sliced roast pork
8 oz sliced roast beef
1 (8-oz) can mixed
   vegetables, drained
4 sweet dill pickles
½ cup sour cream
3 tablespoons mayonnaise
1 teaspoon dry mustard
1 teaspoon sugar
2 tablespoons chopped chives
Garnish
parsley sprigs
tomato wedges
mixed pickled vegetables

Arrange the slices of meat attractively on a large dish, leaving the center empty.

Mix the canned vegetables with the chopped dill pickles. Mix the sour cream with the mayonnaise, mustard, sugar and chives. Mix with the vegetable mixture and spoon into two small dishes. Place in the center of the serving dish. Serve garnished with parsley, tomato and pickled vegetables.
Serves 6

Cook's Tip
This dish may be prepared in advance, but cover the platter with plastic wrap or foil so that the edges of the meat do not dry. Store in the refrigerator.

Charleston Balls

2 slices white bread
½ cup ground beef
1 can sardines
1 teaspoon salt
½ teaspoon celery salt
1 teaspoon paprika pepper
pinch cayenne pepper
pinch curry powder
5 tablespoons chopped
   parsley
2 eggs
½ cup oil
5 tablespoons chopped fresh
   herbs
½ cup whipping cream

Soften the bread slices in water and then squeeze dry. Mix with the ground beef, drained sardines, seasonings, parsley and

eggs. Form the mixture into small balls and fry in the heated oil until browned on all sides. Drain on paper towels. Cool and spear with a toothpick. Mix together the herbs and cream and serve with the meatballs.
Serves 4

Cook's Tip
The meat mixture may be prepared in advance and stored in the refrigerator. Fry and cool just before serving.

Quick Veal Rolls

 cup liver sausage
5 tablespoons chopped
    parsley
6 pickled onions, chopped
¼ cup chopped walnuts
3 tablespoons raisins
4 sweet dill pickles, chopped
5 tablespoons port
6 slices roast veal
Garnish
parsley sprigs

Mix the liver sausage with
the parsley, chopped
onions, walnuts, raisins
and chopped pickles.
Mix in the port. Divide
the mixture between the
slices of veal, form into
rolls and secure with a
toothpick. Arrange on

a serving dish and garnish
with parsley sprigs.
Serves 4

Variation
If liver sausage is not
available, cooked chopped
chicken may be used
instead. Other cooked sliced
meat may be used in place
of the veal.

Tasty Fish Pie

1 can anchovy fillets
1½ teaspoons salt
1 lb fish fillets, skinned and
    cubed
2 teaspoons Worcestershire
    sauce
½ teaspoon white pepper
1 teaspoon prepared
    mustard
3 tablespoons oil
1 small onion, diced
2 cups pie pastry (made
    with 2 cups flour, etc.)
1 green pepper, seeded and
    chopped
2 tomatoes, peeled and
    chopped
5 tablespoons chopped
    parsley
4 slices Edam cheese
6 tablespoons butter

Drain the anchovy fillets,
chop and mix with the
salt, fish, Worcestershire
sauce, pepper, mustard,
oil and diced onion; leave
for 30 minutes.
Roll out the pastry thinly
and use to line an 8-inch
flan ring on a baking sheet.
Drain the fish cubes
from the marinade and
place in the pastry case.
Sprinkle over the pepper,
tomatoes and parsley; pour
over the marinade and top
with the cheese slices. Dot
with butter and bake in a
moderately hot oven
(400° F) for 30 minutes.
Serve warm.
Serves 4–6

23

Sausage and Orange Salad

1 head lettuce
2 oranges
1 cup prepared vegetable
  salad
1 sweet dill pickle
1 cup liver sausage
4 oz continental sausage,
  sliced
5 tablespoons mayonnaise
5 tablespoons chopped
  parsley
4 slices cooked ham
Garnish
lemon slices
parsley
sweet dill pickle fans

Arrange the lettuce leaves on a serving platter. Cut the oranges across one end so that a flat base is formed, then slice one-third from the other end. Scoop out the flesh, chop roughly and mix with the prepared salad. Fill the oranges with this mixture and replace the lids. Stand the oranges in the center of the platter. Chop the pickle finely and mix with the liver sausage. Chill until firm, then form into oval balls and arrange around the oranges. Arrange slices of continental sausage between the liver sausage balls. Mix the mayonnaise with the parsley and spread over the ham slices. Roll up. Arrange on the dish. Serve garnished with lemon slices, parsley and pickle fans.
Serves 6

Pickled Herring Rolls with Salad

20 pickled herring fillets
¼ cup milk
6 tablespoons vinegar
¼ cup dry white wine
2 tomatoes
2 pears
2 apples
1 canned pimiento, chopped
½ cup mixed corn and pickle
  relish
little sugar
Garnish
parsley

Separate the fish from the bones and cover with cold water. Leave for 4 hours changing the water after 2 hours.
Drain the fish, add the milk, ½ cup water, the vinegar and wine. Leave to marinate. Peel and chop the tomatoes, pears and apples. Mix with the pimiento, relishes, a little sugar to taste, and a little of the fish marinade.
Remove the fish from the marinade and drain. Roll each fillet into a large ring, place on a serving dish and fill the center with the salad mixture. Serve garnished with parsley.
Any extra salad mixture can be mixed with a little mayonnaise and served separately.
Serves 6

Tasty Sausage Sticks

1½ lb sausagemeat
2 teaspoons paprika pepper
1 teaspoon all-purpose flour
1 teaspoon pepper
½ teaspoon cayenne pepper
½ teaspoon caraway seeds
1 clove garlic, crushed
1 tablespoon cottage cheese
⅔ cup plain yogurt
2 teaspoons celery salt
½ teaspoon sugar
⅔ cup oil
Garnish
parsley

Mix the sausagemeat with the paprika, flour, pepper, cayenne pepper, caraway seeds and garlic. Chill for 15 minutes, then cut into even-sized sticks.

Mix together the cottage cheese, yogurt, celery salt and sugar. Chill for 10 minutes.
Heat the oil in a pan and lightly brown the sausage strips all over. Remove and drain on paper towels. Arrange on a dish and garnish with parsley. To serve, dip the warm sausage sticks into the chilled yogurt sauce.
Serves 4

Cook's Tip
If a smooth sauce is preferred, press the cottage cheese through a nylon strainer or blend it in the blender.

Puff Pastry Pizzas

1 lb frozen puff pastry
12 slices salami
¼ cup chopped cooked ham
2 onions, sliced
2 slices cheese, cubed
2 tomatoes, peeled and sliced
1 teaspoon paprika pepper
1 teaspoon black pepper
⅔ cup oil
5 tablespoons chopped parsley

Thaw the pastry. On a floured board, roll it out thinly and use to line four 4-inch pie pans or flan rings on baking sheets. On the pastry arrange the salami, ham, onion, cheese and tomatoes. Sprinkle with the seasonings and over each pizza spoon 3 tablespoons oil. Bake in a hot oven (420° F) for 20–25 minutes. Sprinkle with chopped parsley and serve hot.
Serves 4

Cook's Tip
These puff pastry pizzas may be prepared and cooked in advance and then frozen. To freeze, wrap each one in freezer foil or film and pack together in a rigid container. Reheat from frozen.

Raclette

6 lb potatoes
½ a whole semi-soft cheese
½ cup butter
3–4 tablespoons coarse salt

Raclette is a Swiss cheese dish, a specialty from Valais. It is made by holding a large piece of the local cheese over the open fire and scraping off the softened part as it melts. The melted cheese is put on a plate and eaten with baked potatoes and a selection of salads. Traditionally, the white wine from Valais is served with raclette.

It is an ideal dish to serve at an informal party and with the potatoes and salads is surprisingly filling.

Scrub the potatoes and bake in a moderate oven (350° F) for 1–1½ hours or until tender. Split, add a pat of butter and sprinkling of coarse salt. Serve with the raclette.

To make the raclette, cut the cheese into serving portions and place under the broiler to melt the cheese.

Each guest has a portion of cheese which is beginning to melt and eats it with the potatoes and a selection of salads.
Serves 8–10

Cook's Tip
Choose a semi-soft cheese with a high fat content, and a thick skin, for this recipe so that it will melt readily.

Curried Chicken Drumsticks

12 chicken drumsticks
1 tablespoon all-purpose flour
5 tablespoons oil
2 onions, sliced
5 tablespoons dry white wine
1–2 tablespoons curry
  powder
1 teaspoon black pepper
1–2 tablespoons mango
  chutney
3 tablespoons chopped
  parsley
½ cup milk
Garnish
parsley
tomato wedges

Toss the chicken drumsticks
in the flour. Heat the oil in
a pan and fry the onions
until softened. Add the
wine and cook for 3
minutes. Remove from the
heat and add the curry
powder, pepper, chutney
and parsley. Spread over
the chicken drumsticks and
leave to marinate for 30
minutes.
Remove the chicken from
the marinade, pat dry and
broil, turning, for 15–20
minutes.
Meanwhile, put the
marinade in the blender
with the milk and blend.
Serve the chicken hot or
cold with the marinade as a
dip. Garnish with parsley
and tomato wedges.
Serves 6

Bean Salad

⅔ cup oil
3 tablespoons wine vinegar
1½ teaspoons salt
½ teaspoon ground black
  pepper
pinch tarragon
1 teaspoon prepared
  mustard
1 (1¾-lb) can navy beans
1 onion
12 oz ground beef
1 egg
3 tablespoons soft bread-
  crumbs
4 tablespoons tomato
  ketchup
1 teaspoon paprika pepper
Garnish
lettuce leaves

Mix half the oil, the vinegar,
1 teaspoon of the salt, the
pepper, tarragon and
mustard together. Mix with
the drained beans. Peel
and grate onion and mix
with the ground beef, egg,
breadcrumbs, tomato
ketchup, paprika and
remaining salt. Form into
small balls and fry in the
remaining oil, until browned
on all sides. Drain on
paper towels and allow to
cool.
Arrange the lettuce leaves
on a serving plate and
around the edge of the dish
place the meat balls. Pile
the bean salad in the
center.
Serves 4–6

Tomato Molds

1½ lb tomatoes
2 envelopes unflavored
  gelatin
3–4 tablespoons water
1 teaspoon salt
¼ teaspoon celery salt
¼ teaspoon pepper
pinch sugar
3 tablespoons tomato paste
1 cup plain yogurt
1 teaspoon sugar
4–5 tablespoons chopped
  parsley

Pour boiling water over the tomatoes, leave for 30–45 seconds, then remove and peel. Chop the tomatoes and blend in the blender. Cover the gelatin with cold water and soak for 10 minutes, then heat to dissolve. Measure the tomato juice and dissolved gelatin and make up to 3 cups with water. Pour into a saucepan, add half the salt, the celery salt, pepper and a little sugar. Beat in the tomato paste and heat gently. Rinse four to six small molds with cold water and fill with the tomato mixture. Allow to set in the refrigerator. Mix the yogurt, sugar, remaining salt and the parsley together. Serve with the tomato molds.
Serves 4–6

Jumbo Shrimp Kebabs

½ cucumber
1 onion
12 oz shelled jumbo shrimp
8 pimiento-stuffed olives
4 bay leaves
3 tablespoons oil
½ cup tomato ketchup
2 teaspoons paprika pepper

Cut the cucumber into thick slices; peel and quarter the onion. Place the shrimp alternately with onion quarters, olives, bay leaves and slices of cucumber on skewers. Heat the oil in a pan and fry the shrimp kebabs for 8–10 minutes over a moderate heat, turning them to cook on all sides. Drain on paper towels. Heat the ketchup with the same quantity of water, and the paprika, stirring well. Serve as a sauce with the kebabs.
Serves 4

Cook's Tip
If preferred, the kebabs can be brushed with oil and cooked under the broiler. The kebabs may be prepared in advance, covered with plastic wrap and stored in the refrigerator. Fry just before serving.

Herring and Apple Salad

8 pickled herrings
3 tablespoons wine vinegar
1 tablespoon sugar
2 red-skinned apples
juice of 1 lemon
2 onions
2 large dill pickles
2 cups sour cream

Lay the fish in a dish and cover with cold water to extract the salt. Leave in the refrigerator for 12 hours, changing the water three times.
Drain and skin the herrings then cut from the head along the backbone and open out both sides. Remove the fins.
Place the fillets in a bowl and add the vinegar and sugar; marinate for 2 hours. Core and slice the apples and sprinkle with lemon juice. Slice the onions and pickles. Mix the apple, onion and pickles with the herring fillets. Spoon over the sour cream and chill for 30 minutes before serving.
Serves 4

Cook's Tip
Pickled herrings, preserved in spiced vinegar, are available from delicatessen counters.

Savory Fish Cakes

2 cups milk
1½ teaspoons salt
2 tablespoons butter
1 small package instant mashed potato
6 tablespoons all-purpose flour
2 eggs
2 teaspoons anchovy paste
1 lb white fish fillets
2 onions, quartered
2 leeks, sliced
3 tablespoons chopped parsley
½ cup fat for frying
Garnish
parsley

Bring the milk to the boil with ½ teaspoon of the salt and the butter. Lower the heat and mix in the potato powder. Turn into a bowl, add the flour, eggs and anchovy paste. Mix well. Lay the fillets in a flame-proof dish, cover with water, the remaining salt, the onions, and leeks. Cover and simmer for 20 minutes. Remove the fish with a slotted spoon and flake the flesh. Then remove the onions and leeks and chop finely. Mix the fish and vegetables together with the potato mixture, and chopped parsley. Form into small cakes, flatten, and chill for 10 minutes.
Heat the fat and fry the fish cakes for 5 minutes on each side. Drain on paper towels and serve garnished with parsley.
Serves 4–6

Maryland Pork Burgers

2 oz Edam cheese
1 lb ground lean pork
¼ cup liver sausage
½ cup sausagemeat
4 tablespoons chopped
 parsley
2 eggs
6 tablespoons oil
1 (1-lb) can corn kernels
2 tablespoons butter
Garnish
parsley
tomato wedges

Dice the cheese and mix
with the ground pork,
liver sausage, sausagemeat,
parsley and eggs. Form the
mixture into eight patties.
Heat the oil in a pan and
cook the patties for 5

minutes on each side.
Drain on paper towels.
Meanwhile, heat the corn,
drain and toss in butter.
Spoon on to a heated
serving dish and arrange
the patties on top. Serve
garnished with parsley and
tomato wedges.
Serves 4–6

Cook's Tip
These Maryland Pork
Burgers freeze well.
Prepare the mixture
and freeze, in layers,
in a rigid container.
Fry, from frozen
but allow 8 minutes
on each side and
cook over a low heat.

Kipper Bake

2 cups milk
6 tablespoons butter
1 teaspoon salt
1 small package instant
 mashed potato
2 large kippers
1 onion
1 tablespoon oil
1 tomato
1 cup dry breadcrumbs
½ cup grated cheese

Heat the milk with 2
tablespoons of the butter
and the salt. Remove from
the heat and beat in the
instant potato. Skin the
kippers and remove the
bones, making sure that all
small ones are removed.
Peel and slice onion and

fry in the heated oil until
golden brown. Grease an
ovenproof dish with 2
tablespoons of the
remaining butter and line
the dish with half the
potato. Layer the kippers,
onion and sliced tomato in
the dish. Top with the
remaining potato, smooth
over and sprinkle with
breadcumbs and grated
cheese. Dot with the
remaining butter and cook
in a moderately hot oven
(400° F) for 20 minutes.
Serves 4

Farmhouse Omelet

4 onions
1 teaspoon salt
½ teaspoon each celery and garlic salt
2 lb cooked potatoes
½ cup oil
½ cup diced bacon
½ cup diced cooked ham
½ cup diced roast beef
12 eggs
2 teaspoons paprika pepper
1 teaspoon black pepper
5 tablespoons chopped parsley
Garnish
parsley

Peel the onions and dice them finely; mix with the salt, celery and garlic salts. Dice the potatoes. Heat half the oil and fry the sliced onions until softened. Add the diced bacon, ham, beef and potatoes, stir well, and cook for a further 5 minutes. Brush a large baking pan with the remaining oil. Beat the eggs with the rest of the ingredients, pour half into the pan, then add the onion mixture. Pour in the rest of the egg mixture. Bake in a moderately hot oven (400° F) for 25–30 minutes, until set. Turn out, garnish with parsley and serve cut into portions.
Serves 6

Stuffed Peppers

10 peppers, tops removed and seeded
4 onions, peeled
1 small can tuna
2 cups diced dill pickles
4 hard-cooked eggs, sliced
1 cup ground pork
1 cup ground beef
½ teaspoon white pepper
6 tablespoons vinegar
⅔ cup oil
½ cup sour cream
2 teaspoons cornstarch
1 cup sausagemeat
¼ cup butter

Blanch the peppers in salted water for 5 minutes, then drain. Slice two of the onions and chop the other two. Flake the tuna and mix with the pickles and eggs. Mix the ground meats with chopped onions and pepper. Heat the vinegar, oil, sour cream and ½ cup water. Thicken with the dissolved cornstarch. Fill three of the peppers with sausagemeat and three with the tuna mixture. Spoon over a little of the sour cream mixture. Fill four peppers with the ground meat mixture. Place all the peppers in an ovenproof dish and pour over the rest of the sour cream mixture. Top with the sliced onion and dot with butter. Cover with a lid and bake in a moderate oven (350° F) for 20–25 minutes.
Serves 6

31

Spare Ribs with Pineapple

4 lb spareribs
4 teaspoons salt
2 teaspoons each allspice
  and black pepper
3 tablespoons oil
3 tablespoons vinegar
3 tablespoons soy sauce
4 teaspoons brown sugar
1 small can pineapple rings
1 teaspoon grated nutmeg
½ teaspoon cayenne pepper

Cut the ribs so that each piece contains three ribs in all. Rub with the salt, allspice, pepper and the oil. Mix together the vinegar, soy sauce, brown sugar, 6 tablespoons pineapple juice from the can, nutmeg and cayenne pepper. Place the ribs on a rack in a roasting pan and spread with the vinegar mixture. Bake in a warm oven (325° F) for 1 hour, basting every 10–15 minutes with the vinegar mixture.
Cut the pineapple rings into small pieces and add to the ribs. Bake for a further 5 minutes. Arrange on a serving dish and spoon over the cooking juices.
Serves 4

Sausages with Orange Dip

1 orange
5 tablespoons horseradish
  sauce
2 teaspoons lemon juice
1 cup whipping cream
1 cup soft breadcrumbs
2 eggs
5 tablespoons chopped
  parsley
1 cup sausagemeat
1 teaspoon black pepper
1–2 teaspoons paprika
  pepper
2 teaspoons all-purpose flour
¼ cup fat

Mix the grated rind and juice of the orange with the horseradish sauce and lemon juice. Whip the cream until stiff and fold in the orange mixture. Place in refrigerator.
Mix the breadcrumbs with the eggs, parsley and sausagemeat. Season with pepper and paprika. Form the mixture into sausage shapes; coat lightly in flour and fry in the hot fat until browned on all sides. Drain on paper towels and serve with the orange-flavored horseradish cream.
Serves 4

Cheesy Meatballs

$\frac{5}{8}$ *cup butter*
$\frac{1}{4}$ *cup cream cheese*
2 onions
1 lb ground pork
1 cup ground beef
$\frac{1}{2}$ *teaspoon celery salt*
$\frac{1}{2}$ *teaspoon black pepper*
2 eggs
2 tablespoons soft bread-
   crumbs
4 tablespoons chopped
   parsley
$\frac{1}{2}$ *cup oil*

Beat $\frac{1}{2}$ cup of the butter with the cream cheese. Peel and slice the onions. Melt the remaining butter and fry the onion slices until softened and golden brown. Mix the meats with the onions, celery salt, pepper, eggs, breadcrumbs and chopped parsley. Form the mixture into balls, placing a knob of the cream cheese mixture in the center of each. Leave to chill for 15–20 minutes in the refrigerator.

Heat the oil and fry the balls for 8 minutes, turning to brown them on all sides. Drain on paper towels and serve with coleslaw.
Serves 4

> **Cook's Tip**
> When forming the mixture into balls, lightly coat your hands with flour.

Stuffed Cucumber

1 large cucumber
1 cup prepared vegetable
   salad
1$\frac{1}{2}$ cups cooked peas
4 tablespoons chopped
   parsley
3 tablespoons wine vinegar
1 teaspoon sugar
$\frac{1}{2}$ *teaspoon salt*
4 slices cooked ham
4 cheese slices
Garnish
onion rings

Cut away the top one-third of the cucumber lengthwise, peel and cut finely. On the underside of the remaining two-thirds, cut lengthwise, so that a level base is formed, and then hollow out the middle, using a spoon. Mix the cucumber flesh with the finely cut one-third, the prepared salad, peas and parsley. Mix the vinegar with 1 tablespoon water, the sugar and salt. Pour into the hollow cucumber and leave for 5 minutes.

Cut the ham slices in halves and form each one into a small roll. Cut the cheese into triangles. Pour the vinegar mixture out of cucumber, and fill it with the salad. Top with the ham rolls and cheese triangles. Garnish with onion rings.
Serves 4

33

Savory Rice Balls

1¼ *cups round-grain rice*
1 teaspoon each salt and
   white pepper
½ *cup grated cheese*
4 oz salami slices
½ *cup ground cooked tongue*
3 tablespoons chopped
   parsley
¼ *cup fat*
Garnish
parsley

Rinse the rice under cold water, then cook in 4 cups water in a saucepan. Drain well. Add the salt and pepper and leave over the heat for 2 minutes, stirring to evaporate the excess moisture. Stir in the cheese. Chop the salami and mix with the tongue and parsley. Mix with the rice. Form the mixture into balls and chill for 20 minutes. Fry in the heated fat for 10 minutes, turning until browned on all sides. Drain on paper towels and serve garnished with parsley.
Serves 4

Cook's Tip
Do not throw away scraps of cheese. Grate them finely and store in a covered container in the refrigerator.

Broiled Cheesy Frankfurters

4 large frankfurters
1 tablespoon oil
1 teaspoon paprika pepper
6 oz Gouda cheese
4 teaspoons each prepared
   mustard and tomato
   ketchup
8 slices bacon

Cut the frankfurters almost in half lengthwise and brush with a mixture of oil and paprika. Cut the cheese into four large slices and put in the frankfurters. Mix the mustard with the ketchup and spoon into the split in each frankfurter. Wrap two slices of bacon around each frankfurter. Secure each one with a wooden toothpick. Cook the filled frankfurters under the broiler for 8 minutes, turning to brown evenly on all sides. Serve hot or cold.
Serves 4

Variation
Omit the cheese, mustard and ketchup and spread the inside of each frankfurter with a spoonful of smooth pâté.

Cook's Tip
These cheesy frankfurters make ideal picnic or barbecue fare. Serve with a tomato and onion salad.

Ham and Cheese Ring

2 onions
1 cup chopped lean cooked
   ham
4 tablespoons chopped
   parsley
3 tablespoons brandy
4 eggs
2 teaspoons salt
2 teaspoons paprika pepper
pinch dry mustard
½ cup cottage or cream
   cheese

Peel and finely chop the onions. Mix the onions and ham with the parsley and brandy; cover and leave for 20 minutes.
Beat the eggs with the salt, paprika, mustard and cottage cheese. Mix the egg mixture with the ham mixture and ladle into a buttered 2-pint fluted ring mold. Stand the mold in a roasting pan half-filled with water and bake in a moderate oven (350° F) for 40 minutes.
Allow to cool, then carefully turn out on to a serving plate. To serve, cut in wedges like a cake. Served with a selection of salads, this ham and cheese ring makes an ideal lunch dish.
Serves 4–6

Party Loaf

1 small uncut white bread
   loaf
¼ cup butter
2 cups cottage or curd
   cheese
1 teaspoon each salt,
   paprika pepper and sugar
1 cup grated cheese
½ cup tomato ketchup
½ cup chopped cooked ham
4 tablespoons chopped
   parsley
4 tablespoons chopped chives
Garnish
wedges hard-cooked eggs
tomato and radish slices
stuffed olives

Remove the crusts from all sides of the loaf. Cut lengthwise in three thick slices. Spread each slice, on one side, with the butter. Mix half the cottage cheese with the salt, paprika, sugar and grated cheese. Spread one slice of bread with this mixture and cover with a second slice. Mix the remaining cottage cheese with the tomato ketchup and ham. Spread the second slice of bread with the cheese and ham mixture and cover with the third slice. Press chopped herbs into the sides of the loaf. Chill for 30 minutes, then cut into slices to serve. Garnish with wedges of hard-cooked egg, tomato and radish slices and stuffed olives.
Serves 4

Quick Spanish Soup

1 onion
1 large tomato
1 tablespoon olive oil
1 clove garlic, crushed
3 tablespoons chopped ham
1 bay leaf
4 tablespoons long-grain rice
½ cup dry white wine
pinch saffron powder (optional)
½ teaspoon lemon juice
3 cups chicken stock
8 shelled prawns
1 small can mussels or clams
3 tablespoons chopped parsley
Garnish
1 hard-cooked egg, chopped

Peel and chop the onion.
Peel and chop the tomato.

Heat the oil in a pan and fry the onion and garlic for 5 minutes. Add the chopped tomato, ham and the bay leaf. Simmer for 5 minutes. In another pan, place the rice, wine, saffron powder (if used), lemon juice and stock. Bring to the boil and simmer until the rice is cooked. Add the contents from the frying pan, the prawns and mussels or clams and simmer for a further 3 minutes. Check the seasoning, remove the bay leaf and stir in the parsley. Ladle the soup into bowls and serve garnished with chopped hard-cooked egg.
Serves 4

Bean Soup

1¾ cups dried navy beans
2 onions
¼ cup diced bacon
4 tomatoes
4 tablespoons chopped red pepper
½ teaspoon salt
¼ teaspoon celery salt
¼ teaspoon white pepper

Rinse the beans in cold water, and leave, covered with water, in a saucepan overnight.
The next day, add a further 2 cups water to the beans, cover and cook until softened. Peel and chop the onions. Heat the diced bacon in a pan together with the onions and fry until golden brown. Add the peeled and chopped tomatoes, red pepper and seasonings. Simmer for 5 minutes. Then stir into the cooked beans and liquid. Check the seasoning.
Serves 4

Cook's Tip
If time is short, canned navy beans may be used in place of the dried ones. Add them with the tomatoes and red pepper with sufficient water to make a soup consistency. Continue as recipe.

Hungarian Goulash Soup

2 onions
1 small carrot
1 green pepper, seeded
4 tablespoons oil
¾ cup cubed lean pork
½ cup cubed chuck
1 small can tomatoes
1 teaspoon paprika pepper
¼ teaspoon salt
pinch each pepper and
*   garlic salt*
½ cup sour cream

Peel the onions and cut into rings. Peel and slice the carrot; slice the pepper. Heat the oil in a large pan and fry the onion until golden brown. Add the meats and fry for a further 5 minutes. Add the carrot, green pepper, tomatoes, paprika, salt, pepper and garlic salt. Stir well. Add 2 cups water, cover and simmer for 1 hour, adding more liquid if necessary. Before serving, add the sour cream.
Serves 2

Variation
This traditional Hungarian soup recipe may be varied by adding a pinch of cumin and some potatoes. Peel and cube 2 potatoes and add them to the soup for the last 30 minutes of cooking.
Croûtons of bread fried in butter may be sprinkled over the soup just before serving.

Cauliflower Salad

1 cauliflower
2 teaspoons salt
1 small package frozen peas
1 small package frozen
   mixed vegetables
1 head lettuce
1 cucumber, sliced
4 tomatoes, peeled
1 small can pimientos,
   drained
½ cup mayonnaise
1 teaspoon prepared
   mustard
1 teaspoon paprika pepper
Garnish
chopped parsley
hard-cooked egg quarters

Prepare and cook the
cauliflower, whole, in
salted water until tender.

Remove. Cook the peas
and mixed vegetables
together in the same water.
Drain.
Arrange the lettuce leaves
on a serving plate and
place the cauliflower in the
center. Around the cauli-
flower place a circle of
cucumber slices, the whole
tomatoes and the mixed
vegetables and pimientos.
Mix the mayonnaise with
mustard and paprika, and
spoon over the cauliflower.
Garnish with chopped
parsley and hard-cooked
egg quarters.
Serves 6

Shrimp and Fruit Salad

2 ripe bananas
1 small can mandarin
   oranges
1 orange
1 pear
1 apple
12 shelled shrimp
12 walnut halves
¼ cup mayonnaise
   or sour cream
1 tablespoon orange juice
juice of 1 lemon
1 teaspoon sugar
1 tablespoon whipping cream

Peel and slice the bananas.
Drain the mandarins. Peel
and cube the orange, pear
and apple. Mix the shrimp
with the prepared fruit and
walnuts. Mix the mayon-

naise with the orange and
lemon juice, the sugar and
cream and spoon over the
salad.
Serves 4

Variation
This salad looks most
attractive if served in a
glass bowl lined with
lettuce leaves. Add a sprig
of watercress to garnish.

Cook's Tip
When preparing
apples, bananas and
pears for a dish,
sprinkle the cut
surfaces with lemon
juice to prevent them
from discoloring.

Chicken and Rice Salad

1 small package frozen peas
1 small can bamboo shoots
3 oranges
2 cups cooked long-grain rice
4 eggs, hard-cooked
2 cloves garlic, crushed
6 tablespoons olive oil
½ teaspoon salt
1 teaspoon paprika pepper
¼ teaspoon cayenne pepper
pinch each ground ginger
  and dry mustard
1 tablespoon wine vinegar
¼ cup dry white wine
1 cup chopped cooked
  chicken
1 small can artichoke hearts
Garnish
lemon wedges
parsley

Cook and drain the peas. Drain the bamboo shoots. Peel the oranges and cut the flesh into bite-size pieces. Mix the rice, peas, bamboo shoots and orange pieces together. Chop the eggs. Mix the chopped egg with the garlic, oil, salt, paprika, cayenne pepper, ginger and mustard. Add the vinegar and wine, and stir well. Fold into the rice mixture and add the chicken. Pile into a serving dish and arrange a ring of artichokes around the edge of the dish. Garnish with lemon wedges and parsley.
Serves 4–6

Fennel and Apple Salad

4 heads fennel
¼ cup wine vinegar
½ teaspoon salt
pinch garlic salt
1 teaspoon pepper
½ cup olive oil
½ cup ham, cut in strips
1 apple, sliced
1 orange, diced

Clean the fennel and cut into strips. Put in a large salad bowl, pour over the vinegar and sprinkle with the salts and pepper; finally add the oil. Mix well and then add the strips of ham, apple and lastly the diced orange.
This dish should be served immediately.
Serves 4–6

Variation
The apple and orange may be replaced by 1 grapefruit. If available, proscuitto, cut into strips, goes well with fennel.

Cook's Tip
If it is more convenient to prepare the salad ahead of time, do not add the oil and vinegar, but toss the apple slices in a little lemon juice to prevent them from discoloring.

Asparagus Salad

1 small can mushrooms
2 bananas
1 lb canned asparagus tips
1½ cups cooked ham, cut
    into strips
6 tablespoons dry red wine
1 tablespoon wine vinegar
1 teaspoon salt
pinch garlic salt
½ teaspoon ground black
    pepper
pinch cayenne pepper
1 teaspoon dried rosemary
1¼ cups whipping cream
¼ cup mayonnaise
lettuce leaves
4 rings canned pineapple

Drain and slice the
mushrooms. Peel and slice
the bananas. Drain and

chop the asparagus tips.
Mix together the bananas,
asparagus, ham and mush-
rooms. Stir the wine,
vinegar, salts, peppers and
rosemary together. Lightly
whip the cream, fold in the
mayonnaise and the red
wine mixture. Mix this
sauce with the asparagus
salad.
Arrange the lettuce leaves
and pineapple rings on a
serving plate and spoon on
the asparagus salad.
Serves 4–6

Tuna Salad

2 small onions
1 small can tuna
juice of 1 lemon
1 red pepper, seeded and
    chopped
1 green pepper, seeded and
    chopped
2 oranges
1 tablespoon orange liqueur
⅔ cup mayonnaise
¼ teaspoon pepper
1 teaspoon salt
pinch paprika pepper
1 teaspoon Worcestershire
    sauce
4 lemons
Garnish
onion rings

Peel and chop the onions.
Drain and flake the tuna

and sprinkle with the
lemon juice. Mix with the
peppers and onion.
Peel the oranges, removing
a thick layer of skin, and
chop the flesh. Mix with the
orange liqueur.
Mix the mayonnaise,
seasonings and Worcester-
shire sauce. Halve the
lemons and scoop out the
center. Mix the pepper and
orange mixtures and spoon
into the scooped-out
lemons. Top with a
spoonful of mayonnaise
mixture and serve the
remainder separately.
Garnish with onion rings.
Serves 4

Mussel Salad

1 lb canned mussels
1¼ cups dry white wine
8 stuffed olives
1 onion
⅔ cup mayonnaise
1 tablespoon tomato paste
1 teaspoon paprika pepper
1 tablespoon chopped
  tarragon

Drain the mussels and pour over the wine. Leave in a cool place for 30 minutes. Slice the olives and onion. Drain the wine from the mussels and mix into the mayonnaise with the tomato paste and paprika. Mix the mussels, onion, olives and tarragon in a salad bowl. Either serve the mayonnaise separately, or spoon it over the salad.
Serves 4–6

Variation
If available, fresh mussels may be used in this recipe. Use 5 pints fresh mussels and after cleaning leave them in cold salted water for 30 minutes.

Cook's Tip
It's a good idea to make up a batch of mayonnaise and store it in a covered rigid container in the refrigerator. It will keep for up to a week.

Savory Rice Salad

1 cup long-grain rice
1 onion
1 tablespoon oil
¾ cup cooked peas
½ teaspoon salt
½ teaspoon paprika pepper
4 eggs
½ cucumber
⅔ cup mayonnaise
1 tablespoon tomato paste
½ teaspoon sugar
⅔ cup plain yogurt
1 head lettuce

Cook the rice in boiling salted water until tender. Drain and rinse in cold water.
Dice the onion finely and fry in the oil, until softened. Add to the rice, with the peas, salt and paprika. Leave to cool.
Hard-cook and quarter the eggs; cut the cucumber into thin slices. Mix the mayonnaise with the tomato paste, sugar and yogurt. Spoon the rice mixture on to a serving dish and garnish with lettuce, cucumber slices and egg quarters.
Either spoon over the mayonnaise mixture, or serve it separately.
This savory rice salad is a good accompaniment to a selection of cold meats.
Serves 4

Variation
The plain yogurt may be replaced by sour cream.

Dutch Cheese Salad

8 oz Gouda cheese
½ green pepper
1 red pepper
1 sweet dill pickle
1 cucumber
1 apple
1 cup diced cooked ham
⅔ cup plain yogurt
1 tablespoon sour cream
1 tablespoon lemon juice
½ teaspoon grated fresh
   horseradish root
2 teaspoons chopped dill
1 teaspoon each salt, pepper
   and sugar

Cut the cheese into strips.
Seed and dice the peppers;
chop the pickle, dice the
cucumber, and chop the
apple. Mix together the

prepared cheese, ham,
peppers, pickle and apple.
Blend together the yogurt,
sour cream, lemon juice
and horseradish. Add the
dill and season with the
salt, pepper and sugar.
Mix the salad ingredients
with the sauce and leave to
chill for 30 minutes.
Serves 4

Variation
Use ½ cup diced cooked
ham and ½ cup diced
continental sausage or
salami.

Bean Sprouts Salad

1 (1-lb 2-oz) can bean
   sprouts
¼ cup wine vinegar
juice of 2 lemons
1 teaspoon sugar
½ teaspoon salt
¼ cup oil
few lettuce leaves

Rinse the bean sprouts in
cold water, drain and put in
a bowl. Mix together the
wine vinegar, lemon juice,
sugar, salt and oil and toss
the bean sprouts in the
dressing.
Arrange the lettuce leaves
on a serving dish and spoon
on the salad.

Variation
Mix 1½ cups finely chopped
cooked chicken or ham with
the bean sprouts before
adding the dressing.
Sprinkle the salad with 2–3
tablespoons chopped
parsley.
Use fresh bean sprouts
(8 oz or 4 cups is enough).
Serves 4

Cook's Tip
Once this salad
has been dressed it
should be served
immediately.

Stuffed Avocados

4 avocados
juice of 1 lemon
1 cup shelled shrimp
pinch each salt and pepper
1 small can celery hearts
2 eggs, hard-cooked
few drops Tabasco sauce

Avocados are not always ready for eating when purchased. To test for ripeness, press the flesh gently at the rounded end – it should yield slightly.
Cut the avocados in half, remove the seeds and immediately sprinkle the avocados with lemon juice to prevent them discoloring.
Mix together the shrimp and salt and pepper and use to fill four of the avocado halves.
Drain and slice the celery hearts and mix with the chopped hard-cooked eggs and Tabasco sauce. Use this mixture to fill the other four halves.
Serve with mayonnaise or dressing.
Serves 8

Variation
Other fillings may be used – try canned or frozen lobster meat mixed with whipping cream, black pepper and a squeeze of lemon juice; or scoop out the flesh and mix it with sour cream and a few chopped almonds or walnuts. Return to the avocado shells and serve garnished with chopped parsley.

Piquant Cheese Salad

2 onions
6 tomatoes
6 sweet dill pickles
1 cup diced cheese
¾ cup diced salami
¼ cup brown sugar
3 tablespoons pineapple juice
pinch cayenne pepper
3 drops Tabasco sauce
1 teaspoon ground black
    pepper
3 tablespoons dry white wine
5 tablespoons oil
¼ cup finely chopped
    pineapple
Garnish
chopped chives

Peel the onions and cut into rings. Dice the tomatoes; slice the pickles. Mix together the cheese, onions, salami and pickles.
To make the dressing, mix together the sugar, pineapple juice, cayenne pepper, Tabasco sauce, pepper, wine and oil and stir in the pineapple.
Just before serving, toss the salad in the dressing and serve garnished with chopped chives.
Serves 4–6

Variation
Cheeses to try in this salad are Brick, Monterey Jack or Cheddar.

Sausage Salad

8 oz white grapes
12 stuffed olives
1 onion
1 cup cubed continental
    sausage
½ cup cubed cooked tongue
⅔ cup vinegar
5 tablespoons oil
½ teaspoon salt
½ teaspoon dry mustard
½ teaspoon ground mace
1 teaspoon sugar

Halve and seed the grapes. Slice the olives. Finely chop the onion. Mix the grapes, olives, onion, sausage and tongue together and place in a serving bowl. Make a dressing with the vinegar, oil, seasonings and sugar and just before serving pour over the salad.
Serves 4

Variation
The cooked tongue may be replaced by cubes of cooked ham.

Cook's Tip
An easy way to make a dressing is to put all the ingredients into a screw-topped jar and shake until well mixed.

Gourmet's Salad

6 heads French or Belgian
  endive
1½ cups cooked duck, cut
  into strips
½ cup cooked tongue, cut
  into strips
⅔ cup mayonnaise
1 teaspoon paprika pepper
few drops Tabasco sauce
2 teaspoons wine vinegar
pinch sugar
3 tablespoons chopped
  parsley

Garnish
lemon slices
parsley sprigs

Wash the endive heads,
then cut into thin slices.
Place in a bowl. Add the
strips of duck and tongue.

Mix the mayonnaise with 2
teaspoons of hot water, stir
in the paprika, Tabasco
sauce, vinegar, sugar and
chopped parsley.
Add to the endive mixture
and toss lightly.
Turn into a serving dish
and garnish with lemon
slices and parsley sprigs.
Serves 4–6

Variation
If endive is not available,
a head of celery, chopped,
may be used instead. With
the celery add ½ cup
chopped walnuts and 1
dessert apple, cored and
chopped.

Liver Sausage Salad

12 oz liver sausage
1 red pepper
2 large sweet dill pickles
4 celery stalks
2 onions
1½ cups cooked peas
¼ cup oil
1½ tablespoons wine vinegar
½ teaspoon salt
1 teaspoon sugar
¼ teaspoon white pepper
pinch garlic salt

Cut the liver sausage into
slices. Seed and slice the
pepper and cut the pickles
into strips. Chop the
celery; peel and slice the
onions. Mix together the
sliced sausage, pepper,
pickles, celery, peas and

onions in a salad bowl.
Mix the remaining ingre-
dients together, to form a
dressing, and toss into the
salad just before serving.
Serves 4

Variation
Before placing the salad
ingredients in the serving
bowl, rub the inside of the
bowl with a cut clove of
garlic to give the salad a
slight flavor of garlic.

Cook's Tip
Served with French
bread, this salad
makes a refreshing
lunch dish.

Pasta Salad

12 oz pork luncheon meat
2 celery stalks
2 red-skinned apples
4 sweet dill pickles
2 cups cooked pasta
   (macaroni, pasta shells,
   spirals or bows)
¼ cup sliced stuffed olives
2 anchovy fillets
⅔ cup mayonnaise
1 teaspoon soy sauce
juice of 1 lemon
½ teaspoon salt
pinch cayenne pepper
1 teaspoon apple pie spice

Slice the pork luncheon meat; slice the celery. Core and slice the apples and slice the pickles. Mix together the pasta, luncheon meat, olives, celery, apples and pickles.
Chop the anchovy fillets and mix into the mayonnaise together with the soy sauce, lemon juice and seasonings. Chill lightly in the refrigerator before serving with the pasta salad.
Serves 4–6

Cook's Tip
Any cooked leftover pasta may be used for this salad.

Mixed Vegetable Salad

1 (8-oz) package frozen
   mixed vegetables
1 small cauliflower
1 cup green beans
6 tomatoes
1 cup cooked ham, cut into
   strips
⅔ cup mayonnaise
¼ cup chopped parsley
3 tablespoons vinegar
1 teaspoon paprika pepper
½ teaspoon white pepper
pinch curry powder
pinch dry mustard
1 head lettuce
Garnish
1 egg, hard-cooked
parsley sprigs

Cook the mixed vegetables, cauliflower and green beans in boiling salted water until just tender. Drain and cool, breaking the cauliflower into flowerets. Peel and chop the tomatoes. Mix together the prepared vegetables and ham and chill while preparing the dressing.
Mix together the mayonnaise, parsley, vinegar, paprika, white pepper, curry powder and mustard. Line a salad bowl with the lettuce leaves and spoon in the salad. Spoon over the mayonnaise mixture and serve garnished with hard-cooked egg quarters and parsley sprigs.
Serves 4–6

Salads

Cheese and Fruit Salad

4 canned pear halves
1 (8-oz) can cherries
1 small can mandarin
 oranges
8 oz blue cheese
2–3 soaked prunes
1 cup sour cream
juice of 1 lemon
1 teaspoon sugar
½ teaspoon salt
pinch pepper
3–4 tablespoons chopped
 parsley
4 lettuce leaves

Drain and chop the pear halves; drain the cherries and mandarin oranges, reserving a little of the juice. Dice the cheese and mix with the pears, cherries, mandarin oranges and prunes.

Lightly beat the sour cream and mix with the lemon juice, 2 teaspoons reserved mandarin juice, the sugar, salt, pepper and parsley.

Line a salad bowl with the lettuce leaves and spoon in the salad. Serve the sour cream dressing separately.
Serves 4–6

Variation
Blue cheese is particularly good in this salad, but cubes of Cheddar, Longhorn or Brick cheese may be used instead.

Herring and Beet Salad

10 pickled herring fillets
4 sweet dill pickles
2 onions
2 apples
1 egg, hard-cooked
1 cup chopped cooked ham
⅔ cup chopped cooked beets
1 tablespoon mayonnaise
3 tablespoons half-and-half
1 teaspoon white pepper
1 teaspoon sugar
Garnish
hard-cooked egg slices
tomato wedges

Chop the herring fillets. Dice the pickles. Peel and chop the onions. Peel, core and chop the apples. Chop the hard-cooked egg. Mix together all these ingredients with the ham and beets and place in a salad bowl.

Mix the mayonnaise, cream, pepper and sugar together and fold into the salad. Leave to chill for 1 hour.

Serve garnished with slices of hard-cooked egg and tomato wedges.
Serves 4

Cook's Tip
Buy Bismarck herrings for this recipe which are flat fillets preserved in a spiced vinegar.

Macaroni al Pesto

1 clove garlic
few sprigs fresh basil
4 teaspoons salt
1 tablespoon finely chopped
*   pine nuts or walnuts*
5 tablespoons grated
*   Parmesan cheese*
pinch cayenne pepper
6 tablespoons olive oil
1 lb macaroni

Peel and crush the garlic and chop the basil with a little salt, to prevent it from discoloring. Place the nuts, garlic, basil, cheese and cayenne pepper in a mortar and crush until a fine mixture is formed. (If you do not have a pestle and mortar, the ingredients can be blended in the blender.) Gradually beat 5 tablespoons of the oil into the cheese and basil mixture. The sauce should be of the same consistency as creamed butter.
Cook the macaroni in boiling salted water until *al dente* (just tender, but not soggy). Drain, toss in the remaining oil and spoon into a hot dish. Spoon over the *pesto* (the herb sauce) and serve at once.
Serves 4

Variation
This traditional Italian sauce may be served with any type of pasta.

Kidneys with Saffron Rice

½ cup oil
2 onions, chopped
1¼ cups long-grain rice
2 beef bouillon cubes
2 strands saffron
½ teaspoon white pepper
1½ lb calf kidneys
1 tablespoon salt
1 tablespoon all-purpose
*   flour*
2 teaspoons paprika pepper
1 teaspoon black pepper
2 tomatoes

Heat 4 tablespoons of the oil in a pan and fry the onions until softened. Add the rice and fry for a further 3 minutes.
Mix 2 pints boiling water with the bouillon cubes and pour over the rice. Add the saffron strands and white pepper. Cover and simmer for about 20 minutes, until the liquid has been absorbed.
Slice the kidneys, sprinkle with salt and leave for 20 minutes. Rinse under cold water and then drain. Dry. Mix the flour with the paprika and black pepper and toss the kidneys in the seasoned flour. Heat the remaining oil and fry the kidneys over a high heat. Halve tomatoes and cook under the broiler.
Garnish the rice and the kidneys with the broiled tomatoes. If liked, mayonnaise mixed with chopped fresh herbs may also be served.
Serves 4

Rustic Pork Pie

2 eggs
¾ cup frozen peas
salt
1 jar pickled baby corn
  (optional)
1 small can button
  mushrooms
2 canned pimientos
4 cooked carrots
2 dill pickles
2 envelopes unflavored
  gelatin
2 pints stock
2 teaspoons vinegar
10 black peppercorns
1¼ lb sliced roast pork

Hard-cook the eggs for 10 minutes, drain and cool in cold water.
Cook the peas in boiling salted water for about 3–4 minutes according to the directions on the package. Drain and refresh under cold water. Drain the baby corn if used and the mushrooms. Slice the mushrooms and pimientos thinly.
Slice the carrots and dill pickles with a fancy cutter if liked to give a fluted effect. Soften the gelatin in a little cold water. Heat the stock and add the softened gelatin. Allow to dissolve completely. Add the vinegar and pepper-corns. Allow to cool until on the point of setting.
Shell the eggs and slice. Arrange slices of the meat with the egg, corn, if used, mushrooms, peppers, carrots, pickles and peas attractively in a serving dish. Pour over the stock carefully and allow to set for 5–6 hours in the refrigerator.
Serve with French bread.
Serves 4

Artichoke Pizza

8 oz frozen puff pastry, or
  pizza dough (see page 57)
4 tomatoes
8 oz canned artichoke
  hearts
10 black olives
¼ cup grated Parmesan
  cheese
1 clove garlic
1 tablespoon chopped parsley
3 tablespoons oil

Thaw the pastry. Roll out
the pastry or pizza dough
and use to line an 8-inch
shallow pie pan.
Skin and halve the tomatoes
and place in the pan.
Drain the artichokes and
place between the tomatoes.
Dot with the olives and
sprinkle over the Parmesan
cheese, crushed garlic and
parsley. Brush with oil.
Bake in a hot oven (425° F)
for 20–25 minutes. Serve hot
with a salad.
Serves 4

Cook's Tip
This pizza may be
frozen either unbaked
or baked. If freezing
unbaked do not add
the garlic, parsley and
oil until the reheating
stage. Reheat (or
cook) from frozen in
a hot oven.

Swedish Meat Loaf

3 cups pie pastry (made with
  3 cups flour, etc.)
½ cup diced cooked tongue
½ cup diced cooked ham
1 lb ground pork
8 oz ground beef
5 tablespoons Madeira
½ cup liver sausage
3 egg yolks
4 tablespoons soft bread-
  crumbs
1 small pork tenderloin
1 tablespoon oil
1 teaspoon salt
1 teaspoon white pepper
6 prunes, pitted and chopped

Roll out the pastry thinly
to a rectangle and use to
line a 9 × 5 × 3-inch loaf
pan. Mix together the
tongue, ham, pork, beef,
Madeira, liver sausage, egg
yolks and breadcrumbs.
Fry the pork tenderloin in
the heated oil for 5 minutes,
until browned on all sides.
Season and leave to cool.
Bake the pastry blind in a
moderately hot oven
(400° F) for 20 minutes.
Place half the meat mixture
in the pastry-lined pan, add
the tenderloin, then the
chopped prunes.
Cover with the remaining
meat mixture, pressing it
down well. Smooth the
surface and bake for a
further 45 minutes, covering
with foil after 20 minutes.
Leave to cool, turn out and
serve cut in slices.
Serves 6–8

Liver and Bacon Rolls

1 lb calf liver
8 oz lamb liver
1 tablespoon all-purpose flour
½ teaspoon salt
½ teaspoon dried marjoram or oregano
½ teaspoon dried thyme
16–20 slices bacon
¼ cup oil

Cut liver into pieces about 1 inch thick. Sprinkle with flour, salt and herbs. Wrap each piece of liver in a slice of bacon and secure with a wooden toothpick. Place the liver and bacon rolls in the broiler pan and brush with oil. Broil for 3 minutes on each side. Serve with broiled tomatoes and baked potatoes.
Serves 4

Variation
These liver and bacon rolls may be placed on a baking sheet, brushed with oil, and baked in a moderately hot oven (400° F) for 10–15 minutes.

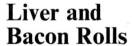

Cook's Tip
These liver and bacon rolls may be served with pre-lunch or pre-dinner cocktails. Make them bite-sized for this occasion.

Pork en Croûte

8 oz frozen puff pastry
4 oz canned mushrooms
½ cup liver sausage
3 tablespoons chopped parsley
1 12-oz piece pork tenderloin
4 tablespoons oil
½ teaspoon each salt and white pepper
beaten egg to glaze
Garnish
parsley
tomato wedges

Thaw the pastry and roll out thinly to a rectangle. Cut off 2 or 3 small strips. Drain and slice the mushrooms. Mix with the liver sausage and spread over the pastry. Sprinkle over the parsley.
Trim the pork tenderloin and brown on all sides in the heated oil. Season with salt and pepper. Cool. Place the pork tenderloin in the center of the pastry and bring up the pastry to make a neat package, sealing the joins well. Decorate with the pastry strips and brush with beaten egg. Bake in a moderately hot oven (400° F) for 20–25 minutes. To serve, cut in slices. Garnish with parsley, and tomato wedges.
Serves 3–4

Beef with Noodles

1 lb beef tenderloin
2 teaspoons salt
1 tablespoon cornstarch
3 tablespoons dry sherry
3 tablespoons soy sauce
2 teaspoons sugar
2 oz Chinese rice stick
*   noodles*
1 onion
7 tablespoons oil
¾ cup frozen peas

Cut beef into strips about 1½ inches by ½ inch. Make a marinade with the salt, cornstarch, sherry, soy sauce, sugar and 1 tablespoon water. Pour over the meat and leave to marinate for 2 hours. Cook the noodles in boiling salted water for 6 minutes. Drain and rinse in cold water.
Peel and slice the onion. Heat the oil in a pan and lightly fry the onion for 1 minute. Add the strips of meat, plus the marinade, and fry for a further 5 minutes, stirring continuously. Lastly, mix in the noodles and peas. Allow to heat through and serve at once.
Serves 4

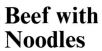

Cook's Tip
Beef tenderloin should be used for this recipe. The other prime cuts may not be sufficiently tender.

Chicken Breasts on Rice and Walnuts

2 onions
2 tomatoes
1 leek
¼ cup butter
3 tablespoons chopped
*   parsley*
4 chicken breasts
1 cup long-grain rice
¼ cup oil
½ cup chopped walnuts
Garnish
parsley

Peel and finely dice the onions. Peel and chop the tomatoes. Wash and slice the leek. Melt the butter and fry the vegetables for 5 minutes. Mix in the chopped parsley.
Slice each breast crosswise, almost through and fill each pocket with some of the fried vegetables. Secure with wooden toothpicks.
Cook the rice in boiling salted water until tender. Drain, rinse and keep warm. Heat the oil in a pan and fry the chicken breasts over a moderate heat for 5 minutes on each side. Remove the toothpicks. Arrange the rice on a serving dish and top with the chicken breasts. Sprinkle with chopped walnuts and serve garnished with parsley.
Serves 4

Chinese Beef

1 lb beef tenderloin
5 tablespoons soy sauce
1 tablespoon dry sherry
1 teaspoon salt
2 onions
1 tablespoon all-purpose
  flour
6 tablespoons oil
1 clove garlic, crushed
1 teaspoon white pepper
1 (1-lb 2-oz) can bean
  sprouts
4 teaspoons sugar
2 teaspoons cornstarch

Cut meat into thin slices or strips. Mix with 2 tablespoons of the soy sauce, the sherry and salt and leave to marinate for 30 minutes.

Peel and chop the onions. Remove the meat from the marinade and toss in the flour. Heat the oil in a frying pan and fry the onions and meat for 4 minutes. Add the marinade, the remaining soy sauce, the garlic, pepper, drained bean sprouts and sugar. Mix together and cook for a further 3–4 minutes. Thicken with the cornstarch, dissolved in 1 tablespoon water, check the seasoning and serve.
Serves 4

Variation
Pork tenderloin may be used in place of the beef. Other prime cuts of meat may not be sufficiently tender for this recipe.

Stuffed Eggplants

4 large eggplants
7 tablespoons oil
10 oz ground pork
10 oz ground beef
1 teaspoon garlic salt
¾ teaspoon black pepper
1 tablespoon soft
  breadcrumbs
5 tablespoons brandy
3 egg yolks
5 tablespoons grated cheese

Cut the eggplants in half, lengthwise. Place cut-sides upwards on a baking sheet, brush with oil and bake in a moderately hot oven (400° F) for 30 minutes. Carefully remove the flesh from the eggplants. Chop finely and mix with the ground meats, garlic salt, pepper, breadcrumbs, brandy and egg yolks. Return the mixture to the eggplant shells. Sprinkle the tops with cheese and return to the oven for a further 30 minutes. Serve with baked tomatoes.
Serves 4

Variation
The ground meats may be replaced with flaked, canned tuna. Omit the brandy and use the oil from the tuna to moisten the mixture.

Lasagne

1 onion
¼ cup olive oil
8 oz ground beef
1 teaspoon salt
½ teaspoon white pepper
5 tablespoons red wine
1 tablespoon tomato paste
6 tablespoons whipping
　cream
pinch dried oregano
1¼ lb lasagne
¼ cup butter
pinch grated nutmeg
¼ cup grated Parmesan
　cheese

Peel and dice onion. Heat
the oil in a pan and fry
the meat and onions for
5 minutes, until browned.
Add the salt, pepper, wine
and tomato paste and cook
until thick. Stir in the

cream and oregano.
Cook the lasagne in boiling
salted water until just
tender (*al dente*). Drain
and rinse under cold water.
Dry with paper towels.
Arrange the lasagne and
meat sauce in layers in a
greased ovenproof dish,
ending with a layer of
lasagne. Dot with butter
and sprinkle with nutmeg
and grated cheese. Bake in
a moderate oven (350° F)
for 10 minutes.
Serves 3–4

Veal Scallops with Rice

2 bouillon cubes
2 cups dry white wine
2 medium onions
½ cup butter
1 cup long-grain rice
½ teaspoon white pepper
1 lb veal cutlets or scallops
1 teaspoon salt
1 tablespoon all-purpose
　flour
2 eggs
6 tablespoons dry
　breadcrumbs
½ cup grated Parmesan
　cheese
Garnish
tomato wedge
parsley sprig

Dissolve the bouillon cubes
in 3 cups hot water. Add

the wine.
Peel and chop the onions.
Heat ¼ cup of the butter
in a pan and fry the onions
for 3 minutes. Stir well, and
add the rice and pepper.
Pour in the bouillon
mixture, cover and simmer
for 20 minutes, until the
liquid is absorbed.
Pound the veal, cut into
pieces, then toss in the salt
and flour. Coat in beaten
egg and breadcrumbs. Heat
the remaining butter and
fry the veal until browned
on both sides.
Spoon the rice into a
serving dish and arrange the
veal on top. Pile the
Parmesan cheese in the
center and serve garnished
with a tomato wedge and
parsley.
Serves 4

Pork with Pineapple

1 lb pork tenderloin
8 oz canned bamboo shoots
4 slices canned pineapple
1 tablespoon soy sauce
1 teaspoon each salt and
*   black pepper*
5 tablespoons vinegar
¼ cup sugar
1 tablespoon canned
*   pineapple juice*
6 tablespoons oil
3 tablespoons cornstarch

Trim the pork and cut into cubes. Drain the bamboo shoots; drain and chop the pineapple slices.
Mix together the soy sauce, salt, pepper, vinegar, sugar, pineapple juice and 2 tablespoons of the oil. Pour over the cubes of meat and turn until they are all moistened. Remove the meat from the marinade and sprinkle with 1 tablespoon of the cornstarch. Heat the rest of the oil in a frying pan and fry the meat until browned on all sides. Remove and keep warm.
Pour the marinade into the frying fat and add the bamboo shoots and pineapple. Cook for 2–3 minutes. Mix the remaining cornstarch with 1 tablespoon cold water and add to the pan. Stir until thickened. Check the seasoning, stir the meat back into the pan and serve.
Serves 4

Indonesian Rice

2 onions
2 cups oil
2 chicken bouillon cubes
1¼ cups long-grain rice
1 large apple
¼ cup butter
¼ cup curry powder
1 cup chopped cooked
*   chicken*
1 cup chopped cooked ham
To serve
fried eggs
shredded coconut
mango chutney
sweet dill pickles

Peel and chop the onions. Heat the oil and fry the onions over a high heat for 3 minutes.
Dissolve the bouillon cubes in 2 pints boiling water. Pour over the onions; add the rice, cover and simmer for 20 minutes, until all the liquid is absorbed.
Peel, core and chop the apple. Melt the butter in a pan and fry the curry powder and apple for 5 minutes. Add the chopped chicken and ham and the cooked rice and onions and cook for another 5 minutes, stirring continuously.
Serve the rice with fried eggs, shredded coconut, mango chutney and sweet dill pickles.
Serves 4

Nasi Goreng

1 cup long-grain rice
3 small onions
1 clove garlic
1 small red pepper
2 cups oil
1 tablespoon curry powder
1 cup cooked chicken, cut into strips
$\frac{3}{4}$ cup shelled prawns
$\frac{3}{4}$ cup crabmeat

Garnish
chopped parsley

Cook the rice in boiling salted water for 15 minutes. Drain, return to pan and stir over a low heat until dry.

Peel and chop the onions; crush the garlic. Seed and chop the pepper. Heat the oil in a pan, and over a medium heat, fry the onions, garlic and pepper for 3–4 minutes. Add the curry powder, and cook, stirring, for a further 2–3 minutes. Stir in the chicken and rice and cook for a further 5 minutes. Finally, stir in the prawns and crabmeat and allow to heat through. Spoon the mixture onto a serving dish and sprinkle with chopped parsley. Serve with a selection of the following side dishes: chili sauce, sweet dill pickles, mango chutney, pineapple and banana slices, shredded coconut.
Serves 4

Variation
The traditional Indonesian dish is sometimes garnished with an egg mixture. Lightly beat 2 eggs with salt and pepper and cook as for an omelet in a little heated oil. Turn the cooked egg mixture out and cut into strips. Arrange the strips over the top of the rice dish.

Loin of Pork, Provençale Style

3 teaspoons salt
1 teaspoon dried rosemary
3 tablespoons chopped parsley
3 tablespoons grated fresh horseradish root
1 3-lb pork tenderloin
2 eggs
4 tablespoons dry breadcrumbs
4 tablespoons oil

Mix 1 teaspoon of the salt with the rosemary, parsley and horseradish. Rub into the meat so that a crust is formed around the meat. Beat the eggs. Dip the meat into the beaten eggs, and then in the breadcrumbs, pressing them on well.
Place the meat in a greased roasting pan, pour over the oil and roast in a moderately hot oven (400° F) for 1½–1¾ hours, covering the meat with foil if the breadcrumb mixture becomes too brown. Serve the pork with baked tomatoes and baked potatoes which can be cooked in the oven with the meat.
Serves 4–6

Traditional Pizza

2 cups all-purpose flour
1 cake (⅔ oz) compressed yeast
½ teaspoon sugar
1¼ cups milk
6 tablespoons olive oil
1 teaspoon salt
4 tomatoes
1 teaspoon celery salt
1 teaspoon black pepper
2 teaspoons dried oregano
4 oz Mozarella cheese
2 onions, chopped
10 anchovy fillets
few capers

Sift the flour and make a well in the center. Cream the yeast with the sugar, 7 tablespoons of the luke-warm milk and 1 tablespoon of the flour. Leave covered in a warm place for 10 minutes, until frothy.
Pour into the well in the flour; leave for 30 minutes. Stir the yeast, flour, remainder of the warm milk, half the oil and the salt together, until a dough is formed. Roll out thinly to a large circle. Place on a greased baking sheet and turn up the edges slightly. Peel and slice the tomatoes and place on the dough. Add the celery salt, pepper, oregano, and slices of cheese. Scatter over the onions, anchovies, capers and the remaining oil. Bake in a moderately hot oven (400° F) for 30 minutes. Serve hot.
Serves 4

Fondues

Burgundy Meat Fondue

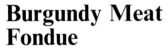

2 lb fillet of beef
oil for deep frying
Herb mayonnaise
5 tablespoons mayonnaise
1 tablespoon each chopped
   tarragon, parsley and dill
1 tablespoon half-and-half
Pepper and tomato sauce
2 tablespoons butter
2 green peppers, chopped
1 onion, chopped
4 tomatoes, peeled
5 tablespoons water
few drops Tabasco sauce
pinch each salt and pepper

Mix together the mayonnaise, herbs and cream and spoon into a small dish.
To make the pepper sauce, heat the butter in a frying pan and fry the peppers and onion until softened. Add chopped tomatoes and the remaining ingredients and simmer for 10–15 minutes. Cool, then spoon into a second small dish.
Trim the beef and cut into small cubes. Two-thirds fill a metal fondue pan with the oil and heat on the stove. Bring the heated oil to the table and place on the spirit burner.
The guests spear a cube of meat on the fondue fork and cook it in the heated oil. The cooked meat is then dipped in the chosen sauce. With a burgundy meat fondue serve baked potatoes, salads and stuffed olives.
Serves 4

Mediterranean Fondue

1 lb shelled shrimp
juice of 1 lemon
2 onions
8 oz Gruyère or Emmenthal
   cheese
2 pints chicken stock
¼ cup chopped dill
pinch cayenne pepper
½ teaspoon pepper
½ teaspoon sugar

Sprinkle the shrimp with lemon juice and leave for 10 minutes.
Peel and chop the onions. Grate the cheese. Pour the stock into a metal fondue pan and heat on the stove. Add the grated cheese and stir over a low heat until melted, but do not allow the mixture to boil. Remove from heat and stir in the onions, dill, cayenne pepper, pepper and sugar.
Bring the fondue pan to the table and place on the spirit burner. Drain the shrimp and pat dry with paper towels. Spear on the fondue forks, dip in the fondue for 1 minute, then eat.
Serve with slices of crusty hot French bread.
Serves 4–6

Paprika Fondue

8 tomatoes
1 green pepper
¼ cup butter
1½ lb Emmenthal cheese, grated
½ teaspoon black pepper
½ teaspoon paprika pepper
pinch dried marjoram
½ teaspoon celery salt
¼ cup tomato paste
½ cup whipping cream
1 teaspoon cornstarch
5 tablespoons dry white wine
16 thick slices white bread

Place the tomatoes in boiling water for 30–45 seconds, then peel and halve. Seed and chop the pepper.
Melt the butter in a fondue pan or flameproof dish placed on the stove and fry the tomatoes for 5 minutes. Add the pepper and fry for a further 5 minutes. Add the grated cheese and allow it to melt over a low heat, stirring all the time. Add the pepper, paprika, marjoram, celery salt, tomato paste and cream. Stir in the cornstarch dissolved in a little of the wine. Stir in the remaining wine. Bring the fondue pan to the table, and place on the spirit burner. Serve cubes of bread to dip into the fondue.
Serves 4–6

Cheesy Herb Fondue

2 lb Roquefort or Gorgonzola cheese
8 oz Brie cheese
¼ cup butter
5 tablespoons dry white wine
¼ cup brandy
1 cup sliced button mushrooms
¼ cup chopped herbs
½ teaspoon grated nutmeg
2 loaves French bread

Crumble the blue cheese and dice the Brie.
Place the butter in a metal fondue pan and melt on the stove. Add the wine and brandy and heat. Add the cheese and allow to melt over a gentle heat, stirring all the time. Stir in the mushrooms, herbs and nutmeg. Bring the fondue pan to the table and place it on the spirit burner.
Serve cubes of bread to dip into the fondue. A selection of salads, olives and pickles may also be served with this fondue.
Serves 6

Cook's Tip
When making cheese fondues, it is essential to allow the cheese to melt slowly over a gentle heat, stirring all the time with a wooden spoon.

59

Beer Fondue

2 cups pale ale
1¼ cups brown ale
6 tablespoons butter
1½ lb Cheddar cheese, grated
few drops Tabasco sauce
1 teaspoon prepared mustard
2 teaspoons Worcestershire
  sauce
1 teaspoon cornstarch

Place the pale and brown ales in a metal fondue pan and add 2 cups water, the butter and cheese. Heat gently on the stove, until the cheese melts, stirring. Add the Tabasco sauce, mustard and Worcestershire sauce.
Mix the cornstarch with a little cold water to form a smooth paste, and then pour into the hot fondue; stir well, until thickened. Bring the fondue pan to the table and place it on the spirit burner.
Serve with French bread and a selection of chopped raw vegetables to dip into the fondue.
Serves 6

Cook's Tip
When giving a fondue party, make sure that the fondue pan and spirit burner are placed safely in the center of the table.

Veal and Wine Fondue

1½ lb veal cutlets or scallops
3½ pints dry white wine
pinch allspice
12 coriander seeds
1 cinnamon stick
5 black peppercorns
1 teaspoon sugar
1 teaspoon salt
½ teaspoon celery salt
¼ teaspoon garlic salt

Cut the meat into thin slices. Place the wine and allspice in a metal fondue pan and bring to the boil on the stove.
Tie the coriander seeds, cinnamon stick and peppercorns in a square of cheesecloth and suspend it in the wine. Add the sugar to the wine and allow to simmer for 5 minutes. Discard the cheesecloth bag. Move the fondue pan to the spirit burner on the table. Spear the veal on the fondue fork and cook in the simmering wine. Serve sprinkled with the mixed salts and accompany with French bread and sauces.
Serves 4

Cook's Tip
If your fondue set has an earthenware pan and not a metal one, heat the oil or stock in a saucepan on the stove and then transfer it.

Breton Cheese Fondue

½ cup butter
2 lb (4 cups) cottage cheese
2 teaspoons all-purpose
   flour
2 cups milk
¼ teaspoon salt
pinch celery salt
pinch cayenne pepper
1 teaspoon paprika pepper
4 egg yolks
½ cup cooked tongue, cut
   into strips

Place the butter in a metal fondue pan and melt on the stove. Mix in the cottage cheese, flour and milk and, stirring all the time, bring just to the boil. Season with the salt, celery salt, cayenne pepper and paprika. Beat in the egg yolks, making sure the fondue does not boil. Stir the tongue into the fondue.
Bring the fondue pan to the table and place it on the spirit burner. Serve squares of bread and a selection of raw vegetables to dip into the fondue.
Serves 4

Cook's Tip
It is advisable to stand the spirit burner on a tray or mat to protect the table.

Oriental Fondue

8 oz sweetbreads
pinch salt
few drops vinegar
8 oz calf kidneys
8 oz veal cutlets or scallops
8 oz sirloin steak
8 oz lean pork
8 oz calf liver
3½ pints chicken stock
½ teaspoon dried mixed herbs
⅔ cup dry sherry

Put the sweetbreads in a pan, cover with water and add a pinch of salt and a few drops of vinegar. Bring to the boil and drain.
Cut the kidneys, veal, steak, pork, liver and sweetbreads into thin slices and place in separate containers.
Place the chicken stock, herbs and sherry in a metal fondue pan and bring to the boil on the stove. Bring to the table and place on the spirit burner.
Spear the individual slices of meat and cook in the liquid.
Serve with crusty French bread and a selection of salads and sauces.
Serves 6

Cook's Tip
With the oriental fondue keep the flame on the spirit burner high, as the cooking liquid must be kept at boiling point.

Fondues

Turkish Meat Fondue

1 lb veal cutlets or scallops
1 lb pork tenderloin
4½ pints chicken stock
Sauce
1 onion, chopped
*2 green peppers, seeded
    and chopped*
*2 tablespoons chopped
    sweet dill pickles*
2 tablespoons butter
5 tablespoons water
salt and pepper
few drops chili sauce

Cut the meats into thin
slices and place in separate
bowls.
Fry the prepared onion,
peppers and pickles in the
butter until softened. Add
the remaining sauce

ingredients, bring to the
boil, and simmer for 5
minutes, stirring occasionally. Pour into a small dish
and leave to cool.
Pour the stock into a metal
fondue pan and bring to the
boil on the stove, then place
on the spirit burner. Spear
the meat on fondue forks
and dip into the stock for
about 30 seconds. Dip into
the sauce and eat.
Serve with French bread
and a selection of salads.
Serves 4
Note Any of the sauces on
pages 72–77 may also be
served with this fondue.

Fish Fondue

8 oz flounder fillets
1 lb smoked haddock fillets
8 oz halibut fillets
*1 tablespoon all-purpose
    flour*
2 egg whites
1 teaspoon paprika pepper
½ teaspoon salt
¼ teaspoon white pepper
oil for deep frying
Sauce
*2 teaspoons Worcestershire
    sauce*
*3 tablespoons soft
    breadcrumbs*
¼ cup tomato ketchup
6 tablespoons oil
3 tablespoons vinegar
1 teaspoon sugar

Skin and cut the fish into
small pieces. Mix the flour
with the egg whites, paprika,
salt and pepper. Toss the
fish in this mixture.
Mix together the ingredients
for the sauce and place in a
small dish.
Two-thirds fill a metal
fondue pan with oil and
heat on the stove. Bring
to the table and place on the
spirit burner. Spear the
pieces of fish and cook in
the oil for 30 seconds, until
they are golden brown; dip
in the sauce before eating.
Serve with French bread
and a green salad.
Serves 6–8

Chocolate Fondue

2 oranges
2 bananas
2 pears
1½ cups pitted cherries
juice of 1 lemon
1 lb semisweet chocolate
pinch ground cinnamon
⅔ cup whipping cream
1 cup confectioners' sugar,
*   sifted*

Peel the oranges, bananas and pears. Cut the flesh into cubes and mix with the cherries. Sprinkle with lemon juice and place in a serving dish.
Grate the chocolate and place in the fondue pan with the cinnamon. Place on the spirit burner and allow to melt, stirring from time to time. Stir in the cream.
Spear the pieces of fruit, dip in the confectioners' sugar then into the chocolate fondue.
Serve with lady fingers.
Serves 4

Variation
For a mocha fondue, stir 2 teaspoons strong liquid coffee into the melted chocolate, before adding the cream. Marshmallows and cubes of plain cake may be served, in addition to the fruits, to dip into the fondue.

Cheese Fondue

8 oz Camembert cheese
1½ lb Gruyère or Gouda
*   cheese*
1 cup milk
6 tablespoons butter, melted
½ teaspoon white pepper
1 teaspoon paprika pepper
1 onion, finely chopped

Remove the Camembert from refrigerator before using and leave it at room temperature for 4 hours. Grate the Gruyère or Gouda cheese coarsely and dice the Camembert. Place the cheeses in a metal fondue pan, together with the milk, butter, seasonings and onion. Place on the stove and heat gently, stirring, until the cheese melts. Do not allow the fondue to boil.
Bring the fondue pan to the table and place on the spirit burner. Serve cubes of bread to dip into the fondue, and accompany with bowls of olives, pickles and potato chips.
Note With a cheese fondue serve a lightly chilled dry white wine.
Serves 6

Cook's Tip
If a cheese fondue should curdle, due to overheating, stir in a little lemon juice to rectify it.

Veal Cutlets with Garlic

8 oz green beans
3 tablespoons oil
½ teaspoon sugar
1½ tablespoons wine vinegar
4 cloves garlic
1 teaspoon salt
½ teaspoon black pepper
4 thick veal cutlets
Garnish
chopped chives

Cook the beans in boiling salted water until just tender. Drain, cool and mix with half the oil, the sugar and vinegar.
Peel the garlic and leave whole. Rub the salt and pepper into both sides of the veal and push a clove of garlic into each cutlet; brush both sides with the remaining oil. Broil or barbecue the cutlets for 2–3 minutes on each side. Serve sprinkled with chopped chives and with the bean salad.
Serves 4

Variation
In place of the veal cutlets, use boneless pork slices cut from the leg. Cook for 5 minutes on each side.

Cook's Tip
For a less pronounced garlic flavor, halve the cloves and rub the cut sides over the veal before cooking.

Balkan Meat Rolls

1 lb ground beef
½ teaspoon salt
¼ teaspoon black pepper
4 onions
1 clove garlic
2 tablespoons oil
1 tablespoon all-purpose flour
5 tablespoons chopped parsley
1 teaspoon paprika pepper
Garnish
parsley

Mix the meat with the salt and pepper. Peel the onions and garlic and chop together finely, then add to the meat. Mix in the oil, the flour, parsley, and paprika.

Form the mixture into small sausage shapes and broil for 5–8 minutes, turning to brown them on all sides. Garnish with parsley and serve with a cabbage salad mixed with a few caraway seeds, and French bread.
Serves 4

Variation
Ground pork may be used in place of the ground beef. Add a pinch of dried rosemary.

Fruity Meat Kebabs

8 oz fillet of beef
8 oz pork tenderloin
8 oz veal cutlet or scallops
1 large banana
juice of 1 lemon
8 canned apricot halves
½ teaspoon salt
pinch garlic salt
1 tablespoon oil

Kebabs are ideal to serve when entertaining as they can be prepared in advance and kept in the refrigerator. Cut the meat into fairly large cubes. Peel the banana, cut into 12 thick slices and sprinkle with lemon juice.
Arrange the meat, apricot halves and slices of banana alternately on four skewers. Season with salts, then brush with oil.
Broil or barbecue for 5–8 minutes, turning to brown the kebabs on all sides. Serve with rice and a green salad.
Serves 4

Variation
In place of the apricots and bananas, use canned pineapple cubes and figs, or cooked prunes and cubes of apple.

Cook's Tip
If you choose a less expensive cut of meat for these kebabs, allow the cubes of meat to marinate in a mixture of oil and vinegar for 1 hour.

Fish with Herbs

2 haddock fillets
1 teaspoon lemon juice
3 tablespoons chopped
   parsley
3 tablespoons chopped
   chives
salt
2 teaspoons oil

Sprinkle the haddock with
lemon juice, herbs, salt and
oil. Leave in the refrigerator
to marinate for 30 minutes.
Broil or barbecue for about
4 minutes on each side,
brushing with more oil
from time to time.
Serve with a tomato and
onion salad.
Serves 2

Variation
Other white fish fillets may
be used in place of the
haddock – try flounder, cod
or turbot.

Cook's Tip
If you prefer to use
frozen fish for this
recipe, be sure to
allow it to thaw
completely before
cooking. The result
may be dryer.

Cheesy Pork Chops

3 heads French or Belgian
   endive
1 bulb fennel
$\frac{2}{3}$ cup plain yogurt
juice of 1 orange
juice of 1 lemon
1 teaspoon sugar
pinch each salt and white
   pepper
2 onions
2 tablespoons butter
$\frac{1}{3}$ cup dried apricots
$\frac{1}{2}$ cup liver sausage
$\frac{1}{2}$ cup diced cheese
4 boneless pork chops
1 tablespoon all-purpose
   flour
$\frac{1}{4}$ cup oil

Trim and cut the endive
and fennel into strips. Mix
the yogurt with the orange
and lemon juices, sugar, salt
and pepper and spoon over
the mixed endive and
fennel. Chill.
Peel and chop the onions.
Melt the butter in a pan and
brown the onion. Chop the
apricots. Mix together the
liver sausage, browned
onions, diced cheese and
apricots. Trim and flatten
the chops. Spread with the
liver sausage mixture and
fold each chop in half.
Secure with wooden tooth-
picks. Coat with flour, and
brush both sides with oil.
Broil or barbecue for about
8 minutes on each side.
Remove the toothpicks
and serve with the endive
and fennel salad.
Serves 4

Broils and Barbecues

Ranch-Style Chicken

1 cup soft breadcrumbs
3 tablespoons chopped parsley
1 red pepper, seeded and chopped
1 green pepper, seeded and chopped
1 onion, chopped
2 teaspoons chopped basil
1 egg
pinch each salt and black pepper
¼ cup grated cheese
2 broilers
3 tablespoons oil
2 teaspoons paprika pepper

Mix together the breadcrumbs, parsley, peppers, onions, basil, egg, seasonings and cheese to form a stuffing. Use to stuff the chickens.
Place the chickens in a roasting pan and brush with oil. Cover with foil and roast in a moderately hot oven (400° F) for about 30 minutes.
Remove the foil, brush with a little more oil and sprinkle with paprika. Return to the oven for a further 10 minutes to brown.
Split each broiler in half and serve with a tangy barbecue sauce.
Serves 2–4

Spit-Roasted Lamb

4½ lb boned and tied leg of lamb
⅔ cup oil
1 teaspoon paprika pepper
¼ teaspoon cayenne pepper
2 teaspoons salt
1 tablespoon Worcestershire sauce
5 tablespoons red wine
1 teaspoon black pepper
1 bay leaf
12 juniper berries
8 oz bacon slices

Remove the skin from the lamb and place the meat in a large dish. Mix together the oil, peppers, salt, Worcestershire sauce, wine and pepper. Pour over the lamb, add the bay leaf and leave to marinate in the refrigerator for up to 6 hours.
Remove the meat from the marinade, pat dry with paper towels and push the juniper berries into the lamb. Cover with bacon and secure with wooden toothpicks.
Place the meat on the rotisserie spit so that the weight is evenly distributed. Place the spit on the rotisserie and cook the meat for 1½–2 hours. While the meat is cooking, from time to time spoon over a little of the marinade. To serve, remove the bacon slices and toothpicks and place the lamb on a carving board.
Serves 6

Salmon Steaks

1 piece candied ginger
juice of 1 lemon
¼ cup soy sauce
3 tablespoons canned
*   crushed pineapple*
1 teaspoon curry powder
½ teaspoon salt
4 salmon steaks
4 leeks
1 tablespoon all-purpose
*   flour*
½ teaspoon black pepper
2 tablespoons butter

Chop the ginger finely.
Make a marinade with the
lemon juice, soy sauce,
pineapple, curry powder,
salt and chopped ginger.
Spoon over the salmon
steaks and leave to

marinate for 20 minutes.
Slice the leeks.
Remove the salmon from
the marinade and toss in
flour. Broil or barbecue
for 6 minutes on each
side, brushing with the
marinade from time to time.
Meanwhile, cook the leeks
in boiling salted water until
just tender. Drain and toss
in black pepper and butter
and serve with the salmon
steaks.
Serves 4

Fish and Ham Rolls

1¾ lb haddock fillets
½ teaspoon salt
1 teaspoon paprika pepper
3 tablespoons grated cheese
2 teaspoons chopped parsley
2 teaspoons chopped dill
4 thin slices cooked ham
1 tablespoon oil
Garnish
parsley sprigs
dill sprigs

Cut the fish into four equal
pieces and sprinkle with the
salt, paprika, grated cheese
and herbs. Roll a slice of
ham around each piece of
fish and secure with a
wooden toothpick.
Brush the rolls with oil and

broil or barbecue for about
15 minutes, turning the rolls
halfway through the
cooking time. Before
serving, remove the
toothpicks and garnish
with parsley and dill sprigs.
Serves 4

Variation
Use flounder instead of the
haddock and cook for a
total of about 12 minutes.
If liked, the slices of ham
may be lightly spread with
a little mild mustard.

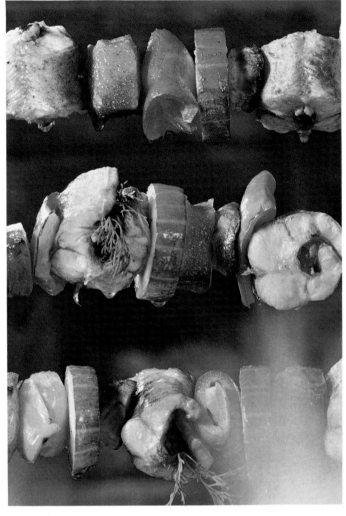

Halibut Steaks

4 halibut steaks
½ teaspoon salt
1 tablespoon grated cheese
1 teaspoon paprika pepper
¼ cup oil
1 carrot
2 onions
1 leek
1 celery stalk
¼ cup butter
4 slices cooked ham

Sprinkle the halibut steaks with the salt, cheese, paprika and oil. Broil or barbecue for about 15 minutes, turning the steaks halfway through the cooking time.
Meanwhile, chop the vegetables finely and fry in the butter until softened.
Place a spoonful of fried vegetables on each slice of ham and form into a roll; secure the ham rolls with a wooden toothpick.
Place beside the halibut and cook for 5 minutes. Remove the toothpicks before serving.
Serve with fresh spinach.
Serves 4

Eel Kebabs

1½ lb fresh eel, skinned and cut into small pieces
½ teaspoon celery salt
½ cucumber
1 red or green pepper
4 oz bacon slices
few dill sprigs
12 button mushrooms
juice of 1 lemon
¼ cup oil
½ teaspoon paprika pepper

Sprinkle the eel with the celery salt.
Cut the cucumber into ½-inch slices. Seed and cut the pepper into cubes.
Make the bacon into rolls. Thread pieces of eel, dill, cucumber, bacon rolls, mushrooms and pepper on to skewers. Sprinkle with lemon juice, oil, and paprika. Broil or barbecue the kebabs for 5 minutes, turning to brown them evenly.
Serves 4

Variation
If fresh eel is not available, smoked eel may be used instead.

Broils and Barbecues

Lobster with Garlic Toast

2 cooked lobsters
8 oz mushrooms
½ cup butter
2 teaspoons dry mustard
4–6 slices bread
1 clove garlic
1 teaspoon lemon juice
pinch white pepper
pinch onion salt

Cut the lobsters in half lengthwise. Remove the meat, chop roughly and mix with the chopped mushrooms, ¼ cup of the butter and the mustard. Fill the lobster shells with the mixture. Place under the broiler and cook for 5 minutes.
Toast the slices of bread.

Crush the garlic and blend with the remaining butter, the lemon juice and seasonings. Spread on the toast, cut in halves or quarters, and serve with the lobster.
Serves 4

Cook's Tip
When purchasing lobster, choose one of medium size which feels heavy for its size. Avoid ones with white shells as this is a sure sign of an old lobster. The tail should curl back up after being pulled, showing it was alive when cooked.

Stuffed Veal Cutlets

4 thick veal cutlets or
  scallops
½ teaspoon celery salt
½ teaspoon paprika pepper
pinch white pepper
2 onions
¼ cup butter
½ cup liver sausage
¼ cup chopped parsley
¼ cup chopped chives
1 tablespoon soft
  breadcrumbs
1 tablespoon oil

Trim the veal and cut each cutlet three-quarters of the way through, making a pocket. Mix the celery salt, paprika and pepper, and rub into the cutlets.
Peel and chop the onions.

Heat the butter in a frying pan and cook the onions until softened. Remove from the heat and add the liver sausage, herbs and breadcrumbs, stirring well. Leave to cool.
Spread the stuffing in the pocket of each cutlet and secure with wooden toothpicks. Brush the cutlets with oil and place in the broiler pan or on the barbecue rack. Broil or barbecue for 4 minutes on each side.
Remove the toothpicks and serve the veal cutlets with peas.
Serves 4

Broils and Barbecues

Stuffed Pork Chops

4 thick boneless pork chops
2 slices white bread
¼ cup whipping cream
½ teaspoon salt
¼ teaspoon white pepper
¼ cup chopped parsley
1 tablespoon chopped chives
1 tablespoon chopped chervil
¼ cup oil
1 teaspoon paprika pepper

Slit each chop horizontally so that a small pocket is formed.
Dice the bread and mix with the cream, salt, pepper and herbs. Mix thoroughly and use to fill the pocket in each chop. Secure with wooden toothpicks. Brush the chops with oil and sprinkle with paprika, then broil or barbecue for 10–15 minutes on each side. Remove the toothpicks and serve the chops on a · bed of braised cabbage, or sauerkraut.
Serves 4

Variation
In place of the chopped chives and chervil use a pinch of dried rosemary, or cook the chops with a sprig of fresh rosemary.

Trout with Dill Butter

4 trout
1 teaspoon salt
½ teaspoon allspice
1¼ teaspoons white pepper
juice of 2 lemons
¼ cup chopped dill
¼ cup butter
6 tablespoons oil
1 lb tomatoes
1 onion, finely chopped

Trout is available all the year round, fresh or frozen. Allow frozen trout to thaw before using.
Rub the insides of the trout with salt and allspice, ¼ teaspoon of the pepper and half the lemon juice. Mix the dill with the butter and spread inside the trout.
Lay the fish on the broiler pan or barbecue rack, brush · with oil and broil or barbecue for about 5 minutes on each·side. Meanwhile, peel the tomatoes, halve or slice and sprinkle with the remaining lemon juice and pepper and chopped onion. Serve with the trout.
Serves 4

Cook's Tip
If lake trout are available, they are particularly delicious cooked this way. Be careful not to overcook the fish or it will be dry.

71

Sauces for Fondues and Broils

Piquant Malaga Sauce

2 eggs, hard-cooked
2 eggs
1 teaspoon ground black
   pepper
½ teaspoon cayenne pepper
⅔ cup olive oil
1 cup chopped almonds
⅓ cup golden raisins
1 tablespoon clear honey
¼ cup wine vinegar
¼ cup tomato ketchup

Chop the hard-cooked eggs
and mix with the raw eggs,
pepper, cayenne pepper and
oil.
Stir in the chopped almonds,
the raisins and remaining
ingredients. Leave in a cool
place for 20 minutes to
allow the flavors to blend.

Serve this sauce with
broiled fish, kebabs or meat
fondues.
Serves 6

Variation
Red or white wine may be
used in place of the wine
vinegar. Instead of the
tomato ketchup use 2
tablespoons tomato paste
blended with 1 tablespoon
water.

> **Cook's Tip**
> Always check the
> seasoning of sauces
> just before serving
> and adjust if
> necessary.

Spanish Sauce

1 red pepper
1 green pepper
1 cup sour cream
3 tablespoons wine vinegar
½ cup olive oil
1 teaspoon white pepper
⅔ cup dry white wine
1 teaspoon salt
1 teaspoon garlic salt
2 eggs, hard-cooked
3 tablespoons chopped
   chives
¼ cup soft breadcrumbs

Halve, seed and chop the
peppers.
Mix together the sour
cream, vinegar, oil, pepper,
wine, salt and garlic salt
with ½ cup warm water;
blend until smooth. Chop

the eggs and add to the
sauce with the chopped
chives, breadcrumbs and
peppers. Serve this sauce
with broiled or fried meats
or kebabs.
Serves 6

Variation
Whipping cream may be
used in place of the sour
cream. Add 1 teaspoon
lemon juice.

Sauces for Fondues and Broils

Garibaldi Sauce

2 egg yolks
2 teaspoons prepared
*   mustard*
½ teaspoon garlic salt
2 teaspoons anchovy paste
pinch cayenne pepper
1¼ cups oil
3 tablespoons wine vinegar
1 tablespoon tomato ketchup
1 tablespoon capers

Place the egg yolks,
mustard, salt, anchovy
paste and cayenne pepper
in a bowl. Beat lightly,
then drop by drop, beat in
the oil until the mixture is
thick. Thin the mayonnaise
with 1 tablespoon boiling
water and the vinegar.
Stir in the tomato ketchup

and capers.
Serve this sauce with
broiled or fried herrings or
mackerel, and meat
fondues.
Serves 6

Cook's Tip
This sauce may be
made in advance and
stored for 1–2 days in
a covered plastic
container in the
refrigerator.

Provençale Sauce

2 onions
1 cup tomato ketchup
6 tablespoons capers
3 tablespoons chopped
*   chives*
½ cup whipping cream
2 teaspoons dried rosemary
1 teaspoon dried marjoram
2 eggs, hard-cooked
½ teaspoon garlic salt
3 tablespoons oil
1 tablespoon wine vinegar

Peel and finely chop the
onions. Mix with the
tomato ketchup, capers,
chives, lightly whipped
cream, rosemary and
marjoram.
Chop the eggs and mix with
the garlic salt, oil and wine

vinegar until thoroughly
combined.
Just before serving the
sauce, blend the hard-
cooked egg mixture into the
tomato mixture.
Serve this sauce with meat
fondues and broiled or
fried lamb chops.
Serves 6

Variation
A clove of garlic may be
used in place of the garlic
salt. Peel and crush the
garlic before using.

Cucumber Sauce

2 eggs
½ cucumber
2 onions
4 dill sprigs
3 tarragon sprigs
1 tablespoon Pernod
(optional)
1 teaspoon Worcestershire
sauce
3 tablespoons oil
¼ cup wine vinegar

Hard-cook the eggs for 10 minutes, shell and chop finely. Peel the cucumber and cut the flesh into small pieces. Chop the onions. Place the cucumber, herbs and onions in the blender and blend until smooth. Pour the purée into a bowl and add the Pernod Worcestershire sauce, oil and vinegar. Sprinkle the chopped hard-cooked egg on the top of the sauce. Serve this sauce with broiled turbot, halibut or salmon, or with broiled veal or lamb or with meat fondues.
Serves 6

Cook's Tip
If you do not have a blender, grate the cucumber and onions and then mix with the other ingredients. Use a pinch each of dried dill and tarragon.

Garlic Mayonnaise

4 large cloves garlic
¼ teaspoon salt
pinch celery salt
2 teaspoons lemon juice
2 egg yolks
1 cup olive oil

This is a specialty in Spain where it is served with broiled fish and meat.
Peel and crush the garlic, then mix with the salts and lemon juice.
Place the egg yolks in a bowl with the garlic mixture. Beating all the time, add the oil, drop by drop, until a thick sauce is formed. Do not add the oil quickly as the sauce will separate. If the mayonnaise is too thick, thin it down with a little wine vinegar, but do not make it a pouring consistency.
Garlic mayonnaise may be made successfully in the blender. Place the garlic mixture and egg yolks in the goblet, switch on to high speed and, in a steady stream, pour in the oil, to form a thick sauce.
Serves 4–6

Cook's Tip
When making mayonnaise, have all the ingredients at room temperature. Do not use eggs straight from the refrigerator.

Sauces for Fondues and Broils

Piquant Tomato Sauce

2 onions
¼ cup oil
¼ cup dry white wine
4 tomatoes
¼ cup cooked ham, cut into strips
½ teaspoon garlic salt
2 teaspoons sugar
2 teaspoons grated fresh horseradish root
½ teaspoon white pepper

Peel and chop or grate the onions. Mix with the oil and wine and stir thoroughly.
Peel and chop the tomatoes. Stir the tomatoes and ham into the sauce, together with the salt, sugar, horseradish and pepper.
Serve this sauce with broiled

fish, pork or lamb or with meat fondues.
Serves 4

Variation
Ready-made horseradish sauce may be used in place of the fresh horseradish.

Cook's Tip
For this recipe use large, fully-ripe tomatoes. The sauce may be prepared in advance and stored in the refrigerator.

Rose Hip Sauce

5 oz rose hips
1 cup cream
¼ cup oil
½ cup port
grated rind and juice of 1 lemon
1 teaspoon salt
2 teaspoons paprika pepper
pinch cinnamon
pinch ground cloves
2 teaspoons sugar
1 teaspoon Worcestershire sauce

Wash and slit the rose hips, then crush them in the blender, or with a fork.
Mix with the cream, oil and port.
Put the lemon rind and juice, the salt, paprika,

cinnamon, cloves and sugar in a small bowl and mix together. Mix into the rose hip mixture. Finally, stir in the Worcestershire sauce.
Leave for 20 minutes for the flavors to blend.
Serve this sauce with broiled pork or veal, and with meat fondues.
Serves 6

Variation
If preferred the sauce may be strained to remove the seeds.

Sour Cream Sauce

2 onions
6 dates
¼ cup capers
¼ cup wine vinegar
1 teaspoon sugar
¼ cup oil
1 cup sour cream
3 tablespoons chopped
   parsley

Peel and chop the onions;
pit and chop the dates.
Mix together the onions,
dates, capers, vinegar and
sugar and blend in the
blender until smooth.
Transfer to a bowl and
beat in the oil, sour
cream and parsley.
Serve this sauce with baked
potatoes, broiled pork
chops or steaks, or meat
fondues.
Serves 4–6

Cook's Tip
If you want to make
your own sour cream
substitute, add 3–4
drops of lemon juice
to ⅔ cup whipping
cream and leave it at
room temperature for
30 minutes.

Madeira Sauce

¼ cup smooth liver pâté
1¼ cups chicken stock
½ cup Madeira
1 cup button mushrooms
¼ cup sour cream
2–3 tablespoons soft
   breadcrumbs
2 tablespoons butter

Blend the liver pâté with
the stock and bring to the
boil. Stir in the Madeira and
sliced mushrooms and
simmer for 5 minutes.
Add the sour cream,
breadcrumbs and butter.
Reheat, but do not boil.
Serve this sauce with veal,
venison, game, or kidney
and bacon rolls.
Serves 4–6

Variation
If preferred the breadcrumbs
and butter can be omitted
and the sauce thickened
with beurre manié. Knead
together ¼ cup flour and
2 tablespoons butter to
form a paste. Beat small
amounts of the flour and
butter paste into the sauce
and cook, stirring until
thickened. Add the sour
cream, but do not allow the
sauce to boil.

Spicy Apple Sauce

¼ cup raisins
1 lb cooking apples
1 teaspoon salt
½ teaspoon white pepper
pinch cayenne pepper
2 teaspoons cinnamon
1 tablespoon horseradish
    sauce (optional)
¼ cup half-and-half

Soak the raisins in hot water.
Peel, core and slice the apples and cook in a small amount of water until softened. Beat the cooked apple to a purée and mix with the drained raisins, the salt, peppers, cinnamon and horseradish sauce. Reheat and just before serving stir in the cream. Serve this sauce with broiled pork chops, ham steaks or meat fondues.
Serves 4–6

Cook's Tip
Keep a few raisins stored in a jar containing 3–4 table-spoons dry sherry. The dried fruit will be plump and impart a delicious flavor to dishes.

Blender Barbecue Sauce

1 onion
4 tomatoes
1 clove garlic, crushed
1¼ cups red wine
1 tablespoon wine vinegar
few drops Tabasco sauce
1 tablespoon brown sugar
1 teaspoon Worcestershire
    sauce
1 teaspoon black pepper
1 tablespoon red currant jelly
pinch salt

Chop the onion; peel and chop the tomatoes. Place in a pan with the remaining ingredients, bring to the boil and simmer for 10 minutes. Cool slightly, then blend in the blender. Return to the pan, check the seasoning and reheat. Serve this sauce with sausages, steaks or broiled chicken.
Serves 4

Cook's Tip
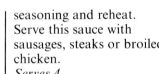
To crush a clove of garlic, sprinkle a little salt on to a board, add the peeled clove of garlic and crush it with the salt using the tip of a round-bladed knife.

Jellied Tomato Cocktail

2 envelopes unflavored
  gelatin
3–4 tablespoons water
1 teaspoon celery salt
1 teaspoon white pepper
1 teaspoon Worcestershire
  sauce
pinch garlic salt
3 cups tomato juice
Garnish
orange and lemon slices
3 tablespoons chopped chives

Soften the gelatin in cold
water. Add the celery salt,
pepper, Worcestershire
sauce and garlic salt to the
tomato juice and heat.
Dissolve the gelatin in the
heated tomato juice. Pour
into a shallow container,

cool and allow to set.
Just before serving, cut the
tomato gelatin into cubes
and arrange in chilled
serving dishes. Garnish with
orange and lemon slices and
a sprinkling of chopped
chives. Serve with hot toast.
Serves 4

Cook's Tip
A speedy way
of cutting chives is
to snip them with
a pair of scissors.

Cream Cheese Cup

1 cup cream cheese
⅔ cup plain yogurt
little milk
1 teaspoon anchovy paste
½ teaspoon caraway seeds
1 teaspoon celery salt
½ teaspoon white pepper
2 eggs, hard-cooked
4 tomatoes
Garnish
3 tablespoons chopped herbs
2 teaspoons caviar
1 celery stalk, chopped

Mix the cream cheese and
yogurt together until
smooth and creamy, adding
a little milk if necessary to
make a soft consistency.
Add the anchovy paste,
caraway seeds, celery salt

and pepper. Shell the eggs
and peel the tomatoes and
cut into slices. Put the egg
and tomato slices into four
glasses. Spoon over the
cream cheese mixture and
garnish with the herbs,
caviar and chopped celery.
Serves 4

Cook's Tip
To peel tomatoes,
nick the skins,
plunge into boiling
water and leave for
30–45 seconds. The
skins will then easily
peel off.

Lobster with Truffles

2 cooked lobsters, each weighing about 1–1¼ lb
Garnish
1 small can truffles
1 orange
parsley sprigs
1 egg, hard-cooked
2 tablespoons mayonnaise

With a sharp knife cut each lobster in half down the middle joint mark, first towards the head, then towards the tail. Remove the claws from the body. Crack the claws with the flat side of the knife until they split.
Take the meat from the tail. From the inside of the lobster remove and discard the gut – a dark-looking thread – with the tip of the knife. Cut the meat from the tail into slices.
Slice the truffles thinly and lay them on the top of the lobster alternately with the tail meat. Halve the orange and place the halves, cut side up, on a large dish. Arrange the body of the lobster on the dish with the claws beside it.
Halve the hard-cooked egg, remove the yolk and mix it with the mayonnaise. Pipe the mixture back into the egg whites and arrange on the dish with the lobster.
Garnish with parsley.
Serve with freshly made toast and butter.
Serves 6

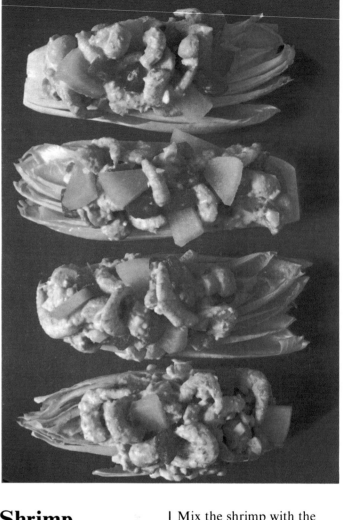

Halibut Vol-au-Vents

*1 lb halibut or other firm-
    fleshed white fish*
⅝ cup butter
*juice of 1 lemon or 3 table-
    spoons dry white wine*
*4 large or 8 small baked
    vol-au-vent cases (patty
    shells)*
4 egg yolks
1 teaspoon paprika pepper
½ teaspoon salt

Skin the fish and cut into
pieces. Place in an oven-
proof dish with 2 table-
spoons of the butter and
half the lemon juice or
wine. Cover and poach in
a cool oven (300° F) for
15 minutes. Remove the
bones and flake the fish;

keep warm. Heat the vol-au-
vent cases in the oven.
In a bowl, beat the egg
yolks with the remaining
lemon juice, the paprika,
salt and 5 tablespoons of
water; place the bowl over
a pan of hot water and
continue to beat the
mixture until it begins to
thicken. Melt the remaining
butter and gradually add to
the beaten mixture.
Continue beating until the
butter is completely
absorbed.
Fill the vol-au-vent cases
with the flaked fish and
pour over the sauce. Serve
any remaining sauce
separately.
Serves 4

Shrimp Salad

1½ cups shelled shrimp
juice of 1 lemon
1 teaspoon onion salt
2 eggs, hard-cooked
4 small tomatoes
*1 small can pear halves,
    sliced*
*½ cup canned button
    mushrooms, drained*
3 tablespoons milk
5 tablespoons mayonnaise
¼ cup Drambuie (optional)
pinch chili powder
⅔ cup whipping cream
*1 tablespoon finely chopped
    sweet dill pickle*
1 teaspoon paprika pepper
salt
*2 heads French or Belgian
    endive*

Mix the shrimp with the
lemon juice and onion salt.
Shell and chop the eggs.
Peel and chop the tomatoes.
Mix the eggs, pears,
tomatoes and mushrooms
with the shrimp. Mix the
milk, mayonnaise, liqueur
and chili powder into the
lightly whipped cream.
Add the pickles and season
the mixture with paprika
and salt. Stir into the
shrimp mixture. Wash and
halve the endive heads,
removing the coarse outer
leaves. Arrange the shrimp
mixture in the endive leaves.
Serves 4–6

Egg Rolls

2 dried Chinese mushrooms
10 oz lean pork, sliced
seasoned flour
½ cup oil
8 oz canned bamboo shoots,
*   sliced*
3–4 tablespoons soy sauce
2 teaspoons cornstarch
2½ cups all-purpose flour
1 teaspoon salt
1 egg
1 egg white

Soak the mushrooms in hot water then cut into thin strips. Coat the meat in seasoned flour.
Heat 2 tablespoons of the oil in a frying pan and fry the mushrooms and bamboo shoots; add 1 teaspoon of the soy sauce, cook for 3 minutes.
Fry the meat slices in 3 tablespoons of the oil, add 3 tablespoons water and the remaining soy sauce and stir in the vegetables. Thicken with the dissolved cornstarch. Cool.
Sift the flour and salt. Mix with ½ cup boiling water. Add the egg and knead to form a dough. Roll out very thinly and cut into eight squares. Put some of the filling on each square and make into packages; seal the edges with egg white. Heat the remaining oil and fry the rolls until golden. Drain and serve hot.
Serves 8

Danish Toasts

1 apple
lemon juice
4 eggs, hard-cooked
⅔ cup whipping cream
2 teaspoons dry mustard
3 tablespoons mayonnaise
5 tablespoons chopped fresh
*   dill (optional)*
4 slices toast
4 oz smoked salmon

Peel, core and slice the apple; dip in lemon juice. Shell and slice the hard-cooked eggs. Lightly whip the cream and mix with the mustard, mayonnaise and dill, if used.
Remove the crusts from the slices of toast and arrange the smoked salmon slices on each piece. Top with an apple slice and slices of hard-cooked egg. Finally, spoon over the mayonnaise mixture.
Serves 4

Cook's Tip
If smoked salmon is not available, canned salmon mixed with freshly ground black pepper and a squeeze of lemon juice may be substituted.

Palm Hearts with Salmon

1 small can palm hearts
1½ tablespoons wine vinegar
3 tablespoons oil
3 tablespoons white wine
8 thin slices smoked salmon
Sauce
5 tablespoons mayonnaise
1 teaspoon paprika pepper
½ teaspoon Tabasco sauce
1 tablespoon chopped green
  pepper
1 tablespoon chopped red
  pepper
1 tablespoon chopped chives
1 tablespoon chopped
  beets
3 tablespoons wine vinegar
3 tablespoons sour cream
½ teaspoon sugar
Garnish
1 tablespoon chopped truffles

Drain the palm hearts. Mix the vinegar with the oil and wine, pour over the palm hearts and leave, covered in the refrigerator for 30 minutes to marinate. Remove from the marinade and wrap a slice of smoked salmon around each palm heart. Arrange on a dish and sprinkle with the chopped truffles.
Mix the ingredients for the sauce together and serve separately.
Serves 4

Cook's Tip
If canned palm hearts are not available, they may be replaced by canned or fresh asparagus tips, artichoke hearts or celery.

Celebration Appetizers

Chilled Fish Salad

4–6 pickled herrings
2 apples
2 onions
1 canned pimiento, sliced
⅔ cup sour cream
⅔ cup plain yogurt
juice of ½ lemon
¼ teaspoon salt
pinch pepper
Garnish
onion rings

Soak the herrings in cold water for 1 hour. Drain and cut into strips. Peel and core the apples and slice thinly. Peel the onions and grate finely. Mix the herrings, apple slices, onions and pimiento together. Mix together the sour cream, yogurt, lemon juice and salt and pepper. Arrange the fish salad in a serving bowl and chill in the refrigerator for 20 minutes. Spoon over the sauce and serve garnished with onion rings.
Serves 4–6

Special Stuffed Eggs

8 eggs, hard-cooked
2 tablespoons butter
1 tablespoon mayonnaise
1 teaspoon curry powder
4 tablespoons cream cheese
1 tablespoon half-and-half
4 stuffed olives
3–4 pieces canned or fresh
  peach
2 teaspoons caviar
8 candied cherries

Halve the hard-cooked eggs. Melt the butter. Remove the yolks from eight of the egg halves and mix with the melted butter, mayonnaise and curry powder. Chill for 30 minutes. Mix the yolks from the remaining halved eggs with the cream cheese and cream. Pipe into eight of the egg whites. Garnish with sliced olives, pieces of peach and the caviar. Pipe the chilled curried mixture into the remaining egg halves and garnish with a candied cherry.
Serves 4

Abalone Soup from China

1 teaspoon cornstarch
1 teaspoon soy sauce
1 teaspoon dry sherry
6 oz filleted tenderized
   abalone
2 cups chicken stock
about 1 teaspoon salt
Garnish
chopped parsley

Mix the cornstarch with the soy sauce and sherry. Pour over the abalone slices and allow to marinate for 30 minutes, turning from time to time. Place the chicken stock in a pan and bring to the boil. Add the abalone slices plus the marinade and simmer for 2 minutes.

Season with salt. Serve sprinkled with chopped parsley.
Note If liked, pieces of cooked chicken may also be added to the soup.
Serves 4

Cook's Tip
If fresh abalone is not readily available, use canned. Do not let the fish boil – it should just be allowed to heat through.

Spanish Tomato Broth

4 small tomatoes
1 (15-oz) can consommé
3 tablespoons chopped
   chervil
5 tablespoons chopped
   parsley
salt and pepper
1–2 teaspoons paprika
   pepper
Garnish
tomato strips

Nick the tomato skins, plunge into boiling water, leave for 30–45 seconds, then peel off the skins and cut the tomatoes into quarters.
Put the consommé in a pan and bring almost to the boil, add the tomatoes,

chervil and parsley. Simmer for 5 minutes. Add the seasoning and paprika. Serve garnished with tomato strips.
To make this soup more substantial serve it with slices of brown bread, spread with pâté and sandwiched with lettuce. Top each sandwich with a slice of orange.
Serves 4

Cook's Tip
If fresh chervil is not available replace it with chopped fresh basil, which blends well with tomato dishes.

Rice Soup

3 cups beef bouillon
1 cup cooked long-grain rice
1 (15-oz) can turtle soup
½ cup cooked tongue, cut into strips
5 tablespoons flaked almonds
4 butter pats

Place the bouillon and rice in a pan, bring to the boil and simmer for 5 minutes. Rub through a fine strainer, or blend in a blender. Return to the pan and reheat. Add the turtle soup and allow to heat. Divide the tongue between four soup bowls. Pour over the rice soup and sprinkle with flaked almonds. Add a pat of butter to each bowl before serving.

Variation
Heat the cooked rice in 3 cups beef bouillon. Cut ⅔ cup cooked ham into thin strips, add to the soup and heat through. Peel and chop 4 small tomatoes. Divide between four bowls and pour over the hot soup. Sprinkle each serving with 1 tablespoon grated mild cheese.
Serves 4

Italian Tomato Soup

3 bouillon cubes
6 tomatoes
2 tablespoons butter
salt and pepper
1 tablespoon vinegar
4 eggs
Garnish
strained hard-cooked egg yolk
5 tablespoons chopped parsley
3 tablespoons chopped chives

Dissolve the bouillon cubes in 3½ pints water and bring to the boil. Nick the tomato skins, plunge into boiling water for 30–45 seconds and peel off the skins. Halve the tomatoes and squeeze out the seeds. Add to the bouillon and leave on a low heat. Add the butter and allow it to melt. Season to taste.
In another pan bring 2 pints water to the boil with the vinegar. Break the eggs, one at a time, on to a wet saucer and let them slip into the water. When all 4 eggs are in the water lower the heat and simmer the eggs for 5 minutes, until they are firm. (Alternatively, use an egg poacher.)
Ladle the soup into deep soup plates. To each serving add some strained hard-cooked egg yolk and a poached egg. Sprinkle with chopped parsley and chives.
Serves 4

Soups

Liver Dumpling Soup

3 stale rolls
salt
½ cup lukewarm milk
1 onion
2 tablespoons oil
3 tablespoons chopped
  parsley
½ cup ground liver
1 egg
pinch white pepper
pinch dried marjoram
grated rind of ¼ lemon
2 pints bouillon
Garnish
chopped chives

Cut the rolls into very thin slices. Sprinkle over ½ teaspoon of salt and pour over the lukewarm milk to soften them.

Peel the onion and chop finely. Heat the oil in a frying pan and fry the chopped onion until transparent; add the parsley. Mix together the onion, softened bread, liver, egg, pepper, marjoram, lemon rind and ½ teaspoon salt. With wet hands, form the mixture into balls about the size of a tomato. Bring the bouillon to the boil and simmer the liver dumplings, covered, for about 15 minutes. Spoon into soup bowls and serve garnished with chopped chives.
Serves 4

French Onion Soup

6 large onions
½ cup butter
1 teaspoon pepper
3½ pints beef bouillon
2 slices bread, crusts
  removed
⅔ cup dry white wine
½ cup grated cheese

Peel the onions and cut into thin rings. Heat 6 tablespoons of the butter in a pan. Add the onion rings and fry until they are transparent. Add the pepper and bouillon, bring to the boil and simmer for 10 minutes. Meanwhile, melt the rest of the butter in a frying pan. Cut the bread into small cubes and fry in the butter

until brown. Drain on paper towels.
Stir the white wine into the soup, check the seasoning and reheat. Ladle into a tureen or individual soup bowls. Sprinkle the croûtons and the grated cheese over the top.
Serves 4

Cook's Tip
If you ladle the hot soup into ovenproof soup bowls you can sprinkle over the croûtons and grated cheese, dot with butter and heat under the broiler until the cheese melts and turns golden brown.

Winter Soup

2 pints milk
1 cup chicken stock
1 bay leaf
6 peppercorns
3 cloves
1 small onion
½ cup pork sausagemeat
3 tablespoons fresh breadcrumbs
¼ teaspoon dried mixed herbs
2 teaspoons chopped parsley
salt and pepper
3 tablespoons butter or margarine
6 tablespoons all-purpose flour
¾ cup cooked peas

Place the milk and chicken stock in a saucepan with the bay leaf, peppercorns, cloves and peeled and quartered onion. Bring very slowly to the boil; remove from the heat and allow to infuse for 20 minutes. Meanwhile, make up the meat balls by mixing the sausagemeat, breadcrumbs, herbs, parsley, salt and pepper together. Make into eight even-sized balls. Strain the milk into a measuring jug. Melt the butter or margarine in a large pan, add the flour and cook for 1 minute, then gradually blend in the strained milk. Bring to the boil, stirring. Add the meatballs and simmer for 10–15 minutes. Stir in the cooked peas. Taste and adjust seasoning if necessary.
Serves 4

Gazpacho

1 medium cucumber
12 oz tomatoes
1 red pepper
1 green pepper
2 large Bermuda onions
1 teaspoon finely chopped garlic
2 cups soft white breadcrumbs
3 tablespoons red wine vinegar
2 teaspoons salt
2 teaspoons olive oil
½ teaspoon paprika pepper or chili sauce

Wash the cucumber, tomatoes and peppers. Chop the cucumber, peel and chop the tomatoes, seed and chop the peppers. Peel and chop the onions.

In a bowl mix the vegetables with the garlic, breadcrumbs, about 2 cups water, the vinegar and salt. Blend the mixture in a blender. Beat the oil and paprika or chili sauce into the tomato mixture and leave, covered, in the refrigerator for 2 hours. Before serving, stir well and ladle into chilled soup bowls.
Serve with separate bowls of cubes of bread, finely chopped onion, chopped cucumber and chopped red and green peppers.
Serves 4

Chilled Cucumber Soup

1⅓ *cups plain yogurt*
½ *cucumber*
½ *teaspoon salt*
¼ *teaspoon black pepper*
2 cups buttermilk
2 cups chicken stock
1 egg, hard-cooked
½ *teaspoon paprika pepper*

Place the yogurt in a bowl. Peel and grate the cucumber. Mix the yogurt and grated cucumber, cover and leave in the refrigerator overnight.
The following day, add the salt and pepper, pour in the buttermilk and the stock and mix well. Shell the egg and chop finely. Ladle the soup into bowls and sprinkle with chopped egg and paprika.
Serves 4

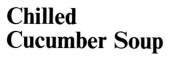

> **Cook's Tip**
> If preferred, you may chop the cucumber, instead of grating it, and blend the soup in the blender.

Princess Soup

½ *cup long-grain rice*
1 lb cooked chicken
2 tomatoes
5 tablespoons chopped fresh herbs
salt and pepper
Garnish
chopped parsley

Cook the rice in boiling salted water until tender. Drain and rinse under cold running water. Finely chop or grind the chicken. Add 2 pints water to the chicken and simmer for 5 minutes. Meanwhile nick the skins of the tomatoes, plunge into boiling water for 30–45 seconds and peel; chop coarsely and stir into the chicken with the herbs. Season to taste and stir in the rice. Allow to heat through, then serve garnished with chopped parsley.
Serves 4

Variation
To the above soup, add 1 small can of asparagus tips, chopped, and ¾ cup frozen peas. Simmer for 5 minutes.

Cream of Vegetable Soup

1–1½ lb vegetables as
available
½ teaspoon salt
1 tablespoon butter
1–2 tablespoons all-purpose
flour
2 cups milk
2 egg yolks
½ cup half-and-half
salt and pepper
Garnish
chopped parsley

Suitable vegetables would
be cauliflower, white
asparagus stalks, or green
asparagus tips, peas,
tomatoes, carrots or
potatoes.
Prepare the vegetables
according to kind. Cook in
a small amount of salted
water until tender. Rub
through a strainer with the
vegetable water or purée in
a blender.
Melt the butter in a saucepan, add the flour and cook
for 2–3 minutes, stirring.
Gradually stir in the milk,
bring to the boil and add
the vegetable purée; reheat.
Beat the egg yolks with the
cream. Put a few spoonfuls
of hot soup into the yolk
and cream mixture, remove
the soup from the heat and
stir the yolk and cream
mixture into the soup.
Season to taste and serve
sprinkled with chopped
parsley.
Serves 4

Cook's Tip
The flavor of this
vegetable soup may
be varied by stirring
in 3–4 tablespoons
chopped fresh herbs.
Grated cheese may be
sprinkled over, or the
soup may be topped
with a spoonful of
sour cream.

Devilled Shrimp

1 teaspoon garlic salt
1 teaspoon celery salt
about 1½ lb shelled shrimp
⅔ cup long-grain rice
¾ cup frozen peas
5 tablespoons oil
2 bay leaves
juice of 1 lemon
½ teaspoon cayenne pepper
Garnish
1 bay leaf

Sprinkle the garlic and celery salts over the shrimp. Cook the rice in boiling salted water until tender. Drain and keep warm. Cook and drain the peas; keep warm.
Heat the oil in a shallow pan, put in the shrimp very closely together in a single layer and cook for 3 minutes. Turn over, place the bay leaves on top and sprinkle with the lemon juice; dust evenly with the cayenne pepper. Cook for a further 3 minutes.
Mix the rice with the peas and arrange around the edge of a serving dish. Remove the shellfish from the pan, drain on paper towels and spoon into the center of the rice. Serve garnished with a bay leaf.
Serves 4

Danish Fishballs

2 rolls
4 onions
1 lb white fish fillets, skinned
3 tablespoons capers
1 teaspoon anchovy paste
5 tablespoons all-purpose flour
2 eggs
⅔ cup cream
pinch each cayenne, nutmeg and curry powder
1½ teaspoons salt
¼ cup butter
3 cups milk
¼ teaspoon white pepper
1 tablespoon horseradish sauce
2 cups soft white breadcrumbs
juice of ½ lemon

Soften the rolls in water. Peel and quarter the onions. Grind the fish, onions, capers, anchovy paste and softened rolls. Place in a bowl and mix with the flour, eggs, cream and seasonings.
Bring 2 pints water and 1 teaspoon of the salt to the boil. Form the fish mixture into balls and simmer for 5 minutes. Remove and keep warm. Melt the butter and add the milk, the remaining salt and pepper. Beat in the horseradish sauce, bread-crumbs and lemon juice until the mixture has thickened. Serve with the fishballs.
Serves 4

Stuffed Flounder

4 whole small flounder
5 tablespoons chopped chives
¼ cup butter
1 teaspoon salt
juice of 1 lemon
1 teaspoon Worcestershire
sauce
1 teaspoon horseradish sauce
1 teaspoon dry mustard
1 teaspoon sugar
1¼ cups dry white wine
4 tomatoes

Make a cut on the darker side of the flounder along the spine as far as the middle bone and make an incision to make a pocket. Mix together the chives, butter, salt, lemon juice, Worcestershire sauce, horseradish sauce, mustard and sugar. Put the seasoned butter into the incisions in the flounder.
Place the fish in an oven-proof dish and pour in the wine. Nick the skins of the tomatoes and lay them on the fish. Cover and cook in a moderately hot oven (400° F) for 15–20 minutes. Lift on to a heated serving dish and spoon over the cooking juices.
Serves 4

Fishballs with Shrimp

1 lb white fish fillets,
skinned
2 onions
salt
¼ teaspoon white pepper
2 teaspoons paprika pepper
2 eggs
⅔ cup cream
¾ cup shelled shrimp
1¼ cups white sauce
⅔ cup dry white wine
5 tablespoons chopped dill

Cut the fish fillets into small pieces. Peel and chop the onions. Place the fish pieces, salt, pepper, paprika, eggs, onions and cream in the blender. Blend to a purée. Bring a pan of salted water to the boil. Form the fish mixture into balls and drop into the boiling water, lower the heat and simmer for 5 minutes. Remove with a slotted spoon and place in an ovenproof dish. Mix the shrimp with the white sauce, wine and dill and pour over the fishballs. Cover and bake in a moderately hot oven (400° F) for 20 minutes. Serve with boiled rice.
Serves 4

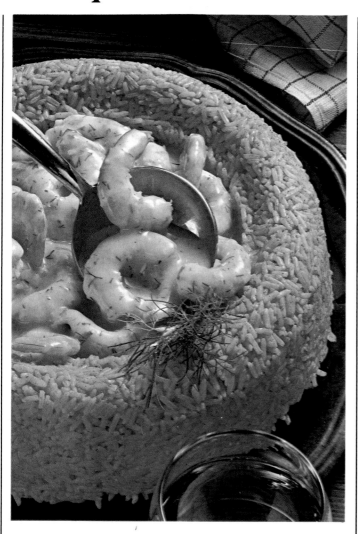

Shrimp with Dill and Rice

1 cup long-grain rice
7 tablespoons half-and-half
½ teaspoon salt
¼ teaspoon sugar
¼ teaspoon white pepper
2 tablespoons butter
1 tablespoon all-purpose flour
3 tablespoons chopped dill
1 lb shelled shrimp
7 tablespoons oil
1–2 teaspoons paprika pepper
dill sprigs

Cook the rice in boiling salted water until tender. Rinse in cold water and drain. Reheat in a colander, placed over a pan of hot water.

Heat the cream with 2 cups water, the salt, sugar and pepper. Work the butter into the flour to form a paste and whisk small amounts into the sauce until it thickens. Stir in the chopped dill and shrimp. Keep hot.

Mix the rice with the oil and paprika and press into an oiled ring mold. Turn out on to a heated dish, and spoon the shrimp sauce into the center. Serve garnished with dill sprigs.
Serves 4

Pike Balls

2 lb pike or carp
1 onion
1¼ cups dry white wine
1 bay leaf
4 eggs
pinch salt
pinch pepper
pinch grated nutmeg
⅝ cup butter
1 cup all-purpose flour
1 cup milk

Skin and bone the fish. Peel the onion. Place the fish trimmings in a pan with 1¼ cups water, the wine, onion and bay leaf. Bring to the boil and simmer for 15 minutes. Strain and season the fish stock. Cut the fish into pieces and purée in a blender, or chop finely. Separate the yolks from the egg whites and beat the whites until firm. Mix in the puréed fish, season with salt, pepper and nutmeg and leave in refrigerator for 30 minutes. Make a thick sauce with the butter, flour and milk. Cool, then gradually add the egg yolks and fish purée. Shape the mixture into balls and cook in the fish stock for 15 minutes. Remove with a slotted spoon and serve with spinach and buttered potatoes.
Serves 4

Trout with Almonds

4 trout
⅔ cup milk
1 teaspoon salt
¼ cup all-purpose flour
½ cup butter
¼ cup flaked almonds
Garnish
tomato wedges
lemon wedges
sprigs parsley

Marinate the trout in the milk and salt for 10 minutes. Remove and roll in the flour. Melt 6 tablespoons of the butter in a frying pan and cook the trout for 4–6 minutes over a medium heat. Place on a heated dish and keep warm. Add the remaining butter to the pan and fry the flaked almonds until they are golden brown. Scatter over the trout. Garnish with the tomato and lemon wedges and parsley.
Serves 4

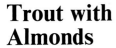

> **Cook's Tip**
> An easy way to coat the fish in flour is to place the flour in a plastic bag, add one trout and shake the bag until the fish is evenly coated.

Sweet and Sour Fish with Mushrooms

3 dried Chinese mushrooms
1–1¼ lb cod fillets
1 tablespoon monosodium glutamate
3 tablespoons soy sauce
2 onions
3 tablespoons cornstarch
1 tablespoon all-purpose flour
2 pints oil
7 tablespoons tomato ketchup
3 tablespoons wine vinegar
4 teaspoons sugar

Soak the mushrooms in hot water. Cut the fish into 1½-inch cubes. Sprinkle over the mono- sodium glutamate and soy sauce and leave for 10 minutes.
Peel and slice the onions; drain the mushrooms. Mix 1½ tablespoons of the cornstarch with the flour. Roll the fish cubes in the flour mixture. Heat the oil and fry the fish cubes in the oil until golden brown. Drain on paper towels and keep warm. Fry the onion slices in 3 tablespoons oil in a frying pan. Add the mush- rooms, heat through and mix with the fish cubes. Mix the ketchup, vinegar, sugar and remaining corn- starch together. Cook, stirring, over a moderate heat until the sauce thickens. Serve separately.
Serves 4

Fish Fillets in Batter

1½ lb white fish fillets
1½ teaspoons salt
2 teaspoons paprika pepper
½ teaspoon white pepper
few drops Angostura bitters
2 tomatoes
4 oz cheese, sliced
5 tablespoons all-purpose flour
2 eggs
½ cup butter

Cut each fillet into 3–4 pieces, making 6 or 8 portions. Dust each piece with salt, paprika pepper and white pepper and sprinkle over a few drops of Angostura bitters. Nick the tomato skins, plunge into boiling water for 30–45 seconds; peel off the skins and cut into thick slices. Place a slice of cheese and tomato on 3 or 4 of the fish pieces. Cover each with another piece of fish, making a sandwich. Press together and secure with a wooden toothpick. Sift the flour into a bowl and make a thick batter with the eggs and a little water. Melt the butter in a pan. Dip the prepared fish in the batter and cook in the butter until golden brown, turning at least twice during cooking. Do not turn the heat up too high or the fish will not cook through. Drain on paper towels and serve with potato salad. *Serves 4*

Liver Sausage-Stuffed Flounder

8 flounder fillets
¼ cup liver sausage
5 tablespoons chopped parsley
5 tablespoons grated cheese
6 tablespoons butter

Place the fillets on a board and spread each one with some liver sausage, then sprinkle on the parsley and cheese. Sandwich two fillets with the sausage sides together, and secure with a wooden toothpick. Melt the butter in a frying pan and brown the fish on each side, until cooked through.

Drain on paper towels and serve at once.
Serves 4

Cook's Tip
Save scraps of cheese, grate them finely and store in an airtight container in the refrigerator. Different varieties of cheese may be mixed together to give a good flavor.

Prawns with Vegetables

1 leek
5 tablespoons oil
1¼ lb shelled prawns
¾ cup frozen peas
½ teaspoon cayenne pepper
½ teaspoon celery salt
1 teaspoon ground ginger
1 teaspoon sugar

Clean, trim and finely slice the leek. Heat the oil in a pan and cook the prawns until they are pale brown. Add the leek and peas and cook for a further 5 minutes. Sprinkle with the cayenne pepper, celery salt, ginger and sugar. Turn into a heated dish and serve.
Serves 4

Variation
Frozen prawns may be used if fresh ones are not available.

Cook's Tip
This dish doesn't benefit by being kept hot and should be served immediately it is cooked.

Haddock in Mustard Sauce

2 lb haddock steaks
1 teaspoon paprika pepper
1 teaspoon salt
½ teaspoon white pepper
½ cup butter
5 tablespoons chopped parsley
2 ripe bananas
3 tablespoons hazelnuts
3 tablespoons currants
¼ cup all-purpose flour
2 cups milk
½ cup prepared mild mustard
1 tablespoon sugar
juice of ½ lemon
few drops Tabasco sauce
5 tablespoons dry white wine
Garnish
parsley sprigs

Dust the haddock steaks with the paprika, salt and pepper and place in an ovenproof dish. Dot with half the butter and sprinkle over the parsley. Slice the bananas and place on top. Coarsely chop the hazelnuts; wash the currants. Melt the remaining butter in a saucepan, stir in the flour and lightly brown; add the milk and stir until thickened. Then stir in the mustard, sugar, lemon juice, Tabasco sauce, nuts and currants. Pour the sauce over the fish to cover completely. Pour over the wine. Bake in a cool oven (300° F) for 25–30 minutes. Garnish with parsley and serve with buttered potatoes.
Serves 4

Ragoût of Carp

1 carp, weighing 1¾ lb,
    cleaned
6 medium onions
1 clove garlic
salt
½ cup oil
all-purpose flour
5 tablespoons paprika pepper
1 teaspoon beef extract
4 cups hot cooked noodles
4 tablespoons sour cream

Thoroughly clean the inside of the fish under running water. Cut thick slices across the body and then cut them in half on the middle bone. Peel the onions and slice thinly. Peel the garlic and crush with a little salt with the tip of a knife. Heat the oil in a flameproof casserole. Lightly brown the onions, stirring all the time. Add the crushed garlic. Roll the pieces of carp in a little flour, place on top of the onions and sprinkle over the paprika. Cover with a lid and cook for 25 minutes. Stir in the beef extract and check the seasoning. Arrange the noodles on four serving plates and spoon over the ragoût. Top with a spoonful of sour cream. Serve with creamed potatoes.
Serves 4

Stuffed Herrings

4 herrings
4 slices bread
⅔ cup milk
2 eggs
½ teaspoon salt
½ bouillon cube
½ teaspoon black pepper
½ teaspoon cayenne pepper
½ cup chopped parsley
2 tablespoons butter, melted
⅔ cup oil
Garnish
parsley sprig

Score the herrings. Slit open on the underside, gut and wash thoroughly in cold water. Dry with paper towels.
Cut the bread into cubes and heat the milk. Put the bread in a bowl with the heated milk to soften it. Beat in the eggs, salt, bouillon cube, pepper and cayenne. Lastly add the parsley and melted butter. Use to stuff the herrings. Brush the broiler pan and the herrings with oil and broil for 12–15 minutes. Serve garnished with parsley, and a potato salad sprinkled with chopped chives.
Serves 4

Special Occasion Dishes

Stuffed Fish Fillets

1¼ lb white fish fillets
juice of 1 lemon
½ teaspoon salt
1 onion
4 tomatoes
few sprigs rosemary
4 thin slices hard cheese
Garnish
rosemary sprigs
lemon wedges

Wash the fillets under cold running water and pat dry with paper towels. Squeeze the lemon juice over the fillets and rub in the salt. Peel the onion and slice into rings.
Nick the skins of the tomatoes, plunge into boiling water, leave for 30–45 seconds and then peel. Cut into thick slices.
Place half the fillets in an ovenproof dish. Then place the onion rings, sliced tomatoes, rosemary and cheese slices on top and cover with the remaining fillets. Cover and bake in a hot oven (425° F) for 15–20 minutes.
Arrange the cooked fish on a dish and garnish with rosemary and lemon wedges. Serve with cooked long-grain rice, and peppers and corn.
Serves 4

Cook's Tip
The best type of cheese to use for this recipe is either Gruyère or Gouda. They are both mildly flavored cheeses and go particularly well with fish.

Kebabs

Fish Kebabs

8 oz each of fresh eel, perch,
   sole and flounder
2½ teaspoons salt
½ teaspoon white pepper
2 teaspoons dry mustard
1 teaspoon Worcestershire
   sauce
few drops Tabasco sauce
½ teaspoon caraway seeds
12–16 shallots
¼ cucumber
1 cup long-grain rice
1 cup button mushrooms
4 oz bacon slices
½ cup oil

Skin and bone the eel.
Wash all the fish, remove
any skin or bones, cut into
cubes (not too small) and
put in a bowl. Add the salt,
pepper, mustard, Worcestershire sauce, Tabasco sauce
and caraway seeds; toss the
fish cubes in the seasoning.
Peel and halve the shallots.
Slice the unpeeled cucumber
thickly. Cook the rice in
boiling salted water until
tender. Rinse, drain and
keep warm.
Meanwhile, remove the
fish from the marinade and
arrange alternately with the
cucumber slices, shallots,
mushrooms and bacon
slices, made into rolls, on
skewers. Heat the oil in a
frying pan. Add the kebabs
and fry for 10 minutes on
each side. Drain on paper
towels and serve with the
rice.
Serves 4

Beef Kebabs

2 teaspoons seasoned salt
1 teaspoon pepper
3 tablespoons chopped dill
16 very thin slices beef
   tenderloin
2 large leeks
1 red pepper
1 cucumber
4 oz bacon slices
oil for deep frying

Mix together the seasoned
salt, pepper and dill and
rub over the beef. Allow
the flavors to penetrate.
Meanwhile, wash the leeks
and seed the pepper. Cut the
leek, pepper, cucumber and
the bacon into 16 narrow
strips as long as the pieces
of meat and put one on
each slice. Roll up and
thread on to skewers.
Heat the oil in a deep fat
fryer and fry the beef rolls
for 5 minutes, turning
occasionally. Drain on
paper towels and arrange
on a serving dish.
Serve with a green salad.
Serves 4

Cook's Tip
To test the tempera-
ture of the oil for
deep frying, drop in a
cube of white bread.
If the oil is the
correct temperature,
the bread will turn
golden brown in
1 minute.

Eggplants in Batter

3 eggplants
1 teaspoon paprika pepper
1 cup all-purpose flour
5 tablespoons cream cheese
2 eggs
3 tablespoons grated cheese
2 apples
1 teaspoon celery salt
oil for deep frying
5 tablespoons chopped
    parsley
Garnish
tomato wedge
parsley sprig

Peel the eggplants and cut into bite-sized pieces.
Make a thick batter with the paprika, flour, the cream cheese, 5 tablespoons cold water, the eggs and the grated cheese. Peel, core and slice the apples.
Sprinkle the celery salt over the apple slices and eggplant pieces.
Heat the oil in a deep fat fryer. Dip the eggplant and apples slices in the batter; thread several pieces alternately on to skewers and deep fry in the heated oil. Remove the fried kebabs with a slotted spoon, sprinkle immediately with the chopped parsley and keep warm until all the kebabs are cooked.
Serve garnished with tomato and parsley.
Serves 4

Serbian Kebabs

1 lb ground beef
2 pork link sausages
1 egg
2 large onions
1 green pepper
1 teaspoon garlic salt
2 teaspoons salt
4 teaspoons paprika pepper
1 teaspoon black pepper
pinch cayenne pepper
3 tablespoons dry
    breadcrumbs
2 dill pickles
4 tablespoons oil

Mix the ground beef and sausages (squeezed out of their skins) with the egg.
Peel and finely dice the onions. Halve, seed and chop the pepper.
Mix the onions and pepper with the meat. Add the garlic salt, salt, paprika, pepper and cayenne. With floured hands, form the mixture into small sausage shapes and roll in the breadcrumbs.
Slice the pickles thickly.
Push the sausages alternately with the pickle slices on to skewers and brush with the oil. Broil for 7 minutes, turning occasionally.
Serve with tomato sauce and baked potatoes topped with herb butter.
Serves 4

Kebabs

Chicken Kebabs

1 lb chicken breasts
1 teaspoon celery salt
$\frac{1}{2}$ teaspoon garlic salt
$\frac{1}{2}$ teaspoon allspice
3 tablespoons oil
1 orange
$\frac{1}{2}$ cup mayonnaise
$\frac{1}{2}$ cup sour cream
2 teaspoons dry mustard

Cut the chicken breasts into pieces about 2 inches wide. Mix together the celery salt, garlic salt and allspice and rub over the chicken pieces.
Push these slices on to skewers; place in an oven-proof dish and sprinkle over the oil. Bake the kebabs in a hot oven (425° F) or under the broiler for 8 minutes. Meanwhile, peel the orange, cut into small pieces and remove the seeds. Mix the mayonnaise with the sour cream and mustard. Stir in the orange slices.
Serve with the kebabs.
Serves 4

Cook's Tip
Chicken breasts are available fresh or frozen. If using frozen chicken breasts allow them to thaw completely before preparing the recipe.

Swiss Liver Kebabs

1 lb lamb liver
4 oz bacon slices
2 small onions
5 tablespoons oil
1 teaspoon salt
2 teaspoons paprika pepper
4 button mushrooms
2 tomatoes
5 tablespoons tomato paste
$\frac{2}{3}$ cup bouillon
$\frac{1}{4}$ cup butter
1 tablespoon all-purpose flour

Chop the liver into small pieces. Cut the bacon into pieces the same size as the liver and peel and quarter the onions. Heat the oil in a frying pan. Dust the liver with the salt and paprika and cook for 4 minutes, turning constantly. Remove. Fry the bacon until well browned with the onions, mushrooms and halved tomatoes.
Thread the prepared pieces of food on to skewers, arranging them colorfully. Keep hot. In a bowl mix the tomato paste with the bouillon. Bring to the boil. Work the butter into the flour to form a paste and whisk into the bouillon until a thick, smooth sauce is formed. Season, and pour over the kebabs. Serve with rice.
Serves 4

Prawn Kebabs

$\frac{1}{4}$ cucumber
4 oz smoked eel
4-oz piece bacon
16–20 shelled prawns
12 stuffed olives
$\frac{1}{2}$ cup canned button
   mushrooms
2 teaspoons paprika pepper
$\frac{1}{2}$ teaspoon salt
$\frac{1}{4}$ teaspoon white pepper
pinch monosodium glutamate
1 teaspoon dill powder
$\frac{1}{2}$ cup oil

Slice the cucumber thickly. Skin the eel, remove the bones and cut into bite-sized pieces. Cube the bacon.
Thread the prawns on to skewers with the olives, cucumber slices, eel, bacon and mushrooms. Mix the paprika, salt, white pepper, monosodium glutamate and dill together and sprinkle over the kebabs, turning them all the time so that they are seasoned all over. Leave in the refrigerator for 30 minutes. Place the kebabs in a shallow oven-proof dish, pour over the oil and bake in a moderately hot oven (400° F) for 10–15 minutes.
Serves 4

Caucasian Kebabs

1 lb sirloin steak
$\frac{1}{2}$ teaspoon salt
$\frac{1}{2}$ teaspoon meat tenderizer
4 onions
2 teaspoons paprika pepper
$\frac{1}{2}$ teaspoon black pepper
12 button mushrooms
$\frac{2}{3}$ cup oil
Garnish
strips red pepper
strips onion

Cut the meat into even bite-sized cubes. Mix the salt and the meat tenderizer together and rub all over the meat cubes. Leave for 15 minutes.
Meanwhile, peel and quarter onions. Rub the paprika into the onions and sprinkle the black pepper on the mushrooms. Thread the meat cubes, onions and mushrooms on to skewers. Brush the kebabs with oil and place on the broiler rack. Broil for 8 minutes, turning to cook them evenly. Serve on a bed of turmeric-flavored rice and garnish with pepper and onion strips.
Serves 4

Filet Mignon Cussy

4 thick filet mignon steaks
½ cup oil
1 teaspoon coarsely ground
  black pepper
1–2 teaspoons paprika
  pepper
1 can artichoke hearts
½ cup unsweetened chestnut
  purée
½ cup button mushrooms
6 tablespoons Madeira
1 teaspoon salt
½ teaspoon garlic salt
Garnish
chopped parsley

Trim the steaks if necessary.
Spoon over 3 tablespoons
of the oil, sprinkle with
black pepper and paprika.
Leave to marinate in the
refrigerator for 2 hours.
Fill the center of each
artichoke with some
chestnut purée and heat
gently in the liquid from the
can for 10 minutes.
Heat the remaining oil in a
frying pan and fry the steaks
for 3 minutes on each side.
Remove and keep warm.
Add the mushrooms and
fry for 1–2 minutes.
Sprinkle over the steaks.
Add the Madeira, the salt
and garlic salt to the pan
and cook for 30 seconds;
pour over the steaks.
Arrange a filled artichoke
on each steak and serve
garnished with chopped
parsley.
Serves 4

Wine-merchant's Beefsteak

1 cup butter
1 onion, cut into rings
1¼ cups red wine
½ bay leaf
¼ teaspoon dried thyme
4 sprigs parsley
2 teaspoons beef extract
4 sirloin steaks
3 tablespoons vegetable oil
1 teaspoon salt
freshly ground black pepper

Melt 2 tablespoons of the
butter, over a moderate
heat, in a frying pan. When
the butter stops bubbling
fry the onions for 5 minutes,
until they become trans-
parent. Pour on the red
wine and simmer for 15
minutes with the bay leaf,
thyme and parsley.
Dissolve the meat extract
in 3 tablespoons warm
water and stir into the
sauce. Soften ½ cup of the
remaining butter and stir
into the sauce.
Fry the steaks in the
remaining butter and the
oil for 1 minute on each
side to seal them, then
again for 1½ minutes on
each side. Place on a warm
dish and season with salt
and pepper. Pour the wine
sauce into the steak pan.
Stir round to mix in the
sediment, then serve with
the steaks. Serve with peas
and potatoes.
Serves 4

Entrecôte Westmorland

1 small cauliflower
4 entrecôte steaks
1½ teaspoons seasoned salt
1 teaspoon black pepper
1 teaspoon dry mustard
oil for deep frying
1 teaspoon salt
Sauce
1¼ cups brown sauce
4 teaspoons prepared mild
  mustard
5 tablespoons white wine
5 tablespoons brandy
Garnish
sprig parsley

Wash the cauliflower and break into flowerets. Trim the steaks and rub with the salt, pepper and mustard.

Heat 4 tablespoons of the oil in a frying pan and fry the steaks for 3 minutes on each side. Remove and keep warm.
Heat the rest of the oil in a deep fat fryer and deep fry the cauliflowerets for 6 minutes, until golden brown. Drain on paper towels and sprinkle with salt. Place the cauliflower with the steaks.
Heat the sauce, add the mustard, wine and the brandy and cook for 2 minutes. Pour over the steaks and serve with the cauliflowerets. Garnish with parsley.
Serves 4

Sirloin Steaks on Pastry

12 oz frozen puff pastry
beaten egg yolk to glaze
4 carrots, diced
2 celery stalks, chopped
8 oz asparagus
2 (1-lb) sirloin steaks
4 tablespoons oil
1½ teaspoons salt
1 teaspoon black pepper
½ cup butter
5 tablespoons brandy
2 egg yolks
5 tablespoons whipping
  cream
Garnish
1 small canned truffle
  (optional)

Thaw the pastry, divide in half and roll out each half to a round about ⅛ inch thick. Place on two baking sheets. Brush with egg yolk and bake in a moderately hot oven (400° F) for 20 minutes. Cook the prepared vegetables in a little salted water. Drain and keep hot. Trim the steaks and fry in the heated oil for 5–8 minutes on each side. Remove, season and keep warm. Add the butter to the pan. Pour the brandy into the melted butter, mix the egg yolks with the cream and stir into the pan. Reheat (but do not boil). Arrange each steak on a pastry round. Top with the vegetables and garnish with grated truffle, if liked. Serve the sauce separately.
Serves 4

Steaks Melba

4 medium tomatoes
½ cup grated cheese
4 strip or boneless loin
   steaks
5 tablespoons oil
1 teaspoon salt
½ teaspoon black pepper
5 tablespoons port
Garnish
lettuce leaves

Cut the tomatoes in half, hollow out and fill with the grated cheese. Brown under the broiler.
Fry the steaks in the heated oil for 3 minutes on each side, lowering the heat after 1 minute. Season with salt and pepper and keep warm. Stir the port into the frying pan, scraping up all the sediment. Bring to the boil and pour into a sauceboat. Arrange the steaks on a serving dish and garnish with lettuce leaves and the tomatoes.
Serve the sauce separately.
Serves 4

> **Cook's Tip**
> When frying steaks, they should be sealed on each side over a high heat for 1 minute and the heat then lowered until the steaks are cooked to your liking.

Steaks Mirabeau

4 strip or boneless loin
   steaks
6 tablespoons butter
2 tablespoons anchovy paste
juice of 1 lemon
6 stuffed olives
5 tablespoons oil
1 teaspoon salt
½ teaspoon ground black
   pepper
8 anchovy fillets

Trim the steaks.
Beat 4 tablespoons of the butter (which should be at room temperature) with the anchovy paste and lemon juice. Chill.
Slice the olives. Heat the oil in a pan and fry the steaks for 3 minutes on each side. Place on a serving dish, season with salt and pepper and keep warm.
Melt the rest of the butter in the pan, scrape up the sediment and pour over the steaks. Arrange the anchovy fillets, crosswise, and olives on top. Serve slices of the anchovy butter separately. Serve with French fried potatoes and salad.
Serves 4

> **Cook's Tip**
> Strip or boneless loin steaks (from the sirloin) are Porterhouse steaks with fillet, and bone, removed. (On West Coast called New York strip.)

Tournedos Helder

1 teaspoon black pepper
1 teaspoon garlic salt
4 tournedos
4 tomatoes
6 tablespoons butter
1 teaspoon salt
½ teaspoon white pepper
3 tablespoons chopped
  parsley
4 tablespoons oil

Press the black pepper and garlic salt on to each side of the steaks.
Nick the skins of the tomatoes, plunge them into boiling water for 30–45 seconds and peel off the skins. Cut into quarters and squeeze out the juice and the seeds. Chop the

flesh and put in a saucepan with the butter, salt, white pepper and parsley; cook for 5 minutes, over a moderate heat, stirring occasionally.
Heat the oil in a frying pan and fry the steaks over a high heat for 2–3 minutes on each side. Arrange the steaks on a heated dish and spoon the tomato mixture on top.
As an accompanying vegetable, serve asparagus tips coated with a cheese sauce.
Serves 4

Entrecôte Meyerbeer

4 entrecôte steaks
4 tablespoons oil
1 teaspoon garlic salt
1 teaspoon black pepper
1 lamb kidney
1 teaspoon salt
½ cup Madeira
1 beef bouillon cube
5 tablespoons cream
3 tablespoons chopped
  canned truffles (optional)
Garnish
parsley sprig

Trim the steaks. Heat the oil in a frying pan and fry the steaks for 2 minutes on each side, remove and season with the garlic salt and pepper; keep warm.
Slice the kidney thinly,

sprinkle with salt and fry for 1 minute in the frying pan. Arrange on the steaks.
Stir the Madeira into the sediment in the frying pan and dissolve the bouillon cube in it. Bring to the boil. Remove from the heat and stir in the cream and truffles, if used. Spoon over the steaks. Serve garnished with parsley.
Serves 4

Steaks

Classic Steaks

*2 strip or boneless loin
    steaks*
4 tablespoons oil
salt
ground black pepper
Garnish
*few sliced mushrooms or
    onions*
chopped parsley

Trim the steaks.
Heat the oil in a frying pan
and fry the steaks for
1 minute on each side.
Reduce the heat and fry for
a further 3 minutes on each
side. (If you prefer your
steaks rare, cook them for
a total of 5 minutes.)
Season with salt and pepper.
Remove and keep warm.
Add the sliced mushrooms
or onions and cook until
softened. Spoon over the
steaks and sprinkle with
chopped parsley.
Serve with a selection of
vegetables in season, or a
salad.
Serves 2

Variation
Tournedos are cut from the
center of the fillet.
These steaks are very tender.
Brush the steaks with
melted butter or oil, season
and broil for about 4–5
minutes on each side. Serve
with herb butter and corn-
on-the-cob.
Porterhouse steaks are cut
from the chump end of the
sirloin, containing part of
the fillet. Brush the steaks
with oil and broil for 3–5
minutes on each side.

Cook's Tip
The cooking times
given for the steaks
will give a medium
steak. If you prefer
a rare or well done
steak adjust the times
accordingly.

Broiled Steak with Herbs

1–2 cloves garlic
4 thick strip or boneless loin
   steaks
1 tablespoon finely chopped
   onion
1 teaspoon each salt and
   pepper
½ cup dry sherry
1 egg, hard-cooked
5 tablespoons chopped fresh
   herbs (chives, parsley,
   dill)
2 teaspoons dry mustard
½ cup butter

Peel and crush the cloves of garlic and press into the steaks. Place the steaks in a shallow dish, sprinkle over the onion, seasoning and sherry and leave to marinate in a cool place for up to 4 hours.

Chop the hard-cooked egg and mix with the herbs, mustard and butter. Remove the steaks from the marinade and broil for 7–9 minutes, brushing with the marinade, until cooked to your liking. Spread each steak with the herb butter and serve with broiled tomatoes.

Serves 4

Cook's Tip
Before broiling whole tomatoes, make a cross in the skins to prevent the tomatoes bursting during cooking.

Filet Mignon Verdi

3 large onions
6 tablespoons oil
1 tablespoon all-purpose
   flour
1 beef bouillon cube
½ cup whipping cream
4 slices liver pâté
1 teaspoon salt
½ teaspoon white pepper
4 filet mignon steaks

Garnish
parsley

Slice the onions. Heat 4 tablespoons of the oil in a pan and fry the onions until softened. Stir in the flour and cook for 2–3 minutes. Dissolve the bouillon cube in 1¼ cups boiling water.

Gradually add the bouillon to the pan, stirring until the mixture has thickened. Stir in the cream and leave on a low heat.

Heat the remaining oil in a separate pan and cook the pâté until browned on both sides. Remove and keep warm. Season the steaks and cook in the pan for about 3 minutes on each side. Arrange the steaks in a heatproof dish, top each one with a slice of pâté, then spoon over the sauce. Quickly brown under the broiler and serve garnished with parsley.

Serves 4

Tournedos Flambé

2 peppers
½ cup mushrooms
6 large tomatoes
4 tablespoons oil
4 tournedos
½ cup butter
1 teaspoon each salt, garlic salt and black pepper
5 tablespoons brandy

Cut the peppers in half and remove the stalk and the seeds; slice the mushrooms; peel and chop the tomatoes. Heat the oil in a pan and fry the steaks on a medium heat for 3 minutes on each side.
In a separate pan, heat the butter and fry the tomatoes with ½ teaspoon each of salt, garlic salt and pepper. Add the peppers and mushrooms and cook until softened. Add the remaining seasoning to the steaks. Pour over the brandy and ignite. Shake the pan backwards and forwards over the heat, until the flames die down. Arrange the steaks on a serving dish and pour over the cooking juices. Arrange the vegetables around the steaks.
Serves 4

Variation
½ cup cooked green beans may be fried with the other vegetables.

Tournedos Rossini

1 teaspoon black pepper
4 tournedos
8 thin bacon slices
4 tablespoons oil
1 teaspoon salt
½ teaspoon garlic salt
½ cup Madeira
4 oz liver pâté

Rub the pepper into the steaks. Put 2 bacon slices around each steak and secure with a skewer. Heat the oil in a pan and fry the steaks on a medium heat for 3 minutes on each side; take out of the pan and remove the skewer and bacon. Season the steaks with salt and garlic salt, place on a dish and keep warm. Pour off any excess oil from the pan and add the Madeira. Stir well and boil for 30 seconds, then pour over the steaks. Top the steaks with 1 or 2 slices of pâté.
Serve with peas and French fried potatoes.
Serves 4

Cook's Tip
When purchasing steaks choose ones which have tiny flecks of fat running through the lean part. This is a good indication that the steaks will cook well.

Pork Chops with Mustard and Mushroom Sauce

1½ tablespoons wine vinegar
3 tablespoons oil
pinch salt
ground black pepper
1 teaspoon prepared mustard
2 pork chops
1 small can button mush-
   rooms
1 tablespoon finely chopped
   parsley

Mix the wine vinegar with 1½ tablespoons of the oil, the salt, pepper and mustard. Trim the chops. Spread the mustard mixture on both sides of the chops and leave for 1 hour.
Heat the rest of the oil in a frying pan. Remove the chops from the marinade and, without letting them drain, fry in the hot oil for 5 minutes on each side, until browned and crisp. Remove and keep warm. Drain and slice the mush-rooms and add to the pan with any leftover marinade and the parsley. Stir well to mix with the sediment and heat the mushrooms. Arrange the chops on a serving dish and spoon over the mushroom mixture. Serve with creamed potatoes and peas.
Serves 2

Balkan Chops

3 medium-sized onions
3 red peppers
1 (8-oz) can corn kernels
½ cup olive oil
4 lamb or veal chops
1 teaspoon salt
½ teaspoon cayenne pepper
¼ teaspoon garlic salt
¼ teaspoon paprika pepper
¼ teaspoon celery salt

Peel and dice the onions. Seed the peppers and cut into strips. Drain the corn. Mix the prepared vegetables together.
Heat the oil in a pan and fry the chops for 3–5 minutes on each side, depending on the thickness. Sprinkle with the seasonings

and arrange on a serving dish. Spoon some of the salad mixture in the center and serve the rest separately.
Serves 4

Variation
If preferred the chops may be brushed on each side with oil and broiled for 4–5 minutes on each side.

Cook's Tip
When turning chops or steaks during cooking use a pair of tongs. A sharp-pointed knife will pierce the meat and lose natural juices.

French Veal Chops

about 3 slices white bread
½ cup milk
4 oz calf liver
1 onion
½ cup mushrooms
1 cup ground pork
3 eggs
2 tablespoons oil
½ teaspoon salt
pinch white pepper
¼ cup butter
6 small veal chops
1 cup grated Gruyère cheese

Remove the crusts from the bread and soak the slices in the milk. Chop the liver finely. Peel and slice the onion; slice the mushrooms. Mix the ground pork with the soaked bread,

chopped liver, onions and mushrooms. Beat the eggs with the oil, salt and pepper and add to the meat mixture.
Heat the butter in a frying pan and fry the chops for 2 minutes on each side, then place in a roasting pan and spread with the meat mixture. Sprinkle over the cheese and bake in a hot oven (425° F) for 10 minutes. Serve with new potatoes, tossed in melted butter and chopped parsley, and peas.
Serves 4–6

Paprika Pork Chops

1 leek
1 carrot
1 celery stalk
3 tablespoons all-purpose flour
2 teaspoons paprika pepper
1 teaspoon garlic salt
1 teaspoon celery salt
1 teaspoon white pepper
4 loin pork chops
4 tablespoons oil
5 tablespoons whipping cream
Garnish
parsley

Prepare the vegetables and cut into fine strips.
Mix the flour with the seasonings and coat each chop in the seasoned flour.

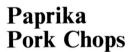

Heat the oil in a frying pan and fry the chops on a moderate heat for 5 minutes on each side, depending on the thickness. Remove and keep warm.
Add the cream to the fat in the pan, then the vegetable strips, pour on $\frac{1}{2}$ cup water and simmer for 5 minutes, but do not allow to boil.
Arrange the chops on a serving dish and spoon over the vegetables and cream sauce. Garnish with parsley and serve with a salad.
Serves 4

Variation
Ham steaks may be used in place of the pork chops.

Veal Chops Maryland

1 cup long-grain rice
4 veal loin chops
1½ teaspoons salt
½ teaspoon white pepper
2 teaspoons paprika pepper
¼ cup all-purpose flour
2 eggs
5 tablespoons dry breadcrumbs
½ cup oil
4 bacon slices
2 bananas
Garnish
parsley

Cook the rice in boiling salted water until tender. Drain and keep warm. Trim the chops to a neat shape. Mix together the salt, pepper, paprika and flour.

Lightly beat the eggs. Coat the chops in the flour, then in the beaten egg and finally in the crumbs, pressing them on well.
Heat the oil in a frying pan and cook the chops over a moderate heat for 5–7 minutes on each side, depending on the thickness. Remove and keep warm.
Fry the bacon and halved bananas in the same pan. Arrange the rice on a serving dish. Place the veal chops on the rice, top with the bacon and bananas and garnish with parsley. Serve with corn.
Serves 4

Hungarian Pork

1 green pepper
½ cup cocktail onions
½ cup mushrooms
2 sweet dill pickles
1 tablespoon paprika pepper
4 slices pork tenderloin
½ cup oil
1 teaspoon salt
½ cup tomato ketchup
Garnish
chopped parsley

Wash the pepper, seed and dice finely; chop the onions and slice the mushrooms; slice the pickles. Rub the paprika into the pork. Heat the oil in a frying pan and fry the pork for 5 minutes on each side. Remove, season with salt

and keep hot.
Place the peppers, onion, mushrooms and pickles in the frying pan and cook for 5 minutes. Add the ketchup and bring to the boil. Arrange the pork on a serving dish, spoon over the vegetables and sauce. Serve sprinkled with chopped parsley.
Serves 4

Veal Chops with Kidney Sauce

4 veal loin chops
½ teaspoon onion salt
1½ teaspoons salt
½ teaspoon white pepper
1 teaspoon prepared mustard
3 tablespoons oil
4 eggs
3 tablespoons chopped parsley
1 tablespoon chopped chervil
¼ cup butter
1 calf kidney
5 tablespoons brandy

Trim the chops if necessary. Season with the onion salt, ½ teaspoon of the salt and the pepper;

spread on the mustard. Heat the oil in a frying pan and fry the chops over a medium heat for 3–5 minutes on each side; remove and keep warm. Beat the eggs with ½ teaspoon salt, 5 tablespoons cold water and the herbs. In another saucepan, melt the butter and cook the eggs until lightly scrambled. Keep warm. Slice the kidney and cook in the pan used for the chops for 30 seconds. Sprinkle with the remaining salt. Pour over the brandy and stir into the kidney. Arrange the chops on a serving dish and spoon the scrambled eggs and kidney on top.
Serves 4

Wiener Schnitzel

4 veal cutlets or scallops
1 teaspoon salt
5 tablespoons all-purpose
   flour
2 eggs
1 cup dry breadcrumbs
½ cup oil
Garnish
lettuce leaves
lemon wedges

Pound the scallops as thinly as possible, sprinkle with salt and coat in the flour. Beat the eggs with 3 tablespoons cold water. Dip the veal slices in the egg then coat in the breadcrumbs. Heat the oil in a frying pan and fry quickly, for 2 minutes on each side, to a golden brown color. Drain on paper towels and serve garnished with lettuce leaves and lemon wedges.
Serves 4

Cook's Tip
Breadcrumbs for coating food are made by pressing white bread, with the crusts removed, through a strainer; or make them in the blender. Breadcrumbs can be stored in the freezer in freezer bags.

Minute Steak with Vegetables

8 oz minute steak
8 oz lean pork
¼ cup butter
1 tablespoon oil
1 teaspoon salt
¼ teaspoon white pepper
½ teaspoon paprika pepper
1 sweet dill pickle
3 tablespoons capers
5 tablespoons chopped
   cooked beets
1 small can button
   mushrooms
5 tablespoons whipping
   cream

Trim the meats and cut into strips, or thin slices. Heat the butter and oil in a frying pan and fry the meat strips for 3–4 minutes. Sprinkle over the seasonings and add the pickle, cut into strips, and the capers. Add the diced beets and drained mushrooms. Cook for a further 2–3 minutes. Finally, stir in the cream and spoon into a serving dish.
Serves 4

Variation
If liked, 5 tablespoons Madeira can be added with the mushrooms.

Mixed Grill

2 pork loin chops
2 strip or boned loin steaks
½ teaspoon salt
¼ teaspoon celery salt
¼ teaspoon black pepper
1 teaspoon paprika pepper
2 teaspoons Worcestershire
  sauce
5 tablespoons oil
4 bacon slices
Garnish
parsley

Trim the chops and steaks. Mix together the salt, celery salt, pepper, paprika, Worcestershire sauce and oil. Add the meats and leave in a cool place to marinate for 20 minutes. Brush the broiler rack with oil. Remove the meats from the marinade and dry on paper towels. Broil for 5–8 minutes on each side. Broil the bacon slices until crisp. Arrange the meats on a serving dish and serve garnished with parsley.
Serves 2

Variation
The ingredients for the popular English Mixed Grill may be varied according to what is available. Mushrooms and tomatoes may be included. In place of the pork chops use lamb. Add lamb kidneys and country sausages.

Veal Slices in Marsala

1 cup button mushrooms
1 lb veal cutlets or scallops
½ teaspoon salt
½ teaspoon white pepper
3 tablespoons all-purpose
  flour
6 tablespoons butter
5 tablespoons Marsala
pinch dried basil
pinch dried oregano
Garnish
chopped parsley

Slice the mushrooms. Pound the scallops until they are thin. Mix the salt, pepper and flour and use to coat the veal.
Melt the butter in a frying pan and cook the veal slices quickly on both sides until they are pale brown, 2–3 minutes. Arrange on a serving dish and keep warm. Fry the mushrooms for 2 minutes in the fat remaining in the pan. Pour in the Marsala, add the herbs and cook for another 2 minutes. Pour the wine sauce and mushrooms over the meat and sprinkle with chopped parsley.
Serve with rice, peas and asparagus.
Serves 4

Cook's Tip
When purchasing veal, look for soft, moist flesh. Avoid veal which looks flabby and wet, or dry and brown.

Pork Chops in Burgundy

2 cups red Burgundy
1 bay leaf
5 peppercorns
2 juniper berries
4 pork loin chops
3 tablespoons all-purpose
  flour
½ teaspoon salt
½ teaspoon black pepper
5 tablespoons oil
6 baby onions
4 bacon slices, chopped
3 tablespoons whipping
  cream
Garnish
parsley

Bring to the boil the red wine with the bay leaf, peppercorns, and juniper berries; cover and simmer for 30 minutes, then strain. Trim the pork chops. Mix the flour with the salt and black pepper. Coat the chops in the seasoned flour.
Heat the oil in a frying pan and fry the chops on both sides with the onions and bacon, until lightly browned. Gradually stir in the red wine; cover and simmer for 15 minutes. Remove the chops and onions and keep warm. Boil the wine over a high heat until it has reduced by half. Stir in the cream, check the seasoning then spoon over the chops and onions. Garnish with parsley and serve a pepper and onion salad separately.
Serves 4

Cook's Tip
Serve the same wine with this dish as you use in the cooking.

Veal Cordon Bleu

4 veal cutlets or scallops
4 slices cooked ham
4 slices Edam cheese
4 tablespoons all-purpose flour
1 teaspoon paprika pepper
2 eggs
5 tablespoons oil
Garnish
parsley
tomato wedges

Pound the veal until it is ½ inch thick. On each veal scallop place a slice of ham and cheese. Fold over and secure with a wooden toothpick.
Mix the flour with the paprika. Add the eggs and about 3 tablespoons of water and beat to make a thick batter. Heat the oil in a frying pan. Dip the veal in the batter and cook in the oil over a moderate heat for 5 minutes on each side. Drain on paper towels and remove the toothpicks. Serve garnished with parsley and tomato wedges. Serve a green salad separately.
Serves 4

Cook's Tip
Use a mildly flavored cheese, such as Edam or Gouda, so that it does not overpower the delicate flavor of the veal.

Veal Rolls

4 veal cutlets or scallops
½ teaspoon paprika pepper
2 teaspoons prepared mustard
1 sweet dill pickle
½ cup liver sausage
¼ cup butter
⅔ cup plain yogurt
½ teaspoon salt
½ teaspoon white pepper

Pound the veal scallops until they are very thin, dust with the paprika and spread with mustard. Cut the pickle lengthwise, in four. Spread some liver sausage on each scallop, then place a piece of pickle on each. Roll the slices up and secure with thread or wooden toothpicks.
Melt the butter in a frying pan and brown the rolls on all sides. Then add the yogurt and season with salt and pepper. Cover and cook over a low heat for 20 minutes.
Remove the toothpicks; arrange on a serving dish, spoon over the sauce and serve with rice and a green salad.
Serves 4

Cook's Tip
The veal rolls may be prepared in advance and frozen. Wrap each closely in freezer film or foil. Thaw before frying.

Milanese Calf Liver

8 oz macaroni
6 tablespoons butter
½ cup grated Parmesan
   cheese
½ cup oil
1 teaspoon salt
¼ teaspoon white pepper
pinch dried marjoram
4 thick slices calf liver
4 tablespoons all-purpose
   flour

Cook the macaroni in
plenty of boiling salted
water for 12–15 minutes.
Drain, and while hot mix
in the butter and cheese.
Place on a serving dish and
keep warm.
Heat the oil in a frying pan.
Rub a mixture of salt,

pepper and marjoram into
the liver and then coat in
the flour. Fry the liver
slices in the hot oil for a
total of 5 minutes. Place the
fried liver slices on the
macaroni. Serve with a
tomato sauce.
Serves 4

Cook's Tip
As liver is highly
nutritious and rela-
tively inexpensive,
try to include it in
your menus once a
week. Do not over-
cook the liver as it
will become tough.

Liver with Bacon

2 slices calf liver
1 teaspoon dried rosemary
2 bacon slices
2 bay leaves
2 tablespoons butter
3 tablespoons oil
2 cups cooked green noodles
   or other pasta
Garnish
tomato slices

Sprinkle the liver with
rosemary. Place a bacon
slice on each piece of liver;
top with a bay leaf and
secure with a wooden
toothpick.
Heat the butter and oil in a
frying pan and fry the liver
slices on both sides, for a
total of 5 minutes. Remove

the toothpicks and keep
the liver warm.
Heat the pasta in the same
fat in the frying pan, turning
constantly. Arrange the
liver slices and pasta on a
serving dish. Garnish with
tomato slices and serve
with an asparagus salad.
Serves 2

Cook's Tip
Calf or lamb liver
is more suitable for
broiling and frying.
Use the coarser,
tougher beef liver
in a casserole.

Roast Veal

2-lb veal roast
1 teaspoon salt
½ teaspoon white pepper
2 teaspoons paprika pepper
2 carrots
2 onions
2 tomatoes
5 tablespoons oil
7 tablespoons dry white wine
6 tablespoons whipping cream
Garnish
parsley

If necessary trim the meat, then rub all over with the salt, pepper and paprika. Place the meat in a roasting pan. Peel and chop the carrots, onions and tomatoes and place with the meat. Pour over the oil and wine and roast in a moderately hot oven (400° F) for 1–1½ hours. Transfer the meat to a serving dish and keep warm while finishing the sauce. Either blend the vegetables and cooking liquid in the blender, or rub through a strainer. Reheat, check the seasoning and stir in the cream. Pour around the meat and serve garnished with parsley.
Cooked spinach topped with grated cheese and browned under the broiler would make a good vegetable to accompany this roast veal dish.
Serves 4

Pot-Roast of Beef

1 teaspoon salt
pinch black pepper
1 teaspoon paprika pepper
2-lb piece beef round
5 tablespoons oil
sprig rosemary
½ lb small potatoes
4 baby onions
6 celery stalks
2 tomatoes
few sprigs parsley
¼ cup butter
5 tablespoons red wine

Rub the salt, pepper and paprika into the meat and brush with oil. Place the meat and rosemary in an ovenproof dish.
Cube the potatoes, peel the onions and chop the celery.

Halve the tomatoes. Place the vegetables around the meat and sprinkle over the coarsely chopped parsley. Dot the butter over the meat. Pour in the wine, cover and roast in a moderate oven (350° F) for 1½–1¾ hours. Serve with a salad.
Serves 4–6

Cook's Tip
This method of cooking is particularly suitable for the less prime cuts, such as round.

Loin of Lamb Provençale

1 teaspoon salt
1 teaspoon garlic salt
1 teaspoon black pepper
1 loin of lamb, 6–8 chops
2 onions
⅔ cup oil
2 eggplants
1 teaspoon dried rosemary
5 tablespoons dry white wine
8 small tomatoes
*5 tablespoons fresh
   breadcrumbs*
5 tablespoons grated cheese
¼ cup butter

Rub seasoning into the meat. Peel and quarter onions. Heat the oil in a roasting pan, add the meat and onions; roast in a hot oven (425° F) for 15 minutes.
Slice the eggplants. Lower the oven temperature to moderate (350° F). Place the eggplant slices around the meat, sprinkle with rosemary and pour in the wine. Return to the oven for a further 30 minutes.
Cut the tops off the tomatoes. Mix 1 tablespoon of the breadcrumbs with 1 tablespoon of the cheese and spread on the tomatoes; dot with butter; replace tops.
Lay the meat with the fatty side up in the broiler pan and sprinkle thickly with the remaining cheese and breadcrumbs. Broil for a few minutes. Serve with the vegetables and cooking juices.
Serves 4–6

Beef with Prunes

4 bacon slices
2-lb piece beef tenderloin
1 teaspoon salt
1 teaspoon white pepper
little oil
1 onion
1 tomato
½ lb pitted prunes
piece thinly peeled lemon peel
1 cinnamon stick
5–7 tablespoons port
*7 tablespoons whipping
   cream*
2 teaspoons cornstarch

Cut the bacon into thin strips. Trim the meat and lard with the bacon strips. Rub the meat with the salt and pepper, and place in a roasting pan. Brush the meat with oil and roast in a moderately hot oven (400° F) for 30 minutes. Meanwhile, chop the onion and peel and chop the tomato. Add to the roasting pan after 15 minutes cooking time. Cover the prunes with water, add the lemon peel and cinnamon and simmer for 10 minutes. Lift the meat on to a serving dish and keep warm. Place the roasting pan over the heat and stir in the port. Bring to the boil, scraping up all the sediment. Mix the cream with the cornstarch and pour into the sauce. Reheat, season and pour around the meat. Drain the prunes and use to garnish.
Serves 4–6

119

Glazed Ham

3-lb processed ham
12 cloves
5 tablespoons clear honey
1 tablespoon brown sugar

Place the ham on a rack in a roasting pan. Bake in a warm oven (325° F) for 1½ hours (30 minutes to the pound) or until a meat thermometer registers 160° F.

With a sharp knife, make incisions in the rind in a diagonal pattern. Insert a whole clove in each cross. Spoon the honey over the ham and sprinkle over the brown sugar. Return the ham to a hot oven (425° F) and bake for a further 20 minutes, or until glazed. Serve hot or cold.
Serves 6–8

Cook's Tip
To make the glazed ham look more festive, it can be studded with cloves and candied cherries secured with toothpicks.

Stuffed Breast of Veal

1 onion
½ cup oil
6 tablespoons long-grain rice
1 bouillon cube
1 teaspoon paprika pepper
6 oz calf liver
2 tablespoons butter
¼ teaspoon white pepper
½ teaspoon salt
1 egg
3 tablespoons chopped peanuts
1 lb boned breast of veal
3 tablespoons all-purpose flour

Peel and finely dice the onion and fry in 5 tablespoons of the oil until softened. Add the rice and fry for a further 2 minutes.

Dissolve the bouillon cube in 2 cups boiling water, add to the rice and cook for 20 minutes, until the liquid is absorbed. Mix in the paprika. Cool.

Chop the liver and cook in the butter for 3–5 minutes. Mix into the rice with the seasoning, beaten egg and peanuts. Allow to cool.

Lay the veal flat, spread with the stuffing and form into a roll. Secure. Sprinkle with flour.

Heat the remaining oil in a flameproof casserole and brown the veal on all sides. Add ½ cup water, cover and cook over a moderate heat for 40–50 minutes. adding more liquid if necessary.
Serves 4

Marinated Beef

1 cup wine vinegar
few sprigs parsley
1 bay leaf
1 onion, sliced
2 cloves
3 peppercorns
2-lb piece beef top round
4 bacon slices
1 tablespoon cornstarch
¼ cup half-and-half

Place the wine vinegar, herbs, onion, cloves and peppercorns in a pan together with 1¼ cups water and bring to the boil. Allow to cool.
Place the beef in a bowl, pour over the cold marinade and leave in the refrigerator to marinate for 6 hours (or overnight), turning the meat from time to time.
Remove from the marinade and pat dry with paper towels. Chop the bacon and fry in a flameproof casserole. Add the meat and brown on all sides. Pour over the marinade, together with 1 cup water, cover and simmer over a moderate heat for 1½–2 hours.
Transfer the meat to a serving dish. Strain the cooking juices into a pan and thicken with the dissolved cornstarch. Check the seasoning, stir in the cream and either spoon the sauce over the meat, or serve it separately.
Serves 4–6

Braised Veal Shoulder

3 tablespoons oil
3-lb piece veal shoulder, boned and rolled
1 onion
1 teaspoon salt
½ teaspoon pepper
few sprigs parsley
1 bay leaf
2 cups stock
2 teaspoons cornstarch

Heat the oil in a frying pan and fry the veal until browned on all sides. Transfer to a casserole dish. Peel and slice the onion. Add the seasoning, sliced onion, herbs and stock. Cover and braise in a moderate oven (350° F) for about 1½ hours or until a meat thermometer registers 175° F.
Transfer the veal to a serving dish and keep warm. Strain the cooking liquid into a pan and thicken it with the dissolved cornstarch. Check the seasoning and serve with the veal.
Serves 6

Roast Beef

1 teaspoon salt
½ teaspoon white pepper
2 teaspoons Worcestershire
*   sauce*
5 tablespoons oil
1½-lb piece beef top round
3 tablespoons brandy
½ teaspoon cayenne pepper
1 carrot
2 celery stalks
1 onion
¼ cup butter
pinch grated nutmeg
¼ cup sour cream

Mix the salt, pepper, Worcestershire sauce and oil together. Place the meat in a dish and pour over the oil mixture with the brandy and cayenne pepper. Cover and marinate for 20 minutes. Lift the meat from the marinade. Place in a roasting pan and roast in a hot oven (425° F) for 20 minutes.

Meanwhile, peel and chop the carrot, chop the celery and onion. Add the vegetables to the meat, dot with butter and sprinkle with nutmeg. Roast for a further 30 minutes.

Place the meat on a serving dish and keep warm. Add the marinade to the roasting pan and bring to the boil, scraping up the sediment. Either push the sauce through a strainer or blend in the blender. Reheat and mix in the sour cream.
Serves 4

Braised Leg of Lamb

1 teaspoon salt
1 teaspoon white pepper
1 teaspoon sugar
1 clove garlic
3-lb leg of lamb
½ cup oil
1 cup dry white wine
1 bay leaf
1 teaspoon dried rosemary
1 onion, sliced
4 oz canned navy beans,
*   drained*
4 bacon slices

Rub the salt, pepper, sugar and crushed garlic into the meat. Place in a bowl and pour over the oil and white wine. Add the bay leaf and rosemary and leave to marinate for 20 minutes.

Remove the lamb from the marinade, pat dry with paper towels and place in a roasting pan. Roast in a moderately hot oven (400° F) for 40 minutes. Mix the onion, beans and chopped bacon with the marinade and spoon around the lamb. Continue cooking for a further 35–40 minutes or until a meat thermometer registers 175° F. Serve the lamb on the bed of braised beans and vegetables. To add the finishing touch, cover the bone with a paper frill.
Serves 4–6

Roast Loin of Veal

4½-lb loin of veal
pinch salt
pinch pepper
½ cup butter
2 cups hot chicken stock
pinch dried basil
2 teaspoons cornstarch
½ cup dry white wine
1 tablespoon lemon juice

Have the veal boned and rolled with the kidney. Tie with string.
Rub the veal with salt and pepper and place in a roasting pan. Pour over the melted butter and roast in a hot oven (425° F) for 15 minutes. Pour in half the hot stock and roast for a further 1 hour. Lower the heat to moderate (350° F), pour in the rest of the stock and roast for a further 1–1½ hours, basting the meat with the cooking liquid. A meat thermometer should register 175° F.
Place the veal on a serving dish and keep warm. Pour the cooking liquid into a pan and add the basil. Mix the cornstarch with the wine and lemon juice. Pour into the pan and, stirring, bring to the boil. Check the seasoning and serve with the veal. Serve with celery, peas and duchesse potatoes.
Serves 8

Cook's Tip
Do baste veal during cooking, otherwise the meat will become dry.

Rabbit with Red Cabbage

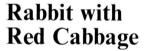

4 rabbit portions
1 teaspoon salt
½ teaspoon white pepper
2 cups red wine
¼ cup butter
4 bacon slices
1 onion, chopped
1 bay leaf
4 juniper berries
1 cooking apple
1 small red cabbage
pinch ground cloves
1–2 teaspoons cornstarch

Place the pieces of rabbit in a bowl and add the salt, pepper and wine. Marinate in the refrigerator for at least 4 hours.
Remove the rabbit from the marinade, and pat dry with paper towels. Melt the butter in a frying pan and fry the rabbit until browned. Place in a flameproof casserole with the chopped bacon, onion, the marinade, bay leaf and juniper berries. Cover; simmer for 2 hours. Peel, core and chop the apple; shred the cabbage. Cook the apple and cabbage in a small amount of salted water. Drain, sprinkle with ground cloves and keep hot. Lift out the pieces of rabbit and keep warm. Boil the cooking liquid for about 5 minutes, then thicken with dissolved cornstarch. Check the seasoning and spoon over the rabbit. Serve the cabbage separately.
Serves 4

Roast Wild Boar

2¼–3-lb loin wild boar
1 teaspoon salt
2 teaspoons paprika pepper
4 oz bacon slices
10 cloves
1 cup oil
1 tablespoon all-purpose flour
1 cup apple juice
1 cup stock
5 tablespoons cranberry sauce
1 teaspoon black pepper

Wild boar used for this recipe should be young. Venison may be used instead.
Trim the meat and rub in the salt and paprika. Wrap the bacon slices around the meat and stick with cloves. Place in a roasting pan with the oil and roast in a moderately hot oven (400° F) for 1–1½ hours. Transfer the meat to a serving dish. Remove the excess fat from the pan and stir in the flour. Cook for 1–2 minutes, stirring. Gradually stir in the apple juice and stock. Bring to the boil, stirring, and cook for 1–2 minutes. Stir in the cranberry sauce and seasoning. Serve with the boar. Potato croquettes are a good accompanying vegetable to this dish.
Serves 6

Braised Venison Steaks

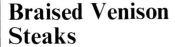

½ teaspoon garlic salt
1 teaspoon salt
1 teaspoon black pepper
1 teaspoon prepared mustard
½ cup red wine
2 teaspoons sugar
½ cup oil
4 young venison steaks
2 onions
1 bulb fennel
1 red pepper
1 small can sauerkraut
⅔ cup sour cream
1 tablespoon paprika pepper

Mix together the garlic salt, salt, pepper, mustard, wine and sugar with 3 tablespoons of the oil and use to marinate the steaks for about 30 minutes.

Slice the onions and fennel; seed and slice the pepper. Heat the rest of the oil in a flameproof casserole and brown the drained steaks. Remove. Stir in the onions, fennel, peppers and sauerkraut and fry for 3–4 minutes. Replace the venison. Add the sour cream, paprika and the marinade, lower the heat and simmer for 30 minutes. Serve from the casserole dish.
Serves 4

Cook's Tip
Venison, like other game meats, must be hung for at least a week before cooking to tenderize the flesh.

Venison Rolls

8 thin slices venison steak
3 tablespoons port
½ teaspoon salt
¼ teaspoon coarsely ground black pepper
8 slices salami
1 tablespoon oil
5 tablespoons red currant jelly
2 teaspoons prepared mustard
2 teaspoons paprika pepper

Pound the venison slices and marinate in the port, salt and pepper for 15 minutes.
Place a slice of salami on each piece of venison, roll up and secure with a wooden toothpick.

Place the venison rolls in the oiled broiler pan, brush with oil and cook under the broiler for 8 minutes, turning to brown the rolls on all sides.
Meanwhile, heat the red currant jelly with the mustard, paprika, and marinade.
Allow to simmer for 2–3 minutes. Remove the toothpicks from the venison rolls and arrange the meat on a bed of cooked rice and peas. Spoon over the sauce.
Serves 4

Cook's Tip
Well-hung venison may be frozen for up to 12 months. Thaw before using.

Roast Saddle of Hare

1 saddle of hare
4 bacon slices
1 teaspoon salt
2 teaspoons paprika pepper
¼ cup pork drippings or
   3 tablespoons oil
1 onion, sliced
½ teaspoon sugar
3 tablespoons tomato paste
5 tablespoons red currant
   jelly
4 juniper berries
1 cup chicken stock
4–5 tablespoons half-and-
   half

Lard the saddle with strips of bacon. Rub the salt and paprika all over the saddle. Heat the drippings in a roasting pan and brown the saddle on all sides. Add the onion slices and roast in a moderate oven (350° F) for 45–50 minutes, until tender. Remove the saddle and keep warm.
Stir the sugar, tomato paste, red currant jelly and juniper berries into the roasting pan. Bring to the boil, scraping up the sediment. Add the stock and simmer for 2–3 minutes. Strain, check the seasoning and just before serving, stir in the cream. Serve with the saddle.
Serves 4

Venison Stroganoff

¾ lb lean venison meat
2 onions
1 cup mushrooms
¼ cup pork drippings or
   3 tablespoons oil
5 tablespoons brandy
5 tablespoons whipping
   cream
juice of ½ lemon
1 pimiento, sliced
½ teaspoon salt
1 teaspoon pepper
5 tablespoons chopped
   sweet dill pickles
1 teaspoon sugar
3 tablespoons chopped
   parsley

Remove any gristle from the meat and cut into thin strips. Peel and slice the onions; quarter the mushrooms.
Heat the drippings in a frying pan and fry the meat until the pieces are evenly browned all over. Add the onions, brandy, cream and lemon juice. Lower the heat and cook for a further 3–4 minutes, stirring the ingredients all the time. Mix in the pimiento, mushrooms, seasoning, pickles and sugar and allow to heat through. Spoon into a serving dish and serve sprinkled with chopped parsley. Serve with rice.
Serves 4

Roast Haunch of Venison

4 bacon slices
1 carrot
2 onions
1¾-lb piece haunch of venison
½ cup oil
1 cup chopped celeriac
½ teaspoon salt
1 teaspoon paprika pepper
2 teaspoons lemon juice
3 tablespoons orange juice
3 tablespoons red currant jelly
grated rind of 1 orange
1 cup half-and-half

Dice the bacon; slice the carrot and the onions. Lightly brown the meat in a flameproof casserole in the oil on all sides, with the bacon, carrots, onions and celeriac. Cover and roast in a moderately hot oven (400° F) for 45 minutes–1 hour. Arrange the venison on a serving dish.
Add the salt, paprika, lemon and orange juices, red currant jelly and orange rind to the casserole. Bring to the boil, scraping up the sediment. Strain into a saucepan, check the seasoning and stir in the cream. Reheat, but do not allow to boil, then pour around the venison. Serve with pasta.
Serves 4

Potted Rabbit

1½ lb rabbit meat
2 onions
1 carrot
1 leek
2 rolls
1 cup dry white wine
4 oz bacon slices
5 tablespoons oil
½ cup chopped almonds
½ cup sausagemeat
1 teaspoon salt
1 teaspoon black pepper
1 bay leaf

Cut the rabbit meat into cubes, removing all the gristle. Cut the onions into quarters, grate the carrot and slice the leek. Soak the rolls in the wine; dice the bacon.

Heat the oil in a flameproof casserole and fry the meat for about 5 minutes, until brown. Add the vegetables and nuts and fry together for a further 5 minutes. Stir in the diced bacon and softened rolls. Remove from the heat and stir in the sausagemeat, salt and pepper. Press the mixture into a greased ovenproof dish, smooth the surface. Add the bay leaf, cover and cook in a moderate oven (350° F) for 35–40 minutes. Serve hot or cold.
Serves 4

127

Broiled Venison Steaks

5 tablespoons oil
½ teaspoon dried sage
½ teaspoon black pepper
½ teaspoon paprika pepper
1 teaspoon salt
4 thin venison steaks
½ cup butter
3 tablespoons chopped
   parsley
juice of ½ lemon
4 canned pear halves
4 tablespoons cranberry
   sauce
4 walnut halves

Mix the oil, sage, pepper, paprika and salt together. Pound the steaks and brush on both sides with the oil mixture; leave to marinate for 10–15 minutes.

Soften the butter and mix with the chopped parsley and lemon juice. Form into a square and chill in the refrigerator.
Broil the venison steaks for 5 minutes on each side. Place on a serving dish. Serve garnished with a pat of herb butter and a pear half filled with cranberry sauce. Top with a walnut half. Serve with duchesse potatoes.
Serves 4

Roast Venison Tenderloin

1¾-lb piece venison tenderloin
4 bacon slices
½ teaspoon salt
¼ teaspoon black pepper
5 tablespoons oil
3 tablespoons brandy
3 tablespoons chopped
   parsley
½ bay leaf
1 tablespoon soft
   breadcrumbs
few drops Tabasco sauce
Garnish
sautéed mushrooms

Trim the venison. Cut the bacon into narrow strips and use to lard the meat. Place the meat in a bowl, sprinkle with salt and pepper and pour over 2 tablespoons of the oil and the brandy. Leave to marinate for 30 minutes. Remove the meat from the marinade, pat dry and brown in a flameproof casserole in the remaining oil.
Cover and roast in a moderately hot oven (400° F) for 45 minutes–1 hour. Remove the meat and place on a serving dish. Stir 1 cup water into the casserole with the marinade, parsley, bay leaf, bread-crumbs and Tabasco sauce. Bring to the boil and simmer for 5 minutes. Remove the bay leaf, pour into a sauceboat and serve with the venison. Serve garnished with sautéed mushrooms.
Serves 4

Rabbit Casserole

6 rabbit portions
2 shallots
4 peppercorns
⅔ cup vinegar
4 bay leaves
¼ cup butter
2 onions, chopped
2½ cups ale
juice of 1 lemon
few sage leaves
1 teaspoon prepared mustard
2 teaspoons sugar
1 teaspoon salt
½ teaspoon black pepper
1 teaspoon tomato paste
2 teaspoons cornstarch

Remove the bones from the rabbit and cut the meat into pieces. Place in a bowl with the halved shallots, the peppercorns, vinegar and bay leaves and marinate in the refrigerator for 6–8 hours, or overnight. Remove the rabbit from the marinade and pat dry with paper towels. Melt the butter in a flameproof casserole and brown the rabbit on all sides. Stir in the onions and fry for a further 2–3 minutes. Strain in the marinade; add the ale, lemon juice, sage, mustard, sugar, seasonings and tomato paste. Bring to the boil, lower the heat, cover and simmer for 1¾–2 hours. Thicken the casserole with the dissolved cornstarch and check the seasoning. Serve from the casserole.
Serves 6

Apple-Stuffed Venison Rolls

4 venison steaks
½ teaspoon salt
¼ teaspoon black pepper
1 carrot
1 onion
2 cooking apples
3 tablespoons oil
1¼ cups red wine
5 tablespoons apple sauce
Garnish
apple slices
2 tablespoons butter

Pound the venison steaks until they are very thin. Mix the salt and pepper and rub into both sides of the venison steaks.
Grate the carrot; peel and slice the onion. Peel and core the apples and cut into slices. Divide the grated carrot, onion and apple slices between the venison, form into rolls and secure with wooden toothpicks. Heat the oil in a flameproof casserole and fry the rolls until browned on all sides. Add the wine and apple sauce. Cover and simmer for 20 minutes. Lift out the venison, remove the toothpicks and place the meat on a serving dish; keep warm. Boil the cooking liquid until reduced by a third. Pour over the venison rolls and serve garnished with the apple slices fried in the butter. Accompany with creamed potatoes or pasta.
Serves 4

Duck with Orange Sauce

1 carrot
1 onion
5 tablespoons oil
1 (5-lb) oven-ready duck
2 oranges
5 tablespoons orange
   liqueur
½ teaspoon salt
1 teaspoon paprika pepper
¼ teaspoon white pepper
⅔ cup duck stock
2 teaspoons cornstarch
Garnish
parsley

Slice the carrot; peel and quarter the onion. Heat the oil in a roasting pan. Add the carrot and onion and place the duck on top. Roast in a moderately hot oven (400° F) for about 1½ hours, turning the duck over halfway through the time.

Cut the orange rind into fine strips and squeeze the juice. Transfer the duck to a serving dish. Skim all but 1 tablespoon of the fat from the pan. Rub the onion and carrot through a strainer and return to the roasting pan. Add the orange juice and rind, the liqueur, salt, paprika, pepper and stock and mix together. Bring to the boil, scraping up the sediment. Thicken with the dissolved cornstarch and serve in a sauceboat. Garnish the duck with parsley.
Serves 4

Braised Turkey

2 turkey portions
½ teaspoon salt
4 bacon slices
2 onions
3 tablespoons chopped
   marjoram or 1 teaspoon
   dried marjoram
5 tablespoons port
1 tablespoon dry bread-
   crumbs
3 tablespoons almonds,
   browned

Sprinkle the turkey portions with salt.
Dice the bacon. Peel and thinly slice the onions. Place the bacon, marjoram and onion slices in an ovenproof dish. Place the turkey portions on top, pour over the port, together with ½ cup water. Sprinkle over the breadcrumbs, cover and cook in a moderately hot oven (400° F) for about 1 hour.

Remove the lid for the last 10 minutes of cooking time to brown the turkey. Arrange on a serving dish with the cooking liquid and vegetables. Sprinkle the turkey portions with the browned almonds.
Serves 2

Variation
Small, whole potatoes and apple quarters may be cooked with the turkey. Add the potatoes for the last 30 minutes of cooking time and the apples for the last 15 minutes.

Turkey Fricassée

1 onion
3 tablespoons oil
½ cup all-purpose flour
2½ cups turkey stock
½ cup canned mushrooms
1 clove garlic
3 cups chopped cooked
*   turkey meat*
8 oz ground pork
½ teaspoon salt
½ teaspoon pepper
juice of 1 lemon
1 can asparagus tips
2 egg yolks
5 tablespoons whipping
*   cream*

Slice the onion.
Heat the oil in a pan and fry the onion until softened.
Mix in the flour and cook for 1–2 minutes, without allowing it to brown.
Gradually add the stock, stirring until the mixture boils.
Stir in the sliced mushrooms, crushed garlic and turkey.
Form the pork into small balls and add to the pan.
Add the seasonings and lemon juice and simmer for 5 minutes. Stir in the chopped asparagus and heat through.
Beat the egg yolks with the cream and gradually blend into the turkey mixture.
Allow to heat through, but do not boil. Check the seasoning and spoon into a heated serving dish.
Serve with rice and peas.
Serves 4–6

Roast Duck – French Style

1 (6-lb) oven-ready duck
1 teaspoon salt
½ teaspoon dried marjoram
12 stuffed olives
2 anchovy fillets
1 apple
4 slices white bread
2 eggs
5 tablespoons Madeira
5 tablespoons golden
*   raisins*
1 small can artichoke hearts

Rub the duck inside with salt and marjoram. Coarsely chop the olives and anchovy fillets. Peel and core the apple and cut into slices. Soak the white bread in water, squeeze dry and mix with the olives, anchovies, apple slices and eggs. Stuff the neck end of the duck with this mixture and secure the opening with a wooden skewer.
Place in a roasting pan and roast in a moderately hot oven (400° F) for 1¾ hours.
Transfer the duck to a serving dish.
Remove the fat from the roasting pan and stir in the Madeira and raisins.
Bring to the boil scraping up the sediment. Heat the artichoke hearts, drain the liquid into the Madeira sauce.
Serve the duck garnished with artichoke hearts. Serve the Madeira sauce separately.
Serves 4–6

Chicken Breasts – Chinese Style

1 lb chicken breasts
½ teaspoon salt
1 tablespoon soy sauce
1 carrot
2 slices canned pineapple
1 teaspoon cornstarch
5 tablespoons oil
2 leeks, thinly sliced
3 tablespoons dry sherry
½ teaspoon sugar

Rub salt on the chicken breasts and sprinkle over the soy sauce. Grate the carrot finely; cut the pineapple slices into small pieces and toss in the cornstarch.
Cut the chicken into thin strips. Heat the oil in a frying pan and fry the chicken for 3 minutes. Add the carrot and leek slices and fry for a further 2 minutes, then add the pineapple pieces. Cover and cook over a moderate heat for 12 minutes.
Stir in the sherry and sugar. Serve with rice.
Serves 4

Cook's Tip
If using frozen chicken breasts, allow them to thaw before cooking. The secret of success with this dish is to cut all the ingredients into fine strips.

Herb-Stuffed Broilers

2 broilers
½ teaspoon salt
few chives
sprigs parsley
sprigs marjoram
sprigs rosemary
1 teaspoon paprika pepper
1 tablespoon all-purpose
  flour
3 tablespoons oil

Broilers are spring chickens, weighing about 2½ lb.
Rub the insides of the broilers with salt. Make two bunches of mixed herbs and tie with thread. Place a bunch in the neck of each chicken and secure the openings with skewers.
Mix together the paprika, flour, and oil to make a smooth paste. Spread over the chickens. Broil or cook on a rotisserie spit for about 40 minutes, turning from time to time. Cut each broiler in half and serve on a bed of rice. Accompany with a mixed salad.
Serves 4

Variation
If possible use fresh herbs for this recipe, but if they are not available use a pinch of each of the herbs, dried, and sprinkle over the broilers before spreading with the paprika mixture.

Exotic Duck

1 (4½-lb) oven-ready duck
½ teaspoon salt
¼ teaspoon pepper
2 large cooking apples
4 oz fresh figs
1 teaspoon curry powder
2 tablespoons butter
¼ cup oil
Garnish
parsley

Rub the inside of the duck with the salt and pepper. Peel, core and slice the apples; dice the figs. Mix together the apples, figs, and curry powder with the butter and use to stuff the neck end of the duck. Sew the openings with thread, or secure with skewers.
Heat the oil in a roasting pan and brown the duck on all sides. Roast the duck, breast-side up, in a moderately hot oven (400° F) for 30 minutes. Turn over, pour in 1 cup hot water and roast for a further 45 minutes–1 hour, basting occasionally with the cooking liquid. Serve the duck on a bed of braised red cabbage and garnish with parsley. If liked, add a garnish of a scooped-out apple filled with apple sauce and topped with a cherry.
Serves 3–4

Delmonico Chicken Parcels

4 chicken portions
1 teaspoon salt
1 teaspoon paprika pepper
3 tablespoons oil
1 cup button mushrooms
1 can artichoke hearts
2 red peppers
⅔ cup whipping cream

Sprinkle the chicken portions with salt and paprika.
Take four pieces of foil each large enough to wrap a chicken portion. Brush each piece of foil with oil and place a chicken portion on each. Slice the mushrooms; drain and slice the artichoke hearts. Wash, seed and chop the peppers. Scatter the prepared vegetables over each chicken portion. Turn the sides of the foil up all the way around and pour some of the cream over each chicken portion. Form the foil into parcels, place on a baking sheet and cook in a hot oven (425° F) for 30 minutes. Open the foil and cook for a further 10 minutes to brown the chicken.
Serves 4

Variation
The peppers may be replaced by 2 tomatoes, peeled and chopped.

Duck – Peking Style

1 (4-lb) oven-ready duck
¼ cup sugar
¼ cup soy sauce
2 cups all-purpose flour
1 tablespoon oil

Dry the duck with paper towels. Dissolve the sugar in a little water and boil for 2–3 minutes. Brush all over the skin of the duck; hang in a cool place overnight. Place the duck on a rack in a roasting pan. Pour over the soy sauce and sufficient water just to cover the bottom of the pan. Roast in a moderately hot oven (400° F) for about 1 hour, basting the duck from time to time. Increase the heat to hot (450° F) and cook for a further 15 minutes.
Sift the flour, and mixing all the time, stir in 1¼ cups boiling water. Turn the dough on to a floured surface and knead for 10 minutes. Roll out thinly and cut into 2-inch rounds. Brush half the rounds with oil and place the remaining rounds on top. Roll each pair out thinly and cook in a lightly oiled frying pan for about 1 minute.
Strip the skin from the duck and cut meat into squares. Serve with the biscuits.
Serves 4

Chicken Cakes

2 cups ground or finely
*   chopped cooked chicken*
3 eggs
1 cup soft breadcrumbs
½ teaspoon salt
½ teaspoon white pepper
¼ cup whipping cream
1 teaspoon paprika pepper
pinch grated nutmeg
¼ cup all-purpose flour
2 tablespoons butter
5 tablespoons oil

Place the chicken in a bowl, add the eggs, breadcrumbs, salt, pepper, cream, paprika, nutmeg and flour and mix well. Melt the butter and stir into the chicken mixture. Divide the mixture into four.

Heat the oil in a frying pan, add one-quarter of the meat mixture, flatten it and cook on each side for 2–3 minutes, until browned. Remove and keep warm while cooking the other three portions.
Serve with a French or Belgian endive salad and rice.
Serves 4

Cook's Tip
This recipe is a particularly good way of using up leftover cooked poultry or game.

Partridge with Sauerkraut and Pears

2 oven-ready partridges
½ teaspoon salt
½ teaspoon celery salt
1 teaspoon paprika pepper
¼ teaspoon white pepper
2 stale rolls
2 onions, chopped
2 tablespoons liver sausage
5 tablespoons oil
½ cup butter
1 bay leaf
2 cups sauerkraut
1 teaspoon sugar
4 ripe pears
3 tablespoons diced bacon

Rub the insides of the partridges with salt, celery salt, paprika and white pepper. Cut the rolls into four, pour over hot water to soften them, then squeeze dry. Beat the softened bread and mix with the diced onions and the liver sausage. Use to stuff the partridges.
Heat the oil in a flameproof casserole and quickly brown the partridges all over. Add the butter and bay leaf, cover and simmer for 30 minutes. Heat the sauerkraut separately with 5 tablespoons water for 10 minutes. Add the sugar, peeled, cored and chopped pears and diced bacon and cook for a further 10 minutes. Arrange the sauerkraut on a serving dish with the partridges on top.
Serves 4

Poultry

Viennese Chicken

4 chicken portions
2 teaspoons salt
5 tablespoons all-purpose
  flour
2 eggs
1⅓ cups dry breadcrumbs
oil for deep frying
Garnish
lemon wedges
parsley sprigs

Rub the chicken portions with salt and coat in the flour. Beat the eggs with a fork and coat the chicken pieces all over, then roll in the breadcrumbs, pressing them on firmly. Heat the oil – if a cube of bread browns immediately, then the oil has reached the correct temperature. Fry the chicken portions until they are golden brown and cooked through. Remove and drain on paper towels. Serve garnished with lemon wedges and parsley sprigs. Serve with a green salad.
Serves 4

Cook's Tip
When serving foods which have been coated in crumbs and deep fried, the garnish of parsley should also be fried in the oil for 2–3 seconds. Drain on paper towels.

Chicken Risotto

1 (5-lb) stewing chicken
1 leek
2 carrots
2 teaspoons salt
1 bay leaf
2 onions
½ cup oil
1 cup long-grain rice
1 red pepper, chopped
¼ cup peas
⅔ cup whipping cream
3 tablespoons butter
1 tablespoon all-purpose
  flour

Place the chicken, prepared leek and carrots in a pan. Cover with 4½ pints water and add the salt and bay leaf. Bring to the boil, cover the pan and simmer for 1½ hours. Peel and finely dice the onions and fry in the oil until they become transparent. Add the rice, and fry, stirring, for 5 minutes. Add 2¼ pints of the chicken stock. Cover and simmer for 20 minutes, until the liquid is absorbed. Stir in the pepper and peas. Strain the rest of the chicken stock and bring it back to the boil. Remove from the heat and stir in the cream. Work the butter into the flour to form a paste and beat small amounts into the sauce. Return to the heat and beat until thick. Arrange the risotto with chicken portions on top and spoon over the sauce.
Serves 4

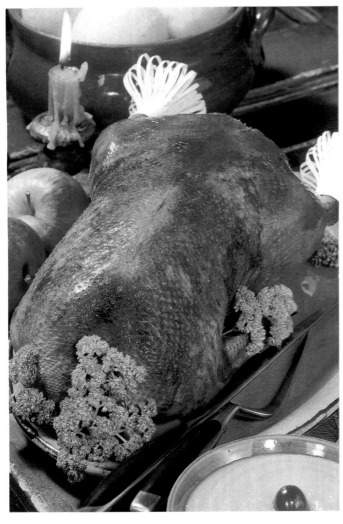

Goose with Apple Stuffing

6 dessert apples
1 onion
1 clove garlic, crushed
1 cup soft breadcrumbs
pinch dried sage
¼ cup port
1 (10-lb) oven-ready goose
salt and pepper
Garnish
parsley sprigs

Peel, core and chop the apples; peel and chop the onion. Mix together the apples, onion, garlic, breadcrumbs and sage. Bind together with the port. Stuff the goose with apple stuffing. Prick the skin all over with a skewer and sprinkle with salt and pepper. Place the goose on a rack in a roasting pan. Roast in a moderately hot oven (400° F) allowing 15 minutes to the 1 lb and 15 minutes extra.
After 1 hour, spoon the fat out of the pan, add ⅔ cup water and continue roasting the goose.
Place the goose on a large platter and garnish with parsley sprigs. Serve with spicy apple sauce (see page 77).
Serves 8

Casseroled Turkey with Fruit

4 turkey portions
½ teaspoon salt
pinch curry powder
¼ teaspoon white pepper
2 teaspoons paprika pepper
1 leek
¼ cup butter
½ tablespoon all-purpose flour
⅔ cup oil
⅓ cup each canned sliced peaches, pineapples and pitted cherries
1 orange, peeled and chopped

Sprinkle the turkey portions with the seasonings; slice the leek. Melt the butter in a pan and fry the prepared leek until it becomes transparent, then sprinkle with the flour. Stir in 6 tablespoons of cold water and leave on a low heat. Heat the oil in a flameproof casserole and brown the turkey portions on all sides. Add the leek, cover and cook in a moderate oven (350° F) for 35–40 minutes. Add the fruits and return to the oven for a further 10 minutes. Serve from the casserole dish, with rice.
Serves 4

Vegetable Dishes

Stuffed Red Peppers

4–6 red peppers
1 cup button mushrooms
4 bacon slices
2 onions
3 eggs
pinch salt
5 tablespoons chopped
    parsley
½ cup oil
¼ cup butter
½ teaspoon black pepper
½ cup sour cream
1 teaspoon sugar

Cut off the tops of the peppers and scoop out the core and seeds. Blanch in boiling salted water for 5 minutes. Leave upside down to drain.
Chop the mushrooms

coarsely; dice the bacon; peel and dice the onions. Place the bacon in a pan, heat until the fat runs, then add the mushrooms and onions and fry for 5 minutes. Lightly beat the eggs with a pinch of salt and the parsley and stir into the vegetables. Cook on a low heat until the eggs are lightly set. Remove from the heat. Use to fill the blanched peppers. Place in a roasting pan with the oil. Cover with foil and cook in a hot oven (425° F) for 25 minutes.
Melt the butter and mix with the black pepper, sour cream and sugar. Spoon over the peppers and cook for a further 5 minutes.
Serves 4

Savoy Cabbage with Yogurt

1 head savoy cabbage
3 onions
1 lemon
1 teaspoon salt
1 bay leaf
2 cloves
1 teaspoon sugar
¼ cup butter
⅔ cup plain yogurt

Cut the cabbage in half and cut out the stalk and the coarse outer leaves; cut the cabbage halves into strips. Peel and slice the onions and lemon.
Place the prepared cabbage, onions and lemon in a pan with 4½ pints water. Add the salt, bay leaf, cloves and sugar. Bring to the

boil, cover and simmer for 30 minutes. Melt the butter, stir in the yogurt and allow to heat through, but do not boil. Drain the cabbage mixture and place in a serving dish. Pour over the yogurt sauce. Serve with broiled or fried pork chops.
Serves 4

Cook's Tip
When buying savoy cabbage, pick one with crisp outer leaves. Reject pale green savoys as they are almost certain to be stale.

Buttered Carrot Sticks

2 lb carrots
1 teaspoon salt
2 onions
½ cup oil
6 tablespoons butter
5 tablespoons chopped
 parsley

Scrap the carrots and cut in four lengthwise, then cut each quarter in 2-inch long strips. Sprinkle with salt; peel and slice the onions. Heat the oil in a pan and fry the onions until they become transparent, then add the carrots together with ½ cup water. Cover with a lid and cook over a moderate heat for 30–35 minutes, until the

carrots are just tender. Using a slotted spoon, transfer to a serving dish and dot with the butter. Sprinkle over the parsley and serve with meatballs or beef casseroles.
Serves 4

Cook's Tip
Although carrots are available all the year round, it's a good idea to freeze young carrots. Remove the tops, wash and scrape but leave whole. Blanch for 5 minutes, drain, cool and pack in freezer bags.

Cucumber with Dill

2 large cucumbers
1 teaspoon salt
juice of ½ lemon
⅔ cup plain yogurt
½ teaspoon sugar
3 tablespoons butter
5 tablespoons chopped dill
1 teaspoon cornstarch

Cucumber is more usually served in salads, but it also makes a very good hot vegetable dish.
Peel and halve the cucumbers; remove the seeds and rinse the halves thoroughly. Cut the cucumber halves into bite-sized pieces. Place in a pan with the salt, lemon juice, yogurt, sugar and

2 tablespoons of the butter; cover and simmer for 10 minutes. Stir in the dill. Make a paste with the cornstarch and the remaining butter; beat into the cucumber and cook, stirring, until thickened. Check the seasoning and serve with fried veal cutlets.
Serves 4

Variation
Tarragon or celery seeds may be used in place of the dill. If fresh herbs are not available, use 1 teaspoon of the dried herbs.

139

Fennel au Gratin

4 bulbs fennel
4 bacon slices
2 cups milk
½ teaspoon salt
3 tablespoons butter
3 tablespoons all-purpose
   flour
5 tablespoons grated cheese

Florence fennel has a distinct anise seed flavor Buy bulbs which have well-rounded roots and avoid ones deep green in color. Trim and slice the fennel; dice the bacon. Heat the milk in a pan with the salt and the bacon; add the fennel and simmer for 20 minutes. Remove the fennel and bacon with a slotted spoon and place in a greased ovenproof dish. Add 1 cup water to the cooking liquid. Work 2 tablespoons of the butter into the flour to form a paste. Beat small amounts of the beurre manié (the flour and butter paste) into the cooking liquid. Stir over a moderate heat until thickened and glossy. Pour over the fennel and bacon. Sprinkle the cheese over the surface, dot with the remaining butter and bake in a hot oven (425° F) for 10 minutes, until the cheese has melted and the surface is lightly browned. Serve with veal cutlets.
Serves 4

Bread Dumplings and Mushrooms

10 stale white rolls
1 teaspoon salt
1½ cups lukewarm milk
1½ lb mushrooms
2 onions
½ cup butter
1 teaspoon pepper
5 tablespoons chopped
   parsley
3 eggs
½ cup whipping cream
Garnish
chopped parsley

Slice the rolls very thinly and sprinkle with the salt. Pour over the lukewarm milk and leave to soak for 15 minutes.

Slice the mushrooms; peel and finely dice the onions. Heat ¼ cup of the butter in a pan and fry the diced onions until softened. Mix the onions, ½ teaspoon of the pepper, the parsley and eggs into the softened bread. Bring a large pan of salted water to the boil. With wet hands, form the bread mixture into dumplings, the size of an apple; simmer them for 15 minutes. Meanwhile, heat the rest of the butter and fry the mushrooms for 10 minutes. Stir in the cream and remaining pepper. Garnish with chopped parsley and serve with the dumplings.
Serves 4

Green Beans with Bacon

2 slices Canadian bacon
1 lb green beans
8 tomatoes
sprig savory
2 tablespoons butter
5 tablespoons half-and-half
½ teaspoon black pepper
1 tablespoon chopped
  parsley

Broil or fry the bacon slices for 4 minutes on each side. Trim the beans and cook in boiling water until just tender. Drain.
Peel and quarter the tomatoes. Cut each bacon slice in half and place in a flameproof casserole with the beans, tomatoes, savory, butter, cream and pepper. Allow to cook over a moderate heat for about 5 minutes. Remove the savory and stir in the chopped parsley.
Serves 4

Variation
In place of the Canadian bacon, 8 oz ordinary bacon could be used. Chop the bacon and fry in its own fat until crisp. Stir into the beans with the tomatoes and other ingredients.

Eggplant and Tomato Bake

2–3 eggplants
3 teaspoons salt
¼ cup all-purpose flour
⅔ cup oil
2 onions, chopped
1 (8-oz) can tomatoes
¼ cup tomato paste
1 teaspoon dried basil
½ teaspoon dried oregano
1 teaspoon sugar
¼ teaspoon black pepper
8 oz Mozzarella cheese,
  sliced
¼ cup grated Parmesan
  cheese

Slice the eggplants into ½-inch slices; sprinkle with 2 teaspoons of the salt and leave aside.
Rinse the eggplant slices and pat dry with paper towels; toss in the flour.
Heat the oil in a frying pan, and fry the eggplant slices until brown on each side. Drain.
Add the onions, tomatoes, remaining salt, the tomato paste, basil, oregano, sugar and pepper to the oil remaining in the pan and cook for 10 minutes. Cool slightly; blend or push through a strainer. Place half the tomato mixture in a greased baking dish. Add a layer of the eggplant slices and a layer of cheese slices. Top with the remaining tomato mixture and sprinkle over the cheese. Cook in a moderately hot oven (400° F) for 20 minutes.
Serves 4

Vegetable Dishes

Oyster Plant au Gratin

2 lb oyster plant
juice of ½ lemon
½ cup butter
3 tablespoons all-purpose
* flour*
2½ cups milk
2 egg yolks
salt and pepper
½ cup cooked tongue, cut
* into strips*
5 tablespoons grated cheese
3 tablespoons dry white
* breadcrumbs*

Oyster plant is a root vegetable which is also called salsify or scorzonera. Scrub the oyster plant in cold water and top and tail. Peel and immediately place in cold water with a few drops of lemon juice added. Drain the oyster plant; cook in boiling salted water for 35 minutes. Drain.

Melt ¼ cup of the butter in a pan. Stir in the flour and cook for 1–2 minutes, without browning. Gradually add the milk and stirring, bring to the boil. Simmer for 1–2 minutes, stirring. Remove from the heat and beat in the egg yolks. Season to taste.

Mix the oyster plant and tongue with the sauce. Pour into a greased ovenproof dish. Sprinkle over the cheese and breadcrumbs and dot with the remaining butter. Cook in a moderately hot oven (400° F) for 10 minutes. Serve with broiled chops.
Serves 4

Tomato-Stuffed Celeriac

2 lb small celeriac
juice of 1 lemon
3 tomatoes
1 onion
¼ cup diced cooked tongue
½ teaspoon salt
½ teaspoon white pepper
3 tablespoons tomato
* ketchup*
½ cup oil
2 cups stock
Garnish
chopped parsley

Celeriac is the edible root of a variety of celery.

Wash and peel the celeriac. Hollow out the centers and dice the scooped-out flesh. Place the celeriac in cold water with a few drops of lemon juice added.

Nick the skins of the tomatoes, plunge into boiling water for 30–45 seconds then peel and chop. Peel and dice the onion. Place the tomatoes, tongue, onions, chopped celeriac, seasoning and tomato ketchup in a bowl and mix. Drain the hollowed-out celeriacs and fill the centers with the tomato mixture. Heat the oil in a flameproof casserole and fry the celeriacs for 10 minutes. Add the stock, cover and simmer for 20 minutes.

Remove from the casserole and serve garnished with chopped parsley.
Serves 4

Stuffed Artichokes

4 globe artichokes
3 tablespoons wine vinegar
½ teaspoon prepared mustard
½ teaspoon pepper
2 eggs
½ cup canned mussels
2 tomatoes
5 tablespoons whipping
  cream
3 tablespoons mayonnaise
½ cup cooked ham, cut into
  strips
Garnish
red pepper strips

Remove the stalks and cook the artichokes in boiling salted water for 50 minutes. Take the artichokes out of the water, drain, and pull out the inner leaves and the choke so that the firm base of the artichoke can be seen.
Stir the wine vinegar into the mustard and pepper; pour into the artichokes and leave for 30 minutes.
Hard-cook the eggs and cut into quarters. Cut the mussels in half.
Peel and chop the tomatoes. Whip the cream lightly and mix with the mayonnaise
Pour in the vinegar mixture from the artichokes and add the ham strips. Fill the artichokes with the tomatoes, mussels and eggs. Spoon over the mayonnaise mixture and serve garnished with red pepper strips. Accompany with thin slices of freshly made toast.
Serves 4

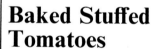

Baked Stuffed Tomatoes

8 large tomatoes
½ teaspoon celery salt
pinch garlic salt
2 slices white bread
¼ cup grated cheese
3 tablespoons chopped
 parsley or chives
5 tablespoons chopped
 cooked ham
2 tablespoons butter
few drops Worcestershire
 sauce
1 teaspoon cornstarch
½ cup sour cream
juice of 1 lemon
1 teaspoon sugar

Cut the tops off the tomatoes and scoop out the centers. Sprinkle the insides with a mixture of celery and garlic salts. Turn upside down and leave to drain.

Soak the bread in hot water, squeeze dry and place in a bowl. Mix in the grated cheese, parsley or chives and ham. Fill the tomato shells with the stuffing and replace the tops. Place in an ovenproof dish.

Melt the butter in a pan, add the Worcestershire sauce, the cornstarch blended with the cream, the lemon juice and sugar and about 5 tablespoons of water. Heat, but do not boil, then pour around the tomatoes. Cook in a moderately hot oven (400° F) for 15 minutes. Serve with rice, peas and buttered new potatoes.
Serves 4

Endive and Ham Parcels

8 heads French or Belgian
 endive
3 tablespoons oil
4 oz bacon slices
8 slices cooked ham
½ teaspoon salt
¼ teaspoon white pepper
¼ cup butter
5 tablespoons whipping
 cream
Garnish
parsley sprigs

Wash the endive heads and remove any damaged outer leaves. Brush four pieces of foil with oil. Dice the bacon and distribute evenly over the slices of ham. Put one head of endive on each slice of ham, sprinkle with salt and pepper and roll up. Put two endive and ham rolls on each piece of foil and turn up the edges of the foil. Dot with butter and spoon over the cream. Close the foil firmly, place the parcels on a baking sheet and cook in a moderately hot oven (400° F) for 30 minutes. Remove the foil and arrange the endive rolls on a serving dish. Garnish with parsley sprigs.
Serves 4

Cook's Tip
When buying endive, choose firmly packed heads. Reject any which are yellow and have curling leaves.

Brussels Sprouts with Sausagemeat Balls

1½ lb fresh or frozen
   Brussels sprouts
4 oz bacon slices
pinch salt
½ teaspoon grated nutmeg
1 cup canned mushrooms
½ cup pork sausagemeat

Trim the fresh sprouts, make a cross in the base of each and blanch in boiling salted water for 3 minutes; drain. (With frozen sprouts, allow them to thaw.)
Dice the bacon, place in a pan, and heat until the fat runs. Add the sprouts and fry for 3–4 minutes with a pinch of salt and the nutmeg. Pour in 2 cups water, cover and cook for 15 minutes.
Halve the mushrooms. Form the sausagemeat into small balls and add to the sprouts, together with the mushrooms. Cook for a further 5 minutes. Check the seasoning and transfer to a serving dish.
Serves 4

Cauliflower with Herbs

1 large cauliflower
1 teaspoon salt
2 tablespoons butter
¼ cup all-purpose flour
5 tablespoons whipping
   cream
5 tablespoons chopped
   parsley
3 tablespoons chopped basil
1 tablespoon each chopped
   borage and lemon balm
Garnish
parsley sprig

Cut off the bottom of the cauliflower stalk, and remove the outer leaves. Cover with cold water and leave for 1 hour.
Bring 2¼ pints of water and the salt to the boil.
Add the whole cauliflower and cook for 15 minutes. Drain and reserve 1 cup of the cooking liquid. Keep the cauliflower warm in a serving dish.
Melt the butter in a saucepan and stir in the flour. Cook for 1–2 minutes without allowing the flour to brown. Gradually stir in the reserved cooking liquid and bring to the boil stirring. Cook for 1–2 minutes. Remove from the heat and stir in the cream and herbs. Pour over the cauliflower and serve garnished with a parsley sprig.
Serves 4

Spinach with Scrambled Eggs

2 lb fresh spinach
1 tablespoon oil
5 tablespoons chopped
  parsley
salt and pepper
4 eggs
2 tablespoons butter

Pick over the spinach very carefully, wash in several changes of water. Leave to drain in a colander.
Heat the oil in a pan, add the spinach and cook for 10 minutes. Drain thoroughly, squeezing out all the liquid. Stir in half the parsley and season with salt. Keep warm.
Beat the eggs in a bowl with the remaining parsley and season with salt and pepper. Melt the butter in a pan and, stirring, cook the eggs until lightly scrambled. Arrange the spinach in a serving dish and spoon the scrambled egg in the center. Serve at once with freshly made toast.
Serves 4

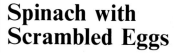

Cook's Tip
Spinach needs careful handling as the tender dark green leaves bruise easily. Choose crisp leaves and reject limp ones which will be stale.

Leeks in a Cream and Raisin Sauce

8 leeks
1 teaspoon salt
8 peppercorns
2 coriander seeds
2 sprigs parsley
2 shallots, sliced
Sauce
$1\frac{1}{4}$ cups cream
2 egg yolks
3 tablespoons raisins
$\frac{1}{4}$ teaspoon pepper

Trim, wash and slice the leeks in half, lengthwise. Place in a pan, cover with water and add the salt, peppercorns, coriander, parsley and shallots. Bring to the boil and simmer for 15 minutes. Drain the leeks well, place on a serving dish and keep warm.
To make the sauce, place the cream and egg yolks in the top of a double boiler. Cook, stirring frequently, until thickened. Stir in the raisins and pepper and spoon over the leeks.
Serves 4

Variation
$1\frac{1}{4}$ cups white sauce could be used in place of the cream. To make the white sauce, use $\frac{2}{3}$ cup of the liquid from cooking the leeks.

Vegetable Dishes

Baked Stuffed Onions

4 large onions
½ cup ground beef
½ cup finely chopped lamb
*   liver*
2 eggs
1 teaspoon salt
1 tablespoon soft
*   breadcrumbs*
1 tablespoon chopped
*   tarragon*
½ teaspoon garlic salt
½ cup oil
1 teaspon paprika pepper
Garnish
parsley sprigs

Peel the onions and scoop out the centers with a sharp-pointed knife; chop the scooped-out onion coarsely and mix with the beef and liver. Add the eggs, salt, breadcrumbs, tarragon and garlic salt. Use this mixture to fill the onion shells, piling it up in the center. Place in a roasting pan and pour in the oil. Cover with foil and cook in a moderately hot oven (400° F) for 35–40 minutes. Transfer to a serving dish and serve garnished with parsley sprigs.
Serves 4

Variation
Other meat fillings may be used to stuff the onions – try 8 oz ground pork (or pork and veal mixed) and use fresh sage in place of the tarragon.

Walnut-Stuffed Cabbage Rolls

3 cups cooked ground pork
¾ cup finely diced cooked
*   tongue*
⅓ cup chopped walnuts
½ teaspoon celery salt
½ teaspoon white pepper
½ teaspoon dried thyme
¼ cup liver sausage
3 tablespoons soft
*   breadcrumbs*
1 egg
1 medium-sized head savoy
*   cabbage*
6 tablespoons vegetable fat
⅔ cup sour cream
3 tablespoons tomato paste

Mix the pork with the tongue, walnuts, celery salt, pepper, thyme, liver sausage and breadcrumbs.

Bind with the lightly beaten egg.
Cook the cabbage, whole, in boiling salted water for 30 minutes. Drain, cool slightly and pull the leaves apart. Arrange the leaves in pairs, with the pairs overlapping each other. Put 3–4 tablespoons of the meat mixture on each pair, form into a roll and secure.
Heat the fat in a frying pan and fry the rolls until browned. Add sufficient water or stock to cover the rolls and simmer for 25–30 minutes. Transfer to a serving dish and keep warm. To make the sauce, heat the sour cream with the tomato paste and spoon over the cabbage rolls.
Serves 4

Parisian Mushroom Salad

8 oz button mushrooms
3 tablespoons mayonnaise
3 tablespoons wine vinegar
½ teaspoon sugar
½ cup chopped cooked ham
Garnish
hard-cooked egg quarters
pinch cayenne pepper

Trim the base of the mushroom stalks and wipe them with a damp cloth. Slice the mushrooms. Mix the mayonnaise with the vinegar and the sugar to make a smooth sauce. Place the prepared mushrooms and ham in a serving bowl and toss in the mayonnaise mixture. Serve garnished with hard-cooked egg quarters sprinkled with cayenne pepper.
Serves 4–6

Variation
If preferred the mushrooms and ham may be tossed in ½ cup French dressing just before serving. To make this dish more substantial, chopped cooked poultry may also be added to the salad.

Leek and Ham Salad

1 egg
1 tomato
1 head lettuce
3–4 cooked leeks
1 bunch garden cress
½ cup cooked ham, cut into strips
1 teaspoon salt
½ teaspoon white pepper
½ teaspoon garlic salt
3 tablespoons wine vinegar
5 tablespoons oil

Hard-cook the egg for 10 minutes; cool, shell and chop finely. Nick the skin of the tomato, plunge into boiling water for 30–45 seconds, then peel off the skin and cut the tomato into strips.

Wash, dry and shred the lettuce leaves. Slice the cooked leeks. Wash and drain the cress. Mix all the prepared salad ingredients together and place in a serving dish.
Mix together the seasonings, vinegar and oil to make a dressing. Sprinkle over the salad just before serving.
Serves 4

Cook's Tip
When preparing the lettuce, tear it into shreds. Do not cut with a knife as this will cause the edges to turn brown.

Cucumber and Dill Salad

½ *cucumber*
4–6 sweet dill pickles
2 zucchini
*3 tablespoons coarsely
    chopped dill*
⅔ *cup shelled shrimp*
1½ cups strawberries
⅔ *cup sour cream*

This salad is particularly
refreshing on a hot day. It
makes a good accompani-
ment to cold salmon.
Peel and thinly slice the
cucumber; slice the pickles
and zucchini. Mix together
the prepared cucumber,
pickles and zucchini and
place in a serving bowl.
Add the chopped dill and
shrimp. Hull and halve the

strawberries and add to the
salad.
Just before serving, spoon
over the sour cream.
Serves 4

Variation
The shrimp may be replaced
by crab meat. Raspberries
may be used in place of the
strawberries. Plain yogurt
could be substituted for the
sour cream.

Roast Beef Salad

4 thick slices roast beef
¼ *cup mayonnaise*
4 tomatoes
½ *cup green beans*
2–3 sweet dill pickles
¼ *head celeriac*
1 head lettuce

Cut the roast beef into strips.
Mix the mayonnaise with a
little of the liquid from the
pickles. Nick the skins of
the tomatoes, plunge into
boiling water for 30–45
seconds, then peel and
chop. Cook the beans in
boiling salted water until
tender. Drain and cool.
Slice the pickles; peel and
cut the celeriac into strips.
Mix all the prepared

ingredients together with
the mayonnaise and leave in
the refrigerator for 10
minutes to marinate.
Wash and dry the lettuce
leaves and use to line a
salad bowl. Spoon in the
beef salad.
Serves 4–6

Variation
This salad is very pleasant
with cabbage instead of
lettuce. Choose a green
variety of cabbage and
shred the leaves, removing
the coarse stalk.

149

Poultry and Orange Salad

¼ cup cream cheese
2 teaspoons grated fresh
    horseradish root
⅔ cup half-and-half
5 tablespoons chopped
    parsley
2 oranges
2 cups finely diced cooked
    chicken

Break up the cheese with a
fork and beat to a smooth
sauce with the horseradish
and the cream. Stir in the
chopped parsley. Halve the
oranges. Scoop out the
orange flesh, discarding the
seeds and membranes, and
cut into small pieces; mix
with the chicken. Stir the
cream sauce into the

chicken and orange mixture.
Pile the mixture into the
orange shells.
Serves 4

Variation
Cottage cheese may be used
in place of the cream cheese.
Use 1 cup diced cooked
chicken and 1 cup chopped
dessert apple and walnuts.

Veal Salad

1 medium head white cabbage
2 onions
5 tablespoons wine vinegar
⅓ teaspoon salt
¼ teaspoon garlic salt
4 tomatoes
½ cucumber
2 cups roast veal, cut into
    thin strips
½ cup oil

Cut the cabbage into
quarters and cut away the
stalks. Using a sharp knife,
shred finely. Wash and
leave to drain. Peel the
onions and slice thinly. Mix
the prepared cabbage and
onions together.
Mix together the vinegar,
salt and the garlic salt and

use to toss the cabbage
mixture. Chill in the
refrigerator for 10 minutes.
Nick the skins of the
tomatoes, plunge into
boiling water for 30–45
seconds, then peel and
quarter. Slice the cucumber
thinly. Place all the salad
ingredients together in a
bowl and mix. Just before
serving, pour over the oil
and toss the ingredients.
Serves 4

Variation
Leftover roast lamb, beef or
pork may be used in place
of the veal.

Brazilian Bamboo Salad

$\frac{2}{3}$ cup milk
$\frac{2}{3}$ cup sour cream
2 teaspoons curry powder
$\frac{1}{2}$ teaspoon salt
1 teaspoon sugar
1 (1-lb 14-oz) can bamboo
   shoots
1 small can peach halves
$\frac{1}{2}$ teaspoon white pepper
$\frac{1}{2}$ teaspoon ground mace
pinch ground cloves
pinch ground cinnamon
3 tablespoons chopped mint

Beat the milk with the sour cream, curry powder, salt and sugar. Leave for 15 minutes to allow the flavors to combine.
Drain the bamboo shoots and slice thinly. Cut the peach halves into strips and mix with the sliced bamboo shoots.
Mix the rest of the spices and the chopped mint into the sauce.
Place the bamboo shoots and peaches in a serving bowl. Pour over the sauce and toss all the ingredients together until evenly coated in the sauce. Allow to chill for 20 minutes before serving.
Serves 4

Eggplant and Orange Salad

2 eggplants
2 onions
5 tablespoons olive oil
2 eggs
2 oranges
5 tablespoons chopped mint
1 teaspoon dried rosemary
5 tablespoons wine vinegar
2 tablespoons sugar
1 teaspoon salt

Place the eggplants on a baking sheet and cook in a moderate oven (350° F) for 10 minutes. Remove and peel off the skins. Slice the eggplants and onions. Heat the oil and fry the eggplant and onion slices together until softened. Leave to become cold.

Hard-cook the eggs for 10 minutes, cool, shell and cut into quarters. Peel and slice the oranges. Mix together the mint, rosemary, vinegar, sugar and salt. Mix the orange slices with the eggplant and onion mixture and pour over the dressing. Leave to marinate for 10 minutes.
Serve garnished with the hard-cooked egg quarters.
Serves 4

Variation
1–2 zucchini may also be added to this salad. Slice the zucchini and fry in the oil with the eggplant and onion slices.

151

Chef's Salad

1 large onion
2 eggs, hard-cooked
1 small can artichoke hearts
1 can anchovy fillets
¼ cucumber
1 bunch garden cress
1 head lettuce
4 tomatoes
½ cup Emmenthal cheese, cut
    into thin strips
½ cup cooked tongue, cut
    into thin strips
12 oz cooked poultry
pinch white pepper
1 teaspoon dry mustard
5 tablespoons wine vinegar
⅔ cup oil

Peel the onion and cut into
rings. Slice the hard-cooked
eggs.
Drain the artichoke hearts
and the anchovies. Form the
anchovy fillets into rings.
Thinly slice the cucumber;
wash and dry the cress and
lettuce.
Peel and cut the tomatoes
into quarters.
Arrange all the salad
ingredients attractively on a
large plate.
Mix the pepper with the
mustard, vinegar and oil to
make a dressing and serve
separately.
Serve with French bread
and butter.
Serves 4

Variation
In place of the artichoke
hearts, drained canned
asparagus spears can be
used.

Bean Salad

1 lb green beans
1 egg
2 tomatoes
1 onion
½ teaspoon salt
5 tablespoons wine vinegar
1 tablespoon chopped savory
3 tablespoons chopped
   borage
2 teaspoons prepared Dijon
   mustard
5 tablespoons oil
1 cup shelled shrimp

Trim the beans and cook in boiling salted water, until just tender. Drain and cool.
Hard-cook the egg for 10 minutes, cool, shell and remove the egg yolk. Press the egg yolk through a strainer. Nick the skins of the tomatoes, plunge into boiling water for 30–45 seconds, peel and cut into slices. Peel and dice the onion and mix with the salt, vinegar, herbs, mustard and the strained egg yolk. Blend in the oil. Arrange the beans, shrimp and tomatoes in a bowl and spoon over the sauce.
Serves 4

Asparagus Salad

1 lb fresh or canned
   asparagus
1 tablespoon wine vinegar
½ teaspoon salt
½ teaspoon sugar
3 tablespoons mayonnaise
5 tablespoons chopped
   parsley
2 slices canned pineapple
½ cup chopped cooked
   chicken
Garnish
tomato wedges
parsley sprigs

If using fresh asparagus, peel, and cook in boiling salted water for 15 minutes. Refresh in cold water, drain and cut into 2-inch lengths. Drain and cut the canned asparagus into 2-inch lengths.
Mix the vinegar with the salt, sugar, mayonnaise and parsley. Cut the pineapple slices into small pieces, add the chicken; mix together. Mix in the asparagus. Pour over the dressing and toss all the ingredients. Spoon into a salad bowl and serve garnished with tomato wedges and a parsley sprig.
Serves 4–6

Variation
The mayonnaise may be replaced by 3 tablespoons sour cream.

Veal Kidneys Monsieur

1 lb veal kidneys
3 teaspoons salt
2 onions
1 tablespoon all-purpose flour
4 tablespoons oil
juice of ½ lemon
2 teaspoons prepared
    mustard
⅔ cup sour cream
1 teaspoon sugar
¼ cup brandy
2 sweet dill pickles
3 tablespoons cocktail
    onions (optional)

Immerse the kidneys in water for about 10 minutes, then remove the gristle and slice into ½-inch thick pieces. Rub about 2 teaspoons of salt into them, rinse and dry. Peel and finely dice the onions. Sprinkle another teaspoon of salt on the kidneys and toss them in the flour.

Heat the oil in a frying pan and fry the kidney slices for 2 minutes, stirring with a wooden spoon so that they brown all over.

Lower the heat. Add the diced onion to the pan. Mix the lemon juice with the mustard, cream and sugar. Trickle the brandy over the kidneys, carefully set alight, let the flame almost go out and then spoon over the cream mixture.

Coarsely chop the pickles, and add with the cocktail onions, if used, to the pan. Stir well and serve immediately.
Serves 4

Flambéed Pork

2 onions
1 lb pork tenderloin
1 teaspoon salt
1 teaspoon paprika pepper
½ teaspoon black pepper
3 tablespoons all-purpose
    flour
1 red pepper
5 tablespoons oil
6 tablespoons Aquavit
¼ cup peas
½ cup sour cream
1 teaspoon sugar

Peel and finely slice the onions. Remove any gristle and surplus fat from the meat and slice thickly. Mix together the salt, paprika, pepper and flour and roll the meat in it. Wash and seed the pepper and cut into strips.

Heat the oil in a frying pan, fry the onion quickly, add the meat slices and fry on each side for 3 minutes. Then pour over the Aquavit, carefully set alight and let the flame go out. Add the peas and pepper strips.

Mix the cream and sugar together and pour into the pan. Let everything bubble for another 5 minutes, then serve immediately on warmed plates.

Serve with a green salad.
Serves 4

Spiced Steak Fillets

4 fillet steaks
½ teaspoon salt
ground black pepper
½ teaspoon paprika pepper
1 onion
5 tablespoons oil
3 tablespoons chopped
*   preserved ginger*
3 tablespoons mango chutney
¼ cup Chartreuse liqueur
5 tablespoons cream
3 tablespoons chopped
*   parsley*

Pound the steaks very thinly and rub the salt, pepper and paprika into them. Peel and very finely slice the onion. Heat the oil in a frying pan and fry the meat for 1 minute on each side. Put the onion slices, chopped ginger (with the syrup) and mango chutney into the pan. Let the mixture get hot, turning constantly with a wooden spoon. Pour over the liqueur and carefully set alight. Extinguish the flames after 30 seconds with the cream. Finally sprinkle over the parsley. Serve immediately on warm plates, accompanied by sautéed potatoes.
Serves 4

Variation
Use sirloin steak or pork tenderloin instead of fillet steak. Fry for 2 minutes on each side in the heated oil.

Riviera Trout

2 fresh or frozen trout
1 teaspoon salt
3 tablespoons all-purpose
*   flour*
1 teaspoon rosemary sprigs
*   or ½ teaspoon dried*
*   rosemary*
5 tablespoons oil
3 tablespoons butter
5 tablespoons Ricard or
*   Pernod*
5 tablespoons cream
Garnish
lemon slices
rosemary sprigs

Thaw the trout if using frozen. Dry with paper towels and roll in the salt and flour. Rub the rosemary inside the trout. Heat the oil in a frying pan with the butter. Lay the trout in the pan and fry for 5 minutes, turning several times. Then pour over the Ricard and carefully set alight; let it almost go out. Extinguish the drying flames with the cream and mix with the juices in the pan.
Serve immediately on warmed plates with French fried or creamed potatoes and a cucumber salad. Garnish with halved slices of lemon and sprigs of rosemary.
Serves 2

Flambéed Dishes

Escargots on Toast

24 canned snails
¼ cup butter
½ teaspoon garlic salt
¼ teaspoon white pepper
½ cup brandy
2 slices wholewheat bread
Garnish
parsley sprigs

Drain the snails in a strainer over a bowl, reserving the juice.
Heat the snails with the butter, garlic salt and pepper in a frying pan for 2 minutes, without letting them burn. Then pour over the brandy and carefully set alight. Let it almost go out and extinguish the last flames with the juice from the can of snails.
Toast the bread and cut diagonally, place on two warmed plates. Spoon the snails with the butter sauce on to the bread. Garnish with parsley and serve immediately, accompanied by a tomato salad.
Serves 2

Variation
Canned snails are delicious served in their shells with garlic butter. Cream ½ cup butter with 2 crushed garlic cloves, 5 tablespoons chopped parsley and salt and pepper. Place a snail in each shell, add a little butter and cook in a moderately hot oven (400° F) for 10 minutes.

Louisiana Chicken

1 chicken, cooked
5 tablespoons oil
pinch saffron
½ teaspoon salt
¼ cup canned corn kernels
¼ cup peas
1 tomato
5 tablespoons whiskey
3 tablespoons brandy
¼ cup butter
½ cup cream

Cut the chicken into wings, legs and breast pieces and remove the largest bones. Heat the oil in a frying pan and reheat the chicken thoroughly. Sprinkle over the saffron and salt. After 2–3 minutes add the drained corn and the peas; cover and cook for a further 2 minutes. Slice the tomato. Mix the whiskey and brandy, pour over the chicken pieces and carefully set alight; let the flames almost go out.
Add the tomato slices to the pan and stir in the butter. Finally stir in the cream. Serve immediately on warmed plates, accompanied by a green salad.
Serves 4–6

Variation
If liked, use canned corn to which diced green and red peppers have been added. This will give even more color to the dish.

Steak au Poivre avec Cognac

24 black peppercorns
2 fillet steaks
½ teaspoon salt
5 tablespoons oil
few drops Tabasco sauce
5 tablespoons brandy
2 tablespoons butter

Crush the peppercorns with the blade of a heavy knife or with a pestle. Salt the steaks. Sprinkle the crushed peppercorns on both sides of the steaks and press in well with a knife. Heat the oil in a frying pan and fry on each side for 1–2 minutes, or longer according to taste. Pour the Tabasco sauce and brandy over the steaks, carefully set alight and let the flames go out. Add the butter and allow to melt in the pan juices. Serve immediately on warmed plates, with French fried potatoes and a mixed salad.
Serves 2

Cook's Tip
When you are flaming food it is better to use high proof spirits as they will burn better. Whatever spirit you use should in any case have an alcohol content of 38%.

Breast of Chicken Flambé

4 fresh or frozen chicken
   breasts
¼ cup butter
4 slices cooked ham
¼ teaspoon garlic salt
1 teaspoon white pepper
6 tablespoons oil
8 oz canned fruit cocktail,
   drained
½ cup brandy

Thaw the chicken breasts if frozen. Place the chicken between 2 sheets of damp wax paper and pound the meat flat.
Divide the butter and ham into 4 equal portions and season with the garlic salt and pepper. Place a portion on each chicken slice. Roll up and fasten the chicken breasts with fine string, thread or wooden toothpicks. Heat the oil in a shallow flameproof casserole, fry the chicken breasts for 3 minutes all over and then lower the heat and continue cooking for a further 10 minutes, turning from time to time. Add the fruit cocktail, pour over the brandy, set alight very carefully with a match and serve while still flaming. Serve with buttered rice.
Serves 4

Sirloin Steaks with Bananas

1 onion
1 banana
2 sirloin steaks
5 tablespoons oil
1 teaspoon prepared
    mustard
½ teaspoon curry powder
¼ cup port
½ cup vodka
½ teaspoon salt
⅔ cup white sauce
1 tablespoon Worcestershire
    sauce
5 tablespoons cream
2 tablespoons butter

Peel and slice the onion and banana. Pound the sirloin steaks very thin. Heat the oil in the frying pan and lightly brown the onion for

2 minutes; then push to one side of the frying pan. Put in the steaks and fry on each side for 2–3 minutes, or longer, according to taste. Push to one side.
Stir the mustard and curry powder into the oil in the pan and add the banana. Pour on the port and vodka, carefully set alight and allow almost to go out. Add the salt, white sauce, Worcestershire sauce and cream and stir into the pan juices. Finally melt the butter in the sauce and spoon over the steak and onion. Serve immediately on warmed plates. Accompany with potatoes and celery salad, if liked.
Serves 2

Scotch Chicken

1 small chicken, roasted
2 onions
8 slices salami
6 sweet dill pickles
2 tomatoes
½ cup frozen peas
5 tablespoons oil
¼ cup Scotch whisky
⅓ cup chopped pickled beets
3 tablespoons chopped
    parsley
1 teaspoon salt
½ teaspoon sugar
1 teaspoon paprika pepper

Divide the chicken into fairly large pieces and remove the larger bones. Peel and finely slice the onions. Cut the salami slices in half. Cut the

pickles into matchsticks. Nick the skins of the tomatoes, plunge into boiling water for 30–45 seconds, peel and quarter. Thaw the peas.
Heat the oil in a frying pan and brown the chicken pieces quickly on all sides. Add the onion and salami and cook for 2 minutes. Pour over the whisky, carefully set alight and allow almost to go out. Add the pickles, tomatoes, beets, peas and parsley and season with the salt, sugar and paprika. Heat through then serve immediately, with potatoes and a green salad.
Serves 4

Orange Crêpe

¼ cup all-purpose flour
1 egg
1 teaspoon sugar
pinch salt
¼ cup butter
2 oranges
12 sugar lumps
6 tablespoons Grand Marnier liqueur
5 tablespoons brandy

Beat the flour with enough cold water to make a thick batter; then add the egg, sugar and salt and stir until smooth. Heat half the butter in a shallow pan. Pour in the batter; after 5 minutes turn the crêpe over, cook for 2 more minutes then slide on to a board and cut into small pieces or 1-inch squares.

Rub the orange peel with the sugar lumps; then grate the rind and squeeze out the juice from the oranges. Melt the remaining butter in the pan with the orange rind, juice and the sugar lumps. Add the crêpe and stir well. Mix the liqueur and the brandy together and pour over, carefully set alight and allow to go out. Serve immediately on warmed plates, with vanilla ice cream.
Serves 2

Cherries Jubilee

1 (15-oz) can pitted cherries
¼ cup butter
1 tablespoon Campari
5 tablespoons sugar
6 tablespoons rum
5 tablespoons cream
1 cup crushed macaroons

Drain the cherries, reserving 5 tablespoons of the juice. Melt the butter in a frying pan, but do not let it get hot. Stir in the Campari and sugar and mix well. Add the cherries and heat for 4–5 minutes, moving around in the pan. Now add the rum to the pan juices and set carefully alight. After 30 seconds extinguish the flames with the cream and the reserved cherry juice. Cook for a further 30 seconds. Put the crushed macaroons into individual dishes, spoon over the cherries and sauce and serve immediately. Serve macaroons separately.
Serves 2

Variation
You can make a delicious dessert if, using the above recipe, you substitute fresh or frozen (thawed) blackberries for the cherries. However, use a blackberry liqueur or brandy to flambé.

159

Zabaglione with Grapes

4 oz black grapes
4 oz white grapes
2 cups medium dry white
*   wine*
½ cup sugar
grated rind of 1 lemon
2 teaspoons lemon juice
5 egg yolks
2 teaspoons cornstarch

Wash the grapes, halve and remove the seeds. Put all the ingredients except the grapes in the top of a double boiler. Mix well together and place on the heat. Beat until the mixture becomes frothy. Take care not to let the water boil, or the mixture will curdle. When the mixture begins to get creamy and frothy, remove immediately from the heat and pour into 4 glasses while still hot. Place the grapes on top of each glass and allow to sink into the zabaglione. Serve with frosted grapes.
Serves 4

Cook's Tip
Frost grapes by dipping them into lightly beaten egg white and then toss in sugar. Allow to dry completely on wax paper.

Ice Cream Melba

1 (14½-oz) can peach halves
*   or 4 fresh peaches*
1 cup confectioners' sugar
⅔ cup brandy
⅔ cup whipping cream
few drops vanilla extract
4 individual bricks vanilla
*   ice cream*
⅔ cup raspberry jam,
*   strained*

Drain the peach halves. If using fresh peaches plunge them into boiling water for 2 minutes, remove and peel off the skin with a small knife. Cut in half and remove the pits.
Put the peaches in a bowl, sprinkle with the confectioners' sugar and brandy and leave for 30 minutes, to marinate.
Whip the cream with the vanilla extract until stiff.
Put the ice cream bricks into 4 individual glass dishes.
Place the peach halves on top. Mix the brandy marinade with the raspberry jam and pour over.
Decorate with piped whipped cream and serve with ladyfingers.
Serves 4

Variation
Instead of raspberry jam you could use fresh or frozen raspberries, puréed with a little sugar.

Melon Filled with Fruit Salad

(in foreground of picture)

juice of 1 lemon
3 tablespoons clear honey
1 large honeydew melon
1 (11-oz) can mandarin
  oranges
1 apple
1 banana
8 oz white grapes
⅓ cup candied cherries
1¼ cups whipping cream
few drops vanilla extract

Mix the lemon juice with the honey. Slice the top third off the melon, remove the seeds and scoop out the flesh with a small spoon or melon baller, to form little balls. Drain the mandarin oranges and stir 3 tablespoons of the juice into the lemon and honey mixture. Peel, core and slice the apple. Slice the banana and halve and seed the washed grapes.
Mix all the fruit together with the honey juice. Whip the cream with the vanilla extract until thick and add to the fruit salad. Arrange in the scooped-out melon.
Serves 4

Variations
Mixed Fruit Salad *(center)*
Mix several different fruits which have been diced or sliced the same size. Sweeten and add lemon, orange, or apple juice.

Raspberry Cups *(top right)*
Stir slightly sweetened raspberries into lightly whipped cream and natural yogurt, and arrange in tall glasses.

Strawberry Curd *(bottom right)*
Halve and sweeten fresh strawberries. Mix together with cottage cheese.

161

Desserts

East Frisian Pears

1½ cups round-grain rice
½ teaspoon salt
2 pints milk
3 tablespoons sugar
grated rind of 1 lemon
3 eggs
few drops vanilla extract
fine dry white breadcrumbs
oil for deep frying
candied angelica strips

Bring the rice to the boil with the salt, milk, sugar and lemon rind. Cook for 20 minutes.
Mix the cooked rice with 1 egg and the vanilla extract and allow to become cold. With wet hands mold into pear shapes. Beat the remaining eggs. Dip the pears in the egg, then roll in the breadcrumbs. Heat the oil to 360° F and fry the pears until a golden brown color. Drain well on paper towels.
Place strips of angelica in the pears to represent stalks.
Serve with canned cherries, frosted grapes and cream.
Serves 4

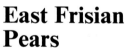

Cook's Tip
Before shaping, spread the mixture in a shallow dish and allow to chill in the refrigerator.

Charlotte Cream

1½ cups confectioners' sugar, sifted
6 egg yolks
2 envelopes unflavored gelatin
1 cup milk
few drops vanilla extract
2½ cups whipping cream

Place 1 cup of the sugar and the egg yolks in the top of a double boiler. Beat over the heat until creamy. As soon as it begins to thicken, remove the mixture from heat and continue beating until really thick.
Dissolve the gelatin in 4 tablespoons water over a low heat. Heat the milk in another pan, remove from the heat and add the vanilla extract and the dissolved gelatin. Stir a few spoonsful of the hot milk into the egg mixture, then pour the egg mixture very carefully into the milk. Allow to cool until on the point of setting. Meanwhile, whip the cream fairly stiffly with the rest of the sugar and fold into the cooled mixture. Rinse a 2½ pint capacity mold and fill with the cream mixture. Put in the refrigerator and leave until set. To serve, invert the mold over a serving dish, cover with a hot cloth and carefully lift the mold off.
The charlotte can be decorated with piped cream and candied fruit.
Serves 4–6

French Sabayon

6 eggs
½ cup confectioners' sugar
½ cup marsala
½ lemon
2 sugar lumps
½ cup ground hazelnuts

Break the eggs, separate the yolks from the whites. Put the yolks in the top of a double boiler. Sift the sugar and add to the egg yolks with the marsala. Rub the lemon peel with the sugar lumps and add to the egg yolk mixture. Beat the mixture over the heat until frothy. Squeeze the juice from the lemon and stir in. Beat the egg whites stiffly and fold into the egg mixture. Finally fold in the ground hazelnuts and pour into individual glasses. Sprinkle chocolate flakes and a little sifted confectioners' sugar on top. Serve immediately with crisp cookies.
Serves 4–6

Cook's Tip

A Sabayon sauce of egg yolks, sugar and wine may be thickened with a little arrowroot and served separately as a delicious accompaniment to fruit puddings.

Cranberry Cream Trifle

1½ lb fresh or frozen
  cranberries
1 cup sugar
juice of 1 lemon
1 cinnamon stick
10 slices brown bread, crusts
  removed
2½ cups whipping cream
few drops vanilla extract
1 tablespoon chopped
  pistachio nuts

Pick over the cranberries, wash in cold water and cook for 20 minutes with all but 2 tablespoons of the sugar, the lemon juice and the cinnamon stick. Some of the liquid should evaporate. Cool and remove the cinnamon stick.

Make the brown bread into fine breadcrumbs. Arrange a layer of these on the bottom of a glass bowl. Whip the cream with the vanilla extract and the remaining sugar until fairly stiff. Put a layer of the cooled cranberries with their juice on top of the layer of breadcrumbs, then spread over a layer of the whipped cream. Repeat these layers, finishing with a layer of cream. Chill in the refrigerator for 2 hours. Sprinkle the chopped pistachio nuts on top.
Serves 4–6

Desserts

Floating Meringues

6 eggs
1 cup milk
2 tablespoons butter
grated rinds of 1 orange and
   1 lemon
$\frac{2}{3}$ cup sugar
$\frac{1}{2}$ cup all-purpose flour
5 tablespoons confectioners'
   sugar

Separate the egg yolks from
the whites. Warm the milk
in a large 2-pint flameproof
dish, add the butter and
grated orange and lemon
rinds. Heat through in the
oven. Beat the egg whites
stiffly, add half the sugar
and beat again until stiff.
Then carefully fold in the
rest of the sugar, the egg

yolks and the sifted flour.
Place large spoonsful of this
mixture in the warm milk,
remove from the heat and
sprinkle with the confec-
tioners' sugar.
Bake in the centre of a hot
oven (450° F) for 5–8
minutes, then reduce the
temperature to 300° F for a
further 15–20 minutes.
Serve at once.
Serves 4–6

Cook's Tip
This dish will not
stand any draft when
it comes out of the
oven. It should be
served immediately
before the topping
sinks.

Apple Fritters

4 cooking apples
juice of 1 lemon
$\frac{1}{4}$ cup sugar
few drops vanilla extract
$\frac{2}{3}$ cup brandy
pinch each ground
   cardamom, cinnamon and
   cloves
$\frac{1}{2}$ cup all-purpose flour
2 eggs
$\frac{1}{2}$ teaspoon salt
5 tablespoons currants
oil for deep frying
1 teaspoon cornstarch

Peel and core the apples and
cut into thick rings. Place
in a flat dish and sprinkle
with the lemon juice, 3
tablespoons of the sugar,
the vanilla extract, brandy

and spices. Leave for 1
hour to marinate.
Mix all but 2 tablespoons of
the flour with 1$\frac{1}{4}$ cups water
until smooth. Then add the
eggs, salt, remaining
sugar and the currants.
Heat the oil to 350° F. Pick
each apple ring from its
marinade with a fork,
drain, toss in the remaining
flour, then dip in the batter.
Fry in the oil until golden.
Drain on paper towels.
Strain the marinade and
heat in a saucepan. Mix the
cornstarch with a little
water. Use to thicken the
marinade and bring to the
boil. Cool and serve as a
sauce. Serve the apple
fritters with vanilla ice
cream.
Serves 4

164

Austrian Apricot Dumplings

1 lb small apricots
sugar lumps
⅔ cup butter
1¼ cups all-purpose flour
2 eggs
½ teaspoon salt
1½ cups soft breadcrumbs
¼ cup confectioners' sugar

Halve the apricots and remove the pits. Place a sugar lump in each cavity. In a saucepan bring to the boil 1½ cups water with 2 tablespoons of the butter. Sift the flour and put all at once into the boiling water. Beat well with a wooden spoon until the lump of dough comes away from the sides of the pan and the surface is shiny. Remove from the heat and beat in the eggs. Shape the still warm dough into rolls and slice into 1-inch thick slices. Flatten a little and mold each one around an apricot. Leave to dry for 5 minutes. Bring 4½ pints of water to the boil with the salt. Drop in the dumplings and cook over a medium heat for 8–10 minutes.

Brown the breadcrumbs in the rest of the butter. Lift the dumplings out of the water with a ladle, drain well, toss in the breadcrumbs and sprinkle with the confectioners' sugar.
Serves 4

Caramel Pudding

4 eggs
1 cup sugar
1 teaspoon vanilla extract
1⅔ cups whipping cream
1 tablespoon confectioners' sugar
Decoration
chocolate curls

Lightly beat the eggs with ⅓ cup of the sugar. Add the vanilla extract and 1 cup cream and stir.

Melt the remaining sugar in a saucepan and cook until it turns a pale caramel color. Pour the caramel into a 2½-pint capacity steaming mold and pour over the egg mixture. Cover tightly with wax paper and foil and place the mold in a saucepan of water. Steam gently for 1¼ hours. The water should bubble quietly. Cool the pudding and tip out on to a serving plate.

Stiffly whip the remaining cream with the confectioners' sugar.

Decorate the caramel pudding with piped cream and chocolate curls.
Serves 4

Note To make chocolate curls, melt 4 (1 oz) squares semisweet chocolate. Spread onto a sheet of wax paper. When cooled and set, scrape the chocolate up into curls with the blade of a knife.

Poires Belle Hélène

4 ripe dessert pears
1 cup medium dry white
  wine
½ cup sugar
few drops vanilla extract
½ stick cinnamon
4 (1 oz) squares semisweet
  chocolate
⅔ cup whipping cream
1 pint vanilla ice cream
Decoration
few candied cherries

Peel and halve the pears.
Remove the core and the
stalk. Lay the pear halves
in a flameproof dish and
add the wine, sugar, vanilla
extract and cinnamon stick
and simmer over a medium
heat for 10 minutes. Remove
from the heat and allow to
cool in the liquid. When
cold, remove the pears and
drain. Meanwhile, put 4
glass bowls in the
refrigerator to chill.
Break the chocolate into
small pieces and melt in a
saucepan, add the cream
and stir well. Divide the
vanilla ice cream into 4
portions and place in the
chilled dishes. Arrange 2
pear halves on top of each
and pour over the hot
chocolate sauce. Decorate
with candied cherries and
serve immediately.
Serves 4

Creamy Rice Mold

1 cup plus 2 tablespoons
  round-grain rice
½ teaspoon salt
2 envelopes unflavored
  gelatin
1¼ cups milk
½ cup sugar
few drops vanilla extract
½ cup Maraschino liqueur
  or cherry brandy
1¼ cups whipping cream
3 tablespoons chopped
  pistachio nuts

Cook the rice in a saucepan
with 6 cups water and the
salt for 20 minutes. Dissolve
the gelatin in 3 tablespoons
water. Warm the milk and
add the dissolved gelatin,
the sugar and vanilla
extract. Stir well to mix.
Drain the rice, stir into the
milk mixture and add the
liqueur. Allow to cool
slightly. Whip the cream
stiffly and fold into the rice.
Pour into a rinsed mold and
chill in the refrigerator.
Turn out onto a serving
dish and sprinkle with
chopped pistachio nuts.
Serve with strained rasp-
berry jam or raspberry
purée made with fresh
raspberries.
Serves 4

Variation
Fruit may also be added to
the cooked, drained rice.
An excellent combination is
chopped cherries and nuts
or seedless raisins and nuts.

Rum Savarin

3 cups all-purpose flour
¾ cake compressed yeast
1¼ cups lukewarm milk
4 eggs
⅔ cup sugar
few drops vanilla extract
½ teaspoon salt
⅔ cup butter, softened
3 tablespoons rum
5 tablespoons white wine
*1 (15-oz) can cherries,
    drained*
⅔ cup whipping cream

Butter and flour a plain
(9-inch) savarin (ring) mold.
Sift the flour into a bowl,
make a well in the center
and add the yeast mixed
with the warm milk. Leave
for 15 minutes.
Beat the eggs with 3 tablespoons of the sugar, stir in
the vanilla extract, salt and
the softened butter. Stir into
the yeast and flour mixture
to form a dough. Leave to
rise for a further 10 minutes.
Spoon the dough into the
savarin mold, until half
full. Leave the dough in a
warm place for 30–60
minutes, until it has doubled
in volume. Bake in a hot
oven (425° F) for 40
minutes. Turn out and cool
on a cake rack.
Place the rum, white wine,
⅔ cup water and the
remaining sugar in a saucepan and bring to the boil.
Pour carefully over the
savarin until all the syrup
has been absorbed. Arrange
the cherries in the middle of
the savarin.
Whip the cream until stiff
and pipe small rosettes
around the savarin.
Serves 6

Chinese Cabbage Soup

12 oz lean pork (tenderloin or from the leg)
2 pints water
2 teaspoons salt
2 teaspoons cornstarch
3 tablespoons soy sauce
2 teaspoons sugar
1 teaspoon white pepper
3 tablespoons oil
8 oz Chinese cabbage

Put the meat, water and salt in a saucepan and bring to the boil. Simmer for 1 hour, or until the meat is cooked and tender. Drain the meat, reserving the cooking liquid. Cut the meat into thin slices and mix with the cornstarch, soy sauce, sugar, pepper and oil. Leave to marinate for 30 minutes. Wash the cabbage and cut into thin strips. Bring the pork cooking liquid back to the boil and add the cabbage strips. Simmer for 15 minutes, then stir in the meat slices with the soy sauce mixture. Continue to simmer for 10 minutes. Serve hot.
Serves 4

Potato and Meat Soup

1 lb boned brisket of beef
4½ pints water
2 teaspoons salt
1 teaspoon celery salt
1½ lb potatoes
¼ cup butter
5 tablespoons finely chopped chervil
⅔ cup cream

Trim off any fat, then put the meat in a saucepan with the water, salt and celery salt. Bring to the boil. Simmer for 45 minutes–1 hour, until the meat is cooked and tender. Meanwhile, peel and finely dice the potatoes. Melt the butter in a frying pan. Add the potatoes and fry lightly for 10 minutes. Remove from the heat.
Remove the meat from the pan, reserving the cooking liquid, and dice finely. Return the diced meat to the pan and stir in the fried potatoes. Bring back to the boil and simmer for 20 minutes, until the potatoes are tender.
Add the chervil and cream and heat without boiling. Serve hot.
Serves 6–8

Variation
One-third of the potatoes may be replaced by 2 carrots and 1 onion. Chop the vegetables and cook them with the potatoes.

Meatball Soup

2 onions
1 cup white wine
2 pints stock
2 cups sauerkraut
½ teaspoon sugar
8 oz lean ground beef
pinch dried mixed herbs
pinch salt
pinch black pepper
1 teaspoon tomato paste
3 tablespoons chopped
   parsley
½ teaspoon black pepper
⅔ cup natural yogurt

Peel and thinly slice the onions. Put the wine and stock in a saucepan and bring to the boil. Add the sauerkraut, onion and sugar and simmer for 40 minutes.

Mix the ground beef with the herbs, salt, pepper and tomato paste. With wet hands form the mixture into small balls. Add to the pan and cook for 5 minutes, or until the meatballs are firm when pressed.
Pour the soup into individual bowls. Sprinkle with parsley and pepper and put a spoonful of yogurt in the center of each.
Serves 4

Variation
Sour cream can be used instead of yogurt.

Provençale Fish Soup

1 lb mussels
2 lb mixed fish (shellfish,
   halibut, turbot, sole,
   flounder)
4 onions
5 tablespoons oil
4½ pints fish or chicken stock
4 tomatoes, peeled
4 thin slices Canadian bacon
2 large potatoes
½ cucumber
½ cup crabmeat
½ cup spiral noodles
1 tablespoon chopped parsley

Scrub the mussels, removing beards. Discard any which are open or do not shut when tapped. Soak for 1 hour in cold water, then drain. Remove all shell or

skin and bones from the fish. Cut the flesh into small pieces. Peel and slice the onions. Heat the oil in a large saucepan, and fry the onion for 5 minutes, then add the fish and mussels. Cook for 5 minutes. Remove the mussel flesh from the shells and return the flesh to the pan with the stock. Bring to the boil and simmer for 15 minutes. Quarter the tomatoes. Dice the bacon. Peel and finely chop the potatoes and cucumber. Add the crab meat, tomatoes, bacon, noodles and potatoes to the pan and simmer for a further 20 minutes. Stir in the cucumber and parsley.
Serves 6–8

Beef Soup

12 oz shank or chuck beef
5½ pints water
1 teaspoon salt
1 bouquet garni
2 carrots
2 red peppers
1¼ cups ribbon noodles
½ teaspoon celery salt
2 teaspoons chopped
  parsley

Remove any fat from the
meat and dice. Put into a
saucepan with the water,
salt and bouquet garni
(3 bay leaves, 3 sprigs
parsley, 1 sprig thyme, tied
together) and bring to the
boil. Simmer gently for
2 hours, until the meat is
tender.

Meanwhile, peel the carrots
and cut into sticks. Remove
the pith, seeds and core
from the peppers and cut
into strips. Add the carrots,
peppers, noodles and celery
salt to the pan and continue
to simmer for about 20
minutes, until the vegetables
are tender. Remove the
bouquet garni. Pour into a
heated soup tureen,
sprinkle over the parsley
and serve.
Serves 6–8

Variation
Add 8 oz canned, drained
butter beans and use string
beans instead of the
noodles.

Leek Soup

4 leeks
2 onions
¼ cup butter
2 pints chicken stock
½ teaspoon sugar
1½ teaspoons all-purpose
  flour
3 tablespoons water
½ cup crumbled cheese
½ cup cooked ham, cut into
  strips
1¼ cups cream
Garnish
5 tablespoons grated
  Parmesan cheese

Wash the leeks, and cut into
strips 1 inch wide. Peel and
slice the onions. Melt the
butter in a saucepan and
add the leeks and onions.

Fry for 5 minutes. Stir in
the stock and bring to the
boil. Simmer for 5 minutes,
then add the sugar. Stir
well and leave to simmer for
15 minutes.
Mix the flour with the
water, and stir into the soup.
Continue to simmer,
stirring, until the soup
thickens. Stir in the cheese,
ham and cream. Heat
gently without allowing to
boil. Pour the soup into
individual bowls and
sprinkle over the Parmesan
cheese.
Serves 4

Minestrone

2 potatoes
2 carrots
2 onions
½ celery stalk
1 leek
1 small head white cabbage
1 clove garlic
2 bacon slices
¼ cup peas
½ cup green beans
4 pints beef stock
1 teaspoon salt
½ teaspoon white pepper
5 tablespoons chopped parsley
3 tablespoons chopped celery leaves
⅔ cup cooked long-grain rice
Garnish
grated Parmesan cheese

Peel the potatoes and carrots and cut into strips.

Peel and slice the onions. Cut the celery into strips. Wash and slice the leek. Core and chop the cabbage. Crush the garlic. Chop the bacon.
Put the bacon in a saucepan and fry until the fat runs. Add the onion and garlic and fry for 5 minutes, adding a tablespoon of oil if necessary. Stir in the vegetables and stock and bring to the boil. Simmer for about 20 minutes, until the vegetables are just tender. Add the salt, pepper, parsley, celery leaves and rice and simmer for a further 5 minutes.
Serve garnished with the Parmesan cheese.
Serves 6–8

Swiss Cheese Soup

1 onion
4 bacon slices
2 pints chicken stock
8 oz Emmenthal cheese
4 cups fresh white breadcrumbs
1¼ cups dry white wine
3 tablespoons each chopped chives, parsley and chervil
salt

Peel the onion and slice very thinly. Fry the bacon until the fat runs. Add the onion and fry together until the bacon is crisp and the onion golden brown. Remove from the heat and keep warm. Meanwhile, heat the chicken stock to boiling. Grate the cheese and put in

a warmed soup tureen with the breadcrumbs. Pour over the boiling stock and leave to soak for 3 minutes, stirring occasionally. The breadcrumbs should disintegrate and the cheese melt. Stir in the wine, herbs and salt to taste. Garnish with the bacon and onion and serve immediately.
Serves 4

Variation
Smoked meat or cooked ham may also be added to the garnish. It should be cut into small strips and fried together with the bacon and onion.

Cream of Tomato Soup

(in foreground of picture)

2 thick slices white bread
1 tablespoon butter
1 clove garlic, crushed
2 cans condensed cream of
   tomato soup
1 tablespoon chopped parsley

Remove the crusts from the bread and cube. Melt the butter and fry the crushed garlic and bread cubes until golden brown. Heat the soup with an equal quantity of milk and garnish with the croûtons and parsley.
Serves 4

Variations
Cream of Asparagus Soup
(extreme right)
Drain a 15-oz can of artichoke hearts. Melt 1 tablespoon butter and fry the artichoke hearts for 2–3 minutes. Add to portions of heated asparagus soup, with 1 tablespoon cream per portion.

Cream of Chicken Soup
(bottom left)
Heat 2 cups frozen peas in cream of chicken soup for 5 minutes. Whip 5 table-spoons whipping cream with 1–2 teaspoons curry powder until stiff and use to top each portion of soup.

Cream of Onion Soup
(top left)
Peel and slice 1 onion. Seed a green pepper and slice into rings. Fry in butter until tender. Heat diced corned beef with cream of onion soup and garnish with the fried onion and pepper.

Pea Soup *(top center)*
Heat 1 cup frozen peas with canned cream of pea soup. Add small cocktail sausages and sprinkle with parsley.

Creamy Asparagus Soup

1 lb fresh asparagus
2 tablespoons butter
3 tablespoons cream
5 tablespoons sour cream or plain yogurt
4 egg yolks

Peel the asparagus and trim off the woody ends. Break into small pieces, about 1 inch long. Cook in boiling salted water until just tender. Reserve the tips, and blend the remaining asparagus to a purée with 2½ pints of the cooking liquid and the butter in a blender. Return the puréed soup to the saucepan and stir in the cream and sour cream. Heat gently for 5 minutes.

Beat the egg yolks in a bowl and gradually add 3 spoonsful of the hot soup. Stir the egg mixture into the remaining soup and heat. Do not allow to boil. Add the reserved asparagus tips and serve.
Serves 4

Cook's Tip
Canned asparagus can be used, in which case it should be blended with the liquid from the can and then thinned down with chicken stock to the required consistency.

German Fish Soup

8 oz halibut fillets or boned salmon steaks
8 oz herring or cod's roe
4–6 onions
½ leek
1 teaspoon salt
3 cups water
2 celery stalks
½ cup chopped parsley
1 teaspoon grated fresh horseradish root
3 tablespoons finely chopped sweet dill pickles
3 tablespoons sour cream
2 tablespoons butter or margarine
dry white wine
finely chopped dill

Skin the fish fillets or steaks and the roe. Chop the roe. Peel and thinly slice the onions. Wash and slice the leek. Put the fish, roe, salt, onion, leek and water in a saucepan and bring to the boil. Simmer for 20 minutes. Dice the celery and add to the pan with the parsley, horseradish, pickles, sour cream and butter or margarine. Cook gently for a further 10 minutes. Add a dash of white wine and sprinkle with the dill.
Serves 4

Variation
If fresh horseradish is not available substitute 1 teaspoon horseradish sauce.

Pork with Yogurt Sauce

2 lb pork tenderloin (in two pieces)
4 oz Gruyère or Emmenthal cheese
$\frac{1}{2}$ teaspoon salt
1 teaspoon paprika pepper
$\frac{1}{2}$ cup all-purpose flour
$\frac{1}{4}$ cup butter
$\frac{1}{2}$ small onion
$\frac{2}{3}$ cup chicken stock
$\frac{2}{3}$ cup plain yogurt
Garnish
parsley sprigs

Remove any excess fat from the pork tenderloin. Slit each piece to make a pocket. Cut the cheese into matchsticks and put half into each pocket. Close with a skewer or trussing needle and

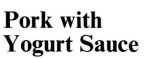

string. Mix together the salt, paprika and flour. Coat the meat in this mixture. Melt the butter in a flameproof casserole. Add the meat and brown on all sides. Peel and grate the onion and add to the casserole with the stock. Stir to mix and bring to the boil. Stir in the yogurt. Cover and cook gently for 45 minutes–1 hour, until the pork is tender. Garnish with parsley sprigs and serve with Brussels sprouts.
Serves 4

Hungarian Meatballs

4 oz bacon slices
3 onions, chopped
3 tablespoons all-purpose flour
1 lb ground pork
$\frac{1}{2}$ cup ground beef
$\frac{1}{4}$ cup chopped parsley
2 eggs
$\frac{1}{4}$ cup fresh breadcrumbs
1 teaspoon salt
$\frac{1}{2}$ teaspoon black pepper
3 teaspoons paprika pepper
5 tablespoons oil
$1\frac{1}{4}$ cups beef stock
5 tablespoons whipping cream

Finely dice the bacon. Put half in a frying pan and heat until the fat runs. Add two-thirds of the onion

and fry until golden brown. Sprinkle with half the flour and stir well. Tip into a bowl. Mix in the ground meats, parsley, eggs, breadcrumbs, salt, pepper and 2 teaspoons paprika. Form the mixture into small balls. Heat the oil and brown the meatballs. Reduce the heat and cook for 10 minutes. Heat the remaining bacon until the fat runs. Add the rest of the onion and fry until soft. Sprinkle with the remaining flour and paprika and stir well. Stir in the stock and bring to the boil. Simmer until thickened, stir in the cream and meatballs. Cook gently for 10 minutes.
Serves 4

Ham with Sauerkraut

1 (3-lb) processed ham
¼ cup honey
1 onion
2 cooking apples
3 tablespoons drippings
2 cups sauerkraut, drained
½ teaspoon salt
1¼ cups stock
⅔ cup red wine
5 tablespoons sour cream
1 teaspoon cornstarch

Put the ham on a rack in a roasting pan and roast in a warm oven (325° F) for 1½ hours or until a meat thermometer registers 160° F.
Remove the rind and most of the fat. Brush the ham with honey and return to a moderately hot oven (400° F) for 20 minutes. Meanwhile, peel and dice the onion. Peel the apples and chop finely. Melt the drippings, add the sauerkraut and onion and fry for 5 minutes. Stir in the apple, salt and stock and bring to the boil. Cover and simmer for 20 minutes.
Drain the sauerkraut, reserving the liquid, and keep warm.
Add the wine to the sauerkraut cooking liquid, boil until reduced to about ⅔ cup and stir in the cream and dissolved cornstarch. Simmer until thickened, season and serve separately.
Serves 4

Pork Rolls in Tomato and Wine Sauce

1 red or green pepper
2 large tomatoes
4 slices pork tenderloin, each
  weighing 4 oz
1 teaspoon salt
½ teaspoon ground caraway
  seeds
2 onions, finely chopped
2 tablespoons butter
⅔ cup dry white wine
5 tablespoons plain yogurt
1 teaspoon cornstarch
¾ cup grated cheese

Cut the pepper into strips. Peel and chop the tomatoes. Pound the pork slices until quite thin. Sprinkle with salt, caraway, pepper strips and some of the onion. Roll up and secure with wooden toothpicks. Melt the butter and brown the pork rolls. Add the remaining onion, the tomatoes and the wine, and cook gently for 40 minutes, turning occasionally.
Transfer the pork rolls to an ovenproof serving dish. Mix together the yogurt and cornstarch and stir into the frying pan. When thickened, pour over the rolls. Sprinkle the cheese on top and bake in a moderately hot oven (400° F) for 10 minutes. Serve with boiled potatoes sprinkled with caraway seeds.
Serves 4

Meat Dishes

Bacon-Wrapped Liver with Raisin Sauce

1½ lb beef or pork liver, in
  two pieces
1½ teaspoons salt
2 teaspoons paprika pepper
2 teaspoons Worcestershire
  sauce
1 teaspoon white pepper
4 oz bacon slices
⅔ cup seedless raisins
2 tablespoons butter
1½ tablespoons all-purpose
  flour
⅔ cup dry red wine
⅔ cup stock
1 teaspoon sugar
5 tablespoons whipping
  cream

Rub the liver with the salt, paprika, Worcestershire sauce and pepper. Leave for 20 minutes.

Wrap the bacon around the liver, covering the liver completely. Place in an oiled roasting pan and bake in a moderately hot oven (375° F) for 25–30 minutes. Meanwhile, soak the raisins in warm water for 15 minutes. Drain well. Melt the butter in a pan, stir in the flour and cook for 1 minute. Gradually stir in the wine and stock and bring to the boil. Simmer, stirring, until the sauce thickens. Add the raisins, sugar and seasoning to taste and cook gently for 5 minutes. Remove from the heat and stir in the cream. Serve separately.
Serves 4

Blanquette of Veal with Peppered Rice

2 lb lean boned shoulder
  of veal
1 leek, finely chopped
1 large carrot, diced
2 onions, diced
1 teaspoon salt
2½ cups water
1 cup long-grain rice
2 green peppers
½ cup oil
1 teaspoon paprika pepper
½ teaspoon white pepper
¼ cup butter
3 tablespoons all-purpose
  flour
1 cup frozen peas

Cut the meat into chunks, removing any fat. Put the meat, leek, carrot, onions and salt in a saucepan. Add the water and bring to the boil. Reduce the heat and simmer for 1 hour. Cook the rice. Meanwhile, finely chop the peppers. Heat the oil and quickly fry the chopped peppers, cooked rice, paprika and pepper until the peppers are just tender. Keep warm. Drain the meat, reserving the cooking liquid but discarding the vegetables. Mix the butter and flour to a paste and add in small pieces to the cooking liquid. Simmer, stirring, until the liquid thickens. Add the peas and meat and simmer until the peas are cooked and the meat reheated. Serve with the rice.
Serves 4

176

Sweetbreads with Asparagus

1 lb calf sweetbreads
2 pork sausages
1 cup mushrooms
4 oz canned asparagus
2 tablespoons butter
1½ tablespoons all-purpose
*   flour*
1¼ cups milk
1 teaspoon salt
½ teaspoon white pepper
Garnish
parsley

Soak the sweetbreads in water for 2 hours, then drain. Blanch in boiling water for 5 minutes, and drain. Remove the skin and ducts and cut the meat into thick slices. Skin the sausages and form the  sausagemeat into small balls. Drop into boiling water and cook for 5 minutes. Drain well. Clean and halve the mushrooms. Drain the asparagus. Melt the butter in a saucepan. Stir in the flour and cook for 1 minute. Gradually add the milk and bring to the boil, stirring all the time. Simmer, stirring, until the sauce thickens. Add the salt, pepper, sweetbread slices, sausagemeat balls, mushrooms and pieces of asparagus. Simmer for 5 minutes. Spoon into a serving dish and garnish with parsley. Serve with a tomato and onion salad.
Serves 4

Braised Veal

2 large onions
5 tablespoons oil
1 teaspoon salt
1 teaspoon black pepper
pinch marjoram
2 teaspoons paprika pepper
1 (2–3lb) boned and rolled
*   shoulder of veal*
1¼ cups stock or water
3 tablespoons tomato paste
1½ tablespoons all-purpose
*   flour*

Peel and chop the onions. Heat the oil in a flameproof casserole. Add the onion and fry for 5 minutes. Stir in the salt, pepper, marjoram and paprika. Lay the veal on the onion and pour in half the stock or water. Cover and braise in a moderate oven (350° F) for 1¼–1½ hours, or until the veal is tender.
Mix together the tomato paste, flour and remaining stock or water in a saucepan. Transfer the veal to a carving board. Cut into slices and arrange on a bed of freshly cooked mixed vegetables. Keep warm. Blend the onion mixture in a blender and add to the saucepan. Bring to the boil and simmer until the sauce thickens, stirring all the time. Pour into a warmed sauceboat and serve with the meat. Accompany with boiled potatoes.
Serves 4

Braised Pork Shoulder

*1 (2-lb) boned and rolled
    shoulder of pork*
1 teaspoon salt
1 teaspoon white pepper
2 onions
2 carrots
¼ celeriac or 2 celery stalks
¼ cup vegetable oil
1¼ cups stock

Score the skin of the pork to mark out squares. Rub the meat with the salt and pepper. Peel and halve the onions. Peel and chop the carrots. Chop the celeriac or celery.
Heat the oil in a roasting pan. Put in the meat and vegetables and roast in a hot oven (425° F) for 1½

hours. After 20 minutes, pour half the stock into the roasting pan. Add the remaining stock after a further 20 minutes.
At the end of the roasting time increase the oven temperature to very hot (475° F) and roast for a further 8 minutes. Transfer the meat to a serving platter and slice. Keep warm. Push the vegetables and liquid from the roasting pan through a strainer or blend in a blender and serve as a sauce. Accompany with Brussels sprouts and creamed or boiled potatoes.
Serves 4–5

Roman Lamb Stew

1 (14-oz) can tomatoes
1 clove garlic
1 onion
2 lb lean lamb
5 tablespoons olive oil
1¼ cups white wine
½ teaspoon dried rosemary
¼ teaspoon dried thyme
1 teaspoon salt
1 teaspoon pepper
1 lb spaghetti
*¾ cup grated Parmesan
    cheese*
Garnish
rosemary sprigs

Drain the tomatoes and chop roughly. Finely chop the garlic. Finely chop the onion. Cut the meat into 1-inch chunks.

Heat the oil in a saucepan. Add the meat and brown on all sides. Stir in the wine, onion, tomatoes, garlic, rosemary, thyme, salt and pepper. Cover and cook for about 20 minutes, until the meat is tender. Stir occasionally and add more wine if the mixture becomes too dry.
Meanwhile, cook the spaghetti in boiling salted water for 12–15 minutes, until just tender. Drain well, then arrange in a ring on a warmed serving dish. Sprinkle the spaghetti with the cheese and spoon the lamb stew into the center. Garnish with fresh rosemary sprigs and serve with a green salad.
Serves 6

Beef Potroast with Horseradish Sauce

1 leek
3 carrots
1 onion
2 whole cloves
2 lb lean bottom round or
  plate beef
1 teaspoon salt
½ teaspoon celery salt
¼ bay leaf
4 pints water
1–2 tablespoons freshly
  grated horseradish root
juice of 1 lemon
1 teaspoon sugar

Wash and chop the leek. Peel the carrots and cut into sticks. Peel the onion and stud with the cloves. Put the meat in a saucepan and add the salt, celery salt, bay leaf, leek, carrots and onion. Pour over the water and bring to the boil. Simmer for 1¼–2 hours, until the meat is tender.
Meanwhile, mix the grated horseradish with the lemon juice and sugar.
Cut the meat in thick slices and garnish with vegetables from the pan. (The cooking liquid makes a good basis for soup.) Serve with the horseradish sauce and a green vegetable such as spinach.
Serves 4

Pork and Green Beans

1 (2-lb) boned shoulder of
  pork
1 teaspoon salt
½ teaspoon white pepper
pinch cayenne pepper
1 red pepper
6 tomatoes
1 lb fresh or frozen green
  beans
1 bouillon cube
2 tablespoons butter
1 tablespoon all-purpose
  flour

Cut the meat into 1-inch chunks. Put in a flameproof casserole and cover with cold water. Add the salt, pepper and cayenne and bring to the boil. Simmer for 20 minutes. Remove the pith, core and seeds from the pepper and cut into strips. Add to the pot and continue cooking for 15 minutes.
Peel and chop the tomatoes. If using fresh beans, trim and cut into pieces. Add the beans and tomatoes to the casserole with the bouillon cube, cover and cook for a further 25 minutes. If using frozen beans, add just before the end of the cooking time.
Mix the butter and flour together to form a paste. Add in small pieces to the casserole. Simmer, stirring, until the liquid thickens. Serve with potatoes.
Serves 4

Meat Dishes

Oxtail Stew

3 lb oxtail, cut into pieces
   2 inches long
1 clove garlic
1 teaspoon salt
$\frac{1}{2}$ bay leaf
10 juniper berries
juice of 1 lemon
2 teaspoons sugar
1 teaspoon dried rosemary
1 teaspoon dried marjoram
3 tablespoons brandy
$\frac{1}{2}$ cup all-purpose flour
$\frac{1}{2}$ cup drippings or oil
$1\frac{1}{4}$ cups red wine
$1\frac{1}{4}$ cups stock or warm water
3 tablespoons tomato paste
1 tablespoon paprika pepper

Lay the pieces of oxtail in a
shallow dish. Crush the
garlic. Mix the salt, garlic,
bay leaf, juniper berries,
lemon juice, sugar, herbs
and brandy, and pour over
the meat. Cover and leave
to marinate for 1 hour.
Remove the oxtail pieces,
dry with paper towels and
coat with the flour. Heat
the drippings or oil in a
flameproof casserole. Add
the oxtail pieces and brown
quickly.
Mix the wine, stock or
water, tomato paste and
paprika with the marinade
and pour into the casserole.
Bring to the boil, stirring,
then cover and simmer for
3–4 hours, until the oxtail
is tender. Serve with
noodles and a green salad.
Serves 4

Stuffed Pork Rolls

6 tablespoons pork drippings
2 onions, sliced
$\frac{1}{2}$ cup sauerkraut
1 teaspoon salt
2 teaspoons sugar
$\frac{2}{3}$ cup water
1 large green pepper
3 bacon slices
4 slices pork tenderloin
$\frac{1}{2}$ cup all-purpose flour
2 teaspoons paprika pepper
1 teaspoon white pepper
$\frac{2}{3}$ cup buttermilk
$\frac{2}{3}$ cup beef stock

Heat half the drippings in a
frying pan and fry the
onions until golden brown.
Add the drained sauerkraut,
salt, sugar and water.
Simmer for 30 minutes.

Meanwhile, remove the
pith, core and seeds from
the pepper and cut into
strips. Chop the bacon and
fry in another pan until the
fat runs. Add the strips
of pepper and fry for 5
minutes.
Pound the pork slices. Top
each with the sauerkraut
and pepper mixtures. Roll
up and secure with wooden
toothpicks. Mix together
the flour, paprika and
pepper. Coat the meat rolls
with this.
Heat the remaining drip-
pings in the frying pan. Add
the meat rolls and brown on
all sides. Pour in the buttermilk and stock, mixing in
any juices from the pan.
Cover and cook for about
40 minutes, until tender.
Serves 4

Piquant Heart Casserole

1½ lb lamb hearts
1 onion
4 pints water
½ teaspoon salt
3 allspice berries
3 black peppercorns
1 bay leaf
1 large cucumber
1 teaspoon Worcestershire
   sauce
2 teaspoons sugar
1 tablespoon lemon juice
3 tablespoons all-purpose
   flour
3 tablespoons finely chopped
   dill

Remove the gristle and tubes from the hearts. Peel the onion and slice thinly. Put the water, salt, allspice berries, peppercorns, bay leaf, hearts and onion in a large saucepan and bring to the boil. Cover and simmer for 3 hours. Meanwhile, peel the cucumber and halve lengthwise. Remove the seeds with a spoon and cut the halves into finger-width slices.
Remove the hearts from the pan and cut into chunks. Strain the cooking liquid and return 1 pint to the pan. Bring back to the boil and add the cucumber. Cover and cook gently for 15 minutes.
Stir in the heart chunks, Worcestershire sauce, sugar and lemon juice. Dissolve the flour in 4 tablespoons of the hot liquid and add to the pan. Simmer, stirring, until thickened, then cook gently for a further 5 minutes. Sprinkle over the dill and serve with boiled rice.
Serves 4

Variation
In place of lamb hearts, you could use beef or veal hearts.

Savory Scotch Eggs

2 slices white bread
5 tablespoons water
2 onions, finely chopped
1 lb ground beef
1 teaspoon salt
1 teaspoon paprika pepper
½ teaspoon white pepper
4 eggs
¼ cup butter

Sprinkle the bread with the water and leave to soak. Squeeze out and crumble into small pieces. Mix with the onions, meat, salt, paprika and pepper. Hard-cook the eggs, then plunge into cold water. When they are cool, shell them and pat dry with paper towels. Divide the meat mixture between each egg, pressing it on firmly and rounding into a ball. Melt the butter in a frying pan. Add the balls and fry, turning carefully, for 10–15 minutes, until well browned and cooked through. Serve hot with buttered noodles, carrots and peas.
Serves 4

Variation
Lay half the meat mixture on the bottom of an oven-proof dish, press in the hard-cooked eggs and top with the remaining meat mixture. Press on firmly and smooth the top. Bake in a moderately hot oven (375° F) for 25–30 minutes, until the meat is cooked through.

Madrid Style Kidneys

2 onions
1 red pepper
1 clove garlic
5 tablespoons olive oil
½ bay leaf
3 tablespoons all-purpose flour
⅔ cup stock
1½ lb veal kidneys
2 teaspoons salt
1 teaspoon black pepper
2 cups frozen peas
5 tablespoons dry sherry

Peel and finely chop the onions. Remove the pith, core and seeds from the pepper and cut into strips. Crush the garlic. Heat 3 tablespoons of oil in a saucepan. Add the onion, pepper, garlic and bay leaf and fry for 5 minutes. Sprinkle over the flour, stir well, then stir in the stock. Simmer for 5 minutes. Meanwhile, remove the fat from the kidneys, halve and remove the core and ducts, then slice. Heat the remaining oil in a frying pan. Add the kidneys and fry until lightly browned. Add the salt, pepper, peas and sherry. Pour over the onion sauce and stir well. Simmer gently for a further 2 minutes. Serve hot with saffron rice.
Serves 4

Hamburgers with Capers

1 large onion
1½ lb lean ground beef
3 tablespoons capers
1 teaspoon salt
½ teaspoon celery salt
½ teaspoon garlic salt
½ teaspoon Tabasco sauce
2 eggs
¼ cup butter
3 tablespoons chopped chives
2 teaspoons prepared mustard
Garnish
parsley sprigs
onion rings

Peel and finely chop the onion. Mix together the beef, onion, capers, salt, celery and garlic salts, Tabasco sauce and eggs. With wet hands, divide the meat into four portions and form each into a patty. Melt the butter in a frying pan. Add the patties and brown quickly on each side. Then reduce the heat and cook for a further 3–4 minutes on each side. Drain on paper towels, transfer the hamburgers to a warmed serving dish. Keep hot.
Remove any excess fat from the pan, add the chives and stir in the mustard. Cook for 1–2 minutes, then pour over the hamburgers and garnish with the parsley sprigs and onion rings. Serve with a tomato salad.
Serves 4

Pork Chops with Celeriac

4 thick pork chops
1 teaspoon salt
¼ teaspoon white pepper
2 teaspoons dry mustard
5 tablespoons all-purpose flour
¼ cup pork drippings
¼ celeriac
1 leek
2 tablespoons butter
4 tablespoons grated cheese

Rub the chops on both sides with the salt, pepper and mustard, then coat with the flour. Heat the drippings in a frying pan, and add the chops. Brown on each side, then reduce the heat and cook for a further 4–5 minutes on each side.

Meanwhile, peel the celeriac, and cut into thin strips or grate. Wash and chop the leek. Melt the butter in a pan and add the celeriac and leek. Fry for about 5 minutes, until the vegetables are just tender.
Place the chops on a warmed serving plate. Top each with a spoonful of the celeriac and leek mixture and a tablespoon of cheese.
Serves 4

Cook's Tip
Use the rest of the celeriac to make a delicious salad; simply peel, grate and mix with mayonnaise and seasoning to taste.

Kidneys in Wine Sauce

12 oz veal kidneys
2 slices white bread
5 tablespoons water
½ cup ground beef
1 teaspoon salt
1 teaspoon paprika pepper
6 tablespoons butter
2 onions, finely chopped
¼ cup all-purpose flour
⅔ cup stock
⅔ cup red wine
salt and black pepper
1 tablespoon chopped
    parsley

Halve the kidneys, cut out the cores and ducts. Wash and dry, then slice thickly. Soak the bread in the water then squeeze out and crumble into small pieces.

Mix together the ground beef, bread, salt and paprika. Form the mixture into small balls.
Melt ¼ cup of the butter in a saucepan. Add the meatballs and onion. Fry until the meatballs are lightly browned, then remove. Stir the flour into the pan and cook for 1 minute.
Gradually stir in the stock and wine, bring to the boil and simmer, stirring, until thickened. Season to taste. Return the meatballs and simmer for 10 minutes.
Melt the remaining butter in a frying pan and fry the kidney slices, turning, for 8 minutes. Stir into the meatball mixture and cook for 2 minutes. Sprinkle with parsley.
Serves 4

Pork with Pepper Ragoût

2 green peppers
2 red peppers
2 celery stalks
2 bacon slices
¼ cup butter
4 onions, finely chopped
1 clove garlic, crushed
3 tablespoons chopped
    parsley
1 medium eggplant
1½ lb lean pork
2 teaspoons paprika pepper
1 teaspoon salt
½ teaspoon pepper
5 tablespoons oil

Remove pith, core and seeds from the peppers, then cut into thin strips. Cut the celery into thin strips. Finely chop the bacon.

Melt the butter in a saucepan and add the onion, peppers, garlic, celery, parsley and bacon. Cook gently until the bacon has rendered its fat.
Meanwhile, chop the eggplant. Cut the pork into thin strips.
Add the eggplant, paprika, salt and pepper to the pan and cook for about 20 minutes, until the vegetables are quite soft. Add a little stock or water if the mixture gets too dry.
Heat the oil in a frying pan. Add the pork strips and fry until they are well browned and tender. Arrange the vegetable mixture on a warmed serving dish and pile the pork in the center.
Serves 4

Hamburgers with Onions

1 lb ground beef
2 teaspoons grated fresh
* horseradish root*
¼ cup chopped parsley
⅔ cup pork sausagemeat
1 teaspoon celery salt
5 tablespoons fresh bread-
* crumbs*
1 egg
1 tablespoon grated celery
1 tablespoon grated carrot
1 tablespoon grated onion
2 tablespoons butter
3 tablespoons oil
2 onions

Mix together the meat,
horseradish, parsley,
sausagemeat, celery salt,
breadcrumbs, egg and
grated vegetables. With wet
hands, divide into four
portions and shape each
into a patty.
Melt the butter with the oil
in a frying pan. Add the
patties and brown quickly
on each side. Then reduce
the heat and cook for 3–4
minutes more on each side.
Meanwhile, peel and slice
the onions. Add to the pan
and continue to fry for a
further 5–6 minutes, until
the onions are golden
brown and the hamburgers
are cooked through.
Top each hamburger with
the fried onion, and serve
with a mixed salad.
Serves 4

Variation
Ground veal or pork may
be used in place of the
ground beef.

Deep-Fried Veal

2 lb veal cutlets or scallops
1 egg
5 tablespoons all-purpose
* flour*
1 teaspoon salt
1 teaspoon pepper
⅔ cup dry breadcrumbs
oil for deep frying
Garnish
1 lemon, sliced
parsley sprigs

Cut the meat into small
pieces. Beat the egg. Mix
the flour with the salt and
pepper. Coat the meat
firstly in the flour, then in
the egg and finally in the
breadcrumbs, so that the
pieces are well covered.
Heat the oil in a deep-fat
fryer until it is 350° F. Fry
the meat for 6 minutes, or
until golden brown and
crispy. Drain on paper
towels. Arrange on a
warmed serving plate and
garnish with slices of lemon.
Deep fry individual sprigs
of parsley in the oil for 30
seconds and use to garnish
the veal. Serve with potato
and tomato salads.
Serves 4

Steak and Onions

4 sirloin steaks
2 teaspoons salt
1 teaspoon white pepper
½ cup all-purpose flour
2 tablespoons butter
3 tablespoons oil
1 Bermuda onion
⅔ cup beef stock
parsley sprig

Season the steaks with the salt and pepper and coat lightly in the flour.
Melt the butter with the oil in a frying pan. Add the steaks are brown quickly on each side. Peel the onion and slice thinly. Add to the pan and fry the steaks for a further 2–3 minutes on each side, or longer according to

taste. Transfer the steaks to a warmed serving dish, overlapping them slightly, and keep warm.
Continue frying the onions until they are golden brown, then arrange over the meat. Add the stock to the pan, stir well and bring to the boil. Simmer, stirring frequently, for 3 minutes, then pour this sauce over the meat. Garnish with the parsley sprig.
Serves 4

Variation
To make a piquant sauce for the steak, fry some sliced peppers and mush-rooms with the onion. Add 1 tablespoon tomato paste, the stock, salt and pepper and a good dash of red wine.

Hamburgers with Herb Butter

2 slices white bread
5 tablespoons water
1½ lb ground beef
1 teaspoon salt
1 teaspoon white pepper
2 teaspoons paprika pepper
1 egg yolk
6 tablespoons butter
1 tablespoon chopped parsley
1 tablespoon chopped dill
1 tablespoon lemon juice
½ teaspoon celery salt
Garnish
tomato wedges
dill sprigs

Sprinkle the bread with the water and leave to soak, then squeeze out the water

and crumble the bread into small pieces. Mix together the beef, bread, salt, pepper, paprika and egg yolk. With wet hands, divide the dough into eight portions and shape each into a patty.
Cream the butter with the parsley, dill, lemon juice and celery salt. Make a hollow in each patty and fill with a pat of this herb butter. Bring the meat mixture up over the herb butter to cover it.
Broil the hamburger patties for 3–4 minutes on each side or until they are well browned and cooked through. Garnish with tomato wedges and dill and serve with a potato and red pepper salad.
Serves 4

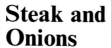
186

Baked Ham Rolls

2 thick slices white bread
2 eggs, beaten
½ teaspoon grated nutmeg
½ teaspoon paprika pepper
1 tablespoon oil
3 tablespoons fresh bread-crumbs
3 tablespoons chopped parsley
3 tablespoons chopped chives
½ teaspoon salt
¼ teaspoon pepper
4 slices proscuitto or cooked ham

Remove the crusts from the bread, toast and place in a mixing bowl. Cover with the beaten eggs and leave to soak for 2–3 minutes. Beat in the nutmeg, paprika, oil, breadcrumbs, parsley, chives, salt and pepper. Spread out the slices of ham and cover thickly with the bread mixture. Roll up and, if necessary, secure with wooden toothpicks or skewers. Place in a greased ovenproof dish, cover and bake in a moderate oven (350° F) for 20 minutes. Serve hot, with a mixed salad.
Serves 4

Variation
For a more substantial dish, make up 1¼ cups basic white sauce, stir in 1 cup grated cheese, season to taste and pour over the ham rolls. Sprinkle with cheese and bake as above.

Stuffed Pork Chops

1 clove garlic
4 thick boneless pork chops
½ teaspoon salt
4 small slices cooked ham
4 thin slices Gruyère or Cheddar cheese
1 teaspoon dried rosemary
1½ tablespoons all-purpose flour
2 eggs
5 tablespoons grated cheese
1 teaspoon paprika pepper
¼ cup butter

Finely chop the garlic. Cut a deep pocket in each chop and rub with salt and garlic. Fill each pocket with a slice of ham and cheese and a little rosemary.
Mix together the flour, eggs, grated cheese and paprika to form a paste. Coat the chops in this paste.
Melt the butter in a frying pan. Add the chops and fry gently for about 6 minutes on each side, until crisp and golden brown. Do not cook too quickly or the outside will be brown before the meat is cooked through. Serve hot, with boiled potatoes and asparagus.
Serves 4

Variation
For a change, try filling the pork chops with any of your favorite stuffing mixes; sage and onion, rice and mushroom or apple and raisin. Then coat in the paste and proceed as above.

187

Luncheon Dishes

Liver Risotto

2 onions
1 lb calf or lamb liver
1 large cooking apple
1 cup long-grain rice
5 tablespoons all-purpose
  flour
5 tablespoons oil
2 teaspoons salt
1 teaspoon sugar
3 tablespoons raisins

Peel and finely chop the onions. Finely chop the liver. Peel and core the apple, then chop. Cook the rice according to the instructions on the package. Meanwhile, toss the liver in the flour. Heat the oil in a pan and add the salt and liver. Fry, turning constantly, for 3 minutes. Add the apple and fry for a further 3 minutes. Stir in the sugar, rice and raisins and cook for a further 3 minutes. Serve hot.
Serves 4

Cook's Tip
To tenderize lamb liver, soak it in milk for an hour prior to cooking. Drain and pat dry with paper towels.

Chicken Soup with Rice

1 (2½–3-lb) stewing chicken
1 teaspoon salt
1 bouquet garni
4 pints water
⅔ cup long-grain rice
1 cup frozen peas
½ teaspoon pepper
1 (14-oz) can peeled
  tomatoes

Put the chicken in a saucepan and add the salt, bouquet garni and water. Bring to the boil, half cover and simmer for 2 hours. Remove the chicken from the pan and strain the cooking liquid. Return the cooking liquid to the saucepan and add the rice. Bring to the boil, cover and simmer for 15–20 minutes, until the rice is tender. Meanwhile, when the chicken is cool enough to handle, remove the meat and chop finely. Add to the pan with the peas and pepper and simmer, uncovered, for a further 10 minutes.
Drain the tomatoes and add to the soup. Heat quickly, without stirring, and serve immediately.
Serves 4–6

Fish Stew

1½ lb mixed white fish (cod, eel, halibut, etc.)
1 teaspoon salt
½ teaspoon white pepper
juice of ½ lemon
5 tablespoons chopped parsley
3 tablespoons oil
¼ cup butter
2 leeks, sliced
2 onions, finely chopped
3 tablespoons all-purpose flour
1¼ cups fish stock or water
1¼ cups milk
1 cup sliced mushrooms
1 red pepper, chopped
2 egg yolks
⅔ cup cream

Skin and bone the fish and cut into 1-inch pieces. Mix the salt, pepper, lemon juice, parsley and oil and pour over the fish. Marinate for 2 hours.

Melt the butter in a saucepan and fry the leeks and onions for 2 minutes. Sprinkle over the flour. Cook, stirring, for 3–4 minutes. Gradually stir in the stock and milk, bring to the boil, and simmer, stirring, until thickened. Add the mushrooms, red pepper, fish and marinade. Simmer for 7–8 minutes, until the fish is cooked. Mix the egg yolks and cream with a little of the stew. Add to the remaining stew. Heat through without boiling.
Serves 4

Spanish Meat and Bean Stew

1¼ cups dried red kidney beans
4 oz bacon, in the piece
1 teaspoon salt
4 pints water
1 bay leaf
1 onion
1 clove garlic
1 red pepper
1 green pepper
4 oz garlic sausage
½ cup diced cooked ham
1 cup diced cooked beef
½ cup diced cooked tongue
½ teaspoon black pepper

Soak the beans in water overnight, then drain. Put the bacon in a saucepan with the beans, salt, water and bay leaf and bring to the boil. Simmer for 1 hour, or until the beans are softened.

Meanwhile, peel and finely chop the onion. Finely chop the garlic. Remove pith, core and seeds from the peppers and cut into strips. Slice the garlic sausage. Remove the bacon from the pan and dice. Return to the pan with the onion, garlic, ham, beef and tongue. Simmer for 15 minutes, then stir in the pepper strips and sausage slices. Season with the black pepper and simmer for a further 15 minutes.
Serves 6

Bean and Vegetable Stew

1¼ cups dried white navy
    beans
1 lb bacon, in the piece
1 pint water
8 oz carrots
1 lb potatoes
1½ lb green beans
2 pears
2 dessert apples
1 tablespoon all-purpose flour
1 teaspoon salt

Soak the navy beans in
water overnight. Drain and
put in a saucepan. Cover
with fresh water, bring to
the boil and simmer for 20
minutes or until the beans
are tender.
Meanwhile, put the bacon
in another saucepan with

the water. Bring to the boil
and simmer for 20 minutes.
Peel and slice the carrots
and potatoes. Trim the
green beans. Remove the
bacon from the pan and
dice. Return to the pan with
the carrots, potatoes and
green beans. Drain the
navy beans and add to the
bacon mixture. Simmer for
15 minutes.
Peel and core the pears and
apples, then slice. Add to
the pan and simmer for a
further 5 minutes. Dissolve
the flour in 3 tablespoons of
the hot stew, then stir into
the pan with the salt.
Simmer until slightly
thickened and serve.
Serves 4

Vegetable Soup

2 kohlrabi
2 carrots
1 small cauliflower
10 Brussels sprouts
8 oz green beans
½ head celery
2 leeks
3 potatoes
1 onion
¼ cup butter
1 tablespoon chopped parsley
3 pints beef stock
1 teaspoon salt
½ teaspoon pepper

Peel and chop the kohlrabi.
Peel the carrots and cut into
sticks. Break the cauliflower
into flowerets. Trim the
sprouts and green beans.
Slice the celery. Wash and

chop the leeks. Peel and
dice the potatoes. Peel and
slice the onion.
Melt the butter in a saucepan. Add the onion and
parsley and cook for 5
minutes. Stir in the celery,
carrots and kohlrabi and
cook for a further 2–3
minutes. Stir in the stock
and bring to the boil. Add
the remaining vegetables
with the salt and pepper and
simmer for 20 minutes,
until the vegetables are
tender.
Serves 4

Savory Peppers

4 green or red peppers
6 tablespoons butter
1 cup diced salami
½ cup cooked ham, cut into
  strips
1 sweet dill pickle, chopped
2 onions, sliced
3 tablespoons tomato paste
¼ cup all-purpose flour
1¼ cups beef stock
2 teaspoons Worcestershire
  sauce
5 tablespoons cottage cheese
1 teaspoon sugar
rind and juice of 1 lemon

Cut the tops off the peppers. Seed and blanch in boiling salted water for 5 minutes. Drain and cool. Melt ¼ cup of the butter in a frying pan and add the salami, ham, pickle, onions and tomato paste. Cook gently for 5 minutes.
Melt the remaining butter in a saucepan. Stir in the flour and cook for 1 minute. Stir in the stock, bring to the boil and simmer, stirring, until thickened. Add the Worcestershire sauce.
Stir a third of this sauce into the sausage mixture, simmer for 5 minutes, then fill the peppers and replace tops. Beat the remaining sauce with the strained cottage cheese, sugar, grated lemon rind and juice. Pour into a dish and stand the peppers in it.
Cover and bake in a hot oven (425° F) for 20 minutes.
Serves 4

Portofino Pepper Pot

1½ lb lean pork (from the
  leg)
4 teaspoons paprika pepper
1 teaspoon salt
1 red pepper
1 green pepper
½ cucumber
2 bulbs fennel
5 tablespoons oil
4 onions, sliced
3 tablespoons tomato paste
1 bouillon cube
1¼ cups buttermilk

Cut the meat into strips and rub with the paprika and salt. Remove the pith, core and seeds from the peppers and cut into strips. Peel and dice the cucumber. Trim and slice the fennel.

Heat the oil in a flameproof casserole. Add the pork and onion and fry for 5 minutes. Add the peppers, cucumber and fennel, and stir well. Continue to cook for 2–3 minutes.
Mix together the tomato paste, bouillon cube and buttermilk, then pour into the casserole. Simmer for a further 10 minutes. Serve hot.
Serves 4

Variation
Omit the cucumber and fennel and add instead 2 cups sliced mushrooms. Substitute ⅔ cup sour cream for the buttermilk.

191

Cassoulet

3 cups dried white navy
   beans
4 onions
1 leek, finely chopped
8 oz bacon, in the piece
2 chicken drumsticks
4 pints chicken stock
½ teaspoon garlic salt
1 teaspoon black pepper
1 teaspoon dried thyme
1 bouquet garni
3 large tomatoes
4 oz garlic sausage
3 tablespoons oil
3 celery stalks, chopped
⅔ cup dry white wine

Soak the beans in water
overnight, then drain. Peel
and finely chop 3 onions.
Put the leek, onion, bacon,
chicken, stock, seasonings
and herbs in a saucepan.

Bring to the boil and
simmer for 1¼ hours.
Meanwhile, peel and chop
the tomatoes and the
remaining onion. Slice the
garlic sausage.
Remove the bacon and
chicken from the pan. Dice
the meats and strain the
cooking liquid.
Heat the oil in a pan and
fry the tomatoes, remaining
onion and celery for 3
minutes. Stir in the wine
and navy beans. Layer the
bean mixture, bacon,
chicken and sausage in a
casserole. Pour over the
bacon cooking liquid, cover
and bake in a hot oven
(425° F) for 1¼ hours.
Serves 4

Hunter's Stew

1 lb cooked game
4 bacon slices
2 onions
1½ cups small button
   mushrooms
12 oz potatoes
8 oz carrots
2 tablespoons margarine
½ teaspoon salt
pinch pepper
1¼ cups stock

Cut the meat into chunks.
Dice the bacon. Peel and
finely chop the onions.
Clean the mushrooms. Peel
and slice the potatoes and
carrots. Melt the margarine
in a flameproof casserole.
Add the bacon and fry until
it renders its fat. Add the

meat and onions and fry for
5 minutes, then stir in the
salt, pepper, mushrooms,
potatoes and carrots. Pour
over the stock and bring to
the boil. Cover and simmer
for 1 hour. Serve hot, in the
casserole.
Serves 4

Cook's Tip
Small button
mushrooms lose a lot
of their flavor if
peeled; simply wipe
them with a clean
damp cloth or paper
towels and use as
required.

Pepper and Sausage Soup

4 onions
2 leeks
4 red peppers
6 medium potatoes
4 tomatoes
4 sausages
¼ cup pork drippings
¼ cup butter
4 pints stock
1 teaspoon salt
¼ teaspoon black pepper
pinch rosemary
⅔ cup cream

Peel and slice the onions. Wash the leeks and cut in strips. Remove the core, pith and seeds from the peppers and cut into rings. Peel and dice the potatoes. Peel the tomatoes, then halve, remove the seeds and chop.
Broil the sausages until they are well browned all over. Cut into slices.
Melt the drippings in a flameproof casserole and add the onions. Fry until golden brown, then stir in the leeks, peppers, potatoes, butter, tomatoes and sausages. Pour in the stock and bring to the boil. Add the salt, pepper and rosemary and simmer for 20 minutes.
Stir in the cream and heat gently without boiling.
Serve hot.
Serves 4

Pork and Veal Risotto

6 tablespoons butter
1 cup long-grain rice
1 teaspoon salt
½ teaspoon celery salt
2½ cups stock
2 onions
4 oz lean pork (from the leg)
4 oz lean veal
1 carrot
2 tomatoes
½ cup diced cooked ham
Garnish
3 tablespoons chopped parsley

Melt 2 tablespoons of the butter in a saucepan. Add the rice, salt and celery salt and stir to mix well. Fry for 2–3 minutes, then add the stock. Bring to the boil, cover and cook for 15–20 minutes, until the rice is tender and all the stock has been absorbed.
Meanwhile, peel and thinly slice the onions. Cut the pork and veal into chunks. Grate the carrot. Peel and quarter the tomatoes.
Melt the remaining butter in a saucepan. Add the pork and veal chunks and brown on all sides. Stir in the onions and carrot and fry for 5 minutes, then add the ham, tomatoes and the cooked rice. Continue cooking for 15–20 minutes, until the meat is tender. Sprinkle with parsley before serving with a mixed salad.
Serves 4

Layered Liver Casserole

2 cups frozen peas
3 slices white bread
½ cup water
1 lb lamb liver
3 tablespoons oil
1 onion, chopped
2 tablespoons butter
3 eggs
1 teaspoon salt
½ teaspoon white pepper
3 tablespoons grated cheese
2 bacon slices
1 lb carrots, diced
¼ cup chopped parsley

Thaw the peas. Sprinkle the bread with the water and leave to soak, then squeeze out and crumble the bread into small pieces. Finely chop the liver.

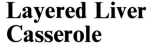

Heat the oil in a saucepan. Add the onion and fry gently for 5 minutes. Add the liver and fry for a further 2–3 minutes. Add the butter and, when it has melted, remove from the heat. Stir in the bread, eggs, salt, pepper and cheese. Dice the bacon. Put the carrots in a baking dish with the parsley, bacon and peas. Cover with the liver mixture. Place the dish on a rack in a pan of hot water and bake in a moderate oven (350° F) for 45–55 minutes. The casserole is cooked when a skewer inserted in the center comes out clean.
Serves 4–5

Italian Fish Bake

2 potatoes, sliced
1 large carrot, sliced
1 small cauliflower
4 oz frozen green beans
2 (7-oz) cans tuna, drained and flaked
2 tomatoes, peeled and sliced
1 beet, sliced
5 anchovy fillets
1 onion, chopped
1 clove garlic, crushed
1 tablespoon capers, chopped
4 eggs, separated
⅓ cup ground hazelnuts
½ cup fresh breadcrumbs
½ cup grated Cheddar cheese
1 tablespoon chopped parsley
salt and pepper

Cook the potatoes and carrots in boiling salted

water for 15–20 minutes. Divide the cauliflower into sprigs and add with the beans for the last 10 minutes. Drain.
Lightly grease a 4-pint capacity ovenproof dish. Layer the cooked vegetables, tuna, tomatoes and beet alternately in the casserole. Finely chop the anchovy fillets and mix with the onion, garlic, capers and egg yolks to a smooth consistency. Stir in the hazelnuts, breadcrumbs and cheese, then fold in the parsley and stiffly beaten egg whites. Season to taste. Spread the topping over the vegetables and bake in a moderately hot oven (400° F) for 20–25 minutes.
Serves 4

Potato Hot Pot

1 lb potatoes
4 eggs
1 lb pork sausages
5 tablespoons sour cream
¼ teaspoon salt
pinch pepper
pinch dried thyme
pinch dried oregano
1 tablespoon butter
½ bunch garden cress
½ teaspoon lemon juice
1 teaspoon oil
pinch sugar
pinch salt

Peel the potatoes and place in a saucepan. Cover with water, bring to the boil and simmer for 15–20 minutes, until tender. Drain and slice. Hard-cook the eggs. Shell and slice. Broil the sausages until well browned on all sides, then slice. Mix together the sour cream, salt, pepper, thyme and oregano.

Layer the potato, egg and sausage slices in a well greased baking pan, finishing with a layer of potatoes. (Reserve a few sausage and egg slices for the garnish.) Pour over the sour cream mixture and dot with the butter, cut into small pieces. Bake in a moderately hot oven (400° F) for 30 minutes. Meanwhile, cut the cress, rinse in cold water, and dry well. Mix the lemon juice, oil, sugar and salt with the cress.

Garnish the hot pot with the reserved slices of egg and sausage and the cress salad.

Serves 3–4

Cabbage and Meat Layered Casserole

1 small head white cabbage
1 stale roll
$\frac{1}{4}$ cup water
1 lb ground meat
pinch grated nutmeg
$\frac{1}{2}$ teaspoon celery salt
2 teaspoons paprika pepper
1 teaspoon salt
1 red pepper, sliced
2 tablespoons butter
3 tablespoons all-purpose flour
$\frac{2}{3}$ cup beef stock
5 tablespoons cream
5 tablespoons grated cheese

Core the cabbage and separate the leaves. Cook these in boiling salted water for 15 minutes. Drain. Soften the roll in the water, then squeeze out and break into small pieces. Mix the meat with the bread, nutmeg and seasonings. Arrange half the cabbage leaves in a greased ovenproof dish. Top with half the meat mixture and half the sliced pepper, then repeat these layers.
Melt the butter. Stir in the flour and cook for 1 minute. Stir in the stock, bring to the boil and simmer, stirring, until thickened. Remove from the heat and stir in the cream. Pour over the meat mixture and sprinkle on the cheese. Bake in a moderately hot oven (400° F) for 35 minutes.
Serves 4–5

Turkish Chicken

2 oranges
4 tomatoes
5 tablespoons raisins
4 slices white bread
2 tablespoons butter
$\frac{2}{3}$ cup milk
1 teaspoon salt
$\frac{1}{2}$ teaspoon white pepper
2 eggs
1 onion, grated
3 tablespoons oil
4 chicken portions
3 tablespoons finely chopped almonds

Peel and slice the oranges. Peel the tomatoes. Soak the raisins in warm water to cover. Toast the bread and butter it. Cut into small pieces and spread over the base of an ovenproof dish. Mix together the milk, salt, pepper, eggs and grated onion. Pour into the baking dish.
Heat the oil in a frying pan and cook the chicken portions for 10 minutes, turning frequently, until lightly browned. Drain the chicken and arrange with the tomatoes on the bread, then cover with the orange slices. Drain the raisins and sprinkle over the oranges with the almonds. Cover with foil and bake in a moderately hot oven (375° F) for 45 minutes–1 hour, until the chicken is tender. Serve hot.
Serves 4

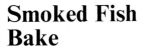

Smoked Fish Bake

6 large kippers, cooked
2 smoked mackerel
2 lb potatoes
1 tablespoon butter
2½ cups milk
1 teaspoon salt
6 eggs
⅔ cup cream
1 cup finely chopped ham
4 tomatoes
5 tablespoons grated cheese

Skin the fish and remove the large bones. Mash the fish with a fork. Peel and boil the potatoes, then mash with the butter, 5 tablespoons milk and the salt. Hard-cook 3 eggs, shell and chop.
Heat the remaining milk in a saucepan and stir in the mashed fish. Remove from the heat and stir in the remaining eggs, the cream and ham.
Spread a thick layer of the mashed potato, about 1 inch deep, over the bottom of a greased oven-proof dish. Cover with half the fish mixture, then some of the chopped egg. Repeat the layers and finish with a layer of mashed potato. Slice the tomatoes and arrange in two overlapping rows down the center. Sprinkle with the grated cheese. Bake in a moderately hot oven (400° F) for 20–25 minutes.
Serves 8

Amsterdam Cod Cake

2 lb thick cod fillets
1 teaspoon salt
½ cup all-purpose flour
2 teaspoons paprika pepper
½ teaspoon white pepper
4 oz bacon slices
4 onions
½ cup small button mush-
  rooms
1 leek
3 tablespoons oil
1 cup grated Edam or Gouda
  cheese
2½ cups milk
4 eggs
pinch grated nutmeg

Remove any bones from the fish, then cut into chunks. Mix together half the salt, the flour, paprika and pepper. Coat the fish chunks with this mixture. Dice the bacon. Peel and slice the onions. Quarter the mushrooms. Slice the leek.
Put the diced bacon in a frying pan and heat until the fat runs. Add the oil, heat, then add the fish chunks and onions, and brown the fish on all sides. Remove from the heat. Transfer the bacon, fish and onion to a greased oven-proof dish. Sprinkle over the mushrooms and leek.
Mix together the cheese, milk, eggs, nutmeg and remaining salt. Pour over the fish. Bake in a moderate oven (350° F) for 20–25 minutes.
Serves 4

Pepper and Pork Hot Pot

1 green pepper
1 red pepper
2 slices white bread
5 tablespoons warm water
1 lb ground pork
1 teaspoon salt
1 teaspoon black pepper
2 teaspoons paprika pepper
10 medium potatoes
1 pint beef stock
⅔ cup sour cream
5 tablespoons grated cheese

Halve the peppers and remove the cores, pith and seeds. Blanch in boiling salted water for 5 minutes. Drain. Sprinkle the bread with the water and leave to soak, then squeeze out the water and crumble the bread into small pieces. Mix together the bread, pork, salt, pepper and paprika.
Peel and thinly slice the potatoes. Put half the slices in the bottom of a greased ovenproof dish. Cover with two of the pepper halves. Spoon over the meat mixture, then cover with the remaining pepper halves. Arrange the rest of the potato slices on top. Mix together the stock and sour cream and pour over the potatoes. Sprinkle on the cheese. Cover lightly with foil and bake in a moderate oven (350° F) for 45 minutes–1 hour, until the potatoes are tender.
Serves 4

Veal and Vegetable Pie

1½ lb boned shoulder of veal
¼ cup pork drippings
4 onions, chopped
1 teaspoon salt
½ teaspoon white pepper
¼ head celery with leaves
2 eggs, hard-cooked
½ cup mushrooms
3 tablespoons all-purpose flour
⅔ cup stock
2 carrots, sliced
11-oz package frozen puff pastry, thawed
1 egg yolk, beaten, to glaze

Cut the veal into ½-inch pieces. Heat the drippings and fry the onions for 5 minutes. Stir in the meat, salt and pepper and cook for 10 minutes.
Meanwhile, cut the celery into strips and chop the celery leaves. Slice the eggs. Quarter the mushrooms. Sprinkle the flour over the meat and stir well, then stir in the stock. Bring to the boil and simmer, stirring, until thickened. Mix in the carrots, celery, celery leaves and mushrooms. Transfer to an ovenproof dish. Cover with the egg slices.
Roll out the pastry to cover the dish. Press the edges to seal and decorate with the pastry trimmings. Brush with the egg yolk and bake in a hot oven (425° F) for 40 minutes. Serve hot or cold.
Serves 4–6

Ham and Vegetable Casserole

2 cups frozen peas
8 oz asparagus
8 oz carrots
8 oz Brussels sprouts
8 oz cooked ham, sliced
3 tablespoons butter
3 tablespoons all-purpose flour
½ cup chopped parsley
4 oz prosciutto

Thaw the peas. Peel and trim the asparagus and cut into pieces. Peel and thinly slice the carrots. Cook the asparagus and carrots in boiling salted water for 8–10 minutes or until tender. Trim the sprouts and cook in boiling salted water for 8–10 minutes. Drain the vegetables, reserving 1¼ cups of the asparagus cooking liquid. Cover the base of a greased ovenproof dish with the ham. Spread over half the vegetables. Melt the butter in a saucepan. Stir in the flour and cook for 1 minute. Stir in the reserved cooking liquid and bring to the boil. Simmer, stirring, until thickened. Stir in the remaining vegetables, the peas and parsley. Pour into the baking dish and top with the prosciutto. Bake in a moderate oven (325° F) for 15 minutes.
Serves 4

Spring Soufflé

½ cup shelled fresh peas
4 tomatoes
1 cup all-purpose flour
1¼ cups water
1 tablespoon chopped parsley
¼ cup chopped chives
1 teaspoon salt
freshly ground pepper
¼ cup grated Parmesan cheese
6 eggs

Cook the peas in boiling salted water for 10–15 minutes until tender. Drain. Scald the tomatoes in boiling water for 30–45 seconds, then peel, remove the seeds and chop the flesh.
Mix the flour with the water, beat to remove lumps then stir in the parsley, chives, salt, pepper and cheese. Separate the egg yolks from the whites. Beat the yolks into the flour mixture, then stir in the peas and tomato flesh. Whisk the egg whites until stiff and fold quickly but thoroughly into the pea mixture. Spoon into a greased 3-pint soufflé dish and bake in a moderate oven (325° F) for 45–50 minutes. Serve immediately.
Serves 4

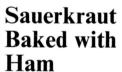

Sauerkraut Baked with Ham

2 lb sauerkraut
1½ lb potatoes
⅔ cup milk
1 teaspoon salt
½ teaspoon pepper
pinch grated nutmeg
8 oz Cheddar cheese
8 oz green grapes
5 tablespoons oil
2 onions, sliced
½ cup diced bacon
2 cups diced cooked ham
⅔ cup browned breadcrumbs
2 tablespoons butter

Drain the sauerkraut, then cook in boiling water for 20 minutes. Drain and cool. Peel the potatoes and cook in boiling salted water for 15–20 minutes, until tender. Drain and mash with the milk, salt, pepper and nutmeg. Dice the cheese. Halve and seed the grapes. Heat the oil and fry the onions and bacon for 5 minutes. Stir in the sauerkraut.
Spoon the potato mixture into a greased ovenproof dish and spread out. Top with the sauerkraut mixture. ham, cheese and grapes. Sprinkle over the breadcrumbs and dot with butter. Bake in a moderately hot oven (400° F) for 20 minutes.
Serves 4

Old-fashioned Cobbler's Pot

2 pickled herrings
4 oz bacon
4 onions
2½ lb potatoes
2 teaspoons salt
1 teaspoon black pepper
1½ cups roast pork, cut into strips
⅔ cup sour cream
1¼ cups milk
3 eggs
1 cup grated Cheddar cheese

Cut the herrings into strips. Chop the bacon. Peel and thinly slice the onions and potatoes. Put the bacon in a frying pan and heat until the fat runs.
Add the onion and fry for 5 minutes, then add the potato slices and fry until lightly browned. Sprinkle over the salt and pepper. Put a layer of this potato mixture in a greased ovenproof dish. Mix the pork with the herring. Spoon on to the potato mixture, then spread over the remaining potato mixture. Smooth the top.
Mix together the sour cream, milk and eggs and pour into the dish. Sprinkle over the cheese. Bake in a moderately hot oven (400° F) for 40 minutes.
Serve hot.
Serves 4

Eggplant and Rice Moussaka

2 eggplants, thinly sliced
2½ cups chicken stock
1 cup round-grain rice
1 lb ground pork
1 teaspoon salt
2 teaspoons paprika pepper
1 teaspoon white pepper
4 tomatoes, sliced
4 eggs
5 tablespoons dry bread-crumbs
5 tablespoons grated cheese
2 tablespoons butter
parsley

Put the eggplant slices in a colander, sprinkle with salt and leave for 20 minutes. Rinse and dry. Bring the stock to the boil and add the rice. Cover and simmer for 15–20 minutes, until tender. Mix together the pork, salt, paprika and pepper.

Mix together half the cooked rice and the meat mixture. Put half this mixture in a greased oven-proof dish. Lay on the eggplant and tomato slices, then spread over the remaining rice meat mixture. Beat the eggs, then pour into the dish. Top with the rest of the cooked rice. Sprinkle over the bread-crumbs and cheese. Dot the butter over the top. Bake in a moderate oven (350° F) for 40 minutes. Serve garnished with parsley.
Serves 4

Spaghetti Carbonara

8 oz spaghetti
4 oz bacon
1 green pepper
5 tablespoons grated Parmesan cheese
5 tablespoons chopped parsley
1¼ cups cream
¼ cup butter
8 slices lean cooked ham
1 teaspoon dried oregano
1 teaspoon dried basil

Cook the spaghetti in boiling salted water for 12–15 minutes, until just tender to the bite. Meanwhile, chop the bacon. Remove the core, pith and seeds from the pepper and chop finely. Put the bacon in a saucepan and heat until it renders its fat and becomes crisp. Stir in the cheese, parsley, cream and green pepper. Cook very gently for 5 minutes. Drain the spaghetti and toss with the butter until well coated. Put the spaghetti in a greased ovenproof dish. Roll up the ham slices and lay on the spaghetti, then cover with the bacon sauce. Sprinkle over the herbs. Bake in a hot oven (425° F) for 10 minutes. Serve hot.
Serves 2–4

Egg Pizza

*4 cups bread dough made
    with 4 cups flour etc. (see
    page 285)*
beaten egg for glazing
3 tablespoons grated cheese
4 eggs
1 (2-oz) can anchovy fillets
4 tomatoes, thinly sliced
3 tablespoons olive oil
pinch curry powder
4 slices cheese

Divide the dough into four
portions. Roll out each
portion on a floured surface
to a round about 8 inches in
diameter. Place on greased
baking sheets. Push up the
edges of the dough rounds
to make a raised border.
Brush with beaten egg and
sprinkle with the grated
cheese. Leave in a warm
place for 15 minutes, then
bake in a hot oven (425° F)
for 12–15 minutes, until
lightly browned.
Hard-cook the eggs, then
shell and slice. Drain the
anchovy fillets and arrange
on the pizza bases. Cover
with the egg and tomato
slices, then sprinkle over
the oil and curry powder.
Cut the cheese into strips
and arrange in a lattice-
work on top of each pizza.
Bake in the preheated oven
for 5 minutes. Serve hot.
Serves 4

Baked Ham and Pea Omelet

1 lb frozen peas
8 eggs
½ teaspoon salt
½ teaspoon celery salt
¼ cup cream
pinch grated nutmeg
1 teaspoon paprika pepper
*½ cup finely chopped cooked
    ham*

Thaw the peas. Beat
together the eggs, salt,
celery salt, cream, nutmeg
and paprika. Add the ham
with the peas. Pour the
mixture into a greased
ovenproof dish.
Cover with foil and bake in
a moderate oven (325° F)
for 30 minutes. Remove the
foil for the last 5 minutes to
allow the top to brown.
Serve hot.
Serves 2–4

Variation
Try this with grated cheese
and canned flaked salmon.
Omit the peas, ham and
paprika and cook as above.

Ham and Egg Rolls

4 slices cooked ham
½ teaspoon paprika pepper
8 eggs
½ cup water
1 teaspoon salt
pinch grated nutmeg
3 tablespoons chopped
   parsley
3 tablespoons chopped
   chervil
¼ cup butter

Spread out the ham slices
on a board and sprinkle
with the paprika.
Beat the eggs with the
water, salt, nutmeg and
herbs until well mixed. Melt
the butter in a large pan.
Add the egg mixture and
cook gently, turning and
stirring frequently, until the
eggs are lightly scrambled.
They should still be moist,
so do not overcook. Re-
move from the heat and
divide the scrambled egg
between the ham slices. Roll
up the ham and, if necessary,
secure the rolls with wooden
toothpicks. Serve warm
or cold with a mixed salad.
Serves 2–4

Variation
Snip 3 tablespoons chives
into the eggs, in place of the
chervil.

Savory Baked Eggs

1 lb potatoes
1¼ cups milk
1 teaspoon salt
½ teaspoon paprika pepper
¼ teaspoon Tabasco sauce
pinch grated nutmeg
10 eggs
¼ cup butter
2 onions, finely chopped
1 lb ground pork
3 tablespoons all-purpose
   flour
½ cucumber, thinly sliced
3 tomatoes, halved
3 tablespoons chopped
   parsley
¼ teaspoon white pepper

Peel the potatoes and cook
in boiling salted water for
15–20 minutes, until tender.
Drain and mash with
5 tablespoons of the milk,
half the salt, the paprika,
Tabasco and nutmeg. Hard-
cook 8 of the eggs. Shell and
halve.
Melt the butter in a pan and
fry the onions and pork until
lightly browned. Sprinkle
over the flour, stir well and
fry for 3 minutes.
Spread the mashed potato
in a greased ovenproof dish.
Cover with the pork mix-
ture, then top with the
cucumber slices and tomato
and egg halves. Beat the
remaining eggs, milk and
salt with the parsley and
pepper, and pour over the
dish. Bake in a moderate
oven (325° F) for 40 minutes.
Serves 4

Egg Dishes

Spicy Soufflé Omelet

5 stuffed green olives
5 anchovy fillets
3 tablespoons milk
½ cup all-purpose flour
½ teaspoon baking powder
1¼ cups water
3 eggs
1 teaspoon salt
2 teaspoons paprika pepper
½ teaspoon dried rosemary
2 tablespoons butter

Slice the olives. Soak the anchovy fillets in the milk for 5 minutes, then drain. Sift the flour and baking powder into a mixing bowl and beat in the water. Separate the egg yolks from the whites. Beat the yolks into the flour mixture with the salt, paprika and rosemary. Beat the egg whites until stiff, then fold into the mixture.

Melt the butter in a large omelet pan and spoon in the egg mixture. Cook, lifting the edges of the omelet to let the liquid egg mixture run on to the pan. Sprinkle over the olive slices and anchovy fillets when the omelet is half cooked. Fold over the cooked omelet and slide out of the pan. Cut in half and serve.
Serves 2

Spinach Crêpes

4 oz frozen spinach
1 cup grated Cheddar cheese
1 cup all-purpose flour
½ teaspoon salt
1 egg
1¼ cups milk
¼ cup oil

Cook the spinach according to the instructions on the package, then drain thoroughly. Chop finely. Add half the cheese to the spinach. Keep warm. Sift the flour into a mixing bowl. Add the salt, egg and half the milk. Beat together until well blended, then beat in the remaining milk and 1 tablespoon of the oil.

Heat a little of the remaining oil in a crêpe pan. Pour in about one-quarter of the batter and tip to cover the pan. Cook for about 1 minute, then turn and cook the other side for about 30 seconds. Slide the crêpe out of the pan. Keep hot while you cook the remaining crêpes in the same way. Spread the spinach mixture over the crêpes and roll them up. Place in a greased ovenproof dish, sprinkle with the remaining cheese and brown quickly under the broiler. Serve hot.
Serves 2–4

Asparagus Omelet with Shrimp

1 (11-oz) can asparagus
⅔ cup shelled shrimp
3 tablespoons butter
6 eggs
3 tablespoons water
½ teaspoon salt
½ teaspoon pepper
Garnish
parsley sprigs

Drain the asparagus and put in a saucepan with the shrimp. Add 1 tablespoon butter and 3 tablespoons of the asparagus can juice. Beat the eggs with the water, salt and pepper until well mixed.
Melt half the remaining butter in an omelet pan. Pour in half the egg mixture and cook, lifting the edge of the omelet to let the egg mixture run on to the pan. While the omelet is cooking place the asparagus and shrimp over a low heat and warm through gently. Slide the cooked omelet out of the pan. Keep hot while you cook the second omelet in the same way, using the remaining butter. Top the omelets with the hot asparagus, fold over and scatter with the shrimp Secure with a wooden toothpick if necessary. Garnish with parsley and serve warm with a green salad.
Serves 2

Variation
Make a cheese sauce using 1¼ cups basic white sauce and ¾ cup grated Cheddar cheese. Fold in the shrimp and pour over the asparagus omelet.

Scrambled Eggs with Salmon

8 large eggs
½ teaspoon salt
¼ teaspoon white pepper
½ cup water
3 tablespoons chopped chives
8 oz smoked salmon
¼ cup butter

Beat the eggs with the salt, pepper and water until well mixed. Add the chives and stir. Cut the salmon into thin strips.
Melt the butter in a frying pan. Pour in the egg mixture and cook gently, turning and stirring frequently, until the eggs are lightly scrambled. They should still be moist, so do not overcook. Spoon the eggs on to a warmed dish and garnish with the salmon strips. Alternatively, the salmon may be added to the eggs when they are half-cooked, and then heated through with the eggs.
Serves 2–4

Variation
Instead of smoked salmon, try 2 cups sliced mushrooms, cooked in butter. Pile on top of the scrambled eggs or fold in.

Fried Eggs with Salami

2 large slices cheese
2 tablespoons butter
12 slices salami
8 eggs
Garnish
paprika pepper
tomato quarters
parsley sprigs

Cut the slices of cheese into quarters. Melt half the butter in a frying pan. Place the salami slices in the pan and fry on each side to heat through. Transfer the salami to a warmed serving dish and keep hot.
Add the remaining butter to the pan and, when it has melted, break in the eggs one at a time. Fry for 1 minute then turn over and fry for 30 seconds. Top each egg with a square of cheese and cover the pan. Cook for a further 30 seconds, or until the cheese is just beginning to melt. Place the eggs on the salami slices. Sprinkle the top of each with a pinch of paprika, then garnish with the tomato quarters and parsley sprigs. Serve hot with crusty bread.
Serves 2–4

Variation
You can substitute slices of garlic sausage or Mortadella for the salami.

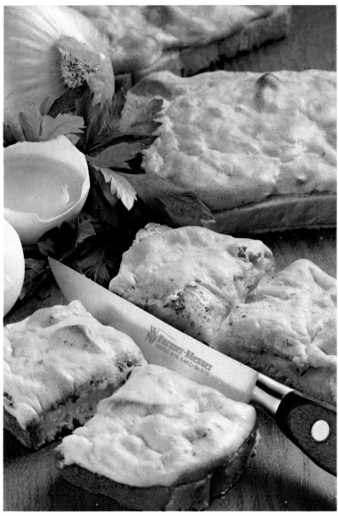

Stuffed Omelets

1 green pepper
¼ cup butter
1 cup chopped mushrooms
8 oz ground beef
½ teaspoon white pepper
8 eggs
1 tablespoon chopped parsley
½ teaspoon salt
½ cup water
½ teaspoon Tabasco sauce

Remove the core, pith and seeds from the pepper and chop finely. Melt half the butter in a frying pan. Add the green pepper, mushrooms, ground beef and half the white pepper. Fry for 6–8 minutes, until the meat is lightly browned and the pepper just tender.

Remove from the heat and keep warm.
Beat together the eggs, parsley, salt, water, Tabasco and remaining white pepper. Melt half the remaining butter in an omelet pan. Pour in half the egg mixture and cook, lifting the edges of the omelet to let the egg mixture run on to the pan. When the omelet is cooked, slide on to a warmed serving plate. Cook the second omelet in the same way, using the rest of the butter.
Spoon the meat mixture on to the first omelet and top with the second omelet.
Serve hot.
Serves 2

Tasty Egg Slices

1 onion
¼ cup butter
¼ cup finely chopped cooked ham
1 tablespoon chopped parsley
dash soy sauce
4 eggs
4 slices toast

Peel and finely chop the onion. Melt half the butter in a saucepan. Add the onion and fry for 5 minutes. Stir in the ham, parsley and soy sauce and cook for a further 3 minutes. Remove from the heat and leave to cool. Separate the egg yolks from the whites and stir the yolks into the ham mixture. Beat the whites until stiff,

then fold into the ham mixture.
Spread the toast with the rest of the butter, then top with the egg and ham mixture and smooth over. Put on a greased baking sheet and bake in a moderately hot oven (400° F) for about 10 minutes, until set and lightly browned. Cut each slice into quarters and serve hot.
Serves 2–4

Egg Dishes

Summer Eggs

8 eggs
1 cup cottage cheese
⅔ cup plain yogurt
⅔ cup cream
juice of 1 small lemon
½ teaspoon salt
¼ teaspoon white pepper
5 tablespoons chopped mixed
   herbs (basil, chervil, etc.)
4 large tomatoes

Hard-cook the eggs, then shell. Push the cottage cheese through a strainer until smooth, then mix in the yogurt and cream. Add the lemon juice, salt, pepper and herbs and stir well.
Pour the herb mixture into a deep serving dish. Halve the eggs and place, cut sides up, in the dish. Peel and halve the tomatoes, then remove the seeds. Slice the flesh into strips and use to garnish the eggs. Serve chilled.
Serves 4

Variation
Substitute cream for cottage cheese for a richer dish.

Cook's Tip
Hold the hard-cooked eggs under cold running water for 1 minute before shelling. This prevents any grey rings forming.

Catalan Beans and Eggs

1 lb dried white haricot
   beans
2 tomatoes
1 large onion
1 red pepper
1 green pepper
¼ cup olive oil
½ cup diced cooked ham
¼ teaspoon cayenne pepper
1 teaspoon salt
4 eggs

Soak the beans in water overnight, then drain. Put in a saucepan and cover with fresh water. Bring to the boil and simmer for 30–45 minutes or until the beans are tender. Drain well.
Peel and chop the tomatoes and onion. Remove the core, pith and seeds from the peppers and chop.
Heat the oil in a saucepan. Add the onion and peppers and fry for 5 minutes. Stir in the ham, tomatoes, cayenne and salt and cook for a further 5 minutes. Mix in the beans and continue cooking for about 5 minutes, until all the ingredients are heated through.
Turn the bean mixture into an ovenproof serving dish. Make four hollows and break an egg into each. Bake in a hot oven (425° F) for 6–8 minutes or until the eggs are cooked. Serve hot.
Serves 4

Spinach Rolls

*1 cup plus 1 tablespoon
    all-purpose flour*
1 teaspoon salt
1 egg
1¼ cups milk
⅔ cup cream
¼ cup oil
2 cooking apples
12 oz frozen spinach
2 teaspoons brown sugar
pinch grated nutmeg
1 tablespoon butter
½ cup grated cheese

Sift the 1 cup of flour into a
bowl. Beat in half the salt,
the egg and half the milk,
then the cream and 1
tablespoon oil.
Heat a little oil in a crêpe
pan. Pour in one-eighth of
the batter. Cook for 1
minute, then turn over and
cook for 30 seconds. Cook
the remaining crêpes in the
same way. Chop the apples,
then cook gently to a purée.
Cook the spinach, drain
and chop. Mix in the apple,
sugar, nutmeg and remain-
ing salt. Spread over the
crêpes, roll up and place in
a greased ovenproof dish.
Melt the butter, stir in the
remaining flour and cook
for 1 minute. Add the
remaining milk and bring
to the boil, stirring, until
thickened. Add the cheese,
pour over the crêpes and
bake in a moderate oven
(350° F) for 15–20 minutes.
Serves 4

Spanish Scrambled Eggs

¾ cup frozen peas
2 onions
3 tablespoons butter
*½ cup cooked ham, cut into
    thin strips*
4 eggs
¼ cup water
½ teaspoon celery salt
½ teaspoon white pepper
1 cup grated cheese
Garnish
*3 tablespoons chopped
    parsley*

Thaw the peas. Peel and
finely chop the onions.
Melt the butter in a frying
pan. Add the onions and fry
for 5 minutes. Stir in the
ham and peas and cook for
a further 3 minutes.

Beat together the eggs,
water, celery salt and
pepper. Stir in the cheese
and pour this mixture into
the pan. Cook gently, turning and stirring frequently,
until the eggs are lightly
scrambled. They should
still be moist, so do not
overcook. Sprinkle on the
parsley and serve.
Serves 2

Cook's Tip

For extra creaminess
stir 1 tablespoon
butter and 1 table-
spoon cream into the
eggs immediately
before serving.

Spiced Cheese Cakes

1 cup cottage cheese
⅔ cup milk
5 tablespoons chopped
  mixed herbs (parsley,
  chives, tarragon, chervil)
¾ cup semolina
5 tablespoons fresh
  breadcrumbs
1 teaspoon salt
1 teaspoon Worcestershire
  sauce
½ teaspoon pepper
½ teaspoon Tabasco sauce
½ cup finely chopped cooked
  ham
beaten egg
dry breadcrumbs
¼ cup butter
3 tablespoons oil

Push the cottage cheese through a strainer until smooth, then mix with the milk, herbs, semolina, breadcrumbs, salt, Worcestershire sauce, pepper and Tabasco sauce. Fold the ham into the cheese mixture. The mixture should be thick, so if necessary add more fresh breadcrumbs. Divide the mixture into 8 portions and form each into a patty-shape. Coat with the beaten egg, then with the breadcrumbs. Heat the butter and oil in a frying pan and fry the cakes for 3–4 minutes on each side, until well browned. Drain on paper towels and serve hot with a cucumber salad.
Serves 4

Liver with Apples

4 dessert apples
¼ cup butter
1 teaspoon paprika pepper
1 lb calf liver
3 tablespoons all-purpose
  flour
½ teaspoon salt
4 slices cheese

Peel and core the apples, then cut into thick slices. Melt half the butter in a frying pan. Add the apple slices and brown lightly. Do not overcook or the apples will break up. Remove from the pan and arrange on a warmed heat-proof serving dish. Sprinkle with ½ teaspoon paprika. Keep warm.

Cut the liver into slices. Mix together the flour, salt and remaining paprika and use to coat the liver slices. Add the remaining butter to the frying pan and, when it has melted, add the liver slices. Cook quickly for 2–3 minutes on each side, until well browned. Do not over-cook or the liver will be tough. Place the liver on top of the apple slices and lay over the cheese slices. Bake in a hot oven (425° F) for 3–5 minutes, until the cheese is beginning to melt. Serve hot.
Serves 4

Celery with Soufflé Topping

2 heads celery
2 tablespoons oil
1 teaspoon prepared mustard
1 teaspoon salt
½ teaspoon white pepper
3 tablespoons warm water
1 cup cottage cheese
¼ cup whipping cream
1 red pepper
1 green pepper
1 onion, chopped
6 green olives, sliced
3 tablespoons chopped
    mixed herbs (basil,
    parsley, chervil, etc.)
3 eggs, separated

Trim and wash the celery, then cook in boiling salted water for 15–20 minutes, until tender. Drain well and slice. Mix together the oil, mustard, salt, pepper and water and stir in the sliced celery. Leave to marinate and keep warm.
Push the cottage cheese through a strainer until smooth and mix with the cream. Remove the cores, pith and seeds from the peppers and chop finely. Stir the onion, peppers, olives, herbs and egg yolks into the cottage cheese mixture. Beat the egg whites until stiff and fold in.
Drain the celery and place in an ovenproof dish. Spoon over the cottage cheese mixture and bake in a hot oven (425° F) for 10 minutes, until golden on top. Serve hot.
Serves 4

Cottage Cheese and Ham Rolls

1 cauliflower
5 tablespoons oil
3 tablespoons vinegar
1 teaspoon prepared mustard
¾ teaspoon salt
pinch sugar
¾ teaspoon white pepper
1 cup cottage cheese
pinch garlic powder
pinch celery salt
5 tablespoons chopped
    mixed herbs (tarragon,
    chives, parsley, etc.)
milk
4 slices prosciutto

Break the cauliflower into flowerets and cook in boiling salted water for 10–15 minutes or until tender. Drain well. Mix together the oil, vinegar, mustard, ½ teaspoon salt, the sugar and ½ teaspoon pepper. Pour over the warm cauliflower then leave to cool and marinate for 20 minutes.
Meanwhile, mix together the cottage cheese, garlic powder, celery salt, herbs and remaining salt and pepper. Add a little milk if the mixture is very stiff. It should be creamy.
Spread the cottage cheese mixture over the ham slices and roll up. Arrange the marinated cauliflower in a serving dish and lay the filled ham rolls on top. Serve chilled.
Serves 2–4

211

Pan-Fried Potato Scones

2 lb potatoes
6 tablespoons butter
½ cup milk
½ teaspoon salt
1 teaspoon pepper
pinch grated nutmeg
2 cups grated cheese
6 tomatoes
5 tablespoons chopped chives
½ teaspoon celery salt

Peel the potatoes and put in a saucepan. Cover with water and bring to the boil. Simmer for 15–20 minutes or until the potatoes are tender. Drain well, then mash with 1 tablespoon of the butter, the milk, salt, pepper and nutmeg. (Add only enough milk to make a smooth mixture: it should be quite stiff.) Stir in the cheese. Slice the tomatoes. Melt a quarter of the remaining butter in a frying pan. Add a quarter of the potato mixture and spread it out in the pan. Cook for 3–4 minutes, then turn the scone over. Top with slices of tomato and sprinkle with chives and celery salt. Cook for a further 3–4 minutes, then slide out of the pan on to a warmed serving dish. Keep hot while you cook and garnish the remaining three scones in the same way, using the remaining butter. Serve hot.
Serves 4

Cheesy Bread

½ long French loaf
¼ cup butter
pinch pepper
pinch garlic salt
4 slices cheese
Garnish
parsley sprigs

Make incisions in the bread, cutting to but not through the bottom, 1½–2 inches apart. Cream the butter with the pepper and garlic salt. Cut the cheese slices in half diagonally to make triangles.
Spread a little seasoned butter on both sides of the bread inside each incision. Place a triangle of cheese in each incision, leaving the point to fold over the top. Place the loaf on a baking sheet and bake in a moderately hot oven (400° F) for 5–10 minutes or until the cheese has melted. Serve garnished with parsley.
Serves 2

Variation
If you enjoy the taste of garlic you could substitute 1 clove of garlic, finely crushed with a little salt, for the garlic salt. 1–2 tablespoons of chopped parsley, creamed into the garlic butter, makes this even more delicious.

Ham and Cheese Sandwiches

4 slices Edam or Gouda
   cheese
4 slices cooked ham
1 tart dessert apple
3 tablespoons all-purpose
   flour
2 eggs
½ teaspoon salt
½ teaspoon paprika pepper
3 tablespoons grated cheese
1 tablespoon tomato paste
¼ cup butter
Garnish
parsley sprigs
tomato quarters

Cut the slices of cheese to
the same size as the ham
slices. Peel and core the

apple, then slice thinly in
rounds. Arrange the apple
slices between the four
pairs of cheese and ham
slices. Mix the flour with
the eggs, salt, paprika,
grated cheese and tomato
paste. The mixture should
be slightly runny.
Coat the ham and cheese
sandwiches with the egg
mixture. Melt the butter in
a frying pan and add the
sandwiches. Fry for 4–5
minutes on each side, until
well browned. Garnish with
parsley sprigs and tomato
quarters. Serve hot with a
green salad.
Serves 2–4

Quick Cheese Snacks

4 slices bread
2 tablespoons butter
2 teaspoons prepared
   mustard
2 slices cooked ham
12 oz ground beef
5 tablespoons grated cheese
3 tablespoons chopped
   parsley
½ teaspoon salt
½ teaspoon pepper
2 slices cheese
5 tablespoons tomato
   ketchup
Garnish
parsley sprigs

Toast the bread, then butter
one side of each slice.
Spread with the mustard.
Dice the ham and mix with

the beef, grated cheese,
parsley, salt and pepper.
Pile this mixture on to the
toast and smooth the tops.
Cut the cheese slices into
thin strips and arrange in a
lattice-work over the tops.
Dot the ketchup in between
the cheese strips. Place on
a baking sheet and bake in a
moderately hot oven
(400° F) for 20 minutes.
Garnish with parsley and
serve hot or cold.
Serves 2–4

Beef Cornucopias

1 (7-oz) can corn kernels
4 tomatoes
1 red pepper
1 green pepper
5 tablespoons mayonnaise
2 teaspoons cider vinegar
½ teaspoon salt
¼ teaspoon white pepper
1 tablespoon chopped onion
8–12 slices roast beef
few lettuce leaves
lemon juice
½ bunch garden cress

Drain the corn. Peel and chop the tomatoes. Remove the cores, pith and seeds from the peppers and cut into thin strips. Mix together the mayonnaise, vinegar, salt and pepper.

Fold in the corn, tomatoes, pepper strips and onion. Chill for 20 minutes. Roll the beef slices into cornucopias and fill with the corn mixture. Place the lettuce leaves on four or six serving plates and sprinkle with a little lemon juice. Place the beef cornucopias on top and garnish with the cress.
Serves 4–6

Variation
For quick Beef cornucopias, fill each with ready-made coleslaw or other salad.

Spicy Texas Beans

1 lb wax beans
1 apple
1 large onion
6 bacon slices
¼ cup oil
5 tablespoons tomato
  ketchup
pinch marjoram
¼ teaspoon cayenne pepper
¼ teaspoon curry powder
pinch paprika pepper
1 teaspoon salt
Garnish
¼ cup chopped parsley
1 tomato, sliced

Trim the beans, then cut into pieces about 1 inch long. Cook in boiling salted water for 10–15 minutes, until tender. Drain and

leave to cool completely. Peel and core the apple, then chop finely. Stir the apple into the drained beans and place in a serving bowl. Peel and finely chop the onion. Fry the bacon until crisp and well browned. Lay on top of the bean mixture. Heat the oil in a saucepan. Add the onion and fry for 5 minutes. Stir in the ketchup, marjoram, cayenne, curry powder, paprika and salt and bring to a simmer. Remove from the heat and allow to cool, then pour over the beans. Garnish with the chopped parsley and tomato slices.
Serves 4–6

Orange and Olive Salad

1 small head Boston or Bibb
  lettuce
juice of 1 orange
salt and white pepper
pinch sugar
1 orange
10 black olives, pitted
1 tablespoon olive oil

Separate the lettuce into
leaves. Wash thoroughly
and pat dry with a dish
towel. Put in a salad bowl.
Mix the orange juice with
the salt, pepper and sugar.
Pour over the lettuce and
toss to coat.
Peel the orange. Slice
thinly, then halve the slices.
Arrange the orange pieces
and olives in the bowl and
sprinkle over the olive oil.
Serve immediately.
Serves 4

Fresh Mixed Salad
Prepare a selection of sliced
salad vegetables, such as
cucumber, tomato, radish
and onion, on a bed of crisp
lettuce leaves and garden
cress. Serve with a dressing
of oil and vinegar, mixed
with salt, pepper and sugar
to taste.

Tasty Salads

Mixed Vegetable Salad

1 large leek
2 large carrots
1 red pepper
½ head celery
2 tomatoes
¼ head white cabbage
½ clove garlic
5 tablespoons wine vinegar
1 teaspoon salt
5 tablespoons water
5 tablespoons oil
2 eggs

Wash and thinly slice the leek. Peel and chop the carrots. Remove the core, pith and seeds from the pepper and cut into thin strips. Trim and thinly slice the celery. Peel and quarter the tomatoes.

Wash the cabbage, then shred finely.
Put the leek, carrots, red pepper, celery, tomatoes and cabbage in a bowl and mix well together.
Crush the garlic clove and put in a saucepan with the vinegar, salt, water and oil. Bring to a simmer, then remove from the heat and pour over the vegetables. Toss well together so the vegetables are coated with the dressing. Allow to cool, then chill well.
Hard-cook the eggs. Cool, then shell and slice. Garnish the salad with the egg slices.
Serves 4

Cauliflower and Egg Salad

1 cauliflower
3 tablespoons mayonnaise
1 teaspoon prepared mustard
⅔ cup plain yogurt
1 teaspoon paprika pepper
½ teaspoon salt
½ teaspoon pepper
pinch sugar
1 tomato
½ head lettuce
4 eggs

Break the cauliflower into flowerets and cook in boiling salted water for 15 minutes or until tender. Drain and place in cold water to refresh.
Mix together the mayonnaise, mustard, yogurt, paprika, salt, pepper and

sugar. Peel the tomato, then halve and remove the seeds. Cut the flesh into small pieces. Separate the lettuce into leaves and wash thoroughly under cold running water. Shake the leaves well to remove excess water, then pat dry with a dish towel. Tear the lettuce into shreds. Hard-cook the eggs. Cool, then shell and quarter.
Drain the cauliflower and put in a salad bowl with the tomato pieces, shredded lettuce and egg quarters. Pour over the yogurt dressing and serve.
Serves 4

Caprice Tomato Salad

4 large tomatoes
1 head lettuce
3 celery stalks
1 (7-oz) can tuna
10 green olives, pitted
10 black olives, pitted
1 tablespoon chopped basil
¼ cup wine vinegar
½ cup olive oil
½ teaspoon salt
½ teaspoon pepper
½ cup Gruyère cheese, cut into very thin strips

Peel and slice the tomatoes. Separate the lettuce into leaves and wash under cold running water. Shake to remove excess water, then pat dry with a dish towel. Trim and chop the celery.

Drain and flake the tuna. Put the tomatoes, lettuce, celery, tuna and olives in a salad bowl and toss well together. Mix together the basil, vinegar, oil, salt and pepper and pour over the salad. Toss to coat the vegetables with the dressing, then scatter over the cheese. Serve immediately.
Serves 4

Bean and Pickled Herring Salad

4 pickled herrings
1¼ cups milk
1 lb green beans
⅔ cup plain yogurt
3 tablespoons tomato ketchup
1 tomato
2 onions
¼ cup chopped parsley
pinch salt
pinch garlic salt

Soak the herrings in the milk for 2 hours. Meanwhile, trim the beans and cut into pieces, then cook in boiling salted water for 10–15 minutes, until tender. Drain and leave to cool.

Drain the herrings, and cut into strips. Mix with the beans.

Mix together the yogurt and ketchup. Peel and finely chop the tomato. Peel the onions and slice into thin rings. Cover the onion rings with boiling water, then drain. Add the tomato and onion rings to the yogurt mixture with the parsley, salt and garlic salt and stir well. Serve this yogurt sauce with the beans and herrings.
Serves 4

Curried Rice and Meat Salad

2½ cups stock
1 cup long-grain rice
½ cup finely chopped roast
   meat (pork, veal, beef)
½ cup finely chopped cooked
   chicken
3 tablespoons mayonnaise
3 tablespoons wine vinegar
3 tablespoons chopped
   mango chutney
1 teaspoon paprika pepper
3 tablespoons concentrated
   curry paste, dissolved in
   3 tablespoons hot water
2 eggs, hard-cooked

Bring the stock to the boil
and add the rice. Cover and
simmer for 15–20 minutes or
until the rice is tender and
has absorbed all the stock.

Mix the meat and chicken
with the cooked rice and
set aside to cool.
Mix together the mayon-
naise, vinegar, chutney,
paprika and dissolved curry
paste. Shell the eggs and
rub the egg yolks through a
strainer. Finely chop the egg
whites. Add both to the
sauce and mix well. Set
aside ¼ cup of the rice
mixture and 1 tablespoon
of the sauce. Mix the
remaining rice with the
rest of the curry sauce.
Combine thoroughly and
spoon into a serving bowl.
Top with the reserved rice
mixture and the spoonful of
sauce. Serve chilled.
Serves 4–6

Herring and Apple Salad

2 large pickled herrings
⅔ cup milk
1 sweet dill pickle
3 celery stalks
2 tart dessert apples
1 small onion
3 tablespoons wine vinegar
5 tablespoons oil
1 teaspoon salt
½ teaspoon paprika pepper
1 teaspoon prepared mustard
3 tablespoons cream
1 head lettuce

Soak the herrings in the
milk for 2 hours, then drain
and cut into thin strips. Cut
the pickle into thin strips.
Trim the celery, then cut
into thin strips. Peel and
core the apples and cut into

thin strips. Peel and finely
chop the onion.
Mix together the vinegar,
oil, salt, paprika, mustard
and cream. Add the
herrings, pickle, celery,
apples and onion and toss
together well. Chill for 20
minutes.
Meanwhile, separate the
lettuce into leaves and
wash under cold running
water. Shake off excess
water, then pat dry with a
dish towel.
Use the lettuce leaves to
line four glass dishes. Spoon
in the salad and serve.
Serves 4

Piquant Fish Salad

2 onions
1½ lb cod fillets
1½ teaspoons salt
2 large dill pickles
4 tomatoes
3 tablespoon capers
¼ cup cottage cheese
5 tablespoons cream
6 tablespoons white wine vinegar
1 teaspoon sugar
½ teaspoon white pepper

Peel and halve the onions. Put in a dry saucepan and fry until browned. Remove from the heat and add the fish and 1 teaspoon salt. Pour over enough water to cover and bring to the boil. Simmer for about 20 minutes, until the fish is cooked. Drain the onions and fish. Slice the onions and flake the fish. Set aside to cool.
Thinly slice the pickles. Peel and quarter the tomatoes. Mix together the fish, onion, pickles, tomatoes and drained capers and place in a serving bowl. Chill for 30 minutes. Push the cottage cheese through a strainer until smooth. Add the cream, vinegar, sugar, pepper and remaining salt and stir well. Pour this dressing over the salad and serve.
Serves 4

Radish Salad

1 lb radishes
1 tablespoon salt
3 tablespoons wine vinegar
¼ cup oil
3 tablespoons chopped parsley
3 tablespoons capers
8 oz Edam cheese

Clean the radishes, then slice very thinly. Put in a bowl and sprinkle with the salt. Cover and leave for 10 minutes, then pour off all the liquid from the bowl. Rinse and pat dry with paper towels.
Mix together the vinegar, oil, parsley and capers. Add the radishes and toss well together. Cut the cheese into thin strips and stir into the salad. Chill for 20 minutes before serving with Melba toast.
Serves 4

Cook's Tip
To make Melba toast, put thin slices of white bread on a lightly oiled baking sheet. Bake in a moderate oven (350° F) for 5 minutes or until crisp. Alternatively, toast thicker slices under the broiler, slice in half to make thin slices and toast the untoasted sides.

Salad Julienne

1 head iceberg lettuce
1 green pepper
3 tomatoes
4 oz Emmenthal cheese
8 oz luncheon meat or
   cooked ham
3 tablespoons chopped
   mixed herbs (parsley,
   chives, basil, chervil, etc.)
$\frac{1}{4}$ cup oil
6 tablespoons apple juice
$\frac{1}{2}$ teaspoon salt
$\frac{1}{4}$ teaspoon pepper
generous pinch sugar

Separate the lettuce into
leaves and wash thoroughly
under cold running water.
Shake off excess water, then
pat dry with a dish towel.
Tear the leaves into small
pieces. Remove the core,
pith and seeds from the
pepper and chop. Cut the
tomatoes into eighths. Cut
the cheese and luncheon
meat or ham into julienne
strips.
Put the lettuce, green
pepper, tomatoes, cheese
and meat into a bowl. Mix
together the herbs, oil,
apple juice, salt, pepper and
sugar and pour over the
salad. Toss together well,
then spoon into four
individual glass dishes.
Serve immediately.
Serves 4

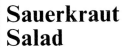

Sauerkraut Salad

1½ cups sauerkraut
2 tart dessert apples
1 small onion
¾ cup diced sweet dill pickles
5 tablespoons chopped mixed
  herbs (dill, parsley, basil,
  borage)
1 teaspoon salt
2 tablespoons sugar
3 tablespoons lemon juice
½ cup oil

Drain the sauerkraut and
rinse well in hot water.
Drain again, pressing out
all the water. Peel, core and
dice the apples. Peel and
finely chop the onion.
Mix together the sauerkraut.
apples, pickles, onion and
herbs. Add the salt, sugar

and lemon juice and toss
together well.
Heat the oil in a pan and
pour carefully over the
salad, so that it mixes. Toss
again and leave to cool.
Serve chilled.
Serves 4

Variation
This salad is also delicious
made with white cabbage
instead of sauerkraut. Cut
away the coarse outer
leaves, remove the core
and shred finely.

Riviera Onion Salad

4 onions
1 red pepper
1 green pepper
4 tomatoes
2 eggs
8 green olives, pitted
¼ cup wine vinegar
¼ cup oil
5 tablespoons hot water
½ teaspoon salt
¼ teaspoon garlic salt
2 teaspoons prepared
  mustard

Peel and thinly slice the
onions. Remove the cores,
pith and seeds from the
peppers and cut into thin
strips. Blanch the onion
slices and pepper strips in
boiling water for 3 minutes.

Drain well and leave to
cool.
Peel and slice the tomatoes.
Hard-cook the eggs. Cool,
then shell and quarter.
Halve the olives.
Arrange the onions and
peppers in a bowl. Add the
tomato slices and olive
halves, and lay the egg
quarters on top.
Mix together the vinegar,
oil, hot water, salt, garlic
salt and mustard. Pour over
the salad and chill for 20
minutes before serving.
Serves 4

Roquefort Dressing

*2 oz Roquefort or any other
   blue-veined cheese*
*grated rind and juice of
   2 lemons*
2 teaspoons sugar
*6 tablespoons cream
   or half-and-half*
¼ cup oil
6 tablespoons milk
6 tablespoons vinegar
¼ cup port or Madeira wine
6 tablespoons hot water
½ teaspoon cayenne pepper

Push the cheese through a
strainer until smooth, then
mix with the remaining
ingredients to form a
creamy dressing.
This dressing may be served
with vegetable salads as well
as chicken, game and pasta
salads.
Makes 1¼ cups dressing

Variation
A thicker Roquefort
Dressing may be made by
mashing 2 oz blue-veined
cheese with 1¼ cups mayonnaise. Add salt, pepper and
lemon juice to taste.

Italian Dressing

¾ cup wine vinegar
⅔ cup red wine
1 clove garlic
1 teaspoon salt
2 teaspoons capers
1 tablespoon mustard seed
2 green or red peppers
*2 teaspoons prepared
   mustard*
1 teaspoon black pepper
1 teaspoon dried rosemary
1 teaspoon dried oregano
½ cup oil

Mix the vinegar and red
wine together, and leave for
1 hour. Finely chop the
garlic, then pound in a
mortar with a pestle. Add
the salt, capers and mustard
seed and pound to a paste.

Remove the cores, pith and
seeds from the peppers and
cut into very thin slivers.
Put the vinegar mixture and
garlic paste in a saucepan.
Bring to the boil, stirring,
then add the mustard,
pepper, pepper slivers,
rosemary and oregano.
Remove from the heat,
stir in the oil and allow to
cool.
This dressing is delicious
with vegetable salads, such
as asparagus, cauliflower,
mushroom, pepper and
artichoke, as well as with
fish and cooked meat salads.
Makes 2 cups dressing

Sauces and Dressings

Thousand Island Dressing

⅔ cup mayonnaise
3 tablespoons tomato
   ketchup
5 tablespoons hot water
1 teaspoon paprika pepper
⅔ cup sour cream
3 tablespoons vinegar
2 teaspoons sugar
1 tablespoon grated fresh
   horseradish root

Beat together the mayonnaise, ketchup and hot water until frothy. Gradually beat in the paprika, sour cream, vinegar, sugar and horseradish.
The dressing should be light and airy and used at once. If it is left to stand before serving, it should be beaten again. Serve with chicory, endive, asparagus and beet salads, as well as with those containing lobster, herring, chicken or turkey, anchovy, cooked veal or eggs.
Makes 2 cups dressing

Variation
If you like, add finely chopped canned pimiento, capers and hard-cooked eggs.

Vinaigrette Sauce

2 eggs
1 egg yolk
2 teaspoons prepared
   mustard
½ teaspoon white pepper
½ teaspoon salt
½ teaspoon celery salt
pinch garlic powder
⅔ cup hot water
1 onion
2 teaspoons capers
¼ cup red wine
¼ cup wine vinegar
½ cup oil

Hard-cook the eggs. Cool, then shell. Separate the yolks from the whites. Mash the yolks with the uncooked egg yolk until creamy. Stir in the mustard, pepper, salt, celery salt and garlic powder. Gradually stir in the hot water and continue stirring until smooth. Peel and finely chop the onion. Add to the sauce with the capers, wine, vinegar and oil. Beat well or blend and leave to cool. Finely chop the hard-cooked egg whites and add to the sauce just before serving. Try vinaigrette sauce with salads such as potato, mixed vegetable, celery, asparagus, artichoke, shrimp, herring, sausage and roast beef.
Makes 2 cups sauce

Spicy Tomato Dressing

6 tablespoons tarragon
    vinegar
1 teaspoon prepared English
    mustard
½ teaspoon salt
½ teaspoon garlic salt
6 tablespoons olive oil
1½ tablespoons tomato
    ketchup
½ teaspoon Tabasco sauce
¼ cup mango chutney

Put all the ingredients in a
blender and blend until
smooth. Taste and add
more Tabasco sauce if you
prefer a hotter, spicier
dressing. Chill for 20
minutes.
Serve with meat salads, such
as beef, sausage, game and
ham, and potato, Chinese
cabbage, herring and pasta
salads.
Makes 1 cup dressing

Cook's Tip
If you don't have an
electric blender sub-
stitute a smooth
chutney such as
peach or apricot for
the mango, place all
the ingredients in a
large screwtop jar
and shake until
blended.

Ravigote Sauce

4 egg yolks
1 teaspoon prepared mustard
1 teaspoon grated fresh
    horseradish root
½ teaspoon salt
½ teaspoon celery salt
½ teaspoon garlic salt
pinch cayenne pepper
2 teaspoons paprika pepper
6 tablespoons apple juice
6 tablespoons wine vinegar
1 teaspoon sugar
⅔ cup olive oil
3 tablespoons capers
3 tablespoons chopped chervil
3 tablespoons chopped chives
1 teaspoon anchovy paste

Mix the egg yolks with the
mustard, horseradish, salt,
celery salt, garlic salt,
cayenne, paprika, apple
juice, vinegar and sugar.
Gradually beat in the oil.
When all the oil has been
incorporated, stir in the
capers, herbs and anchovy
paste.
Serve this sauce with
herring, shrimp, mixed
vegetable, celery, asparagus,
sausage and egg salads.
Makes 1¼ cups sauce

Sauces and Dressings

Russian Sauce

2 egg yolks
juice of 1 lemon
½ teaspoon salt
½ teaspoon dry mustard
⅔ cup olive oil
1½ teaspoons paprika pepper
pinch cayenne pepper
1 teaspoon sugar
½ red pepper
½ green pepper
1 egg, hard-cooked
2 sweet dill pickles
3–4 tablespoons chopped cooked beet

Mix the egg yolks with the lemon juice, salt and mustard. Add the oil, drop by drop, stirring all the time. When half the oil has been added, the remainder may be stirred in more quickly. When all the oil is incorporated, stir in the paprika, cayenne and sugar.
Remove the cores, seeds and pith from the peppers and chop finely. Shell and finely chop the hard-cooked egg. Finely chop the pickles. Add the peppers, egg, pickles and beet to the sauce and stir well. Chill before serving with herring, smoked fish, sausage, cooked meat, chicken and rice salads and fried liver.
Makes ⅔ cup sauce

Escoffier Sauce

⅔ cup mayonnaise
3 tablespoons hot water
grated rind of ½ lemon
juice of 1 lemon
juice of 1 orange
2 teaspoons sugar
4 drops Tabasco sauce
2 teaspoons paprika pepper
3 tablespoons chopped chives

Beat the mayonnaise with the hot water, lemon rind and juice, orange juice, sugar, Tabasco and paprika. Add the chives to the sauce and stir well. Serve chilled with salads, such as pepper, cooked meat, sausage, fish and pasta.
Makes 1¼ cups sauce

Note This sauce may be stored in a covered container in the refrigerator for 3–4 days.

Cook's Tip
This goes especially well with a cold meat and fruit salad. Try chicken with peaches or ham with pineapple, served with the sauce and accompanied by a rice salad.

Caesar Salad Sauce

6 tablespoons oil
5 tablespoons wine vinegar
3 tablespoons red wine
generous pinch garlic salt
1 teaspoon sugar
¼ teaspoon black pepper
1 teaspoon prepared mustard
1 clove garlic
2 slices bread
1 bacon slice

Mix the oil with the vinegar, wine, garlic salt, sugar, pepper and mustard until smooth. Thinly slice the garlic. Cut the bread into cubes.
Finely dice the bacon.
Put in a frying pan and heat until the fat runs. Add the garlic and bread cubes and fry for 5–7 minutes or until the bread cubes are lightly browned on all sides. Remove from the heat and drain the mixture on paper towels.
Mix the salad with the dressing and garnish with the bacon and bread cubes. Suitable salads are lettuce and pepper (Caesar Salad), onion, fennel, fish, potato and beef.
Makes ⅔ cup sauce

Horseradish Cream Sauce

¼ cup whipping cream
⅔ cup mayonnaise
grated rind of 1 lemon
¼ cup grated fresh
   horseradish root
pinch cayenne pepper
¼ cup wine vinegar
2 teaspoons sugar
2 teaspoons anchovy paste
¼ bunch garden cress
   (optional)
3 tablespoons chopped
   parsley

Whip the cream until it is stiff. Stir in the mayonnaise, lemon rind, horseradish, cayenne, vinegar, sugar and anchovy paste.
Wash the cress, then chop finely. Mix into the sauce with the parsley. Serve this sauce chilled with any of these salads: vegetable, potato, mushroom, tomato and cucumber, fish, hard-cooked egg and scallion and cold cooked meat.
Makes 1¼ cups sauce

Cook's Tip
This is an excellent sauce to use for a fondue party or as a dip for a selection of sliced raw vegetables.

Sweet and Sour Dressing

2 onions
¼ cup brown sugar
1¼ cups unsweetened
* pineapple juice*
3 drops Tabasco sauce
½ teaspoon freshly ground
* black pepper*
3–4 tablespoons pineapple
* jam*
⅔ cup vinegar

Peel and finely chop the onions. Put the sugar and pineapple juice in a saucepan and heat, stirring to dissolve the sugar. Add the onion and bring to the boil. Simmer until the onion is tender.
Stir in the Tabasco, pepper, jam and vinegar. Continue

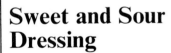

simmering for 10–15 minutes to reduce the sauce and thicken. Allow to cool, then chill and serve with salads such as chicken or turkey, pasta, celery, Belgian endive, fruit, cooked meat and avocado.
Makes 1¼ cups dressing

Variation
For a slightly different flavor, without destroying the balance of sweet and sour, substitute apricot nectar for the pineapple juice and apricot jam for the pineapple jam.

Herb Cream Dressing

3 tablespoons chopped chervil
3 tablespoons chopped
* tarragon*
1 tablespoon chopped parsley
¼ teaspoon salt
½ teaspoon celery salt
1 egg
3 tablespoons cottage cheese
5 tablespoons oil
1 teaspoon prepared mustard
½ cup vinegar
3 tablespoons mayonnaise
5 tablespoons cream

Put the chervil, tarragon, parsley, salt and celery salt in a mortar and pound with a pestle until well mixed to a paste. Hard-cook the egg. Cool, then shell and separate the white from the

yolk. Add the yolk to the herb paste and mix well. Rub the cottage cheese through a strainer until smooth. Beat into it the oil, mustard, vinegar, mayonnaise, cream and herb mixture. Finely chop the egg white and stir into the dressing. Chill well.
Pour this dressing over cold cooked meat and sausages, hard-cooked eggs and cold vegetables such as cauliflower, asparagus, tomatoes and artichokes.
Makes 1¼ cups dressing

Variation
Stir in 1–2 tablespoons of tomato ketchup.

Potato Salad Dressing

2 onions
1¼ cups water
2–3 teaspoons prepared mustard
½ cup cider vinegar
1¼ teaspoons sugar
1 teaspoon salt
1 teaspoon celery salt
½ teaspoon black pepper
½ cup oil
1 tablespoon chopped parsley

Peel and finely chop the onions. Bring the water to the boil in a saucepan. Add the onion, mustard, vinegar, sugar, salt, celery salt and pepper. Simmer for 1 minute, then remove from the heat. Stir in the oil and parsley.

Dress cooked sliced potatoes while they and the dressing are still warm, then allow to cool. Serve at room temperature. This dressing can also be used for celery, tomato, green bean, beet, sausage and fish salads.
Makes 2 cups dressing

Cook's Tip

Tiny new potatoes are ideal for a potato salad. Cook in their skins for maximum flavor, and toss in the dressing while still warm.

Cocktail Sauce

⅔ cup whipping cream
¼ cup milk
¼ cup mayonnaise
¼ cup tomato ketchup
½ teaspoon Tabasco sauce
1 tablespoon confectioners' sugar
1½ tablespoons vinegar
pinch cinnamon
pinch garlic salt
½ teaspoon hot curry powder
¼ cup oil

Whip the cream until thick but not stiff. Add the milk, mayonnaise and ketchup and continue beating for 2 minutes. Stir in the Tabasco sauce, confectioners' sugar, vinegar, cinnamon, garlic salt and curry powder. The sauce should be light pink in color. Finally add the oil and serve at once.
This sauce will enhance many appetizers, such as shellfish cocktail, mushroom salad and oysters.
Makes 2 cups sauce

Variations
This sauce may also be flavored with Worcestershire sauce instead of the Tabasco, and sharpened with lemon juice instead of the vinegar.

Indian Curry Sauce

1 large cooking apple
1 onion
½ cup buttermilk
¼ cup milk
¼ cup mild curry
  powder
1 tablespoon sugar
3 tablespoons white wine
¼ cup oil
2 tablespoons vinegar
2 tablespoons mayonnaise
2 tablespoons hot water
3 tablespoons chopped
  chives

Peel and core the apple, then slice. Peel and finely chop the onion. Put the apple, onion, buttermilk, milk, curry powder, sugar and white wine in a sauce-pan. Bring to the boil and simmer for 15 minutes. By this time, the apple should be a purée. Remove from the heat.

Beat in the oil, vinegar, mayonnaise, then the hot water. Allow to cool, then add the chives.

This sauce can be served with fish salads, chicken or turkey salad, shellfish appetizers, and pasta salad.

Makes 1¼ cups sauce

Sour Cream Mayonnaise Dressing

⅔ cup mayonnaise
⅔ cup hot water
⅔ cup sour cream
¼ cup wine vinegar or lemon
  juice
1 tablespoon sugar
2 teaspoons paprika pepper

Beat the mayonnaise with the hot water, then beat in the sour cream until the mixture becomes creamy. Add the vinegar or lemon juice, sugar and paprika and continue beating for a further 2 minutes.

Serve chilled with lettuce and Belgian endive salad, fish salad, egg salad, smoked salmon and mushroom salad.

Makes 2 cups dressing

Cook's Tip

To introduce a flavor of herbs, try using a herb-flavored vinegar instead of the wine vinegar. Mint and tarragon have an aromatic flavor, but almost any herb such as sage, marjoram, basil or thyme can be used.

229

Sauerkraut and Sausage Hot Pot

4 bacon slices
1¾ cups sauerkraut
1 sugar cube
1 onion, thinly sliced
8 oz salami, sliced
⅔ cup sour cream
2 teaspoons paprika pepper
1 teaspoon cornstarch
1 teaspoon salt

Dice the bacon. Drain the sauerkraut. Put the sauerkraut in a saucepan, cover with water and bring to the boil. Simmer for 20 minutes, then drain well.
Put the bacon in another saucepan and heat until the fat runs. Add the sugar cube and, when it has dissolved, add the onion. Fry for 6–8 minutes, until the onion turns golden brown. Stir in the sauerkraut and salami slices and cook for 5 minutes.
Mix together the sour cream, paprika, cornstarch and salt. Add to the saucepan and bring to the boil, stirring well. Simmer until slightly thickened, then serve hot with Spicy Texas Beans (see page 214).
Serves 2

Tomato-Flavored Liver

1 lb tomatoes
1 lb calf or lamb liver
1 small onion
1½ lb potatoes
3 tablespoons butter
milk
salt and black pepper
3 tablespoons all-purpose flour
1 tablespoon paprika pepper
¼ cup plain yogurt

Peel and slice the tomatoes. Cut the liver into bite-sized pieces. Peel and finely chop the onion. Cook the potatoes in boiling salted water for 15–20 minutes. Drain, then mash with a little butter, milk and seasoning to taste, to make a smooth thick purée. Keep hot.
Coat the liver pieces with the flour. Melt the remaining butter in a frying pan. Add the onion and fry for 5 minutes. Add the liver pieces and brown quickly on all sides. Stir in the tomato slices, paprika, and salt and pepper to taste. Cover and cook for 5–7 minutes.
Meanwhile, spoon or pipe the potato around the edge of a warmed serving dish. Stir the yogurt into the liver mixture and heat through for 1 minute, then pile in the center of the potato ring. Serve immediately, accompanied by peas.
Serves 3–4

Shredded Potato Cake

4 large potatoes
½ teaspoon salt
½ teaspoon white pepper
1 teaspoon all-purpose flour
4 bacon slices
2 egg whites
4 oz German sausage
  (Mettwurst, blutwurst),
  sliced
4 cheese slices

Peel the potatoes and cook in boiling salted water for 8–10 minutes. Drain well and grate. Mix with the salt, pepper and flour. Dice the bacon. Beat the egg whites until they are stiff but not dry and fold into the potato mixture. Put the bacon in a frying pan and heat until the fat runs. Place the potato mixture in the pan and spread out over the bottom. Arrange the sausage slices on top. Cook for 15–20 minutes. Place the cheese on top, cover the pan and cook for a further 2–3 minutes, until the cheese has melted. Serve hot with a sauerkraut and caraway salad.
Serves 2

Chicken and Sausage Ragoût

1 lb chicken breasts
1 large dill pickle
¼ cup butter
2 teaspoons paprika pepper
½ teaspoon salt
½ teaspoon white pepper
⅔ cup stock
⅔ cup white wine
8 oz salami, sliced
5 tablespoons cream

Cut the chicken into bite-sized pieces. Slice the pickle. Melt the butter in a saucepan and add the pieces of chicken, paprika, salt, pepper, stock and wine. Bring to the boil and simmer for 25–30 minutes, until the chicken is tender. Add the salami slices, pickle and cream and heat through gently for 5 minutes. Serve hot.
Serves 3–4

Cook's Tip
The flavor of this dish can be varied according to the type of salami used. Choose from salami made with herbs or garlic or with the minimum of seasonings.

Tortellini with Chicken Livers

12 oz chicken livers
½ onion
12 oz tomatoes
1 lb tortellini
¼ cup olive oil
½ teaspoon salt
½ teaspoon white pepper
½ teaspoon celery salt
2 tablespoons butter
½ cup grated Parmesan cheese

Remove any membrane or gristle from the livers and cut the meat into bite-sized pieces. Peel and finely chop the onion. Peel and chop the tomatoes.
Cook the tortellini in boiling salted water for 12–15 minutes, until just tender to the bite. Meanwhile, heat the oil in a frying pan. Add the onion and liver and fry for 3 minutes. Stir in the salt, pepper, celery salt and tomatoes and continue cooking for 4–5 minutes. Drain the tortellini and add the butter. Toss well to coat the pasta with the butter, then arrange on four warmed serving plates. Top each with a serving of the liver sauce and sprinkle over the Parmesan cheese.
Serves 4

Meat Pizzas

1 stale roll
¼ cup warm water
2 onions
1 lb ground beef
1 egg
salt and pepper
¼ teaspoon cayenne pepper
1–2 tablespoons chili sauce
¼ cup oil
2 eggs, hard-cooked
2 tomatoes
12 stuffed green olives
4 slices cheese
8 anchovy fillets

Soften the roll in the warm water, then squeeze out the water and crumble the roll into small pieces. Peel and finely chop the onions. Mix together the bread, onion, beef, egg, salt and pepper, cayenne and chili sauce. Divide into four portions and form each into a patty. Fry the patties in the oil for 3–4 minutes on each side, until crisp. Transfer to a baking sheet.
Shell and slice the eggs. Slice the tomatoes and olives. Cut the cheese into thin strips. Top each meat patty with egg, tomato and olive slices, anchovy fillets and finally strips of cheese. Bake in a moderately hot oven (400°F) for 5–7 minutes, until the cheese begins to melt.
Serve hot.
Serves 4

Spaghettini with Garlic

1 lb spaghettini (thin spaghetti)
3 cloves garlic
6 tablespoons olive oil
1 teaspoon salt
3 tablespoons chopped parsley
1 teaspoon black pepper

Cook the spaghettini in boiling salted water for 10–12 minutes, until just tender to the bite. Meanwhile, finely chop the garlic.
When the spaghettini is cooked, drain well. Put in a warmed serving dish and keep hot. Heat the oil in a pan and add the garlic. Fry until golden brown.

Stir in the salt, then pour over the spaghettini. Toss well so all the strands are coated, then sprinkle over the parsley and pepper. Serve immediately.
Serves 4

Cook's Tip
The long strands of spaghettini should not be broken up when added to the pan. Hold the spaghettini at one end and lower the strands into the boiling water. As they soften and curl around in the water, carefully push the rest of the strands down.

Caper Steaks

2 minute steaks (6 oz each)
2 tablespoons butter
5 tablespoons sour cream
3 tablespoons prepared mustard
3 tablespoons chopped capers
2 teaspoons finely chopped mixed herbs (parsley, chives)
½ teaspoon salt
½ teaspoon black pepper
Garnish
parsley sprigs

Pound the meat with a mallet to tenderize it. Melt the butter in a frying pan. Add the steaks and brown quickly on both sides. Remove from the pan. Add the sour cream,

mustard, capers, herbs and salt and pepper to the fat in the pan. Stir well and bring this sauce to the boil. Replace the steaks in the pan and spoon the sauce over. Cook for 5–7 minutes longer (for rare steaks) or until the meat is cooked as you like it.
Transfer the steaks to a warmed serving dish and cover with the sauce. Garnish with the parsley and serve hot with mixed vegetables and boiled potatoes.
Serves 2

Veal Scallop Open Sandwiches

2 tablespoons butter
4 slices white bread
1 head lettuce
4 small veal scallops
  (4 oz each)
3 tablespoons all-purpose
  flour
$\frac{1}{4}$ cup oil
4 tomatoes
$\frac{1}{2}$ teaspoon celery salt
$\frac{1}{2}$ teaspoon garlic salt

Butter the slices of bread. Separate the lettuce into leaves, wash thoroughly, pat dry with a dish towel and shred. Pound the veal scallops with a mallet to flatten and tenderize them. Coat with the flour.
Fry the scallops in the oil for 2–3 minutes on each side or until lightly browned. Remove from the pan and keep warm.
Halve the tomatoes and place in the pan, cut sides down. Fry for 3 minutes, then turn over and sprinkle with the celery and garlic salts. Remove from the heat.
Place the bread on four individual dishes. Put a scallop on each slice, then add a layer of shredded lettuce. Top with two tomato halves and serve.
Serves 4

Tongue with Bacon Sauce

1 lb potatoes
2 tablespoons butter
1 teaspoon salt
1 teaspoon pepper
3–4 tablespoons milk
1 small onion
4 bacon slices
3 tablespoons all-purpose
  flour
$\frac{3}{4}$ cup stock
4 slices cooked tongue
3 tablespoons tomato paste

Peel the potatoes and cook in boiling salted water for 15–20 minutes, until tender. Drain and mash with half the butter, half the salt and pepper and enough milk to make a smooth thick purée. Keep warm.
Peel and finely chop the onion. Dice the bacon. Put the bacon in a pan and fry until the fat runs. Add the onion with the remaining butter and fry for 5 minutes. Sprinkle over the flour, then stir well. Gradually stir in the stock, bring to the boil and simmer, stirring all the time, until thick and smooth.
Add the tongue slices and tomato paste with the remaining salt and pepper and simmer gently for 5 minutes.
Arrange the puréed potato in a ring on a warmed serving dish. Spoon the tongue and sauce into the center and serve hot, accompanied by a tomato salad.
Serves 2

Sausage Stroganoff

8 oz German sausage,
 such as Bratwurst
1 small sweet dill pickle
1 small onion
½ cup button mushrooms
3 tablespoons oil
⅓ cup chopped pickled beet
3 tablespoons whipping
 cream
3 tablespoons brandy
1 teaspoon anchovy paste
1 teaspoon freshly ground
 black pepper
3 tablespoons sour cream

Cut the sausage into thin strips. Cut the pickle into strips. Peel and finely chop the onion. Clean and quarter the mushrooms. Heat the oil in a saucepan.

Add the onion, sausage and pickle and cook for 5 minutes. Stir in the mushrooms and beet, then add the cream, brandy, anchovy paste and pepper. Heat through gently for 2–3 minutes, stirring well. Top with sour cream and serve hot with brown bread.
Serves 2

Variation
If preferred, serve the stroganoff as a cold dish accompanied by a crisp green salad or cucumber salad.

Quick Meat, Pepper and Onion Stew

½ red pepper
1 onion
6 bacon slices
¾ cup ground beef
¾ cup ground pork
1 teaspoon black pepper
1 tablespoon celery salt
3 tablespoons brandy

Remove the core, pith and seeds from the pepper and dice. Peel and thinly slice the onion. Cut the bacon into thin strips. Put the bacon in a frying pan and heat until the fat runs. Add the onion and fry for 5 minutes, then stir in the remaining ingredients. Cook

for a further 8–10 minutes, stirring frequently, until the meat is well browned. Serve hot with a potato salad.
Serves 2

Cook's Tip
As a substitute for the potato salad, serve with hot baked potatoes split open and topped with a swirl of sour cream and crisp-fried crumbled bacon.

Vienna Steaks

½ green pepper
2 thick slices lean roast beef
(each about 5 oz)
1 teaspoon salt
½ teaspoon black pepper
1 tablespoon all-purpose
flour
3 tablespoons drippings
1 medium onion, sliced
½ teaspoon caraway seeds
2 teaspoons paprika pepper
1 tablespoon tomato paste
1 teaspoon dried marjoram
1¼ cups hot water
1 large potato, cooked and
sliced
1 dill pickle, sliced

Remove the core, pith and
seeds from the pepper and
cut into thin strips. Cut each
slice of meat into four. Mix
the salt, pepper and flour
and use to coat the meat.
Heat the drippings in a
frying pan. Fry the meat for
2 minutes on each side or
until well browned.
Remove. Add the onion
to the pan and fry until
lightly browned. Stir in the
pepper strips, caraway
seeds, paprika, tomato
paste, marjoram and water.
Bring to the boil and
simmer for 5 minutes.
Add the potato slices and
meat to the sauce and
continue cooking for 5
minutes. Garnish with the
pickle and serve hot with a
sauerkraut or coleslaw
salad.
Serves 2

Quick Supper Rice

1 onion
3 tablespoons oil
1 teaspoon salt
1 teaspoon paprika pepper
1 teaspoon pepper
½ cup diced cooked ham
½ cup diced luncheon meat or
other cooked meat
2 cups cooked long-grain rice
1 cup diced cheese
¼ cup chopped chives

Peel and finely chop the
onion. Heat the oil in a
frying pan and add the
onion. Fry for 5 minutes.
Stir in the salt, paprika and
pepper, then add the diced
ham and luncheon meat.
Fry for 1 minute. Add the
rice and mix thoroughly.

Continue to cook for 4–5
minutes to reheat the rice.
Add a spoonful or two of
water if the mixture is too
dry. Stir in the cheese and
cook for a further 1–2
minutes, until the cheese
begins to melt. Sprinkle
over the chives and serve
hot, with green beans.
Serves 2

Banana Beef Sandwiches

3 large tomatoes
1 banana
lemon juice
1 medium onion
¼ cup butter
8 oz ground beef, or half
  beef and half pork
1 tablespoon all-purpose
  flour
1 teaspoon salt
½ teaspoon pepper
4 rolls

Peel and halve 2 of the
tomatoes. Slice the third
tomato into four. Peel and
slice the banana. Sprinkle
the slices with lemon juice
to prevent them discoloring.
Peel and finely chop the
onion. Melt the butter in
a frying pan.
Add the onion and fry for 5
minutes. Add the ground
meat and peeled tomato
halves and fry until the
meat is well browned,
stirring to break up the
tomatoes. Sprinkle over the
flour, salt and pepper and
stir well. Cook for a further
1 minute.
Slice the tops off the rolls.
Scoop out some of the soft
center and fill with the meat
mixture. Garnish with the
tomato and banana slices
and serve hot with a tomato
cocktail.
Serves 2

Goulash in a Hurry

2 dill pickles
2 tablespoons butter
2 onions, chopped
¼ cup all-purpose flour
2½ cups stock
1 teaspoon each salt, pepper
  and paprika pepper
pinch sugar
1 tablespoon tomato paste
8 oz ground pork
beaten egg, to bind
1 cup diced cooked brisket
  of beef
1 cup diced luncheon meat
2 tomatoes, quartered

Chop the pickles. Melt the
butter in a saucepan. Add
the onions and cook for
5 minutes. Stir in half the
flour and cook for 1 minute,
then gradually stir in the
stock. Bring to the boil,
stirring, and simmer until
thickened. Add the salt,
pepper, paprika, sugar and
tomato paste and continue
to simmer for 5 minutes.
Meanwhile, mix the
remaining flour into the
pork and bind with a little
beaten egg. Form into
small balls. Drop into the
sauce and simmer for 8–10
minutes, until firm. Add the
meat cubes, pickles and
tomato quarters and cook
for 10 minutes to heat
through. Serve hot with
creamed potatoes.
Serves 4

Bavarian Apple Strudel

2½ cups all-purpose flour
½ teaspoon salt
1 tablespoon oil
1 egg
¾ cup lukewarm water
8–10 cooking apples
lemon juice
¼ cup butter, melted
1¼ cups sour cream
3 tablespoons raisins
½ cup sugar
about ⅔ cup milk
confectioners' sugar

Sift the flour and salt into a bowl. Stir in the mixed oil, egg and water. Knead to a dough and continue kneading for about 10 minutes. Cover, leave in a warm place for 30 minutes.

Peel and core the apples. Slice thinly and sprinkle with lemon juice.
Roll out the dough on a floured cloth then stretch it until very thin. Brush with the melted butter then with the sour cream.
Top with the apple slices, raisins and sugar.
Roll up the strudel, using the cloth to lift it. Cut into portions to fit one or two greased baking sheets.
Brush with milk and bake in a hot oven (450° F) for 40–45 minutes, until golden brown. Brush with milk three or four times during baking.
Sprinkle with confectioners' sugar.
Serves 6–8

Emperor's Omelet

½ cup raisins
8 eggs
¼ cup sugar
1¼ cups milk
2 cups all-purpose flour
½ teaspoon salt
6 tablespoons butter
½ cup confectioners' sugar

Cover the raisins with boiling water, then drain. Separate the egg yolks from the whites. Mix the yolks with the sugar, milk, flour and salt and beat until smooth. Beat the egg whites until stiff and fold into the mixture. Add the raisins, but do not stir in. Leave for 10 minutes. Melt a quarter of the butter

in a frying pan. Pour in a quarter of the mixture and cook gently for 2 minutes. Turn the omelet over, adding a little more butter to the pan, and cook for a further 2 minutes. Using two forks, separate the omelet into small pieces and allow to cook for another 30 seconds.
Turn the omelet pieces on to a warmed plate or dish and sprinkle with confectioners' sugar. Keep warm while you cook the remaining omelets in the same way, using the remaining butter. Serve warm with cream.
Serves 4

Jam Omelets

8 eggs
¼ teaspoon salt
6 tablespoons water
¼ cup raspberry jam
¼ cup brandy
½ cup chopped walnuts
3 tablespoons raisins
¼ cup butter
½ cup confectioners' sugar

Beat the eggs in a mixing bowl. Add the salt and water and beat until well mixed. Put the jam, brandy, walnuts and raisins in a saucepan and warm gently over low heat.
Meanwhile, melt a quarter of the butter in an omelet pan. Add a quarter of the egg mixture and cook, lifting the edges of the omelet to allow the liquid egg mixture to run on to the pan. When the omelet is set, slide it on to a warmed plate. Keep warm while you cook the remaining omelets in the same way.
Spread the omelets with the jam mixture. Roll them up and serve hot, sprinkled with confectioners' sugar.
Serves 4

Variation
Try black cherry jam with cherry brandy. Serve hot with thick cream.

Rice Pudding

2½ cups water
1 cup round-grain rice
½ teaspoon salt
⅔ cup raisins
2 cups milk
¼ cup sugar
1 teaspoon grated lemon rind
4 egg yolks
1¼ cups cream
¼ cup butter

Bring the water to the boil and add the rice and salt. Simmer for 10 minutes. Meanwhile, cover the raisins with boiling water and leave for 5 minutes. Drain the rice and raisins. Add the raisins to the rice with the milk, sugar and lemon rind. Pour into a greased baking dish. Mix together the egg yolks and cream and pour over the rice mixture. Cut the butter into small pieces and dot over the top.
Bake in a moderate oven (350° F) for 30 minutes or until the rice is tender and the mixture is creamy. A golden brown crust should have formed on top.
Serves 4

Cook's Tip
Serve with poached fruit, rhubarb, gooseberries or apricots.

239

Cherry Pudding

½ cup sugar
2 cups milk
12 slices bread, crusts
    removed
1 (15-oz) can pitted black
    cherries, drained
4 eggs, separated
juice and grated rind of
    1 lemon
few drops vanilla extract
1 cup whipping cream
¼ cup confectioners' sugar

Dissolve a quarter of the
sugar in half the milk. Dip
the bread slices in the milk
mixture so they are
saturated, but not soggy
and falling apart. Grease a
baking dish and sprinkle
with another quarter of the
sugar. Arrange half the
bread slices in the dish and
cover with the cherries,
reserving a few for decoration. Cover with the
remaining bread.
Mix the egg yolks with the
remaining milk, lemon
juice and rind, vanilla
extract, remaining sugar
and the cream.
Beat the egg whites until
stiff, then fold into the yolk
mixture. Spoon over the
baking dish. Bake in a
moderate oven (350° F) for
30–35 minutes. Do not let
the top become too brown.
Sprinkle with the con-
fectioners' sugar and
decorate with the reserved
cherries.
Serves 4–6

Pear Sponge Pudding

1 (14½-oz) can pears
1 cinnamon stick
½ cup butter
½ cup sugar
4 eggs
2¼ cups all-purpose flour
½ cup cornstarch
1 teaspoon baking powder
pinch salt
grated rind of 1 lemon
a little milk
confectioners' sugar

Drain the pears, reserving
the juice. Put the juice in a
saucepan with the cinnamon
stick. Bring to the boil and
simmer for 10 minutes.
Remove the cinnamon stick
and leave the juice to cool.
Cream the butter with the
sugar until light and fluffy.
Beat in the eggs, adding a
tablespoon of flour with
each. Sift the remaining
flour with the cornstarch,
baking powder and salt and
fold in. Stir in the lemon
rind and enough milk to
give the batter a consistency that will just drop
from the spoon.
Put the pears in a greased
baking dish. Spoon over the
batter and smooth the top.
Bake in a moderate oven
(350° F) for 40 minutes or
until the top is lightly
browned. Sprinkle with
confectioners' sugar and
serve warm with the cinna-
mon-flavored juice.
Serves 4–5

Frankfurt Pudding

2 lb cooking apples
juice of 1 lemon
½ cup sugar
1 teaspoon cinnamon
10–12 slices stale bread
2½ cups apple wine or juice
3 tablespoons raisins
confectioners' sugar

Peel and core the apples and cut into slices. Sprinkle with lemon juice to prevent discoloration, then sprinkle with the sugar and cinnamon.
Toast the bread slices in a moderate oven (350° F) for 10–12 minutes, until they are lightly browned and very dry. Rub through a coarse strainer or grind in a blender. Add enough apple wine to the crumbs to moisten them thoroughly. Put half the bread mixture in a greased baking dish. Spoon over the apple slices and sprinkle with the raisins. Cover with the remaining bread mixture. Bake in a moderately hot oven (375° F) for 45 minutes. Sprinkle with confectioners' sugar and serve warm with cream.
Serves 4

Spanish Apple Slices

2 cups all-purpose flour
½ cup butter
⅓ cup sugar
1 egg
few drops vanilla extract
2 lb cooking apples
1 tablespoon dried pepper-
mint leaves
2 teaspoons cinnamon
pinch ground cardamom
½ cup raisins
1 egg yolk, beaten

Sift the flour on to a working surface and make a well in the center. Add the butter in small pieces with the sugar, egg and vanilla extract. Mix well together with one hand to form a soft pastry dough. Chill for 20 minutes.
Peel, core and thinly slice the apples. Mix with the peppermint, cinnamon, cardamom and raisins. Set aside one-third of the pastry. Roll out the remainder on a floured surface and use to line a well-greased 8-inch square cake pan. Fill with the apple mixture. Roll out the remaining pastry to cover. Press the edges together to seal and prick all over. Brush with the egg yolk.
Bake in a hot oven (425° F) for 45 minutes, until golden. Cool slightly, then remove carefully from the pan. Serve warm.
Serves 4–6

Cherry and Cottage Cheese Cake

3 eggs
6 tablespoons butter
½ cup sugar
⅔ cup semolina
1¾ cups cottage cheese
1 teaspoon baking powder
1 tablespoon rum
grated rind of 1 lemon
1 (15-oz) can pitted cherries
2 cups whipping cream

Separate the egg yolks from the whites. Cream the butter with the sugar until light and fluffy. Beat in the egg yolks and then the semolina. Push the cottage cheese through a strainer until smooth and add to the creamed mixture with the baking powder, rum and lemon rind.

Drain the cherries, reserving the can juice. Stir the cherries into the cottage cheese mixture. Beat the egg whites until stiff, then fold into the mixture. Spoon into a greased baking dish and bake in a moderately hot oven (400° F) for 40 minutes. Whip the cream with 4–5 tablespoons of the reserved cherry juice until stiff. Allow the cherry cake to cool very slightly before serving, topped with the cream.
Serves 6

Cheese Rolls with Cherry Compote

4 soft rolls
½ cup milk, warmed
1 cup cottage cheese
⅔ cup currants
1 tablespoon sugar
few drops vanilla extract
pinch salt
1 (1-lb) can pitted cherries
1 tablespoon cornstarch
1 tablespoon water
⅔ cup cherry brandy

Slice the tops off the rolls to make lids and scoop out the insides. Turn over in the warmed milk so they become saturated not soggy. Strain the cottage cheese until smooth, then mix with the currants, sugar, vanilla extract and salt. Fill the rolls with this mixture and replace the lids. Put on a baking sheet and bake in a moderately hot oven (400° F) for 10–15 minutes, until golden brown.

Meanwhile, drain the juice from the cherries and warm it. Dissolve the cornstarch in the water and add to the cherry juice. Bring to the boil and simmer until clear and thickened. Stir in the cherries and cherry brandy and heat through for 5 minutes.

Serve the cheese rolls and cherry compote hot or cold.
Serves 4

Crêpes with Nut Sauce

1 cup all-purpose flour
pinch salt
1 teaspoon sugar
1 egg
1¼ cups milk
3 tablespoons oil
1½ cups ground hazelnuts
1¼ cups whipping cream
½ cup confectioners' sugar

Sift the flour, salt and sugar into a bowl. Make a well and add the egg and half the milk. Beat until smooth, then gradually beat in the remaining milk and 1 teaspoon oil. Set aside. Mix together half the hazelnuts, 5 tablespoons cream and half the confectioners' sugar. This

filling should be thick. Heat a little of the remaining oil in a 10-inch crêpe pan. Spoon in a quarter of the batter and tip to cover the pan. Cook for 1 minute, then turn over and cook for about 30 seconds. Slide out of the pan and keep hot while you cook the remaining three crepes in the same way.
Spread the crêpes with the hazelnut filling and roll up. Arrange on a warmed serving dish. Gently heat the remaining hazelnuts, cream and confectioners' sugar in a saucepan, and pour over the crêpes.
Serves 2–4

Steam-Baked Apples

4 large apples
5 tablespoons raisins
¼ cup sugar
3 tablespoons butter
1 tablespoon ground almonds
  or walnuts
2 tablespoons brandy
2 tablespoons cherry brandy
4 slices bread
4 eggs
2 cups milk
1 orange, sliced

Slice the tops off the apples to form lids. Scoop out the cores, making a hole about 1 inch wide.
Finely chop the raisins, then mix with the sugar, butter, nuts and brandies. Fill the apples with this and chill

for 10 minutes. Meanwhile, soak a clay cooking pot (schlemmertopf or chicken brick) in water for 10 minutes. Remove and pat dry the inside of the bottom section. Arrange the bread slices on the bottom and pour on the beaten eggs and milk. Place the stuffed apples on top. Lay an orange slice on each apple. Top with the apple lids. Put the lid on the pot and place in a cold oven. Turn the oven to very hot (475° F) and bake for 40 minutes. Serve hot.
Serves 4

Surprise Grapefruit

12 oz blackberries (fresh, frozen or canned)
4 small grapefruit
½ cup confectioners' sugar
3 tablespoons blackberry liqueur or brandy
⅔ cup whipping cream
5 tablespoons sugar
1 egg white
2 tablespoons chopped hazelnuts

If using frozen blackberries, thaw them. Drain canned berries. Cut a slice from the top of each grapefruit and scoop out the flesh. Remove the core, pith and seeds. Chop the flesh and mix with the blackberries. Stir in the confectioners' sugar and liqueur or brandy. Fill the grapefruit with the mixture. Chill for 20 minutes. Meanwhile, whip the cream with half the sugar until it is thick. Beat the egg white until stiff, then fold into the cream. Pile on top of the stuffed grapefruit.
Melt the remaining sugar in a saucepan. Add the hazelnuts and stir well. Sprinkle over the cream topping. Allow to cool slightly before serving.
Serves 4

Cook's Tip
A stiffly beaten egg white folded into whipped cream will make the cream go further. Sweeten to taste with sugar and vanilla extract.

Special Fruit Desserts

Strawberries in Wine

1 lb fresh strawberries
½ cup confectioners' sugar
juice of 1 large lemon
½ cup Marsala
1¼ cups cream

Wash the strawberries carefully and hull, then pat dry with paper towels.
Cut into halves or quarters, depending on size. Arrange in four individual glass dishes and sprinkle with the confectioners' sugar and lemon juice. Leave for 20 minutes.
Pour over the Marsala and chill for 30 minutes before serving, topped with the cream.
Serves 4

Variation
Honeydew Melons in Wine
Halve two small honeydew melons and scoop out the seeds. Peel the melons and cut the flesh into cubes or balls. Put the melon into four glass serving dishes.
Mix together ½ cup Marsala and 3 tablespoons clear honey and pour over the melon. Chill for 30 minutes, then serve with whipped cream flavored with a pinch of ground ginger.

Puff-Topped Apples

2 apples
2 tablespoons currants
2 tablespoons clear honey
2 tablespoons chopped
  walnuts
¼ cup butter
2 eggs
1 teaspoon cornstarch
2 tablespoons confectioners'
  sugar
1 tablespoon chopped
  candied orange peel

Peel the apples. Halve horizontally and remove the cores. Mix together the currants, honey, walnuts and half the butter. Fill the hollows in the apples with this mixture.
Separate the egg yolks from the whites. Beat the yolks with the cornstarch and confectioners' sugar. Beat the whites until stiff, then fold into the yolk mixture. Sprinkle the candied orange peel over the apple halves, then cover each with the egg mixture, piling it up.
Melt the remaining butter in a frying pan. Put the apple halves in the pan, apple sides down, and fry for 3 minutes, then cover the pan and cook for a further 2 minutes. Serve hot.
Serves 2–4

Variation
Fill each apple half with a generous spoonful of mincemeat instead of the honey mixture.

245

Special Fruit Desserts

Cherry and Pear Salad

*1 (15-oz) can pitted black
  cherries or 1 lb fresh
  cherries*
2 juicy pears
juice of 1 lemon
5 tablespoons sugar
3 tablespoons brandy
*3 tablespoons cherry liqueur
  (optional)*
*4 large or 16 small
  macaroons*

If using fresh cherries, remove pits. Drain the canned cherries, reserving the can juice. (This may be used to replace the 3 tablespoons of cherry liqueur.) Peel and quarter the pears, then remove the cores. Slice the pears and mix with the cherries. Stir in the lemon juice, sugar, brandy and cherry liqueur or can juice.
Break the macaroons into small pieces and add to the fruit mixture. Toss together well and spoon into four individual glass dishes. Serve chilled.
Serves 4

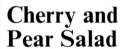

Cook's Tip
Grate the rind of a lemon before squeezing the juice. Keep in the refrigerator and use to flavor cakes and desserts.

Peach Flames

*1 (14½-oz) can peach slices
  or 4 large fresh peaches*
4 large plain cookies
¼ cup brandy
2 egg whites
⅔ cup confectioners' sugar

Drain the canned peaches. If using fresh peaches, scald them in boiling water, then remove the skins. Halve and pit, then cut into slices.
Put a cookie in each of four greased individual baking dishes. Sprinkle the cookies with the brandy and cover with the peach slices. Beat the egg whites until very stiff then fold in the confectioners' sugar. Pipe the meringue on to the peaches to form a peak. Bake in a hot oven (450° F) for 2–3 minutes, until the meringue is lightly browned and firm. Serve hot or warm.
Serves 4

Variation
Use canned peach halves or peeled, pitted fresh peach halves. Arrange the peach halves in a baking dish, cut sides uppermost, and fill the hollows in the peaches with chocolate ice cream or cranberry sauce. (Mix a little brandy with the cranberry sauce, if you like.) Top with the meringue and bake as above.

Apple Salad

3 tablespoons raisins
3 tablespoons currants
5 tablespoons clear honey
juice of 1 lemon
3 tablespoons sugar
2 large dessert apples
1 large pear
8 apricots

Cover the raisins and currants with boiling water and leave for 5 minutes. Warm the honey in a saucepan until it is very liquid. Drain the raisins and currants and add to the honey with the lemon juice and sugar. Remove from the heat.
Peel and quarter the apples and pear. Remove the cores and cut the fruit into thin slices. Halve the apricots, remove the cores and cut into quarters.
Add the fruit to the honey mixture and stir well. Spoon into a serving dish. Cool, then chill for 30 minutes before serving.
Serves 4

Variation
Other fruits may be used with the apples, such as bananas or mandarin oranges. If fresh apricots are not available, use dried ones and soak them in cold water for 4 hours before making the salad.

Peach Meringue

4 large fresh peaches or 8 canned peach halves
4 slices white bread
4 eggs
$1\frac{1}{4}$ cups milk
$\frac{1}{4}$ cup sugar
1 teaspoon cornstarch

Scald the fresh peaches with boiling water, then remove the skin. Halve and pit. Drain the canned peach halves. Arrange the bread slices on the bottom of a greased baking dish. Separate the egg yolks from the whites. Scald the milk, then strain into a bowl. Add 3 tablespoons of the sugar. Allow to cool slightly, then beat in the egg yolks. Pour over the bread slices. Bake in a cool oven (300° F) for 25 minutes.
Meanwhile, beat the egg whites until stiff, then fold in the remaining sugar and the cornstarch.
Put the peach halves, cut sides down, on top of the baked egg custard mixture, spoon over the meringue and bake for a further 8–10 minutes, until the meringue is golden brown. Serve warm.
Serves 4

Vanilla Soufflé

3 tablespoons finely crushed
  graham crackers
4 eggs
$\frac{1}{4}$ cup sugar
$\frac{1}{2}$ teaspoon cornstarch
$\frac{1}{2}$ teaspoon vanilla extract

Press the cracker crumbs on
to the bottom and sides of a
greased baking dish.
Separate the egg yolks from
the whites. Beat the yolks
with the sugar in the top of
a double boiler. Continue
beating until the mixture is
pale and thick and will
make a ribbon trail on
itself when the beater is
lifted. (If you use an electric
mixer, there is no need to
beat over heat.) Fold in the
cornstarch and vanilla
extract.
Beat the egg whites until
stiff and fold into the egg
yolk mixture. Spoon into
the baking dish and smooth
the top. Bake in a cool oven
(300° F) for 30 minutes or
until golden brown.
Serve immediately, with
fruit salad.
Serves 2

Variation
Lemon Soufflé
Beat the egg yolks with
the sugar and the juice of 1
lemon, as described above.
Follow the recipe, substitut-
ing 1 teaspoon grated
lemon rind for the vanilla
extract.

Fruit Muesli

2 dessert apples
1 ripe pear
1 banana
1 orange
juice of 1 lemon
1–2 tablespoons sugar
5 tablespoons muesli
5 tablespoons milk or water

Peel, core and slice the
apples and pear. Peel and
slice the banana. Peel the
orange, removing all the
white pith, and chop. Put
the fruit in a bowl and add
the lemon juice and sugar.
Toss well so the fruit is
covered with the lemon
juice.
Mix the muesli with the
milk or water. Add to the
fruit and stir well. Leave for
10 minutes before serving.
Serves 4

Variation
Substitute clear honey for
the sugar. Add 3 table-
spoons chopped nuts.

Cook's Tip
Put the orange in
a small bowl, cover
with boiling water
and leave for 2
minutes. It is then
easy to peel.

Stuffed Oranges

1 lb strawberries
4 oranges
1 cup cottage cheese
a little milk
grated rind of ½ orange
¼ cup sugar
3 tablespoons orange liqueur

Wash the strawberries carefully and hull. Pat dry with paper towels and cut into quarters. Cut the tops off the oranges to form a lid and scoop out the flesh. Remove all the pith and seeds and chop the flesh. Push the cottage cheese through a strainer until smooth. If it is very thick, add a little milk. Stir in the orange rind, sugar and orange liqueur. Fold in the strawberries and orange flesh. Fill the oranges with the cottage cheese mixture and replace the lids. Chill before serving.
Serves 4

Variation
Grapefruit may be stuffed in the same way.

Cook's Tip
If you have a blender, use this to purée the cottage cheese, adding a little milk, instead of straining it.

Strawberry Stripes

8 oz strawberries
1 package strawberry-flavored gelatin
1 package black cherry-flavored gelatin
⅔ cup whipping cream
1 tablespoon sugar
1 tablespoon finely chopped pistachio nuts

Wash the strawberries carefully and hull. Pat dry with paper towels and cut in half.
Prepare the gelatins separately, according to the directions on the packages. Cool slightly, then pour a quarter of the strawberry gelatin into each of four individual glass dishes.

Chill in the refrigerator until set, then top with the strawberries. Fill the dishes with the still-liquid black cherry gelatin and chill until set.
Whip the cream with the sugar until stiff. Pipe on to the desserts and sprinkle with the pistachio nuts.
Serves 4

Variation
Use other fruit – raspberries, peaches, pears – with complementing gelatin flavors.

Rum Pudding

*2 teaspoons unflavored
  gelatin*
3 tablespoons water
4 eggs, separated
⅓ cup sugar
*grated rind and juice of 1
  lemon*
¼ cup sweet white wine
¼ cup rum
4 small macaroons
*stewed fruit (cherries,
  pineapple, peaches)*

Sprinkle the gelatin over
the water and leave until
spongy. Place the bowl in a
pan of simmering water and
heat until the gelatin
dissolves completely.
Beat the egg yolks, sugar,
lemon rind and juice in the
top of a double boiler.
Continue beating until the
mixture is thick and pale
and will make a ribbon
trail on itself when the
beater is lifted. (If using an
electric mixer, no heat is
needed.) Remove from the
heat.
Strain the dissolved gelatin
into the egg yolk mixture
and stir well. Add the wine
and rum. Fold in the
stiffly beaten egg whites.
Spoon into four individual
glass dishes and chill until
set.
Decorate with the
macaroons and pieces of
fruit and serve.
Serves 4

Chilled Plum Pudding

1 lb ripe plums
1 cup water
*2 envelopes unflavored
  gelatin*
½ cup sugar
rind and juice of 2 lemons
¼ cup brandy
pinch cinnamon
½ teaspoon vanilla extract
1½ cups almonds, chopped
⅔ cup whipping cream
*3 tablespoons finely chopped
  pistachio nuts*

Halve the plums, remove
pits and poach in a saucepan with ½ cup of the water
for 10–15 minutes, until
very soft. Sprinkle the
gelatin over ¼ cup of the
water and leave until
spongy. Purée the fruit in a
blender. Return to the
saucepan and add the sugar,
lemon rind and juice. Taste
and add more sugar if
preferred.
Dissolve the gelatin over
a pan of simmering water.
Strain into the plum purée
and stir well. Add the
brandy, cinnamon, vanilla
extract and remaining
water. Mix well and pour
into a dampened ring mold.
Smooth the top and chill
until set.
Turn out the pudding on a
serving plate. Press on the
chopped almonds. Whip the
cream until stiff, pipe in
rosettes around the base
and sprinkle with the
pistachios.
Serves 4–6

Smyrna Fig Dessert

2 envelopes unflavored
   gelatin
$\frac{1}{4}$ cup water
2 cups sweet white wine
$\frac{1}{4}$ cup sugar
juice of 2 lemons
$\frac{1}{4}$ cup brandy
$1\frac{1}{4}$ cups whipping cream
1 lb ripe figs
chocolate scrolls

Sprinkle the gelatin over
the water and leave until
spongy, then place the bowl
in a saucepan of simmering
water and heat until
dissolved.
Heat the wine in a saucepan
with the sugar, lemon juice
and brandy until the sugar
has completely dissolved.

Remove from the heat.
Strain the gelatin into the
wine mixture and stir well.
Leave to cool.
Whip the cream until stiff.
Peel and chop the figs. Stir
the cream into the wine
mixture, reserving a little
cream for the garnish. Fold
in the chopped figs.
Spoon the fig dessert into
four individual glass dishes.
Chill until set then pipe a
rosette of cream on top of
each serving. Decorate with
chocolate scrolls.
Serves 4

Lemon and Wine Dessert

2 ripe lemons
1 cup sugar
2 tablespoons butter
2 envelopes unflavored
   gelatin
$1\frac{1}{4}$ cups water
1 cup medium-dry white wine
$\frac{2}{3}$ cup whipping cream

Thinly pare the rind from
one lemon. Peel both
lemons, removing all the
white pith. Slice the flesh
thinly and remove any seeds.
Spread the slices on a
baking sheet covered with
aluminum foil. Sprinkle
over all but 2 tablespoons
sugar and dot with the
butter. Bake in a moderate
oven (350° F) for 40 minutes

or until candied. Leave to
cool then arrange in four
glass dishes, reserving any
cooking juices.
Sprinkle the gelatin over
$\frac{1}{4}$ cup of the water and leave
until spongy. Pour the
reserved juices into a
saucepan. Add the remain-
ing water, the wine, lemon
rind and remaining sugar.
Bring to the boil, stirring
to dissolve the sugar.
Discard the lemon rind.
Add the softened gelatin
and stir until completely
dissolved. Cool, then pour
into the glass dishes. Chill
until set, then decorate with
a spoonful of whipped
cream.
Serves 4

Coffee Creams, Budapest-Style

2½ *cups whipping cream*
½ *cup confectioners' sugar*
½ *teaspoon vanilla extract*
1½ *teaspoons instant coffee powder*
¼ *cup hot water*
2 *eggs*
8 *oz ripe cherries*

Whip the cream, confectioners' sugar and vanilla extract together until the mixture is stiff. Dissolve the coffee in the water. Leave to cool then beat into the cream. Separate the egg yolks from the whites. Add the yolks to the cream, and beat in well. Beat the egg whites until stiff and fold into the cream. Divide the cherries between 4 individual glasses, reserving about 12 for the garnish. Spoon in the cream and chill for 30 minutes. Garnish with the reserved cherries just before serving.
Serves 4

Variation
Try dissolved cocoa powder, apricot brandy or orange liqueur instead of the instant coffee.

Cook's Tip
If using canned cherries, drain and dry on paper towels.

Meringue Trifle

2 *lb mixed fruit (goose-berries, raspberries, blackberries, apricots)*
¾ *cup sugar*
8 *oz plain cookies*
¼ *cup maraschino or cherry brandy*
1 *cup milk*
½ *cup cream*
2 *tablespoons custard powder*
4 *egg whites*

Wash the fruit. Remove stalks, pits and skin, then chop or slice as necessary. Put in a large, ovenproof dish and sprinkle with 4 tablespoons of the sugar. Lay the cookies over the fruit and sprinkle with the liqueur to moisten.
Heat almost all the milk in a saucepan with the cream and 4 tablespoons of the remaining sugar. Mix the reserved milk with the custard powder, then pour on the hot milk. Stir well and return to the saucepan. Bring to the boil, stirring all the time, and simmer until thick. Cool, then pour over the cookies and fruit.
Beat the egg whites until frothy. Gradually add the remaining sugar, beating until stiff. Pile over the trifle and bake in a moderate oven (350° F) for 8–10 minutes, until the meringue is set. Serve at room temperature or chilled.
Serves 4–6

Surprise Desserts

Italian Zabaglione

6 egg yolks
¼ cup sugar
3 tablespoons Marsala
maraschino cherries

Put the egg yolks in a heat-proof bowl placed over a pan of simmering water, or in the top of a double boiler. Beat the yolks until they are pale and creamy. Add the sugar and Marsala and continue beating until the mixture is very light and frothy. Do all this as quickly as possible and do not let the bowl become too hot or the eggs will cook and stick to the bowl. Remove from the heat. Spoon into four individual glasses and garnish with the cherries. Serve immediately, with ladyfingers.
Serves 4

Variation
To 'stretch' this dessert, fold 2–3 stiffly beaten egg whites into the finished zabaglione.

Cook's Tip
Egg whites stored in a covered container in the refrigerator will keep successfully for several days. Use to make dessert meringue toppings.

Melting Orange Toasts

2 oranges
6 tablespoons apricot jam
1–2 tablespoons brandy
4 slices bread
¼ cup butter
1 teaspoon cocoa powder (optional)
2 egg whites
5 tablespoons confectioners' sugar

Peel the oranges, slice and remove any seeds. Mix the apricot jam with the brandy. Cut the crusts off the bread and, if liked, cut each slice into four small squares. Melt the butter in a frying pan and fry the bread until golden brown on both sides. Drain on paper towels, then sprinkle with the cocoa powder, if used. Arrange the slices in a flameproof dish. Halve the orange slices and place on the bread slices. Spread with the jam mixture. Beat the egg whites until frothy. Gradually add the sugar, beating until stiff. Pile on to the orange slices. Bake in a hot oven (450° F) for 2–3 minutes, until the meringue is lightly browned. Serve warm or cold.
Serves 4

Variation
This recipe can be prepared using slices of apple, pear, peach or banana. Fruits that discolor should be first sprinkled with lemon juice.

Blackberry Toasts

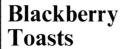

$1\frac{1}{4}$ cups whipping cream, or
    plain yogurt
12 oz blackberries
$\frac{1}{4}$ cup sugar
$\frac{1}{4}$ cup butter
4 slices bread
3 (1-oz) squares semisweet
    chocolate
3 tablespoons warm water
$\frac{1}{4}$ cup egg liqueur (Advocaat)

If using cream, whip until
stiff. Fold the berries and
half the sugar into the
cream or yogurt.
Melt the butter in a frying
pan and dissolve the
remaining sugar in it. Add
the bread slices and fry on
one side. Transfer to four
plates, fried sides up. Spread

with the berry mixture.
Melt the chocolate in a
heatproof bowl placed over
a pan of simmering water,
or in the top of a double
boiler. Stir in the water
until smooth and remove
from the heat.
Top each serving with a
spoonful of egg liqueur and
then pour over the chocolate
sauce. Serve immediately.
Serves 4

Variation
Use blueberries, raspberries
or strawberries instead.

Old Viennese Chestnut Dessert

2 lb fresh sweet chestnuts
$\frac{1}{2}$ cup sugar
$\frac{1}{2}$ cup water
$1\frac{1}{4}$ cups whipping cream
$\frac{1}{3}$ cup confectioners' sugar
$\frac{1}{2}$ teaspoon vanilla extract
candied cherries

With a sharp knife, make a
slit in the hard skin of each
chestnut. Lay the chestnuts
on a baking sheet and bake
in a hot oven (425° F) for 30
minutes. Remove the shells
and skin from the chestnuts.
Put the sugar and water in
a saucepan and bring to the
boil, stirring to dissolve the
sugar. Simmer until a syrup

is formed. Add the chestnuts
and cook for 10 minutes.
Remove from the heat and
leave to cool for 15 minutes.
Grate the chestnuts and pile
in the center of a serving
dish. Whip the cream with
the confectioners' sugar and
vanilla extract until stiff,
then pipe in rosettes around
the grated chestnuts. Cut the
cherries into small pieces
and place on the cream
rosettes.
Serves 4

Variation
Beat the whipped cream
into a small can of
sweetened chestnut purée.

Currant and Semolina Desserts

4⅓ cups milk
¼ cup sugar
grated rind of ½ lemon
½ teaspoon vanilla extract
1½ cups semolina
½ cup ground almonds
½ cup currants
2 eggs
1 (7½-oz) can peach slices
1 (7½-oz) can cherries

Bring the milk to the boil in a saucepan. Add the sugar, grated lemon rind, vanilla extract and semolina and simmer, stirring constantly, for 10 minutes or until the mixture is thick. Remove from the heat and stir in the ground almonds and currants.
Add the eggs and mix well. Pour the semolina mixture into four dampened soup bowls. Smooth the tops and chill for 2–3 hours or until firm.
Drain the peaches and cherries, reserving the juice. Turn the semolina desserts out on to four plates. Spoon over a little of the reserved juice and decorate with the peach slices and cherries.
Serves 4

Variation
Omit the currants and add instead chopped walnuts, pineapple pieces and candied cherries.

Blushing Girls

2½ envelopes unflavored gelatin
½ cup water
4 sugar cubes
2 lemons
½ cup sugar
4½ cups buttermilk
red food coloring
⅔ cup whipping cream

Sprinkle the gelatin over half the water and leave until spongy. Then place the bowl in a saucepan of simmering water and heat until the gelatin has dissolved. Remove from the heat.
Rub the sugar cubes over the skin of one lemon to extract the zest. Put the sugar cubes in a saucepan with the remaining water and the sugar. Heat gently, stirring to dissolve the sugar. Add the juice from the one lemon. Remove from the heat. Strain in the gelatin and stir well, then add the buttermilk. Mix in enough red food coloring to give a good rich color. Pour into individual bowls and chill until set. Pipe small 'nests' of whipped cream on top of each serving. Pare the rind from the remaining lemon into curls and use as garnish.
Serves 4–6

Variation
To make 'Geisha', use oranges instead of lemons and omit the red food coloring.

255

Ice Cream Desserts

Zermatt Ice Coffee

1 pint vanilla ice cream
¼ cup ground hazelnuts
2 pints strong, lukewarm coffee
¼ cup orange liqueur

Soften the vanilla ice cream and mix in the hazelnuts. Spoon the mixture into tall glasses or large coffee mugs. Pour the coffee over the ice cream and then sprinkle with the liqueur.
Serves 4–6

Variation
Boulevard Iced Coffee
Cut 1 pint vanilla ice cream into cubes and divide between four glasses. Fill the glasses with an equal mixture of strong lukewarm coffee and lukewarm cocoa. Top each serving with a tablespoon of brandy and decorate with whipped cream. If you like, sprinkle the top with cocoa powder or grated chocolate.

Cook's Tip
Soften ice cream by transferring to the main part of the refrigerator about 30 minutes before needed.

Citrus Sherbet

juice of 4 large oranges
juice of 4 large lemons
1¼ cups sparkling white wine
1⅓ cups confectioners' sugar
4 egg whites
1 tablespoon sugar
5 tablespoons raspberry jam

Mix together the orange juice, lemon juice, wine and half the confectioners' sugar. Put to one side.
Meanwhile, beat the egg whites with the remaining confectioners' sugar until thick. Dampen a 9 × 5 × 3-inch loaf pan and sprinkle with the sugar. Stir the beaten egg white into the wine mixture. Pour into the pan and put in the freezing compartment of the refrigerator. Freeze for 10 minutes then turn the sherbet into a bowl and beat for 1 minute. Return to the pan and freeze for a further 15 minutes. Beat again, and again after a further 25 minutes. Freeze for 1 hour, beat well, then freeze until solid.
Remove the sherbet from the freezer and allow to soften slightly, then mix in the raspberry jam. Spoon into four tall glasses and serve.
Serves 4

Jubilee Ice Cream Dessert

1⅓ cups mixed candied fruit
3 tablespoons rum
1 tablespoon boiling water
⅔ cup whipping cream
1 pint vanilla ice cream
1 tablespoon finely chopped
    pistachio nuts

Halve the large pieces of candied fruit and leave the smaller ones whole. Mix together the rum and water and pour over the fruit. Leave for 30 minutes. Whip the cream until it is thick. Put two or three spoonsful of ice cream in each of four individual glass dishes. Divide the fruit between the glasses. Pipe a rosette of cream on each serving and sprinkle with the pistachio nuts. Serve immediately.
Serves 4

Variation

Canned apricot halves or poached fresh apricots may be used instead of the candied fruit. Prepare the servings of ice cream and apricots as above, then sprinkle each with a table-spoon of orange liqueur and garnish with grated or flaked chocolate.

Cook's Tip

Cream for piping should be whipped until thick enough to stand in peaks. Over-whipping will curdle the cream.

Cassis Ice

2½ cups blackcurrant juice
½ cup water
juice of 1 large lemon
⅔ cup confectioners' sugar
2½ cups whipping cream
8 wafer cookies

Mix together the black-currant juice, water, lemon juice and confectioners' sugar. Whip the cream until it is thick. Reserve about ¼ cup of cream and beat the remainder with the blackcurrant mixture. Pour into a shallow freezer tray or other container that will fit into the freezing compartment of your refrigerator. Freeze for 3 hours or until firm.

Dip the freezer tray into hot water to loosen the ice. Cut it into squares. Arrange the wafer cookies on a serving dish and top with the cassis ice squares. Spoon over the reserved whipped cream and serve.
Serves 4

Variation
For a special occasion, substitute 3 tablespoons of cassis (blackcurrant liqueur) for 3 tablespoons of the water.

Emma Calvet's Ice Cream Dessert

12 oz frozen raspberries
4 (1-oz) squares semisweet chocolate
⅔ cup whipping cream
3 tablespoons cherry brandy
1 pint vanilla ice cream
1 (15-oz) can pitted black cherries, drained

Chill four glass dishes. Put the raspberries in a strainer and leave to thaw, then push through the strainer. Gently melt the chocolate with the cream. Stir in the cherry brandy and pour into a sauceboat.
Put a spoonful of ice cream into each glass. Top with the cherries, then the remaining ice cream. Pour over the raspberry sauce and serve with the chocolate sauce.
Serves 4

Variation
Instead of raspberries and cherries, use oranges. Peel 2 oranges and chop the flesh. Mix with 5 table-spoons orange liqueur and 3 tablespoons brown sugar. Put a spoonful of ice cream in each of four chilled glasses and top with some of the orange mixture. Add the remaining ice cream and then the rest of the orange mixture. Make a chocolate sauce as above, omitting the cherry brandy.

Nougat Ice Cream Cake

$\frac{1}{2}$ cup ground hazelnuts
16 small wafer cookies
1 (15$\frac{1}{2}$-oz) can pineapple
   chunks or 8 oz candied
   pineapple
1 pint vanilla ice cream
1 pint chocolate ice cream
4 (1-oz) squares semisweet
   chocolate
1 cup chopped nougat
2 cups whipping cream

Sprinkle a greased 4$\frac{1}{2}$ ×
2$\frac{1}{2}$ × 1$\frac{1}{2}$-inch loaf pan with
the ground hazelnuts.
Arrange 12 wafer cookies on
the bottom and sides.
Drain the canned or chop
the candied pineapple.
Soften the two ice creams.
Break the chocolate into
small pieces. Spoon the
vanilla ice cream into the
pan and smooth over. Mix
three-quarters of the pineapple and all the chocolate
into the chocolate ice cream.
Spread smoothly over the
vanilla ice cream.
Sprinkle the nougat over
the chocolate ice cream.
Cover with the remaining
wafer cookies. Put into the
freezer compartment of the
refrigerator for 3 hours.
Whip the cream until thick.
Turn out the ice cream cake
on to a serving plate. Pipe
over the whipped cream and
decorate with the remaining
pineapple.
Serves 4–6

Fruit and Ice Cream Crêpes

$\frac{1}{2}$ cup all-purpose flour
pinch salt
1 teaspoon sugar
1 egg
$\frac{2}{3}$ cup milk
1$\frac{1}{2}$ tablespoons oil
6 tablespoons black cherry
   jam
1 tablespoon orange liqueur
1 tablespoon confectioners'
   sugar
$\frac{2}{3}$ cup whipping cream
1 pint vanilla ice cream
1 (15$\frac{1}{2}$-oz) can fruit salad,
   drained
1 banana, sliced

Sift the flour, salt and
sugar. Beat in the egg and
half the milk until smooth,
then gradually beat in the
remaining milk and $\frac{1}{2}$ teaspoon oil.
Heat a little oil in an 8-inch
crêpe pan. Spoon in a
quarter of the batter and tip
to cover. Cook for 1 minute,
then turn over and cook for
about 30 seconds. Slide out
of the pan. Cook the
remaining crêpes and cool.
Gently heat the jam, liqueur
and confectioners' sugar,
stirring to dissolve the
sugar. Beat in the whipped
cream. Remove from the
heat.
Fold over the crêpes and fill
with the ice cream and fruit.
Spoon over the warm sauce.
Serves 4

Fish Salad

2 (8-oz) white fish fillets
2 medium onions
1 teaspoon Worcestershire
   sauce
1 teaspoon salt
1 teaspoon prepared mustard
1–2 tablespoons white wine
5 tablespoons water
2 tomatoes
2 cups finely chopped mixed
   pickled vegetables
   (cucumber, carrot,
   cauliflower, onion, etc.)
$\frac{1}{4}$ cup wine vinegar
$\frac{1}{2}$ cup oil

Place the fish fillets in a shallow dish. Peel and finely chop the onions. Mix the onions with the Worcestershire sauce, salt, mustard and wine and pour over the fish. Leave to marinate for 1 hour.

Place the fish in a saucepan and add the water. Bring to the boil, cover and steam for 8–10 minutes, until the fish is cooked and will flake easily. Remove the fish from the pan and take off the skin. Flake the fish and leave to cool.

Quarter the tomatoes. Add the vegetables and tomatoes to the fish with the vinegar, oil and fish marinade.

Mix well and place in a serving dish. Chill before serving.

Serves 6 (about 190 calories per serving)

Orange Baskets

1 lb carrots
2 small dessert apples
juice of 1 lemon
$\frac{1}{3}$ cup raisins
4 oranges
4 celery stalks
2 tablespoons sugar
Garnish
$\frac{1}{4}$ cup chopped pistachio nuts

Peel and finely grate the carrots. Peel and core the apples, then slice thinly. Sprinkle with the lemon juice to prevent discoloration. Cover the raisins with boiling water and drain. Halve two of the oranges, cutting in a zig-zag pattern for a more decorative effect. Scoop out the flesh, dis-carding all the white pith and seeds, and chop finely. Peel the other two oranges and finely chop the flesh, discarding all the white pith and seeds.

Grate or finely chop the celery. Mix together the carrots, apples, raisins, orange flesh, celery and sugar. Leave for 20 minutes, then fill the orange halves with this salad. Sprinkle over the pistachio nuts and serve.

Serves 4 (about 200 calories per serving)

Fennel Salad

2 large or 3 medium bulbs
    fennel
1 large onion
1 teaspoon salt
1 teaspoon black pepper
$\frac{1}{4}$ cup wine vinegar
$\frac{1}{4}$ cup oil
1 slice bread
$\frac{1}{2}$ oz butter or margarine
$\frac{1}{2}$ teaspoon garlic salt
4 oz salami, sliced

Trim the fennel and halve
lengthwise. Wash and slice
thinly. Peel and finely chop
the onion. Place the fennel
in a shallow dish. Mix
together the onion, salt,
pepper, vinegar and oil and
pour over the fennel. Leave
to marinate for 20 minutes
in the refrigerator.
Trim the crust from the
bread, then cut into small
cubes. Melt the butter or
margarine in a frying pan.
Add the garlic salt and
bread cubes and fry until
golden brown on all sides.
Drain on paper towels.
Cut the salami into thin
strips and mix with the
fennel. Sprinkle over the
bread croûtons and serve.
*Serves 4 (about 265 calories
per serving)*

Cucumber and Shrimp Salad

8 oz shelled shrimp (fresh or
    frozen)
1 cucumber
salt
5 tablespoons wine vinegar
$\frac{1}{2}$ teaspoon monosodium
    glutamate (optional)
$\frac{1}{2}$ cup oil
2 tablespoons soy sauce
$\frac{1}{2}$ teaspoon sugar
1–2 tablespoons chopped dill
Garnish
1 egg
4–5 tablespoons canned fruit
    cocktail, drained

If using frozen shrimp,
allow them to thaw. Slice
the cucumber very thinly,
using a mandoline or the
slicer on a cheese grater.
Sprinkle the cucumber
slices with salt and leave for
20 minutes. Rinse and
drain well.
Put the cucumber slices and
shrimp in a bowl. Mix
together the vinegar, monosodium glutamate (if used),
oil, soy sauce, sugar and
dill. Pour over the cucumber
and shrimp and toss well.
Chill for 20 minutes.
Meanwhile, hard-cook the
egg. Cool, then shell and
slice. Garnish the salad with
the egg slices and fruit and
serve.
*Serves 6 (about 175 calories
per serving)*

Radish and Beet Salad

1 large white radish
2 medium cooked or pickled beets
2 large onions, sliced
2 teaspoons grated fresh horseradish root
1 teaspoon prepared mustard
2 tablespoons wine vinegar
3 tablespoons water
$\frac{1}{4}$ cup oil
1 teaspoon salt
pinch garlic salt
pinch Tabasco sauce
$\frac{1}{2}$ cup chopped parsley
4 lettuce leaves

Peel the radish, then grate. Peel the beets, making sure you remove a thick layer of outer skin, and coarsely grate.

Mix together the onions, horseradish, mustard, vinegar and water in a saucepan. Bring to the boil, then remove from the heat. Strain the liquid into a bowl and discard the onions. Add the oil, salt, garlic salt and Tabasco sauce to the liquid and mix well. Taste, and if the sauce is too sour, add a little sugar or spoonful of plain yogurt. Stir in the parsley.
Arrange the radish and beets in alternating rows on a serving dish. Garnish with the lettuce leaves and serve with the parsley sauce.
Serves 6 (about 100 calories per serving)

Majorcan Medley

2 anchovy fillets
5 tablespoons milk
12 stuffed green olives
4 sweet dill pickles
2 slices cooked ham
3 tablespoons capers
2 medium onions
3 tablespoons chopped parsley
2 teaspoons sugar
1 teaspoon salt
1 tablespoon dry sherry
3 tablespoons oil
6 lettuce leaves

Soak the anchovy fillets in the milk for 1 hour, then drain and chop. Slice the olives and pickles. Cut the ham into strips. Mix together the anchovies, olives, pickles, ham and capers.
Finely chop 1 onion.
Put with 1 tablespoon parsley, the sugar, salt, sherry and oil in a blender and blend to a purée. Pour into a saucepan and bring to the boil. Boil for 1 minute, then pour over the salad. Mix well. Chop the remaining onion.
Arrange the lettuce leaves on a serving dish. Pile on the salad, sprinkle over the chopped onion and remaining parsley and chill well before serving.
Serves 6 (about 120 calories per serving)

Slimming Salads

Chicken Madeleine Salad

½ *cup frozen peas*
½ *cup frozen green beans*
½ *small onion*
3 tablespoons wine vinegar
1 teaspoon sugar
½ *teaspoon salt*
½ *teaspoon black pepper*
½ *teaspoon prepared mustard*
½ *teaspoon grated fresh*
   horseradish root
3 tablespoons oil
1½ cups chopped cooked
   chicken
lettuce leaves

Cook the peas and beans according to the directions on the packages, then drain and cool.

Peel and finely chop the onion. Put in a saucepan with the vinegar, sugar, salt, pepper, mustard, horseradish and oil. Cook gently until the onion is soft, then remove from the heat. Thin this dressing with a little water if necessary. Allow to cool.
Mix the chicken with the vegetables. Add the dressing and toss well. Chill for 30 minutes.
Arrange lettuce leaves on a serving dish. Pile the salad in the center and serve.
Serves 6 (about 205 calories per serving)

Brussels Salad

8 oz fresh young spinach
2 heads French or Belgian
   endive
2 ripe pears
2 onions
2 slices canned pineapple
¼ *cup pineapple juice (from*
   the can)
2 teaspoons sugar
pinch cayenne pepper
¼ *cup wine vinegar*
½ *teaspoon salt*
Garnish
1 egg

Wash the spinach leaves and shake to remove excess water, then pat dry with a dish towel. Wash and thinly slice the endive. Peel and quarter the pears, remove

the cores and slice thinly. Peel and finely chop the onions. Chop the pineapple slices.
Mix together the pineapple juice, sugar, cayenne, vinegar and salt. Hard-cook the egg, then cool, shell and finely chop.
Put the spinach, endive, pears, onion and pineapple in a bowl. Add the dressing and toss well. Garnish with the chopped hard-cooked egg and serve.
Serves 6 (about 80 calories per serving)

263

Carrot and Apple Salad

1 lb carrots
2 medium dessert apples
8 red radishes
¼ cup raisins
5 tablespoons chopped
   parsley
¼ cup oil
juice of 2 lemons
⅔ cup plain yogurt
½ teaspoon white pepper
1½ teaspoons sugar
½ teaspoon salt

Peel the carrots and cook in boiling salted water to cover for 10 minutes. Drain well and allow to cool, then slice thinly.
Peel and quarter the apples, remove the cores and thinly slice. Wash and thinly slice the radishes. Put the carrots, apples, radishes and raisins in a bowl.
Mix together the parsley, oil, lemon juice, yogurt, pepper, sugar and salt. Pour over the salad and toss well. Chill for at least 20 minutes before serving.
Serves 4 (about 210 calories per serving)

Variation
Instead of cooking the carrots, grate them before mixing with the remaining ingredients.

Chicken and Celery Salad

1½ cups frozen peas
½ head green celery
2 white celery stalks
2 sweet dill pickles
¼ cup wine vinegar
1 teaspoon salt
1 teaspoon white pepper
2–3 tablespoons oil
½ cup cottage cheese
2 cups chopped cooked
   chicken

Cook the peas according to the directions on the package. Drain and allow to cool. Trim and thinly slice the green celery. Trim the white celery and cut into very thin julienne strips. Cut the pickles into strips. Mix together the vinegar, salt, pepper and oil. Push the cottage cheese through a strainer until smooth, then stir into the dressing. Mix thoroughly.
Put the peas, celery, chicken and pickles into a bowl and toss well together. Chill well, then spoon over the dressing.
Serves 4 (about 350 calories per serving)

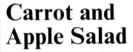

Cook's Tip
To cool peas quickly hold in a strainer under cold running water.

Cabbage and Fruit Salad

1 large head red cabbage
1 head celery
1½ lb head white cabbage
2 grapefruit
2 dessert apples
3 tablespoons mayonnaise
¼ cup sour cream
pinch salt
pinch pepper
Garnish
8 walnut halves

Remove the outer leaves from the red cabbage and cut the stalk close to the leaves. Cut out the middle of the cabbage carefully, so that the outer circle of leaves remains intact, like a bowl. (You can use the inner part of the cabbage for another recipe.) Soak the circle of leaves in cold water for 1 hour, then leave to drain.

Trim the celery and cut into thin strips. Remove the outer leaves from the white cabbage. Quarter it and cut out the core. Shred the cabbage. Blanch the cabbage and celery strips in boiling water for 2 minutes, then drain well and allow to cool.

Peel the grapefruit, removing all the white pith. Separate the segments. Peel and quarter the apples. Remove the cores and slice thinly.

Mix together the mayonnaise, sour cream, salt and pepper. Add the celery and white cabbage strips, most of the grapefruit segments and the apple slices and blend well. Spoon into the red cabbage 'bowl'. Garnish with the remaining grapefruit segments and the walnuts.

Serves 6 (about 130 calories per serving)

Liver and Apple Rings

1 lb dessert apples
1 large onion
2 tablespoons butter
5 tablespoons oil
1½ lb calf or lamb liver,
*   sliced*
½ teaspoon salt

Peel and core the apples, then slice into rings. Peel the onion and slice thinly into rings. Melt the butter with the oil in a large frying pan. Add the onion rings and fry until golden brown. Push to one side and add the liver slices. Fry for 2–3 minutes on each side or until just firm. (If your frying pan isn't large enough, it may be neces-sary to fry the liver in batches.) Remove the liver and onion from the pan and keep warm.

Put the apple rings in the pan and fry quickly until golden brown on each side. Arrange the liver, onion and apple rings on a warmed serving dish and sprinkle with salt. Serve immediately.
Serves 4 (about 445 calories per serving)

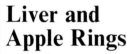

Cook's Tip
Liver is extremely nutritious yet low in calories, even when fried.

Baked Fish with Cheese

1½ lb white fish fillets
½ cup button mushrooms
1 teaspoon salt
1 teaspoon garlic salt
1 teaspoon white pepper
1 teaspoon paprika pepper
1 teaspoon sugar
2 cups buttermilk
1 chicken bouillon cube
3 tablespoons chopped chives
4 oz cheese, sliced
*   (Emmenthal or Gouda)*

Skin the fish and cut into finger-size pieces. Wash and halve the mushrooms. Mix together the salt, garlic salt, pepper, paprika, sugar, buttermilk and bouillon cube. Put the fish in a shallow baking dish. Scatter with the mushrooms and pour over the buttermilk mixture. Sprinkle over the chives and cover with the cheese slices. Bake in a moderate oven (350° F) for 15–20 minutes, until the fish is cooked. If the cheese topping begins to brown too much, cover with aluminum foil. Serve hot.
Serves 4 (about 290 calories per serving)

Sausages with Apple and Raisins

1 onion
2 tablespoons butter or
  margarine
2 large German sausages or 4
  large pork sausages
1 cooking apple
3 tablespoons raisins
3 tablespoons clear honey
1 teaspoon paprika pepper
1 teaspoon salt
½ teaspoon white pepper

Peel and thinly slice the onion. Melt the butter or margarine in a frying pan and fry the onion for 5 minutes, then push to one side. Add the sausages to the pan and fry until well browned on all sides. Meanwhile, peel and core the apple and cut into thick slices.
Remove the sausages from the pan and slice. Keep warm. Add the apple slices to the pan and cook until very soft. Strain off excess fat. Stir in the raisins, honey, paprika, salt and pepper. Mix with the onions. Return the sausage slices to the pan and heat through before serving.
Serves 2 (about 540 calories per serving)

Variation
Add ½–¾ cup canned drained sauerkraut to the apple mixture.

Shrimp and Corn

⅔ cup shelled shrimp (fresh
  or frozen)
1 (7-oz) can corn kernels
2 cups buttermilk
2 tablespoons butter or
  margarine
1 tablespoon cottage cheese
2 teaspoons cornstarch
2 slices cooked ham
½ cup chopped button
  mushrooms
½ teaspoon salt
½ teaspoon white pepper
2 drops Tabasco sauce
Garnish
1 tablespoon chopped parsley

If using frozen shrimp, allow to thaw. Drain the corn and put in a deep frying pan. Add the butter-milk and bring to the boil. Melt the butter or margarine and blend with the cottage cheese and corn-starch. Stir into the butter-milk mixture. Simmer until thickened.
Cut the ham into strips. Add the mushrooms, ham, salt, pepper, Tabasco and shrimp to the pan and cook gently for 5 minutes. Sprinkle with parsley and serve with omelets or crêpes.
Serves 2 (about 440 calories per serving)

Variation
Substitute a (7½-oz) can drained, flaked salmon for the shrimp, and 1 cup thawed frozen peas for the corn.

Easy Paella

2 onions
4 oz mackerel fillets
12 oz flounder fillets
2½ cups water
1 teaspoon salt
1 cup long-grain rice
5 tablespoons oil
2 small tomatoes
⅔ cup shucked, cooked
   mussels or clams
⅔ cup shelled shrimp (fresh
   or frozen)

Peel and slice the onions.
Remove the skin from the
mackerel and flounder fillets
and cut into small pieces.
Bring the water to the boil.
Add the salt and rice, cover
and cook gently for 15–20
minutes, until the rice is

tender and has absorbed all
the water. Remove from the
heat.
Heat the oil in a frying pan.
Add the onions and fry
until golden brown. Stir in
the mackerel and flounder
pieces. Cook for 5–6
minutes, until the fish is
firm and cooked.
Cut the tomatoes into small
pieces and add to the pan
with the rice, mussels or
clams and shrimp. Cook,
stirring, for a further 5
minutes or until all the
ingredients are heated
through. Add a spoonful or
two of water if the mixture
becomes too dry. Serve hot.
*Serves 4 (about 500 calories
per serving)*

Fish and Vegetable Omelet

1 lb cod fillets
½ lemon, sliced
1½ teaspoons salt
1 bay leaf
2 small potatoes, peeled
3 tablespoons butter or
   margarine
1 onion, sliced
1 small sweet dill pickle,
   sliced
2 eggs
2 tablespoons chopped dill

Put the cod in a saucepan
with the lemon slices, 1 teaspoon salt, the bay leaf and
water to cover. Bring to the
boil. Simmer for 15 minutes
or until the fish is cooked.

Meanwhile, cook the
potatoes in boiling salted
water for 15 minutes, until
tender. Drain and slice.
Drain the fish. Remove the
skin and cut into chunks or
flake. Keep warm.
Melt the butter in a frying
pan. Fry the onion for 5
minutes. Add the potato,
pickle, tomato and fish
and stir well. Beat the eggs
with the remaining salt and
the dill and pour into the
pan. Cook, lifting the edges
of the omelet to let the egg
run on to the pan.
When the omelet is set, cut
into two and slide on to
warmed serving plates.
*Serves 2 (about 500 calories
per serving)*

Veal with Vegetables

1½ lb lean veal stew meat
1 teaspoon celery salt
1 teaspoon white pepper
½ cup all-purpose flour
¼ cup butter or margarine
2½ cups chicken stock
1½ cups frozen peas
1½ cups frozen mixed
  vegetables
1 (11½-oz) can corn kernels
¼ cucumber

Cut the veal into chunks. Mix together the celery salt, pepper and flour and use to coat the chunks of veal.
Melt the butter or margarine in a saucepan. Add the veal and brown on all sides. Pour in the chicken stock and bring to the boil, stirring well. Cover and simmer for 1½ hours or until the veal is tender. Thaw the peas and mixed vegetables. Drain the corn. Thinly slice the cucumber. Add the vegetables to the pan, cover and cook for a further 5 minutes. Serve hot with boiled potatoes.
Serves 4 (about 550 calories per serving)

Kidney and Apple Goulash

8 lamb kidneys
2 onions
¼ cup butter or margarine
2 tablespoons all-purpose
  flour
1 teaspoon salt
½ teaspoon white pepper
1¼ cups red wine
2 dessert apples
5 tablespoons cream

Remove any fat and skin from the kidneys. Halve and cut out the cores and ducts. Wash, pat dry with paper towels and cut into slices. Peel and slice the onions.
Melt the butter or margarine in a saucepan. Add the onions and fry for 5 minutes. Add the kidney slices and brown on each side. Sprinkle over the flour, salt and pepper and stir well, then gradually stir in the wine. Bring to the boil and simmer for 10 minutes.
Meanwhile, peel the apples. Quarter them and remove the cores, then slice. Add the apples to the pan and cook for a further 3 minutes. Stir in the cream and heat through gently. Serve hot.
Serves 4 (about 350 calories per serving)

Variation
Omit the cream and top each portion with a spoonful of plain yogurt.

Tolstoy Steak

2 medium potatoes
8 oz fillet steak
2 tomatoes
½ sweet dill pickle
2 tablespoons butter or
   margarine
3 tablespoons oil
1 onion, sliced
3 tablespoons all-purpose
   flour
⅔ cup beef stock
1 tablespoon tomato paste
½ teaspoon black pepper
½ teaspoon salt
3 tablespoons whipping
   cream

Peel the potatoes and cook in boiling salted water for 15–20 minutes, until tender. Drain and slice. Remove

any fat from the meat, then cut into small cubes. Peel and quarter the tomatoes. Cut the pickle into strips. Melt the butter with the oil in a frying pan. Fry the onion for 5 minutes. Add the meat and brown quickly on all sides. Remove the meat from the pan. Sprinkle the flour over the onion and stir well, then gradually stir in the stock. Bring to the boil and simmer, stirring, until thickened. Stir in the tomato paste, pepper and salt. Add the potatoes, tomatoes and pickle and cook for 5 minutes. Return the meat to the pan, heat through then stir in the cream.
Serves 2 (about 670 calories per serving)

Westmorland Delight

1 roll
8 oz ground pork
12 oz lean ground beef
1 teaspoon celery salt
½ teaspoon garlic salt
½ teaspoon black pepper
2 tablespoons oil
3 tablespoons all-purpose
   flour
⅔ cup beef stock
2 teaspoons prepared
   mustard
¼ cup chopped parsley
1 tablespoon chopped chervil
¼ cup cocktail onions
2 teaspoons sugar

Soften the roll in ¼ cup warm water, then squeeze out and crumble into small pieces. Mix with the ground

pork, ground beef, celery and garlic salts and pepper. Shape into 8 patties. Heat the oil in a frying pan and brown the patties well on each side. Remove and keep warm. Stir the flour into the fat in the pan and cook, stirring, for 1 minute. Gradually stir in the stock, bring to the boil and simmer, stirring, until thickened. Add the mustard, parsley, chervil, onions and sugar. Return the meat patties and simmer for a further 3–4 minutes, until cooked through.
Serves 4 (about 550 calories per serving)

Low Calorie Recipes

Stuffed Baked Cucumbers

4 eggs
¼ cup cream
½ teaspoon salt
½ teaspoon white pepper
pinch grated nutmeg
1 tablespoon chopped parsley
1 tablespoon chopped dill
4 small cucumbers
2 small onions
2 tablespoons oil
1½ cups diced cooked ham
⅔ cup hot chicken stock
Garnish
2 tomatoes
few dill sprigs

Hard-cook the eggs, then cool, shell and halve. Rub the whites through a strainer. Mash the yolks and beat in the cream, salt, pepper, nutmeg, parsley and dill. Stir in the egg whites.

Slice off the tops, lengthwise, from the cucumbers. Scoop out the seeds with the tip of a teaspoon. Peel and finely chop the onions. Heat the oil in a saucepan. Add the onions and fry for 5 minutes. Add the ham and brown lightly. Remove from the heat and allow to cool slightly. Stir in the egg mixture. Fill the cucumbers with this mixture and replace the tops. Place the cucumbers in a baking dish and pour in the stock. Cover and bake in a cool oven (300° F) for 40 minutes.

Cut the tomatoes into quarters. Arrange the stuffed cucumbers on a serving plate and garnish with the tomato quarters and dill sprigs. Serve hot.
Serves 4 (about 385 calories per serving)

Bendor Steak

1 lb fillet steak
½ cup oil
1 teaspoon white pepper
½ teaspoon cayenne pepper
1 teaspoon dried rosemary
½ teaspoon celery salt
¼ cup brandy
3 tablespoons all-purpose flour
3 tablespoons grated cheese
1 teaspoon paprika pepper
2 tablespoons butter or margarine
Garnish
rosemary sprig

Remove any fat from the steak and cut into finger-length strips. Put into a shallow dish. Mix together the oil, pepper, cayenne, rosemary, celery salt and brandy. Pour over the steak and leave to marinate for 30 minutes.
Mix together the flour, cheese and paprika. Remove the steak strips from the marinade and coat with the flour mixture. Broil for 5–6 minutes, turning to brown all sides. Pile the steak strips on a warmed serving dish and keep hot.
Melt the butter in a sauce-pan and add the marinade. Stir well and bring to the boil, then pour into a sauceboat. Garnish the meat with the rosemary sprig and serve with the marinade sauce.
Serves 4 (about 540 calories per serving)

Steaks with Stuffed Tomatoes

½ carrot
3 tablespoons capers
1 onion
1½ lb lean ground steak
2 teaspoons salt
2 teaspoons paprika pepper
1 teaspoon black pepper
1 egg
2 large tomatoes
1 tablespoon oil
¼ cup soft breadcrumbs
2–3 teaspoons grated horseradish
parsley sprigs

Peel and grate the carrot. Chop the capers. Peel and finely chop the onion. Mix together the carrot, capers, onion, steak, salt, paprika and pepper. Add the egg and knead together. Form into two large patties. Halve the tomatoes and scoop out the centers. Mix the tomato flesh with 2 teaspoons oil, the bread-crumbs and horseradish. Use to fill the tomatoes. Heat the remaining oil in a frying pan. Add the beef patties and fry for 5–6 minutes on each side, until well browned. Add the tomatoes after the patties have been cooking for 5 minutes. If you prefer, broil the beef patties and tomatoes instead of frying. Garnish with parsley.
Serves 4 (about 380 calories per serving)

Meat Dishes to Keep You Slim

Pernod-Flavored Kidneys

2 dessert apples
4 celery stalks
5 tablespoons chopped
  chervil
1 tablespoon vinegar
2 calf kidneys
2 teaspoons celery salt
2 teaspoons black pepper
1 tablespoon prepared
  mustard
¼ cup oil
¼ cup Pernod
⅔ cup plain yogurt
parsley sprigs

Peel and core the apples, then cut into thin slices. Thinly slice the celery. Mix together the apple, celery, chervil and vinegar. Remove any fat from the kidneys, then skin, halve and cut out the cores and ducts. Wash and pat dry with paper towels. Rub the celery salt and pepper into the kidney halves. Mix together the mustard, oil and Pernod. Put the kidney halves in a shallow dish and pour over the mustard mixture. Leave to marinate for 10 minutes. Remove the kidney halves from the marinade and broil for 2–3 minutes on each side. Baste with the marinade if necessary. Heat the yogurt. Spoon over the kidney halves and garnish with parsley. Serve with the apple salad.
Serves 4 (about 325 calories per serving)

Steaks with Red Peppers

1¼ cups water
½ cup long-grain rice
2 teaspoons salt
2 red peppers
½ cup chopped walnuts
1½ lb fillet steak
½ teaspoon celery salt
1 teaspoon black pepper
¼ cup oil
Garnish
4 parsley sprigs

Bring the water to the boil. Add the rice and 1 teaspoon salt. Cover and simmer for 15–20 minutes, until the rice is tender and has absorbed all the water. Halve the peppers length-wise. Remove the cores, pith and seeds. Mix the walnuts with the rice. Fill the pepper halves with this mixture. Cut the meat into four portions and trim off any fat. Rub with the remaining salt, the celery salt and pepper. Heat the oil in a frying pan. Place the pepper halves in the pan, pepper sides down, and fry for 4 minutes. Add the steaks and fry for 2–4 minutes on each side, according to taste. Place the steaks on the stuffed pepper halves and garnish with the parsley sprigs. Serve hot with a green salad.
Serves 4 (about 595 calories per serving)

Liver Budapest-Style

1 red pepper
1 green pepper
1 egg, hard-cooked
3 tablespoons wine vinegar
5 tablespoons oil
1 tablespoon prepared
* mustard*
½ cup finely chopped chives
1½ lb calf or lamb liver
1 teaspoon salt
1 teaspoon dried marjoram
1 teaspoon dried rosemary
2 teaspoons paprika pepper
3 onions, sliced
rosemary sprig

Remove the cores, pith and seeds from the peppers, then cut into strips. Cover with boiling water and leave to soak for 10 minutes. Finely chop the egg. Drain the pepper strips. Mix together the vinegar, 1 tablespoon oil, the mustard, chives and chopped egg. Add the pepper strips and leave to marinate for 20 minutes. Meanwhile, cut the liver into pieces. Mix together the salt, marjoram, rosemary and paprika and use to coat the liver.
Heat the remaining oil in a frying pan. Add the liver and sliced onions and fry for 6–7 minutes or until the liver is just firm and the onions are golden brown. Serve hot, garnished with a rosemary sprig, accompanied by the pepper salad.
Serves 4 (about 410 calories per serving)

Austrian Chicken

1½ cups frozen peas
2 broilers (1 lb each)
1½ teaspoons salt
1½ teaspoons white pepper
2 eggs
⅔ cup dry breadcrumbs
½ cup ground hazelnuts
2 teaspoons paprika pepper
5 tablespoons oil
⅔ cup plain yogurt

Cook the peas according to the directions on the package, then drain and leave to cool. Cut the chickens in half, using poultry shears or a very sharp knife. Rub the chicken halves with the salt and pepper. Beat the eggs. Mix together the breadcrumbs, hazelnuts and paprika. Coat the chicken halves first with the egg and then with the breadcrumb mixture.
Heat the oil in a frying pan. Add the chicken halves and brown well on each side, then cook gently for 45 minutes or until the chicken is tender.
Meanwhile, mix together the peas and yogurt. Serve the hot chicken with the pea salad.
Serves 4 (about 580 calories per serving)

Variation
This delicious nutty coating can also be used for pork chops or veal scallops.

Meat Dishes to Keep You Slim

Peppered Steaks with Tomatoes

½ teaspoon celery salt
½ teaspoon paprika pepper
4 fillet steaks (about
  4 oz each)
5 tablespoons black
  peppercorns
2 lb tomatoes
3 tablespoons oil
2 tablespoons butter or
  margarine
½ cup beef stock
½ teaspoon salt
1 cup grated cheese
3 tablespoons chopped
  parsley

Rub the celery salt and paprika into the steaks. Roughly crush the pepper-corns and press on to both sides of the steaks. Peel and quarter the tomatoes. Discard the seeds and chop the flesh. Heat the oil in a frying pan. Add the steaks and fry for 3–4 minutes on each side. Meanwhile, put the tomato flesh, butter, stock, salt and cheese in a saucepan and cook gently for 5 minutes. Transfer to a warmed serving dish with the steaks and sprinkle over the parsley. Serve hot.
Serves 4 (about 450 calories per serving)

Gentleman's Steaks

1 (12-oz) can wax beans
1 apple
1 onion
3 tablespoons vinegar
1 teaspoon sugar
½ teaspoon salt
¼ cup cottage cheese
1 tablespoon mayonnaise
1 tablespoon chopped dill
1 tablespoon chopped parsley
1 tablespoon chopped
  tarragon
1 sweet dill pickle, finely
  chopped
4 small, thick slices of lean
  roast beef (4 oz each)
2 teaspoons oil
1 teaspoon black pepper
1 egg, hard-cooked

Drain the beans. Quarter the apple. Remove the core and slice crosswise. Peel and finely chop the onion. Mix together the beans, apple, onion, vinegar, sugar and salt.
Strain the cottage cheese until smooth. Beat in the mayonnaise, dill, parsley, tarragon and 3 tablespoons warm water. Mix the pickle into the sauce with 1–2 tablespoons of the pickle water.
Brush the meat with the oil. Sprinkle with the pepper, then broil for 3 minutes on each side.
Garnish with slices of the egg and serve with the herb sauce and bean salad.
Serves 4 (about 385 calories per serving)

Maltese Chicken Salad

1½ lb frozen mixed vegetables
1 lb cooked chicken
2 oranges
5 tablespoons cottage cheese
⅔ cup plain yogurt
5 tablespoons mayonnaise
1 teaspoon vinegar
1 teaspoon prepared mustard
1 teaspoon sugar
½ teaspoon salt
½ teaspoon pepper
3 tablespoons warm water

Cook the vegetables according to the directions on the package, then drain and leave to cool. Slice the chicken or cut into chunks. Peel the oranges, removing all the white pith, and slice. Push the cottage cheese through a strainer until smooth. Beat in the yogurt, mayonnaise, vinegar, mustard, sugar, salt, pepper and water. Fold the mixed vegetables into the dressing, then turn into a serving dish. Arrange the orange slices on top and then the chicken. Chill for 20 minutes before serving.
Serves 4 (about 395 calories per serving)

Stuffed Cucumber Slices

1 large cucumber (about 1½ lb)
½ teaspoon salt
½ teaspoon celery salt
2 small onions
1 cup cottage cheese
1 teaspoon paprika pepper
5 tablespoons chopped parsley
½ cup finely chopped cooked ham

Wash the cucumber, and halve lengthwise. Scoop out the seeds with the tip of a teaspoon. Rub the inside of one half with the salt and celery salt. Peel and finely chop the onions. Push the cottage cheese through a strainer until smooth, then beat in the paprika and parsley. Stir in the ham and onions. Pile this mixture on the un-seasoned cucumber half. Replace the other half and press on firmly. Chill for 20 minutes. Serve the cucumber, in slices, with a green salad.
Serves 4 (about 155 calories per serving)

> **Cook's Tip**
> Choose straight firm cucumbers no more than 2 inches wide. The skin is perfectly edible.

Asparagus and Egg Salad

1½ *lb asparagus*
4 *eggs*
6 *tablespoons butter or*
    margarine, softened
juice of ½ lemon
¾ *teaspoon sugar*
¼ *cup cooked peas*
1 *red pepper*
¼ *cup all-purpose flour*
½ *teaspoon salt*

Trim and scrape the asparagus. Tie in a bundle and place in a saucepan of boiling salted water, keeping the tips above water. Simmer for 10–15 minutes until tender. Drain and cool.
Hard-cook 2 eggs. Cool, shell and finely chop. Mix with ¼ cup butter, the lemon juice, ½ teaspoon sugar and the peas. Cut the asparagus into pieces. Remove the core, pith and seeds from the pepper, then cut into thin strips. Add with the asparagus to the pea mixture.
Mix the flour with ½ cup water. Beat in the remaining eggs and sugar and the salt. Melt the remaining butter in a frying pan. Pour in the egg mixture and cook, lifting the edges to let the liquid egg run on to the pan. Finish cooking under the broiler to brown the top, then cut into strips. Arrange around a dish and pile in the asparagus salad.
Serves 4 (about 335 calories per serving)

Green-Red Slices

4 *slices brown bread*
2 *tablespoons butter or*
    margarine
½ *cup cottage cheese*
3 *tablespoons milk*
½ *teaspoon paprika pepper*
pinch salt
pinch sugar
3 *tablespoons chopped*
    parsley
3 *tablespoons chopped chives*
1 *tablespoon chopped*
    tarragon
1 *tablespoon chopped chervil*
8 *large red radishes*
4 *tomatoes*
1 *head lettuce*

Spread the slices of bread with the butter or margarine. Mix the cottage cheese with the milk, then beat in the paprika, salt, sugar, parsley, chives, tarragon and chervil. Spread this mixture thickly and evenly on the bread.
Wash the radishes, then cut into slices. Quarter the tomatoes. Arrange the radish slices and tomato quarters in two rows on the slices of bread.
Separate the lettuce into leaves and wash well in cold running water. Shake off excess water, then pat dry with a dish towel. Arrange the lettuce leaves on a serving plate and place the bread slices on top.
Serves 4 (about 190 calories per serving)

Greek Mushrooms

8 oz mushrooms
2 teaspoons salt
juice of 2 lemons
3 tablespoons oil
2 teaspoons paprika pepper
1 cup buttermilk
4 bacon slices
1 teaspoon sugar
1 teaspoon soy sauce

Wash the mushrooms and trim the stalks almost level with the caps. Place in a bowl and sprinkle over the salt and half the lemon juice. Leave for 10 minutes, then rinse in cold water. Shake off excess water and pat dry with paper towels. Heat the oil in a saucepan. Stir in the paprika, then add the mushrooms. Fry for 3–4 minutes, shaking the pan or stirring occasionally. Add the buttermilk, stir well and simmer for 5 minutes.
Meanwhile, fry or broil the bacon slices until they are crisp and golden. Drain on paper towels and allow to cool.
Stir the sugar, soy sauce and remaining lemon juice into the mushroom mixture. Remove from the heat and cool. Place the bacon slices on top and serve cool or chilled.
Serves 4 (about 145 calories per serving)

Madras Chicken Sandwiches

4 slices brown bread
2 tablespoons butter or margarine
3 tablespoons mayonnaise
4 lettuce leaves
1 cup chopped cooked chicken
$\frac{2}{3}$ cup whipping cream
1 teaspoon curry powder
1 dessert apple
1 tablespoon lemon juice

Toast the slices of bread, then spread with the butter or margarine. Cover with the mayonnaise, then place a lettuce leaf on top of each slice.
Arrange the chicken on the lettuce. Whip the cream with the curry powder until it is thick. Spoon over the chicken.
Peel and core the apple. Grate and mix with the lemon juice to prevent discoloration, then place on top of the cream.
Serves 4 (about 420 calories per serving)

Variation
Use cooked turkey or veal instead of chicken.

Cook's Tip
Make a slimmer's mayonnaise by mixing equal quantities of a low calorie salad dressing with plain yogurt.

Veal and Fruit Ragoût

1½ lb veal (from the shoulder
  or breast)
2 tablespoons butter or
  margarine
¾ cup water
3 tablespoons all-purpose
  flour
8 oz green grapes
1 dessert apple
1 ripe pear
½ teaspoon salt
½ teaspoon paprika pepper
3 tablespoons cream

Remove any fat from the
meat and cut into chunks.
Melt the butter or margarine in a saucepan. Add the
veal chunks and fry until
golden brown on all sides.
Add ½ cup of the water,

cover and simmer for 40–45
minutes, until the veal is
tender.
Mix the flour with the
remaining water to form a
smooth paste. Stir into the
veal and cook for a further
5 minutes.
Peel the grapes, halve and
remove the seeds. Peel and
quarter the apple and pear.
Remove the cores and dice.
Stir the salt, paprika and
cream into the veal mixture,
then fold in the fruit. Heat
through gently for 2–3
minutes. Serve hot.
*Serves 4 (about 465 calories
per serving)*

Shrimp and Egg Sandwiches

1 lb shelled shrimp (fresh or
  frozen)
4 eggs
¼ cup oil
1 small onion, chopped
½ teaspoon salt
½ teaspoon paprika pepper
4 slices bread
2 tablespoons butter or
  margarine
4 lettuce leaves
2 tomatoes, quartered

If using frozen shrimp,
allow to thaw. Hard-cook
2 eggs. Cool, shell and cut
into wedges.
Heat the oil in a frying pan.
Add the onion, fry for 5
minutes, then push to one
side. Add the shrimp and

cook for 2–3 minutes to
heat through. Remove the
shrimp from the pan and
keep warm.
Beat the remaining eggs
with the salt and paprika.
Pour into the pan and cook
quickly but gently, stirring
in the onion, until lightly
scrambled.
Meanwhile, toast the bread.
Spread it with the butter
and place a slice on each of
four warmed plates. Place a
lettuce leaf on each slice,
then spoon on the
scrambled egg. Top with the
shrimp and garnish with
the hard-cooked egg wedges
and tomato quarters.
Serve hot.
*Serves 4 (about 470 calories
per serving)*

279

Cottage Cheese Variations

1 lb cottage cheese
½ cup milk
1 teaspoon salt
1 (8-oz) can pitted cherries, drained
1 tablespoon confectioners' sugar
5 tablespoons lemon juice
3 tablespoons chopped herbs
grated rind of 1 lemon
1 teaspoon sugar
2 oranges
5 tablespoons ground hazelnuts
1 egg, hard-cooked, chopped
3 tablespoons chopped sweet dill pickle
1 tablespoon chopped red pepper
½ teaspoon celery salt

Beat the cottage cheese, milk and salt until smooth. Divide into four portions. Chop most of the cherries. Mix with the confectioners' sugar, half the lemon juice and one portion cottage cheese. Garnish with the whole cherries.
Add the herbs, lemon rind and sugar to another portion of cottage cheese. Peel the oranges and cut into chunks. Add to a third portion of cottage cheese with the hazelnuts.
Mix the chopped egg with the pickle, red pepper, celery salt, remaining lemon juice and final portion of cottage cheese.
Serves 4 (about 345 calories per serving)

Plum Wine Soup

8 oz small plums
¼ cup sugar
2 cups red wine
1¼ cups water
2 whole cloves
pinch ground cinnamon
thinly pared rind of 1 lemon
3 tablespoons sago
1 tablespoon cornstarch
8 small macaroons

Halve and pit the plums. Tip into a bowl and sprinkle over 3 tablespoons sugar. Leave for 30 minutes. Put the wine, all but 3 tablespoons of the water, the cloves, cinnamon, remaining sugar and the lemon rind in a saucepan. Bring to the boil. Stir in the sago and simmer for 10 minutes. Add the plums and cook for a further 5 minutes, until very soft. Remove from the heat. Take out and reserve the lemon rind. Discard the cloves. Purée the soup in a blender and return to the pan. Bring back to the boil. Dissolve the cornstarch in the remaining water and add to the pan. Simmer, stirring, until slightly thickened. Return the lemon rind to the soup. Ladle into four bowls and float two macaroons on each. Serve hot or chilled.
Serves 4 (about 285 calories per serving)

Egg and Anchovy Sandwiches

4 eggs
4 slices brown bread
2 tablespoons butter or
*   margarine*
12 anchovy fillets
5 tablespoons milk
2 stuffed green olives
½ teaspoon paprika pepper

Hard-cook the eggs. Cool, then shell and slice thinly. Spread the bread with the butter or margarine. Arrange the egg slices over the bread.
Soak the anchovy fillets in the milk for 5 minutes, then drain. Rinse with water and pat dry with paper towels.

Cut the fillets into thin strips and arrange over the eggs, to form a lattice-work. Finely chop the olives and sprinkle over the egg. Add a pinch of paprika to each serving.
Serves 4 (about 175 calories per serving)

Cook's Tip
To slice hard-cooked eggs successfully, dip the knife blade into a bowl of boiling water between each slice.

Yogurt and Ginger Soup

2½ cups milk
2 tablespoons cornstarch
2 egg yolks
1¼ cups plain yogurt
¼ cup sugar
grated rind and juice of
*   1 lemon*
5 tablespoons slivered
*   preserved ginger*
3 tablespoons ginger syrup
*   (from the jar of preserved*
*   ginger)*
12 small macaroons
*   (optional)*

Put all but ¼ cup of the milk in a saucepan and bring to the boil. Dissolve the cornstarch in the remaining milk. Pour the hot milk over the cornstarch mixture and stir well, then return all to the saucepan. Bring back to the boil, stirring constantly, and simmer until thickened. Beat the egg yolks with the yogurt. Add a spoonful of the hot milk mixture, then stir the yogurt mixture into the saucepan. Heat gently, but do not allow to boil.
Stir the sugar, lemon rind and juice, preserved ginger and ginger syrup into the soup. Pour into 4 bowls and float 3 macaroons on each, if liked. Serve warm or chilled.
Serves 4 (about 340–490 calories per serving)

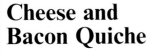

Cheese and Bacon Quiche

2½ cups all-purpose flour
½ teaspoon salt
⅔ cup butter
3–4 tablespoons water
8 oz bacon or cooked ham
4 eggs
1 cup cream
pinch pepper
1 cup grated cheese

Sift the flour and salt into a mixing bowl. Rub in the butter until the mixture resembles breadcrumbs. Stir in enough water to bind together, and form into a dough. Chill for 20 minutes. Roll out the pastry and use to line a greased 10-inch cake pan or flan ring placed on a baking sheet.

Cut the bacon or ham into very thin strips. Lay the strips in the pastry case. Separate the egg yolks from the whites. Beat the yolks with the cream and seasoning to taste. Stir in the cheese. Beat the egg whites until stiff, then fold into the egg yolk mixture. Spread over the bacon. Bake in a moderately hot oven (400° F) for 30–40 minutes, until the pastry is golden and the filling set. Ease the quiche out of the pan and serve.
Serves 6–8

Game Pies

13-oz package frozen puff pastry
4 bacon slices
½ cup chopped cooked game
1 leek, trimmed
1 onion, chopped
¼ cup liver sausage
¼ teaspoon salt
½ teaspoon paprika pepper
¼ teaspoon dried thyme
pinch dried marjoram
beaten egg to glaze

Thaw the pastry. Chop the bacon. Place the bacon in a frying pan and heat until the fat runs. Add the game and fry with the bacon for 5 minutes. Wash and slice the leek, add to the pan with the onion and cook for a further 5 minutes. Cool slightly, then either blend in the blender, or grind finely. Mix in the liver sausage, seasonings and herbs to form a smooth paste.

Roll out the pastry on a floured surface. Cut into an even number of circles with a 2½-inch fluted cookie cutter. Spoon the meat filling on to half the circles. Dampen the edges and press on the remaining circles. Place the pies on a baking sheet and brush with the beaten egg. Bake in a moderately hot oven (400° F) for 20–25 minutes. Serve hot or cold.
Makes 15

Savory Upside-Down Pie

7½-oz package frozen puff
*   pastry*
1½ lb ground beef
1 teaspoon salt
½ teaspoon black pepper
1 large onion, chopped
3 egg yolks
1 cup mushrooms
4 oz bacon slices
½ cup crumbled blue cheese
2 tablespoons each chopped
*   sorrel and chervil*

Thaw the pastry. Mix the ground beef with the salt, pepper and onion; bind with the egg yolks. Wash and quarter the mushrooms. Cover the bottom of an 8-inch loose-bottomed cake pan with the bacon.

Arrange the cheese, herbs and mushroom quarters on top. Cover with the meat mixture, pressing it down firmly and smoothing the top.

Roll out the pastry on a floured surface to a circle large enough to cover the filling. Place over the filling and prick the pastry with a fork. Bake in a moderately hot oven (400° F) for 50 minutes–1 hour.

Remove from the oven, invert the pan over a warm plate or cake rack and turn out the pie.
Serves 6–8

Meat Pasty Morsels

3 red or green peppers
1 lb ground beef
2 cloves garlic, crushed
½ teaspoon white pepper
¼ teaspoon cayenne pepper
1 teaspoon cardamom seeds
1 teaspoon cinnamon
½ teaspoon salt
juice of 1 lemon
1 lb onions, chopped
3 tablespoons oil
13-oz package frozen puff
*   pastry*
oil for deep frying

Remove cores, pith and seeds from the peppers, then chop finely. Put the ground beef, chopped peppers, garlic, spices, salt and lemon juice in a frying pan and fry for 5–10 minutes, stirring,
Fry the onions lightly in the oil, then add to the meat mixture. Allow to cool. Thaw the pastry and roll out to a rectangle about 21 × 13 inches. Trim and cut into strips 2 inches wide and 6 inches long. Place a spoonful of the meat mixture at one end and roll up tightly, pressing the edges together to seal. Deep fry in oil heated to 375° F for 4–5 minutes, until golden brown. Drain on paper towels.
Makes 20

Sausage and Meat Flan

13-oz package frozen puff pastry
1 onion, sliced
¼ cup oil
1 clove garlic, crushed
½ teaspoon salt
¼ teaspoon black pepper
½ cup ground beef
½ cup ground pork
3 tablespoons fresh white breadcrumbs
2 teaspoons anchovy paste
2 beef or pork sausages
2 oz garlic sausage, sliced
2 eggs
1 teaspoon dried marjoram
½ teaspoon dried thyme
¼ cup milk

Thaw the pastry. Roll out on a floured surface, and use to line a 9-inch cake pan or flan ring.

Fry the onion in the oil until soft. Add the garlic, salt and pepper and fry for a further 5 minutes. Mix together the ground beef and pork, the breadcrumbs, anchovy paste and the onion mixture. Spread into the pastry case.

Broil or fry the sausages until well browned, then slice. Arrange the sausage and garlic sausage slices over the ground meat mixture. Beat the eggs with the herbs and milk and pour over. Bake in a moderately hot oven (400° F) for 40 minutes.
Serves 6

Savory Tartlets

1-lb package frozen shortcrust pastry
¾ cup lean ground beef
pinch salt
pinch white pepper
1 egg, beaten
pinch dried thyme
½ cup chopped mushrooms
½ cup diced cheese
¼ cup diced tongue
¼ cup diced garlic sausage
½ cucumber
½ cup liver sausage
3 tablespoons chopped parsley

Thaw the pastry. Grease 12 shallow muffin pans and dust with flour. Roll out the pastry on a floured surface and use to line the pans.

Mix the ground beef with the salt, pepper, egg and herbs, and fill four of the tartlets with this mixture. Mix the mushrooms with the cheese, tongue and garlic sausage and use to fill four more tartlets. Grate the cucumber coarsely. Mix with the liver sausage and parsley and use to fill the remaining tartlets.

Bake in a moderately hot oven (400° F) for 20 minutes. Cool on a cake rack, then carefully remove the tartlets from the pans.
Makes 12

Cheese Twists

1-lb package frozen puff
pastry
1 egg
1 tablespoon milk
½ teaspoon ground cloves
2 tablespoons butter
5 tablespoons fresh brown
breadcrumbs
¼ cup cream
½ cup grated cheese
1 tablespoon anchovy paste
1 teaspoon ground coriander
½ teaspoon grated nutmeg
¼ cup water

Thaw the pastry. Roll out on a floured surface until about ¼ inch thick. Brush with the egg, milk and cloves, beaten together. Melt the butter and stir in the breadcrumbs, cream, cheese, anchovy paste, coriander, nutmeg and water. Spread evenly over the pastry then cut into strips about 1 inch wide. Press two strips together, with the pastry and filling alternating. Holding the ends, twist in opposite directions. Repeat with the remaining strips. Place the twisted strips on a floured baking sheet and bake in a moderately hot oven (400° F) for 25 minutes. Serve warm or cold, cut into 3-inch strips.
Makes about 15

Stuffed Bread

½ cake compressed yeast
¼ cup butter
1 cup milk, warmed
4 cups sifted all-purpose flour
1 onion, sliced
5 tablespoons oil
8 oz white cabbage, chopped
and blanched
1 cup chopped mushrooms
salt and pepper
12 oz ground beef
¼ cup chopped chives
1 egg, beaten

Mix the yeast with 5 tablespoons warm water. Leave in a warm place for 15–20 minutes, until frothy. Melt the butter in the milk and add to the flour with the yeast mixture. Mix to a smooth dough, knead. Leave to rise in a warm place for 1–1½ hours. Fry the onion in the oil until soft, then add the cabbage, chopped mushrooms, salt and pepper and fry for 5 minutes. Add the ground beef and cook for 5 minutes. Stir in the chives. Knead the dough again. Roll into a circle about ½ inch thick. Pile the meat filling in the center. Seal, and place on a greased baking sheet, seam underneath. Rise again for 40 minutes. Brush with the egg and bake at 350° F for 50 minutes.
Serves 4–6

285

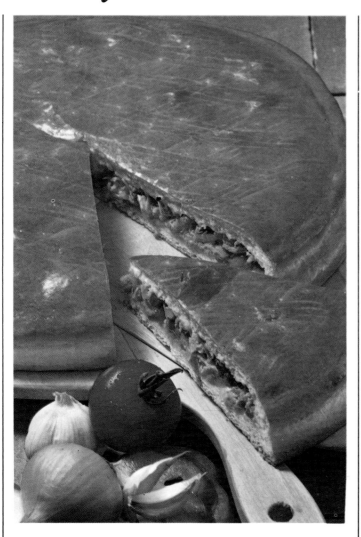

Spanish Chicken Pie

1 red pepper
1 green pepper
1 large onion
8 oz tomatoes
3 tablespoons oil
$\frac{1}{4}$ cup diced cooked ham
$1\frac{1}{2}$ cups diced cooked chicken
$\frac{1}{2}$ clove garlic, crushed
1 teaspoon salt
$\frac{1}{4}$ teaspoon pepper
4 cups bread dough, made with 4 cups all-purpose flour etc (see page 285)
1 egg, beaten

Remove cores, pith and seeds from the peppers, then chop finely. Peel and chop the onion and tomatoes.
Heat the oil and fry the peppers, onion and garlic gently for 10 minutes.
Add the tomatoes, ham and chicken and bring to a simmer. Stir in the salt and pepper. Remove from the heat.
Divide the dough in half and roll out on a floured surface to 2 circles about 12 inches in diameter. Place 1 circle on a greased baking sheet. Spread over the chicken mixture to within $\frac{1}{2}$ inch of the edge. Place the second dough circle on top and press the edges together to seal. Score with a knife, brush with the egg and bake in a moderately hot oven (400° F) for 45 minutes.
Serves 6–8

Cheese and Grape Puffs

1-lb package frozen puff pastry
2 eggs
3 tablespoons water
1 teaspoon paprika pepper
$\frac{1}{4}$ teaspoon black pepper
1 teaspoon allspice
8 oz Cheddar cheese
4 oz white grapes
4 oz salami, sliced

Thaw the pastry. Roll out on a floured surface to a rectangle about $\frac{1}{8}$ inch thick and cut into 2-inch squares. Mix the eggs with the water, paprika, black pepper and allspice, and brush some of this mixture over the pastry squares.
Cube the cheese. Halve the grapes, and seed. Cut the salami slices into small pieces. Place a cube of cheese, grape and piece of salami on each pastry square. Bring the corners of the pastry inwards to form an envelope, and press together firmly. Brush with the remaining egg mixture. Place on a greased baking sheet and bake in a moderately hot oven (400° F) for 15 minutes or until lightly browned. Serve warm.
Makes 35–40

Piquant Cheese Tart

11-oz package frozen
  shortcrust pastry
$\frac{1}{4}$ *cup butter*
2 onions, finely chopped
3 tablespoons all-purpose
  flour
1 cup milk
1$\frac{1}{2}$ cups grated Emmenthal
  or Gruyère cheese
3 eggs, beaten
5 tablespoons chopped chives
3 tablespoons chopped
  parsley
2 teaspoons paprika pepper

Thaw the pastry. Roll
out on a floured surface to a
circle about $\frac{1}{4}$ inch thick.
Use to line a 10-inch cake
pan or flan ring placed on a
baking sheet. Bake in a
moderately hot oven
(400° F) for 10 minutes.
Remove and reduce oven
temperature to 300° F.
Meanwhile prepare the
filling. Melt the butter in a
saucepan. Add the onions
and fry for 5 minutes.
Sprinkle over the flour, stir
well, then stir in the milk.
Bring to the boil, stirring,
and simmer until slightly
thickened. Remove from the
heat, and add the cheese,
eggs, chives, parsley and
paprika.
Pour into the pastry case,
and bake on the bottom
shelf for 40 minutes, until
golden brown.
Serves 6–8

Mushroom Pasties

11-oz package frozen puff
  pastry
4 oz bacon slices
1 small onion
1$\frac{1}{2}$ cups sliced button
  mushrooms
2 teaspoons tomato paste
$\frac{1}{2}$ *teaspoon celery salt*
$\frac{1}{2}$ *teaspoon white pepper*
2 tablespoons butter
1 egg, beaten

Thaw the pastry. Dice the
bacon. Peel and finely chop
the onion. Fry the bacon
and onion together until the
bacon has rendered its fat.
Add the mushrooms, tomato
paste, celery salt, pepper
and butter, and fry until the
liquid evaporates. Remove
from the heat.
Roll out the pastry on a
floured surface. Cut into
4-inch circles. Place a
spoonful of filling on one
half of each circle and fold
over the other half to cover,
forming a half-moon shape.
Press the edges together to
seal, using the prongs of a
fork for decorative effect.
Brush with the beaten egg
and place the pasties on a
floured baking sheet. Bake
in a moderate oven (350° F)
for 25 minutes. Serve hot or
cold, garnished with a sprig
of parsley.
Makes 8–10

Pies, Cakes and Cookies

Autumn Pie

2 cups all-purpose flour
¼ teaspoon salt
½ cup butter
1 egg
½ cup sugar
12 oz blackberries or
  loganberries
2 teaspoons cornstarch
¼ cup gooseberry jam
3 egg whites
½ cup confectioners' sugar

Sift the flour and salt into a bowl. Rub in the butter. Stir in the egg and 3 tablespoons sugar. Form into a dough, chill for 20 minutes. Sprinkle the berries with the remaining sugar. Leave to drain in a sieve over a saucepan. Warm the berry juice. Dissolve the cornstarch in 1 tablespoon water, stir into the berry juice. Bring to the boil, stirring, and simmer until thickened. Add the berries and cool. Roll out the pastry to line a greased 8-inch cake pan or flan ring. Bake at 325° F for 15–20 minutes. Cool.
Spread the jam over the pastry base. Spoon in the berry mixture. Beat the egg whites with the confectioners' sugar until stiff, then pipe over a lattice work. Bake at 350° F for 15 minutes. Cool before serving.
Serves 6–8

Plum Slices

½ cake compressed yeast
⅔ cup milk, warmed
¼ cup butter, softened
½ cup sugar
½ teaspoon salt
grated rind of ½ lemon
1 egg
3 cups all-purpose flour
2 lb plums
½ cup flaked almonds

Mix the yeast with 2 tablespoons of the milk. Leave in a warm place for 15 minutes, or until frothy. Melt the butter in the remaining milk and add to the yeast with ¼ cup of the sugar, the salt, lemon rind and egg.
Sift the flour into a bowl. Pour in the yeast mixture and mix thoroughly. Turn out on a floured surface and roll to fit a greased 9 × 13-inch baking sheet. Leave to rise in a warm place for 1–1½ hours.
Wash the plums. Halve, remove the pits and slice. Arrange the plum slices on the dough and sprinkle with the almonds. Leave in a warm place for 10 minutes. Bake in a moderate oven (350° F) for 40 minutes. Sprinkle over the remaining sugar and cool before slicing.
Makes 15–20

Marble Cake

3 tablespoons dry bread-
   crumbs
$\frac{1}{2}$ cup butter or margarine
$\frac{2}{3}$ cup sugar
grated rind of $\frac{1}{2}$ lemon
2 large eggs
$\frac{2}{3}$ cup milk
$\frac{1}{2}$ cup cornstarch
$1\frac{3}{4}$ cups all-purpose flour
1 teaspoon baking powder
$\frac{1}{4}$ cup cocoa powder
1 tablespoon confectioners'
   sugar

Grease a $7\frac{1}{2}$-inch fluted savarin or kugelhopf mold. Sprinkle in the breadcrumbs and tip the mold to coat the sides. Cream the butter with $\frac{1}{2}$ cup of the sugar and the lemon rind until light and fluffy. Add the eggs, one at a time, with a little of the milk and beat well. Sift the cornstarch, flour and baking powder into the bowl and fold into the creamed mixture with all but 3 tablespoons of the remaining milk.
Spoon half the mixture into the mold. Add the cocoa powder and remaining sugar to the other half and mix well with the remaining milk. Spoon into the mold over the plain mixture, and stir gently with a knife into spirals. Bake in a moderately hot oven (400° F) for 60–70 minutes or until a skewer inserted in the cake comes out clean. Turn the cake out on to a cake rack. Leave to cool, then sprinkle with the confectioners' sugar.
Serves 6–8

Viennese Almond Cookies

3 egg whites
1 cup sugar
½ teaspoon vanilla extract
pinch salt
1¼ cups ground almonds
6 (1-oz) squares semisweet
*   chocolate*
1 tablespoon unsalted butter

Beat the egg whites until they hold a stiff peak. Add the sugar, vanilla extract, salt and ground almonds and fold in quickly with a metal spoon. Place spoonsful of the mixture on baking sheets lined with parchment or rice paper, leaving space between each

spoonful. Bake in a moderate oven (325° F) for 10 minutes. The cookies should dry out rather than bake, and be firm to the touch, not soft. Leave to cool, then remove carefully from the parchment paper. If you have used rice paper, which is edible, just cut around each cookie with scissors. Melt the chocolate with the butter and stir well. Dip the base of each cookie in the chocolate, then leave upside-down to dry.
Makes 15–20

Rice Cake

7½-oz package frozen puff
*   pastry*
½ cup round-grain rice
2½ cups milk
1¼ cups cream
¼ teaspoon salt
¼ cup sugar
2 eggs
2 egg yolks
3 tablespoons finely chopped
*   candied peel*
¼ cup chopped red and yellow
*   candied cherries*
¼ cup chopped almonds
⅓ cup raisins

Thaw the pastry. Put the rice, milk, cream, salt and 3 tablespoons of the sugar in a saucepan and bring to the boil. Cover and simmer

for 20–25 minutes, until the rice is tender and has absorbed all the liquid. Cool then beat in the eggs and 1 of the egg yolks. Roll out the pastry to line a 9-inch cake pan or flan ring. Bake at 400° F for 10 minutes. Mix the rice with the candied peel and spread half in the pastry case. Mix the remainder with the cherries, almonds and raisins, spoon over and smooth the top. Beat the remaining egg yolk and sugar and pour over the rice mixture. Bake at 400° F for about 25 minutes. Cool then sprinkle with confectioners' sugar.
Serves 6–8

Pies, Cakes and Cookies

Fruit Tartlets

2 cups all-purpose flour
¼ teaspoon salt
½ cup butter
1 egg
pinch sugar
fruit (see method)
Filling
2 tablespoons butter
¼ cup all-purpose flour
1 tablespoon sugar
1 egg yolk
⅔ cup milk
¼ teaspoon vanilla extract
5 tablespoons apricot jam

Sift the flour and salt into a bowl. Rub in the butter then stir in the egg and sugar. Form into a dough, adding a little water if necessary. Chill for 20 minutes. Roll out and use to line 12 greased and floured shallow muffin pans. Bake in a moderate oven (325° F) for 20 minutes. Cool on a cake rack.

Any kind of fruit can be used for the filling, fresh, cooked or canned.

Melt the butter in a saucepan and stir in the flour and sugar. Beat the egg yolk with the milk and strain into the pan. Cook, stirring, until the mixture comes to the boil, then remove from the heat. Stir for 1 minute, then add the vanilla extract. Cool and spoon into the pastry cases. Top with the drained fruit, then brush with a glaze of the sieved heated apricot jam.
Makes 12

Apple Cake

2¾ cups all-purpose flour
1 cup sugar
⅔ cup butter
2 egg yolks
pinch salt
1 lb cooking apples
juice of 1 lemon
pinch cinnamon
⅓ cup raisins
½ cup ground almonds
½ cup ground hazelnuts
3 tablespoons apricot jam
¼ cup confectioners' sugar
3 tablespoons kirsch or
*   cherry brandy*

Sift the flour into a bowl. Stir in ⅔ cup of the sugar and rub in the butter. Add the egg yolks and salt and mix quickly to a dough.

Chill for 20 minutes. Roll out half the dough to line a 10-inch cake pan or flan ring. Bake at 400° F for 15 minutes. Peel, core and slice the apples. Mix with the remaining sugar, the lemon juice, cinnamon, raisins and nuts. Moisten with a little water to blend. Spoon into the pastry shell and smooth over.

Roll out the remaining dough to cover the cake. Bake in the preheated oven for 30 minutes. Cool in the pan overnight.

Warm the jam and spread over the cake. Combine the confectioners' sugar and kirsch, spread over the jam and leave to set.
Serves 6–8

291

Uncooked Cheesecake

1½ cups all-purpose flour
½ cup cornstarch
¼ cup butter
2 egg yolks
⅔ cup sugar
1 tablespoon rum
2 cups cottage cheese
⅔ cup cream
grated rind of 1 lemon
2 teaspoons lemon juice
juice of 1 orange
⅔ cup raisins
2 envelopes unflavored gelatin
3 tablespoons apricot jam
½ cup toasted flaked almonds

Sift the flours on to a working surface. Make a well and add the butter, cut into small pieces, the egg yolks, 3 tablespoons sugar and the rum. Mix to a dough and chill for 20 minutes. Press into the bottom of a greased 8-inch loose-bottomed cake pan. Bake at 400° F for 25 minutes. Cool in the pan. Strain the cottage cheese and beat with the cream, lemon rind and juice, orange juice and remaining sugar. Stir in the raisins. Dissolve the gelatin in 5 tablespoons water in a bowl over a pan of simmering water. Strain into the cheese mixture and stir well. Spoon into the cake pan, smooth over. Warm the jam and spread over. Chill in the refrigerator until set. Decorate with the almonds.
Serves 8–10

Viennese Whirls

⅔ cup butter
⅔ cup confectioners' sugar
¼ cup cornstarch
5 tablespoons milk
pinch salt
grated rind of ½ lemon
2 cups all-purpose flour
6 (1-oz) squares semisweet chocolate

Cream the butter with the confectioners' sugar and cornstarch until light and fluffy. Beat in the milk, salt and lemon rind. Sift the flour into the bowl and mix together thoroughly, adding more milk if the mixture is too thick to pipe.
Using a piping bag fitted with a large star nozzle, pipe the mixture on to greased baking sheets in S-shapes or circles. Bake in a moderate oven (350° F) for 10 minutes or until light brown. Cool the cookies on a cake rack.
Melt the chocolate gently in the top of a double boiler. Dip the cookies in the chocolate so they are half-coated. Allow to dry on wax paper.
Makes 20

Variation
Use the melted chocolate to sandwich together pairs of the cookies.

Banana Cake

$\frac{2}{3}$ *cup butter*
$\frac{2}{3}$ *cup sugar*
juice and grated rind of
 1 lemon
2 eggs
1$\frac{3}{4}$ cups all-purpose flour
$\frac{1}{2}$ cup cornstarch
1 teaspoon baking powder
pinch each salt, ground
 ginger, cinnamon, cloves
 and nutmeg
4 bananas

Cream the butter and sugar until light and fluffy. Beat in the lemon rind and eggs. Sift 1$\frac{1}{4}$ cups of the flour, the cornstarch, baking powder, salt and spices into the creamed mixture and fold in. If the mixture is too dry to combine, add a little milk. (It should not be too soft.) Use half the mixture to line the bottom of a greased loose-bottomed 9-inch cake pan. Bake in a moderate oven (350° F) for 25 minutes. Cool.
Peel the bananas and cut or dice them. Sprinkle with the lemon juice, then spoon into the pan and spread out.
Mix the remaining cake mixture with the remaining flour to form a dough. Roll out a circle to cover the pan. Lay over the filling and press to seal the edges. Bake in the preheated oven for 35 minutes. Sprinkle with confectioners' sugar and leave to cool in the pan.
Serves 6–8

Buttercream Fingers

$\frac{1}{2}$ cake compressed yeast
1 cup milk, warmed
4 cups all-purpose flour
$\frac{1}{2}$ cup butter
1 egg
$\frac{3}{4}$ cup sugar
$\frac{1}{2}$ teaspoon grated lemon rind
1 cup chopped almonds
$\frac{1}{2}$ cup unsalted butter
1 cup confectioners' sugar
$\frac{1}{2}$ teaspoon vanilla extract

Mix the yeast with 3 tablespoons warm milk. Leave in a warm place for 15 minutes, until frothy.
Sift the flour into a bowl and pour in the yeast mixture. Melt $\frac{1}{4}$ cup butter in the remaining warm milk and add to the bowl with the egg, $\frac{1}{4}$ cup sugar, and the lemon rind. Form into a dough, knead. Spread out on a greased baking sheet and leave to rise for 1–1$\frac{1}{2}$ hours.
Melt the remaining butter, and stir in the remaining sugar and the almonds.
Mix in 1 tablespoon of milk, cool, then spread over the dough. Bake at 400° F for 40 minutes. Cool and cut into fingers. Split each finger in half through the center. Cream the unsalted butter, confectioners' sugar and vanilla extract until light and fluffy. Use to sandwich together the split fingers.
Makes 25–30

Black Forest Cherry Cake

4 (1-oz) squares semisweet
  chocolate
½ cup butter
½ cup sugar
4 eggs
¾ cup ground almonds
½ cup all-purpose flour
½ cup cornstarch
2 teaspoons baking powder
2 cups whipping cream
1½ lb canned pitted cherries,
  drained
6 tablespoons kirsch
12 red candied cherries
chocolate scrolls

Melt the chocolate in the
top of a double boiler.
Cool. Cream the butter and
sugar until light and fluffy.
Beat in the eggs, almonds
and melted chocolate.
Sift the flour, cornstarch
and baking powder into the
creamed mixture and fold
in, mixing well. Turn into
3 greased 7-inch layer cake
pans. Bake at 350° F for
20–25 minutes, until
cooked. Leave to cool.
Whip the cream until
thick. Dry the cherries on
paper towels. Remove the
cake layers from the pans.
Sprinkle each layer with
2 tablespoons of kirsch.
Sandwich together with the
cherries and cream, leaving
enough cream to spread
over the top and sides of the
cake, and to pipe a border.
Decorate with the candied
cherries and pile chocolate
scrolls in the center.
Serves 8–10

Cinnamon Stars

4 small egg whites
1⅓ cups confectioners' sugar
2¾ cups ground almonds
2 tablespoons ground
  cinnamon
grated rind of ½ lemon
sugar

Put the egg whites into the
top of a double boiler or a
heatproof bowl. Beat until
frothy, then add the con-
fectioners' sugar. Place over
simmering water and
continue beating until the
meringue is thick and will
hold its shape. Remove
from the heat. Put 4–5
tablespoons of the meringue
to one side.
Fold the ground almonds,
cinnamon and lemon rind
into the remaining
meringue. Leave to cool for
1 hour.
Sprinkle a work surface
with sugar and roll out the
meringue until about ¼ inch
thick. This mixture will be
soft and must be rolled out
very carefully. Cut into stars
with a cookie cutter. Place
the stars on a greased and
floured baking sheet.
Spread the reserved
meringue carefully over the
stars and bake in a
moderate oven (325° F) for
15–20 minutes, until just
firm. Transfer the stars
carefully to a cake rack and
leave to cool.
Makes about 60

Jam Rings

4 eggs
1 cup butter
⅔ cup confectioners' sugar
½ teaspoon vanilla extract
pinch salt
2¾ cups all-purpose flour, sifted
½ cup sugar
1 cup chopped almonds
1 egg, beaten
¼ cup black cherry jam

Hard cook the eggs for 10 minutes. Cool and shell. Halve and tip the yolks into a strainer. (Keep the whites for another recipe.) Strain the yolks and beat in the butter, ½ cup confectioners' sugar, the vanilla extract and salt. Add the flour and mix well. Roll out to a thickness of ½ inch. Cut into circles, using a fluted 2-inch cookie cutter. Cut smaller circles from the center of each to form rings. Mix together the sugar and almonds. Brush one side of each ring with the beaten egg, then dip into the almond mixture. Lay the rings, almond side up, on a greased baking sheet, and bake in a moderate oven (350° F) for 10–15 minutes, until browned. Cool on a cake rack. Warm the jam and sandwich together pairs of cookies. Sprinkle over the remaining confectioners' sugar.
Makes 25–30

Sachertorte

7 eggs, separated
¾ cup plus 2 tablespoons sugar
½ cup cocoa powder
1 cup all-purpose flour
½ cup butter, melted
¾ cup crushed plain cookies
5 tablespoons dry bread-crumbs
5 tablespoons apricot jam
8 (1-oz) squares semisweet chocolate
½ cup whipping cream
2 cups confectioners' sugar

Beat the egg yolks with ½ cup sugar until frothy. Fold in the sifted cocoa and flour. Stir in the butter. Beat the egg whites until frothy. Add the remaining sugar and beat until stiff. Fold into the egg yolk mixture with the cookie crumbs. Grease two 9-inch layer cake pans and coat with the breadcrumbs. Spoon in the cake mixture and bake in the center of a moderately hot oven (400° F) for 30 minutes. Reduce heat to 350° F and cook for 15–20 minutes. Cool in the oven for 15 minutes, with the door slightly open, then remove to cool completely. Warm the jam and use to sandwich the layers and spread over the sides of the cake. Melt the chocolate. Cool, then beat in the cream and confectioners' sugar. Spread smoothly over the top and sides of the cake.
Serves 8–10

Strawberry Jelly Roll

8 oz strawberries
⅓ cup sugar
3 large eggs, separated
⅔ cup confectioners' sugar
½ cup plus 2 tablespoons
  all-purpose flour
6 tablespoons cornstarch
⅔ cup whipping cream

Hull and quarter the strawberries. Sprinkle with 3 tablespoons of the sugar and leave for 30 minutes. Beat the egg yolks with the remaining sugar. Beat the egg whites until frothy, then add half the confectioners' sugar. Beat until stiff then fold into the yolk mixture. Sift the flours and fold in quickly but thoroughly. Spread smoothly in a 9 × 12-inch jelly roll pan lined with wax paper. Bake in a moderately hot oven (400° F) for 10–15 minutes. Turn out carefully on to clean wax paper, peel off the first paper and roll up with the clean paper inside. Cool. Drain the strawberry juice and whip with the cream until thick. Fold in the remaining confectioners' sugar and the strawberries. Unroll the cake. Spread over the filling and roll up, using the paper to lift the cake. Sprinkle with extra confectioners' sugar and serve.
Serves 4–6

Anise Seed Cookies

4 eggs
1⅓ cups confectioners' sugar
pinch salt
2¾ cups all-purpose flour
2 teaspoons ground anise
  seed

Separate the egg yolks from the whites. Cream the egg yolks with the confectioners' sugar and salt until pale and frothy. Beat the egg whites until very stiff, then fold into the yolk mixture. Sift the flour and anise seed on to the mixture, and fold in quickly but thoroughly. Grease a baking sheet and sprinkle with flour. Fill a piping bag, fitted with a plain nozzle, with the cookie mixture and pipe in small rounds on the baking sheet. Leave to dry out overnight, then bake toward the top of a moderate oven (325° F) for 20 minutes. Cool on a cake rack.
Makes 36

Variation
To make Vanilla Cookies, substitute 1 teaspoon vanilla extract for the ground anise seed.

Brandy Pretzels

1 cup butter
⅔ cup plus 2 tablespoons
* confectioners' sugar*
1 egg yolk
pinch salt
½ teaspoon vanilla extract
2¾ cups all-purpose flour
3–4 tablespoons brandy

Cream the butter with ⅔ cup of the confectioners' sugar until light and fluffy. Beat in the egg yolk, salt and vanilla extract. Sift the flour into the bowl and mix well. Chill for 2–3 hours. Break off pieces of the dough and roll into 'worms' about ¼ inch thick and 6 inches long. Twist each worm into a pretzel (see photograph) and place on a baking sheet. Bake in a moderate oven (325° F) for 10 minutes or until golden. Cool on the baking sheet. Mix together the brandy and remaining confectioners' sugar and brush over the pretzels. Leave to set on a cake rack until the glaze becomes shiny.
Makes about 45

Cook's Tip
For quick creaming, use soft margarine instead of butter.

Chocolate Macaroons

4 (1-oz) squares semisweet
* chocolate*
4 egg whites
¾ cup plus 2 tablespoons
* sugar*
2 cups ground almonds

Grate the chocolate. Beat the egg whites until stiff. Add the sugar gradually and continue beating until the mixture is thick and glossy. Fold in the ground almonds and grated chocolate. Drop spoonsful of the mixture on to a baking sheet lined with parchment or rice paper, leaving space between each cookie. Bake in a moderate oven (350° F) for 15–20 minutes. Do not let the macaroons become too dark or they will taste bitter. Cool on the baking sheet, then carefully peel the macaroons off the parchment paper or cut around each cookie on the edible rice paper.
Makes about 30

Variation
Topped macaroons
Prepare in the same way as above, but use 5 egg whites and 1 cup sugar. Leave 5–6 tablespoons of the egg white and sugar mixture to one side, and then place a small spoonful on each chocolate macaroon before baking.

Strawberry Yogurt Cake

1¾ cups all-purpose flour
¼ cup margarine
¾ cup sugar
1 egg
4 envelopes unflavored
   gelatin
¼ cup water
1 lb strawberries
3¾ cups plain yogurt
⅔ cup whipping cream
1 small apricot

Sift the flour on to a working surface. Make a well in the center and put in the margarine, cut into small pieces, ½ cup of the sugar and the egg. Mix quickly together to form a dough. Press into the bottom of a greased 9-inch loose-bottomed cake pan. Prick all over with a fork and bake in a moderately hot oven (400° F) for 25 minutes or until cooked. Leave to cool.
Sprinkle the gelatin over the water and leave to soften. Hull the strawberries, then strain or blend three-quarters of them. Mix with the yogurt and the remaining sugar. Dissolve the gelatin in a bowl over simmering water, then strain into the yogurt mixture.
Put aside a few strawberries for decoration and halve the rest. Arrange the halves, cut sides down, on the pastry base. Spoon over the yogurt mixture and chill until set.
Remove from the pan. Whip the cream and pipe on top of the cake. Decorate with pieces of strawberry and apricot.
Serves 6–8

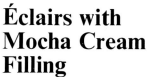

Éclairs with Mocha Cream Filling

⅔ *cup water*
pinch salt
¼ *cup butter*
½ *cup plus 2 tablespoons*
  all-purpose flour
2 small eggs
grated rind of ½ lemon
1¼ *cups whipping cream*
2 teaspoons coffee essence
⅓ *cup confectioners' sugar*
1 teaspoon coffee powder
1–2 *tablespoons warm water*

Put the water and salt in a saucepan and bring to the boil. Add the butter and, when melted, sift in the flour. Remove from the heat and beat well until the mixture leaves the sides of the pan. Cool slightly, then beat in the eggs and lemon rind. Fill a piping bag with the mixture and pipe on to a floured baking sheet in 3-inch strips. Bake in a moderately hot oven (400° F) for 25 minutes. Slit the éclairs lengthwise and leave to cool.
Whip the cream with the coffee essence until thick. Fill the éclairs with the cream, piping it for a more decorative effect.
Combine the confectioners' sugar, coffee powder and warm water and use to glaze the tops of the éclairs. Allow the glaze to set, then serve.
Makes about 15

Butter Cookies with Almond Paste

¾ *cup plus 2 tablespoons*
  butter
½ *cup confectioners' sugar*
¼ *cup almond paste*
grated rind of ½ lemon
2¼ *cups all-purpose flour*
1 egg yolk
sugar

Cream the butter and confectioners' sugar together until light and fluffy. Beat in the almond paste and lemon rind, then sift the flour on to the mixture. Knead well together. Divide the dough in three and form each piece into a roll about 1½ inches thick. Chill for 20 minutes.
Lightly beat the egg yolk and brush over the rolls of dough. Roll them in sugar, then cut into slices ¼ inch thick. Place the slices on greased baking sheets, leaving space between the slices, and bake at 400° F for 8–10 minutes, until lightly browned. Cool on a cake rack.
Makes about 60

Cook's Tip
The rolls of uncooked dough, without the egg yolk and sugar coating, may be wrapped in foil and kept in the refrigerator for up to a week.

299

Almond Paste Hearts

2 cups almond paste
1¾ cups confectioners' sugar
2 egg whites
1 egg yolk
candied angelica
candied cherries

Work the almond paste and 1¼ cups of the confectioners' sugar together. Roll out on a surface dusted with confectioners' sugar until ½ inch thick. Cut out small hearts with a cookie cutter. With the remaining almond paste mixture, cut thin strips long enough to form the heart shape. Brush the edges of the hearts with egg white, then place the strips on top to form a raised border. Flute with the prongs of a fork, then brush the borders with the beaten egg yolk. Place the hearts on a baking sheet and bake in a hot oven (425° F) for 3–5 minutes. Mix together the remaining egg whites and confectioners' sugar and brush in the centers of the hearts. Leave to set, then decorate with the candied fruit.
Makes about 20

Variation
Use a selection of cookie cutters to make different shapes.

Hazelnut and Almond Fingers

1¾ cups all-purpose flour
1 teaspoon baking powder
1 egg
3 tablespoons milk
¾ cup sugar
1 cup ground hazelnuts
½ cup butter or margarine
1 egg yolk
¼ cup ground almonds
¼ cup flaked almonds

Sift the flour and baking powder into a bowl, and make a well in the center. Put the egg, milk and half the sugar into the well and mix together. Add the remaining sugar, the hazelnuts and butter or margarine, cut into small pieces, and mix quickly to a dough. Chill for 20 minutes. Form the dough into small fingers. Brush with the beaten egg yolk and roll in the ground and flaked almonds. Put on a greased baking sheet and bake in a moderately hot oven (400° F) for 12–15 minutes, or until firm and lightly browned.
Makes about 30

Cook's Tip
Keep butter in the refrigerator, and then grate it for easier mixing.

Vanilla Crescent Cookies

2½ cups all-purpose flour
1 cup ground almonds
⅔ cup sugar
*¾ cup plus 2 tablespoons
  butter*
2 egg yolks
1 teaspoon vanilla extract

Sift the flour on to a working surface. Add the almonds, ⅓ cup of the sugar, the butter, cut into small pieces, the egg yolks and vanilla extract. Mix together by hand very quickly, then chill the dough for 2–3 hours. Form the dough into 'worms' about 2 inches long, then curve into crescent shapes. Place the crescents on a greased baking sheet and bake in a moderate oven (350° F) for 8–10 minutes or until golden. Sprinkle the crescents with the remaining sugar while still warm, then cool on a cake rack.
Makes about 60

Cook's Tip
The sugar sprinkled on the cookies may be flavored with vanilla. To make vanilla sugar, put sugar in a stoppered jar. Add a vanilla bean and leave for at least 1 week.

Brandy Snap Ring

1½ cups butter
¾ cup sugar
¼ teaspoon salt
3 eggs
1 tablespoon rum
*juice and grated rind of
  ½ lemon*
1¼ cups all-purpose flour
1 tablespoon baking powder
¾ cup cornstarch
2 cups confectioners' sugar
1 egg yolk
6–8 brandy snaps, crushed
⅔ cup whipping cream
8 red candied cherries

Cream ¾ cup butter with the sugar until light and fluffy. Beat in the salt, eggs, rum, lemon juice and rind. Fold in the sifted flour, baking powder and cornstarch. Pour into a greased 9-inch ring mold and bake in a moderate oven (350° F) for 45–60 minutes. Cool slightly in the mold, then turn out on a cake rack to cool completely. Cut into four layers.
Cream the remaining butter with the confectioners' sugar and egg yolk. Use to sandwich together the four layers and to cover the completed cake. Press on the crushed brandy snaps to cover completely. Decorate with the cream, whipped and piped, and halved candied cherries.
Serves 6–8

Aperitifs

Aperitifs, which are served before a meal, should not be too sweet or strong, but dry. Most aperitifs contain vermouth or wine. They should be served in small, short-stemmed glasses.

Bombarral (*illustrated on the right*)
Put ¾ oz vodka, 1½ oz port and a few ice cubes in the goblet of the blender and blend for about 10 seconds. Pour into a glass, and put a slice of lemon on the rim of the glass.

Berlenga
Mix 1 glass (4 oz) port with ¾ oz gin and some ice cubes; shake well. Pour into a glass and put a slice of lemon on the rim of the glass.

Adonis
Mix ¾ oz sweet vermouth with ice, 1½ oz dry sherry and a dash of Angostura bitters. Strain into a glass.

Sixty-Six (*illustrated on the left*)
Mix ¾ oz Campari, ¾ oz dry vermouth, ¾ oz dry sherry and ¾ oz gin with a few ice cubes. Pour into a glass and add a few drops of lemon juice.

Each of the above recipes makes 1 drink.

Prince of Wales Drinks

The origin of these drinks is not known, but originally they were served in silver glasses. If you do not have any silver or pewter mugs, serve the drinks in tall glasses, with straws.

Prince of Wales (*illustrated on the right*)
Put 4 ice cubes in a silver or pewter mug, or a tall glass. Pour in 1½ oz Curaçao and 2 drops of Angostura bitters. Stir, and top with champagne. Decorate with an orange segment placed on the rim of the glass.

Duke of York (*illustrated on the left*)
Put a few ice cubes in a glass, add the juice of 1 orange and 1 teaspoon of grenadine. Stir, and then top with champagne. Decorate with a thin slice of lemon placed on the rim of the glass.

Eden Rocks
Half fill a glass with crushed ice. Add 1 teaspoon of raspberry syrup and 1½ oz cherry brandy. Stir, and top with champagne. Decorate with an orange wedge placed on the rim of the glass.

Each of the above recipes makes 1 drink.

Fruity Daiquiris

These cocktails are very refreshing and always contain rum, either light or dark. The light rum has a slightly sweeter flavor. Serve in cocktail glasses.

Daiquiri
Mix ice with the juice of 1 lime, 1 teaspoon confectioners' sugar and 1½ oz white rum. Strain into a cocktail glass.

Banana Daiquiri (*left*)
Place 1½ oz lime juice, 1 teaspoon sugar, 1 cup crushed ice, 1½ oz white rum and 1 peeled banana in the goblet of the blender and blend for 10 seconds. Pour into a glass and serve

with a slice of banana placed on the rim.

Martinique Daiquiri (*right background*)
Mix 3 ice cubes with ¾ oz dark rum, 1 teaspoon grapefruit juice, 1 teaspoon pineapple juice, 1 teaspoon lime juice and 1 teaspoon lemon juice. Shake well, then strain into a cocktail glass.

Havana Club (*illustrated on the right*)
Mix a few ice cubes with ½ oz sweet vermouth and 1 oz dark rum. Serve in a cocktail glass and decorate with a cherry if liked.

Each of the above recipes makes 1 drink.

Unusual Highballs

A highball is simple to make and always popular. Any liquor can be used, with ice, soda or ginger ale.

Dundee Highball
(*illustrated on the left*)
Mix 1 teaspoon Curaçao with 2 teaspoons lemon juice, 2 teaspoons sugar syrup and 1½ oz rum. Add some crushed ice, shake well and strain into a glass. Top up with soda.

Eton Highball
Mix 1 teaspoon rum with 2 teaspoons lemon juice, 2 teaspoons sugar syrup and ¾ oz each of cherry brandy and gin. Add some crushed

ice, shake well and strain into a glass. Top up with soda.

Crystal Highball
(*illustrated in the background*)
Mix some crushed ice with ¾ oz dry vermouth and 2 tablespoons orange juice. Strain into a highball glass and top up with soda.

Victory Highball
(*illustrated on the right*)
Mix 2 ice cubes with ¾ oz Pernod and ¾ oz grenadine. Strain into a glass and top up with soda.

Each of the above recipes makes 1 drink.

Piquant Tomato Cocktail

2 lb tomatoes
few sprigs parsley
2 teaspoons paprika pepper
pinch salt
1 small head celery
1 large apple
10 ice cubes
freshly ground black pepper

Peel and quarter the tomatoes; wash and dry the parsley. Place the tomatoes, parsley, paprika and salt in the goblet of the blender and blend until smooth. Pour the mixture into a jug. Chop the celery; peel, core and chop the apple. Blend the apple and celery and mix with the tomato juice. Add the ice cubes. Pour the cocktail into four small glasses and sprinkle with the black pepper.
Makes 4 drinks

Variation
Mix ½ cup cream into the cocktail, and replace the celery with ½ teaspoon celery salt.

Vegetable Cocktail

1 lb carrots
1 tomato
1 sprig parsley
1 cup chopped celery
juice of 1 grapefruit
pinch salt
4 lemon slices

Peel and chop the carrots. Place them in the goblet of the blender together with the peeled and quartered tomato, parsley and chopped celery and blend for 30 seconds. Pour the juice into a jug and add the grapefruit juice and salt, mixing it well. Pour the cocktail into four glasses and place a lemon slice as decoration on the rim of each of the glasses before serving.
Makes 4 drinks

Cook's Tip
Other vegetables may be used in place of the carrots. Orange juice may be used if preferred instead of the grapefruit juice.

Strawberry Milk Shake

8 oz strawberries
¼ cup granulated sugar
3 tablespoons strawberry
  ice cream
2 cups milk
juice of 1 lemon
juice of 1 orange
grated rind of 1 lemon
¼ cup confectioners' sugar
4 ice cubes

Halve the strawberries and place in a bowl. Sprinkle over the granulated sugar and leave for 30 minutes for juice to be extracted. Blend the strawberries and juice in the blender, add the ice cream, milk, lemon juice, orange juice, grated lemon rind and con-fectioners' sugar and blend for a further 30 seconds. Pour into four glasses and add an ice cube to each one. *Makes 4 drinks*

Variation

Pineapple Milk Shake
Replace the strawberries with canned or fresh pineapple. Use vanilla ice cream in place of the strawberry. Pour 1–2 tablespoons chocolate syrup on top before serving.

Honey and Fruit Cocktail

2 dessert apples
¼ cup clear honey
2 cups apple juice
2 cups grape juice
10 hazelnuts, chopped
¼ cup whipping cream

Peel, core and slice the apples. Heat the honey with the apple and grape juices until it has dissolved. Pour the mixture into the goblet of the blender and add the hazelnuts and sliced apples. Blend for 2 minutes and pour into four glasses. Lightly whip the cream and place a spoonful on each drink. Serve at once. *Makes 4 drinks*

Variations
The apples may be replaced with 8 oz pitted plums, or 2 bananas and the juice of 2 oranges and ½ grapefruit. If liked, pieces of fruit may be added to the drink just before serving.

Cook's Tip
If clear honey is not available, use sugar syrup.

Orange Punch

3 large oranges
2 teaspoons confectioners'
*   sugar*
2 bottles dry white wine
1 bottle champange
about 10–15 ice cubes

Peel the oranges and cut away all the pith. Cut the fruit into thin slices, removing the skin and seeds. Place in a punch bowl, then sprinkle with the confectioners' sugar. Pour in the white wine and chill for 20–30 minutes. Just before serving, add the champagne and ice cubes.
Serves 10–12

Variation
The punch may also be prepared using equal quantities of dry red and white wine. Chill the oranges in the white wine and add the red wine just before serving.

Cook's Tip
To reduce cost, substitute a sparkling white wine for the champagne.

Fizzes

Fizzes are made with carbonated beverages. If champagne is used the drink is known as a Royal Fizz. They should be drunk while still fizzy.

Gin Fizz *(left)*
Shake together the juice of $\frac{1}{2}$ lemon, 1 teaspoon confectioners' sugar, 2 oz gin and ice cubes. Strain into a highball glass and top up with carbonated water.

Golden Fizz *(right)*
Mix one egg yolk with ice, juice of $\frac{1}{2}$ lemon, 2 teaspoons confectioners' sugar and $1\frac{1}{2}$ oz gin. Strain into a highball glass and top up with carbonated shater.

Orange Gin Fizz (*illustrated in the background*)
Mix the juice of 2 oranges with ice, 2 teaspoons confectioners' sugar, the juice of $\frac{1}{2}$ lemon and 2 oz gin. Strain into a highball glass and top up with carbonated water.

Apricot Fizz
Mix the juice of $\frac{1}{2}$ lemon and $\frac{1}{2}$ lime with ice, 1 teaspoon confectioners' sugar and 2 oz apricot brandy. Strain into a highball glass and top up with carbonated water.

Each of the above recipes makes 1 drink.

Pre-dinner Cocktails, Long and Short

Quick Fixes

These are relatively simple drinks to make and should be served in highball glasses with straws. The ingredients are just stirred. It is advisable to make these drinks as required, as they do not keep.

Whiskey Fix (*illustrated on the right*)
Shake together 1 teaspoon confectioners' sugar, the juice of $\frac{1}{2}$ lemon and ice. Strain into a highball glass, fill with ice and add $2\frac{1}{2}$ oz whiskey. Stir with a spoon and float a slice of lemon on top.

Brandy Fix (*illustrated on the left*)
Prepare as above, adding

1 teaspoon water to the lemon juice and sugar, and using $2\frac{1}{2}$ oz brandy instead of whiskey.

Gin Fix
Prepare as above, but substitute gin for whiskey.

Rum Fix
Prepare as above, but substitute rum for whiskey.

Cherry Fix
Prepare as above and substitute cherry brandy for whiskey.

Each of the above recipes makes 1 drink.

Special Cucumber Punch

1 medium cucumber
2 bottles chilled dry white wine
$\frac{1}{2}$ cup maraschino liqueur
1 bottle champagne

Wash the cucumber, dry and slice thickly. Place in a punch bowl and pour the chilled wine over the cucumber. Allow to stand for 30 minutes. Add the maraschino liqueur and leave for 5 minutes. Remove the cucumber slices and pour in the chilled champagne. Serve immediately.
Serves 10–12

Variation
The champagne may be replaced by a bottle of sparkling white wine.

Cook's Tip
When making this drink in hot weather, immerse a small jug of ice cubes in the punch. This will cool it down without diluting it.
If liked, extra cucumber may be cut into thin slices and floated on the punch when serving to give added color.

Famous Gin Cocktails

Gimlet
Shake 1 oz Rose's lime juice, 1 teaspoon confectioners' sugar and 1½ oz gin with ice. Strain into a cocktail glass.

Maiden's Prayer
Shake 1½ oz gin, ½ oz triple sec and 1 oz lemon juice with ice. Strain into a cocktail glass.

Queen Elizabeth Cocktail
(*foreground*)
Mix 6 ice cubes with 1½ oz gin, ½ oz dry vermouth and 1½ teaspoons Benedictine. Stir well and strain into a glass over 1 piece of pineapple and a slice of orange.

Gin and Sin (*illustrated in the background*))
Shake 1 oz gin, 1 oz lemon juice, 1 tablespoon orange juice and 1 dash grenadine with ice. Strain into a glass.

Tom Collins
Shake juice of ½ lemon, 1 teaspoon confectioners' sugar and 2 oz gin with ice, then strain into a collins glass. Add ice cubes and top up with carbonated water. Stir and decorate with lemon and orange slices and a cherry. Serve with a straw.

Each of the above recipes makes 1 drink

Coolers for Hot Days

These are cool, refreshing drinks ideal for summer evenings.

Brandy Cooler (*illustrated in the background*)
Mix a few crushed ice cubes with a teaspoon of sugar, the juice of ½ lemon and 2 oz brandy. Shake, strain into a highball glass and top up with ginger ale. Serve with a few maraschino cherries and slices of orange.

Gin Cooler
Prepare as above, but substitute gin for brandy.

Eyebright Cooler
Place 3 ice cubes in a highball glass with the juice of ½ lemon, 2 oz Calvados or applejack and 2 oz red wine. Top up with ginger ale. Stir carefully and serve with two maraschino cherries and pieces of pineapple.

Cablegram Highball
(*illustrated in the foreground*)
Pour the juice of ½ lemon, 1 teaspoon confectioners' sugar and 2 oz whiskey into a highball glass. Add ice cubes, stir well and top with ginger ale.

Each of the above recipes makes 1 drink.

Melon Punch

1 very ripe melon
3 tablespoons confectioners'
  sugar
2 bottles Riesling wine
1 bottle champagne
15 ice cubes (optional)

Quarter the melon; remove the seeds and peel and cut the flesh into small dice. Put the diced melon in a punch bowl and sprinkle with confectioners' sugar. Pour half a bottle of white wine over the pieces of melon and leave covered for 30 minutes. Add the remaining wine, and just before serving pour in the champagne. Add ice cubes if liked.
Serves 10–12

Cook's Tip
When choosing fruit for punches make sure it is really ripe and unblemished, so that it will give a sweet aroma to the punch.
Always add the champagne just before serving as it will lose its sparkle very quickly.

Coffee Fluff

12 candied cherries
2 tablespoons instant coffee
  powder
6 eggs
5 tablespoons confectioners'
  sugar
1½ oz advocaat

Cut the cherries in half. Mix the coffee with 1¾ cups of hot water and cool. Separate the egg yolks from the whites. Mix the yolks with 3 tablespoons of confectioners' sugar and stir until creamy. Pour in half the cooled coffee, stir well and then add the remainder. Beat the egg whites until stiff, then beat in the remaining confectioners' sugar until stiff. Fold the whites into the coffee and add half the cherries. Serve in tall glasses and lace with the advocaat, then top with the remaining cherries. Serve immediately.
Serves 6–8

Variation
Chocolate Fluff
Use cocoa instead of coffee, and Drambuie or Kahlua instead of advocaat.

Spiced Coffee with Prunes

5 tablespoons whipped
  cream
3 tablespoons confectioners'
  sugar
2 cups strong black coffee
1 teaspoon cinnamon
4 cooked prunes
4 tablespoons brandy

Mix the cream with the confectioners' sugar. Heat the coffee and stir in the cinnamon. Place a prune in each of four cups, lace with the brandy and pour over the hot coffee.
Top each up with a tablespoon of whipped cream.
Serves 4

Variation
Use plums instead of prunes, and allow to infuse in a little brandy for a few hours before using. Choose dessert plums with a sweet and juicy flesh. If under-ripe, keep in a cool place for 1–3 days before using.

Oriental Orange Coffee

3 oranges
4 sugar lumps
⅔ cup whipping cream, whipped
⅔ cup confectioners' sugar
2 tablespoons butter
¼ cup granulated sugar
5 tablespoons Grand Marnier
½ cup brandy
2 pints black coffee

Remove thin strips of peel from one of the oranges and then extract the juice. Rub the second orange with the sugar lumps and cut the third orange into 10 thin slices. Mix the whipped cream with the confectioners' sugar. Melt the butter in a saucepan and add the granulated sugar. Add the sugar lumps and orange juice and allow to dissolve slowly. Remove from heat. Add the Grand Marnier and brandy, ignite and let it burn for half a minute. Pour the orange mixture into coffee cups and add 1 strip of orange peel. Heat the coffee and pour into cups, top with whipped cream and garnish with slices of orange.
Serves 6–8

Austrian Coffee

4 egg yolks
1 tablespoon clear honey
3 tablespoons brandy or Cognac
⅔ cup cream
5 cups strong black coffee

Heat 4 large coffee cups by filling them with hot water; leave for a couple of minutes, then pour the water away. Beat the egg yolks with the honey and brandy or Cognac, until well mixed. Pour into the heated coffee cups and pour the cream on top. Heat the coffee and fill each cup. Serve immediately.
Serves 4

Variation
Prince Melange
Instead of mixing the egg yolks with honey and brandy, use 2 tablespoons of confectioners' sugar and 2 tablespoons Drambuie or Kahlua. Pour hot chocolate into the cups instead of coffee. Top with whipped cream and grated chocolate.

Cocktails and Punches

Whiskey Cocktails

Manhattan Cocktail (sweet)
(*illustrated on the right*)
Stir ¾ oz sweet vermouth
with 1½ oz whiskey and ice.
Strain into a cocktail glass
and serve with a cherry.

Manhattan Cocktail (dry)
Stir ¾ oz dry vermouth with
1½ oz whiskey and ice.
Strain into a cocktail glass
and serve with an olive.

Old-fashioned Cocktail
Put a small sugar cube,
dash of Angostura bitters
and 1 teaspoon water in an
old-fashioned glass. Muddle
well, then stir in 2 oz
whiskey. Add a twist of
lemon peel and ice cubes.

Decorate with a slice of
orange and lemon and a
cherry. Serve with a
swizzle stick.

Whiskey Sour
Shake the juice of ½ lemon,
½ teaspoon confectioners'
sugar and 2 oz whiskey with
ice. Strain into a sour glass
and decorate with a slice
of lemon and a cherry.

*Each of the above recipes
makes 1 drink.*

Daisy Cocktails

These are made from
liquor, grenadine (or other
cordials) and lemon or lime
juice. Shaken with cracked
ice, they are served in a
stein, metal cup or old-
fashioned glass and
decorated with fruit.

Star Daisy
(*illustrated in the foreground*)
Shake the juice of ½ lemon,
½ teaspoon confectioners'
sugar, 1 teaspoon raspberry
syrup or grenadine, 1 oz
gin and 1 oz apple brandy
with ice. Strain into a glass
and decorate with fruit.

Gin Daisy (*illustrated in the
background*)
Use 2 oz gin instead of gin
and apple brandy.

Brandy Daisy
Use 2 oz brandy instead of
the gin and apple brandy.

Rum Daisy
Use 2 oz rum instead of gin
and apple brandy.

Whiskey Daisy
Use 2 oz whiskey instead of
gin and apple brandy.

*Each of the above recipes
makes 1 drink.*

Long Drinks Using Tonic and Fruit Juices

Gin and Tonic
Put a few ice cubes in a highball glass, add 2 oz gin and top with tonic water. Serve with a slice of lemon or lime.

Rabbit's Revenge
(*illustrated in the foreground*)
Put several ice cubes in a highball glass, add 2 dashes of grenadine, 1 teaspoon of pineapple juice and 2 oz whiskey, and top with tonic water. Serve with a slice of orange.

Dett Long
Place a little crushed ice in a highball glass and add 2 oz cherry brandy. Top with tonic water and serve with a slice of lemon.

Apple Knocker (*illustrated in the background*)
Half-fill an old-fashioned glass with crushed ice. Add 1½ oz vodka, stir, and then top with apple juice.

Barbed Wire
Pour 2 oz whiskey into a highball glass, add a little crushed ice and top up with apple juice.

Each of the above recipes makes 1 drink.

International Vodka Cocktails

Vodka has a neutral flavor and can be used widely. Most vodka cocktails are mixed with fruit juices, carbonated beverages or other ingredients where the taste of the vodka will not interfere.

Tovarich
Mix 1½ oz vodka with ice, ¾ oz kümmel and the juice of ½ lime. Strain into a cocktail glass.

Olive (*illustrated in the foreground*)
Mix 2 oz vodka with ice and ½ oz sherry. Shake briefly, strain into a cocktail glass and sprinkle with finely grated lemon peel. Serve with a stuffed olive.

Volga Boatman
Mix ½ oz vodka, a few ice cubes, ½ oz cherry brandy and ½ oz orange juice. Shake well and strain into a cocktail glass.

Vodka Martini (*illustrated in the background*)
Mix 1½ oz vodka with a few cubes of ice and ¾ oz dry vermouth. Stir well and strain into a frosty cocktail glass.

Each of the above recipes makes 1 drink.

Cocktails and Punches

Pick-Me-Up's for Parties

These long cocktails are suitable for serving on festive occasions.

Brandy Pick-Me-Up
(*illustrated in the background*)
Mix 4 crushed ice cubes with 2 oz brandy or Cognac. Shake for 30 seconds and then pour into a cocktail glass. Top up with champagne and serve immediately.

Champagne Pick-Me-Up
Prepare as above, but use 1 oz brandy and 1 oz dry vermouth. Shake well and serve immediately.

Pink Carter Pick-Me-Up
(*illustrated in the foreground*)
Place 2 ice cubes in a cocktail glass, add 3 dashes of Angostura bitters and 1 oz gin. Top up with champagne and a little grated lemon peel. Serve immediately.

Hanseatic Pick-Me-Up
(*illustrated center right*)
Mix 2 ice cubes with $\frac{1}{2}$ oz whiskey, $\frac{1}{2}$ oz brandy and $\frac{1}{2}$ oz blackberry brandy. Top up with champagne and serve with a slice of orange and lemon.

Each of the above recipes makes 1 drink.

Brandy Cocktails

Sweet liqueurs and brandy are typical ingredients used to make these drinks.

Sidecar
Mix several ice cubes with 1 oz brandy, $\frac{1}{2}$ oz triple sec and the juice of $\frac{1}{4}$ lemon and shake. Strain into a cocktail glass.

Alexander Cocktail
(*illustrated on the left*)
Mix 1 oz brandy with a little crushed ice, 1 oz crème de cacao and 1 oz cream. Shake quickly. Strain into a glass and top with a spoonful of whipped cream.

Bazooka
Mix 1 oz brandy with a little crushed ice, $\frac{1}{2}$ oz cherry brandy and $\frac{1}{2}$ oz gin. Strain into a cocktail glass and serve with a piece of pineapple.

Femina Cocktail
(*illustrated on the right*)
Mix 1 oz Cognac with a little crushed ice, 1 oz Cointreau and 1 oz orange juice. Strain into a cocktail glass.

Each of the above recipes makes 1 drink.

Bronx Cocktails

Bronx
Mix the juice of ¼ orange, with 3 ice cubes, 1 oz gin, ½ oz dry vermouth and ½ oz sweet vermouth. Strain into a cocktail glass. Serve with a slice of orange.

Dry Bronx
As above, but use all dry vermouth instead of half sweet and half dry.

Bronx Terrace (*illustrated on the left*)
Shake 1½ oz gin, 1½ oz dry vermouth and the juice of ½ lime with ice. Strain into a cocktail glass and add a cherry.

Bronx Silver Cocktail
Shake the juice of ½ orange, 1 egg white, ½ oz dry vermouth and 1 oz gin with ice. Strain into a flip glass.

Each of the above recipes makes 1 drink.

More Highballs

Cuba Libre
Put the juice and rind of ½ lime in a highball glass. Add 2 oz rum and top up with cola and ice cubes.

Bourbon Highball
(*illustrated above*)
Put 2 oz bourbon whiskey in a highball glass. Top up with ginger ale or carbonated water and ice cubes. Serve with a twist of lemon peel.

Gin Highball
Substitute gin for the bourbon.

Angostura Ginger Ale
Place 2 ice cubes in a glass with 1 teaspoon of Angostura bitters. Top up with ginger ale and stir.

Gin Buck
Pour 1½ oz gin and the juice of ½ lemon into a glass. Add some ice cubes, and top up with ginger ale.

Each of the above recipes makes 1 drink.

Swedish Glögg

2 pints red wine
⅔ cup Aquavit
½ cinnamon stick
5 pieces candied ginger
½ teaspoon ground cardamom
10 cloves
1 cup sugar
few raisins

Place all the ingredients in a large saucepan and heat slowly (but do not allow to boil). Allow to stand for 30 minutes so that the flavors can infuse. Reheat slowly, then strain and ladle into heat-proof glasses.
Serves 6–8

Variation
Dissolve the sugar in ⅔ cup water. Omitting the Aquavit, add all the ingredients except the wine. Boil together in a pan until reduced by half. Strain, add the wine and reheat.

Cook's Tip
To avoid having to strain the Glögg, tie the spices and raisins in a piece of cheesecloth and allow to float in the wine while infusing.

Mandarin Punch

⅔ cup orange juice
1¼ cups apple juice
⅔ cup canned mandarin orange juice
2 cups white wine
thinly pared rind of ½ lemon
thinly pared rind of ½ orange
1 tablespoon sugar
4 cloves
1 stick cinnamon
1 (11-oz) can mandarin oranges, drained

Bring the orange, apple and mandarin orange juices to the boil. Add the white wine pared lemon and orange rinds, sugar, the cloves and cinnamon stick. Heat over a moderate heat for 5 minutes, but do not allow to boil.
Stir in the mandarins and reheat. Remove the cloves and cinnamon stick before serving.
Pour into a punch bowl and serve hot.
Serves 6

Variation
This punch can also be served chilled.

Martini Cocktails

Mix martinis in a pitcher filled with hard frozen cracked ice. Stir briskly until very cold, then strain into frosty stemmed cocktail glasses. To serve on the rocks, use chilled old-fashioned glasses. Serve with an olive or a twist of lemon peel.

Martini
(traditional 2-to-1)
Measure $1\frac{1}{2}$ oz gin and $\frac{3}{4}$ oz dry vermouth into the pitcher.

Extra Dry Martini
(*illustrated above*)
Measure 2 oz gin and $\frac{1}{4}$ oz

dry vermouth into the pitcher.

Dry Martini
Measure $1\frac{2}{3}$ oz gin and $\frac{1}{3}$ oz dry vermouth into the pitcher.

Sweet Martini
Measure 1 oz gin and 1 oz sweet vermouth into the pitcher.

Boston Bullet
Use an olive stuffed with an almond.

Tequini
Use tequila instead of gin.

Each of the above recipes makes 1 drink.

Frosted Drinks

These long drinks are served in frosted glasses or glasses with sugar-frosted rims. To frost glasses, chill in the refrigerator. To sugar-frost, the rim of each glass is dipped in lemon juice or egg white, swirled to remove excess moisture and then dipped in sugar to give a frosted effect. If serving a brandy cocktail, grenadine may be substituted for lemon juice when preparing the glass for frosting.

Brandy Crusta Cocktail
Cut the rind of $\frac{1}{2}$ lemon in a spiral and place in the glass. Put 1 teaspoon maraschino, 1 dash bitters, 1 teaspoon

lemon juice, $\frac{1}{2}$ oz triple sec and 2 oz brandy in a pitcher with ice. Stir well and strain into glass. Serve with a slice of orange.

Mint Julep
Put 4 mint sprigs, 1 teaspoon confectioners' sugar and 2 teaspoons water in a silver mug or collins glass. Muddle well, then fill with ice and $2\frac{1}{2}$ oz bourbon whiskey. Stir and decorate with slices of orange, lemon and pineapple, a cherry and several mint sprigs. Serve with a straw.

Each of the above recipes makes 1 drink.

Irish Coffee

1¼ *cups whipping cream*
⅔ *cup Irish whiskey*
6 teaspoons sugar
2 pints black coffee

Warm the glasses by filling with hot water while making the coffee. Whip the cream until fairly stiff.
Pour the whiskey into 6 glasses and add a teaspoon of sugar to each glass. Heat the coffee and pour into the glasses to within ½ inch of the top. Spoon the whipped cream on to the coffee so that it floats.
Serves 6

Variation
Do not whip the cream but

pour it over the back of a teaspoon on to the coffee, so that it floats and finds its own level.

Cook's Tip
Some people maintain that Irish coffee can only be made properly with brown sugar. Try it – it does make a difference. But any sugar in the coffee will help the cream to float.

More After-dinner Drinks

Widow's Kiss
Shake 1 oz brandy, ½ oz chartreuse, ½ oz Benedictine and 1 dash Peychaud bitters with ice. Strain into a cocktail glass.

Black Forest Cocktail
Mix a few ice cubes with 1 oz plum brandy (sliwowitz), ½ oz gin and a dash of maraschino. Shake well. Strain into a glass.

Apri (*illustrated on the right*)
Mix 1 oz apricot brandy with some ice cubes, ½ oz

plum brandy and 2 teaspoons of orange juice. Shake well and strain into a glass.

Alsatian (*illustrated on the left*)
Mix 1 oz cherry brandy with a few ice cubes, 1 oz brandy, 1 teaspoon of cold black coffee and 1 teaspoon of sugar. Shake well and strain into a glass.

Grasshopper Cocktail
Shake ¾ oz green crème de menthe, ¾ oz white crème de cacao and ¾ oz cream with ice. Strain into a cocktail glass.

Each of the above recipes makes 1 drink.

318

Sugar Loaf Punch

*3 bottles red wine
  (preferably full-bodied)*
4 cloves
1 stick cinnamon
few strips lemon rind
juice of 2 oranges
juice of 1 lemon
1 sugar loaf
½ bottle rum

Heat the wine with the cloves, cinnamon and lemon rind in a heatproof punch bowl or a heatproof dish placed over a burner.
Add the orange and lemon juice. Using tongs, hold the sugar loaf over the heated wine and sprinkle a little of the rum carefully over the sugar. When the rum has soaked into the sugar, ignite it.
Gradually pour the remaining rum over the sugar; the sugar loaf should burn until it has completely melted into the wine. Pour into heatproof glasses and serve.
Serves 10–12

Cook's Tip
Jamaican rum, which is heavy-bodied and dark, is more suitable for using in this kind of drink than the lighter Puerto Rican rum.

After-dinner Liqueur Flips

These drinks are called flips as they contain egg yolks. Their attraction is the use of liqueurs.
Serve in small glasses.

Armagnac Flip
Mix 1 oz peach brandy, 1 egg yolk sprinkled with ground almonds, 1 oz Armagnac brandy and ice. Strain into a glass.

Brandy Flip (*illustrated left*)
Lightly beat 1 oz orange Curaçao, 1 egg yolk, 1 oz brandy and ice. Strain into a glass.

Whiskey Flip
Mix 1 oz crème de cacao, 1 egg yolk, 1 oz Irish whiskey and ice. Strain into a glass.

Calvados Flip
Mix 1 oz Benedictine or chartreuse, 1 egg yolk, chopped nuts and 1 oz Calvados.

Chartreuse Flip
Mix 1 oz chartreuse, lemon peel, 1 egg yolk, 1 oz vodka and a dash of maraschino.

Scotch Flip (*illustrated right*)
Mix 1 oz cherry brandy, 1 egg yolk and 1 oz Scotch whisky.

Each of the above recipes makes 1 drink.

Herbs and Spices

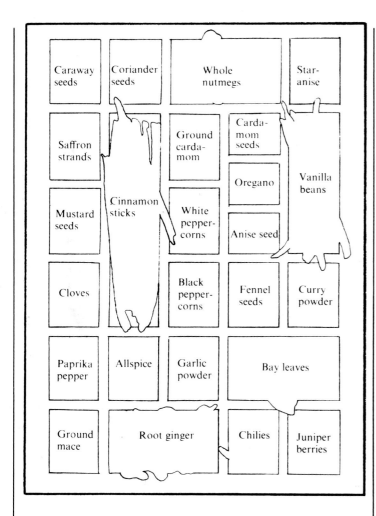

The herbs and spices illustrated left are identified above. A guide to their use in cooking can be found on page 322.

Caraway seeds	Coriander seeds	Whole nutmegs		Star-anise
Saffron strands		Ground carda-mom	Carda-mom seeds	
	Cinnamon sticks		Oregano	Vanilla beans
Mustard seeds		White pepper-corns	Anise seed	
Cloves		Black pepper-corns	Fennel seeds	Curry powder
Paprika pepper	Allspice	Garlic powder	Bay leaves	
Ground mace	Root ginger		Chilies	Juniper berries

The seasoning of dishes is very much a matter of personal and family preference. As there are so many different seasonings to choose from you can change the flavor of a dish by adding varying herbs and spices. First, however, you have to learn the basics – which flavorings have a special affinity with which foods; you need to become acquainted with as many different herbs and spices as possible so that you can identify the flavors which you prefer. With herbs there is some difference between the fresh and dried varieties. It is not difficult to grow herbs and even if you do not have a garden some herbs can be cultivated successfully in pots indoors. The flavor of fresh herbs is certainly preferable to that of the dried variety. Most of the recipes in this book use fresh herbs, unless otherwise stated, and you will see that a larger amount of fresh herbs is used. Do not expect to achieve the same flavor in a finished dish from fresh and dried herbs and do remember to be sparing in the amount of dried herbs you use. Dried herbs should be purchased from a store which has a quick turnover as the flavor of old stock will be impaired.

Herbs

Herbs are plants which provide us with flavored leaves (e.g. mint), flowers (e.g. borage) or stems (e.g. fennel) for use in cooking. Herbs are available fresh or dried.

Spices

Strictly speaking, these are the group of seasonings, many of tropical origin, which come from roots (e.g. horseradish), rootstocks (e.g. ginger), bark (e.g. cinnamon), flowers or parts of flowers (e.g. cloves, saffron), berries (e.g. peppercorns), pods (e.g. vanilla), fruits (e.g. anise seed) or seeds (e.g. nutmeg). Spices are always dried and often crushed or ground when purchased and used.

Using Herbs and Spices

The amount used does depend on your personal preferences and the dish. As a guide, when using fresh herbs allow $\frac{1}{2}$–1 teaspoon, chopped, per portion. Use half the amount of dried herbs, or simply a pinch. Much smaller amounts of spices are used in dishes. For general purposes, allow a pinch of spice per serving.

• Too little seasoning is always better than too much as it can be rectified before serving. Herbs and spices are used to bring out the flavor of a dish, not to overwhelm it. Avoid using too many spices in the one dish.
• Many spices are sensitive to light, so buy them in non-transparent containers and store them in a cupboard.
• Spices quickly lose their aroma if they are not kept in sealed containers. If you buy your spices loose, decant them into airtight containers for storage.
• Buy herbs and spices in small amounts and use them up as quickly as possible.
• When possible buy spices unground, or in leaf form, so that they can be ground or crushed just before being added to a dish. This imparts a better flavor to the dish.
• Immediately after use, re-seal the containers. Do not store different spices in the same container as they will taint each other.
• When using fresh herbs, rinse them in cold water and pat dry with paper towels. Chop them on a board prior to adding them to the dish, or using as a garnish.
• It helps to bring out the aroma of dried herbs if you rub them between your fingertips before use.
• For grinding spices which are in berry form, such as peppercorns, use a mill. Keep separate mills for white and black peppercorns. For nutmeg there is a traditional nutmeg grinder.
• For garlic use a garlic crusher, or crush the clove with a little salt and the blade of a knife.
• One of the best implements for crushing all dried spices, and herbs too, is a pestle and mortar. It is certainly worthwhile investing in one.
• The flavor of certain seasonings in cooked dishes does change when frozen. When preparing a dish for the freezer under-season it and at the reheating stage, taste the dish and adjust the seasoning as necessary.
• Most fresh herbs are excellent freezer candidates – the freezing of herbs does not impair their flavor. To freeze herbs, wash and dry and pack in freezer containers or wrap in freezer foil. Seal and label. When frozen, herbs can be crumbled and added to the dish.

A–Z of Herbs and Spices

The following is a list of the more common herbs and spices used in cooking.

Allspice Is available ground or whole. The whole berries are used in pickling, casseroles and soups. Ground allspice is used in baking.
Anise seed Is available ground or whole. It has a licorice flavor and is used mainly in baking.

Basil Is available fresh or dried. Used in fish, veal, pork and lamb dishes and in salads. Basil goes particularly well in tomato-based dishes such as pizza and bolognese sauce.
Borage Is available fresh or dried, but not so aromatic when dried. Borage goes well in tomato and mustard sauces, salads (particularly cucumber) and with vegetables.
Bouquet garni Made up with a bay leaf, 2-3 sprigs parsley, and a sprig of thyme all tied in a piece of cheesecloth. Use when cooking soups, stews and casseroles and remove before serving. Also available in sachets.

Capers Are preserved in vinegar and sold in jars. Capers go well with fish, veal and poultry dishes and sauces.
Caraway Seeds with a distinctive flavor. Goes with meat dishes, vegetables (potatoes, cabbage and sauerkraut in particular), soups and sauces. Caraway seeds are also used in breads and cookies.
Cardamom Is available ground or whole. The whole seeds are used in pickling and curried dishes; ground cardamom is used mainly in baking.
Cayenne Is the dried spice of the chili, a member of the capsicum family. Used sparingly in fish, beef and pork dishes.
Chervil The leaves are available fresh or dried, and in powder form. Chervil goes with fish, meat, poultry and vegetable dishes. It is also used in soups, salads and sauces.
Chilies Are from the capsicum family and are very hot. Fresh chilies are used in curries and Mexican cooking. Chili powder is also available and should be used sparingly.
Chives Available fresh or dried, chop (or cut with scissors) and add to soups, salads, sauces and egg dishes just before serving. Chives are also used as a garnish.
Cinnamon Available in stick or powder form and used in sweet dishes (milk puddings, stewed fruit), cakes, pastries and cookies.
Cloves Available whole or ground. Used in meat and vegetable dishes, soups, sauces, stewed fruit, pastries and mulled wine. Remove whole cloves from a dish before serving.
Coriander Available as seeds or in powder form. Goes with meat dishes.
Curry powder Is a mixture of spices used in Indian cooking. Curry powder varies in strength according to the spices used. Curry powder can be added to veal, beef, lamb, pork and chicken casseroles; shrimp and vegetable dishes.

Dill The leaves are available fresh or dried; the seeds are available dried. Used in fish, beef and lamb dishes; with vegetables, salads, eggs and egg-based sauces.

Fennel Is available dried or fresh. Use dried fennel in marinades for fish, salads and mushrooms. Use the fresh variety in salads and mayonnaise. Fennel has an anise seed flavor and is interchangeable with dill.

Garlic The cloves are used very finely chopped or crushed. Garlic salt and powder is also available. Garlic is used in fish, meat and poultry dishes, salads, sauces, cheese fondues, salad dressings and mayonnaise.

Ginger Available in root or powder form, or preserved in sugar or syrup. Used mainly in cakes and cookies.

Horseradish Has a strong hot flavor similar to mustard. Use the roots grated, mix with cream and serve as a sauce with beef, sausages and ham. Horseradish sauce is available in jars.

Juniper Available as berries. Used in meat and game dishes and marinades.

Mace Available in blades, or ground. Use in fish and veal dishes, sauces, cakes and pastries.

Marjoram The leaves are available fresh or dried and go with pork, poultry and game stews; also used in soups and sauces.

Mint Better to use the fresh variety. Goes with lamb and veal dishes; stuffings, peas, new potatoes and salads.

Mustard Available ready prepared in various strengths. The whole seeds are used in pickling; ground mustard is used in meat, cheese and poultry dishes, sauces and marinades.

Nutmeg Available whole or ground. It is used with vegetables (potatoes, spinach and cauliflower in particular), in soups, sauces and cheese dishes.

Oregano A herb much used in Italian cooking. It goes with meat and vegetable dishes, meat and tomato sauces and pizzas.

Paprika Available ground in mild, hot and very hot varieties. Good with fish, meat and vegetable dishes, soups, sauces and salad dressings.

Parsley It is better to use the fresh variety, which is available throughout the year, as dried parsley has very little flavor. Parsley can be used in most savory dishes and as a garnish, either chopped or as sprigs.

Pepper Available whole or ground. For a better flavor use the whole peppercorns and grind freshly when needed. Pepper is used in all savory dishes. Use the black variety for dark colored dishes and white pepper for pale colored dishes such as poultry or veal fricassées.

Rosemary Available fresh or dried. To extract the flavor from the fresh spiky leaves, crush them in a pestle and mortar. Rosemary goes with pork, lamb, veal and chicken dishes. It is also used as a garnish.

Saffron Has a distinctive flavor and is sold in strands and powdered form. Used in certain classic dishes (e.g. paella), fish, rice and chicken dishes and in curries. It is also used in baking.

Sage Available fresh or dried. The leaves are used in stuffings for pork, goose and duck; in savory meat dishes and soups.

Savory Available fresh or dried and used in fish, poultry, meat and vegetable dishes. Use sparingly, particularly the dried variety.

Tarragon Available fresh or dried. The fresh leaves are used to flavor vinegar. Also used in egg, fish and poultry dishes, sauces, savory butters, salads and vegetables.

Thyme Available fresh or dried. Used in fish, meat and poultry dishes, stuffings, sauces and soups.

Vanilla The beans are used in sweet dishes (puddings, soufflés, stewed fruit) and in cakes and pastries. Vanilla extract is also available, but the flavor is less acceptable.

Using a Freezer

If you enjoy cooking and eating well, are a busy career girl, a housewife or a bachelor cook, a freezer can often be one of your best investments. You can prepare and cook food when you are less busy and store it perfectly safely in the freezer until required. You can prepare larger quantities of a favorite dish – it takes very little extra time to make, for example, a casserole to serve 12 people than one to serve six portions – serve half of it and freeze the remainder for future use. If you do this once or twice a week it won't be long before there's a good selection of dishes in the freezer all ready for reheating. A further advantage of owning a freezer is that you can store certain foods which can be sometimes difficult to find, and seasonal foods. This way you are able to enjoy the delicious soft fruits during the winter months.

Providing a few basic rules with regard to packaging and selection are adhered to, food stored in a freezer will remain in perfect condition.

The Importance of Temperature

For the successful home freezing of food you need an appliance which is capable of reducing a specified weight of food daily to $-18°$ C ($0°$ F) within a 24-hour period without affecting the food already frozen and stored. The rapid freezing process protects the food from any deterioration and enables it to retain its nutritional quality, value and flavor.

When freezing food, refer to the manufacturer's instructions with regard to the amount which can be frozen at any one time; the smaller the portion, the faster it will freeze. When freezing liquids or semi-liquids remember that you will want to reheat the frozen block, so bear in mind the capacity of your saucepans for reheating. It is often more convenient, and cuts down on the reheating time, to freeze food in, say, two-portion packs rather than in four- or six-portion ones. Obviously this depends on your particular requirements.

The quality, flavor and nutritional value of most foods remain the same after freezing as when fresh, but remember that there is no magic wand inside the freezer to improve the quality of poor food. No amount of freezing is going to turn a scrawny old chicken into a plump young one.

The Right Way to Pack

All foods destined for the freezer must be protected from the cold, dry air inside the freezer cabinet for two main reasons – to prevent dehydration and cross flavors occurring. The packaging materials used must be moisture- and vapor-proof. If using polyethylene containers they must be able to withstand sub-zero temperatures and make sure that the lids give an airtight seal. To ensure a proper seal, freezer tape may be used. Use heavy-duty or freezer foil or film.

No matter what packaging material is used, the same golden rules always apply – make sure that as little air is left inside the package as possible, that the food is tightly and closely wrapped and that there is an airtight seal. Certain delicate foods, such as soft fruits and decorated cakes, should be flash frozen before packing. Put them on a suitable plate or tray and place in the freezer until hard, then pack in bags or containers, seal and return to the freezer.

When packing certain foods, remember to allow a headspace for the expansion of the liquid content on freezing. Fruits and vegetables require very little headspace as there are small areas around them to allow for expansion. Liquid and semi-liquid foods – soups, casseroles and sauces – are a different story. If packed in a shallow container giving a larger surface area, about a $\frac{1}{2}$-inch headspace; in a deeper container with less surface area a $\frac{3}{4}$-inch headspace should be left.

It's very convenient to freeze stock (and other liquids) in ice cube trays. When frozen, the cubes can be packed individually and used as required for soups, stews etc.

To keep your freezer in order every package must be

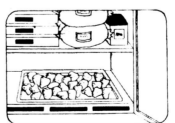

Flash freezing strawberries. Soft fruits should be flash frozen on a tray until hard, then packed.

Foods for freezing should be wrapped closely and tightly, excluding as much air as possible.

marked with its contents, number of servings and date of freezing. It's invaluable to keep a record in a notebook of all the packages in the freezer, but don't forget to cross items off the list when you take them from the freezer.

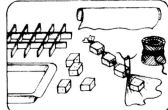

Stock (and other liquids) can be frozen in ice cube trays. When frozen pack individually. Use the frozen cubes for soups, stews, etc.

Careful Thawing

Foods already cooked, to be eaten cold, such as breads, cakes, cold meats etc, must be fully thawed. On removing the package from the freezer, loosen or take off the wrapping and allow the package to thaw in the refrigerator or in a cool place.

Cooked made-up dishes, such as casseroles, may be reheated from frozen. It is usually easier to do this in a suitable container in the oven, because on top of the stove the food needs to be stirred from time to time, to prevent it from sticking. Pre-blanched vegetables may be cooked from frozen. It is most important to allow uncooked frozen poultry to thaw fully before cooking. In an emergency, cuts of meat may be cooked from frozen, but a better result is obtained if the meat is allowed to thaw before cooking. To ensure that a frozen meat cut is sufficiently cooked in the center it is advisable to use a meat thermometer. When preparing food for the freezer and thawing it do remember not to leave it sitting in a warm kitchen as this will encourage the growth of bacteria. Cool it quickly before freezing; thaw it in a refrigerator or cool place.

The question of refreezing foods is one which often worries freezer owners. It is mostly a matter of common sense. If you purchase frozen meat and make a casserole it is perfectly safe for it to be refrozen. Soft fruits, strawberries in particular, do not benefit from being refrozen, but this is due to their nature, not from the safety point of view. Obviously, you wouldn't keep some cooked leftover meat in the refrigerator for 2–3 days and then decide to turn it into a moussaka and freeze it.

A meat thermometer. When cooking a cut of meat from frozen it is advisable to use a meat thermometer so that you can see when the meat is cooked in the center.

What to Freeze

- Fruits in season which can be used for favorite dishes
- Perishable foods that are not always easy to obtain and foods that are advantageous to buy in bulk
- Dishes which can be cooked in larger quantities just as easily as in small quantities, e.g. soups, casseroles, sauces and pâtés
- Any commercially frozen foods
- Vegetables in season – home-grown or bought from the supermarket. Prior to freezing, vegetables should be blanched.
- Home-baked breads, cookies, pies, quiches and cakes
- Sandwiches for packed meals
- Fresh herbs

What not to Freeze

- Green salad vegetables
- Hard- or soft-cooked or poached eggs
- Egg-based sauces e.g. mayonnaise
- Radishes
- Avocados
- Bananas
- Uncooked potatoes

Ten Golden Rules to Freezing

- Select the freshest and best food for freezing
- Package the food correctly and exclude as much air as possible
- Keep utensils and packing materials scrupulously clean
- Prepare, cook, cool, wrap and freeze food quickly
- Label and record all your freezer packages
- Add garlic, cream, yogurt and egg yolks at the reheating stage
- Lightly season dishes for freezing and re-check the seasoning when reheated
- Undercook pasta dishes
- Use your frozen packages in rotation
- Clear out and defrost the freezer at least once a year

A Guide to Entertaining

Today more and more people are entertaining in their own homes due mainly to the ever-increasing costs of eating out. The menu need not be lavish to impress your guests; in fact a simple dish, well cooked and nicely served, can be just as appealing as a more elaborate one. Remember too, that you as the hostess, want to enjoy the evening with your friends, so avoid worrying about the meal and spending all your time in the kitchen. With a little pre-planning and organization and bearing the following points in mind you will be able to produce a meal to delight your friends as well as enjoying their company.

• The ideal menu should offer contrast, color and flavor. Avoid choosing an appetizer, main course and dessert all of which contain cream.
• If you are having a casserole as a main course, don't choose dishes of a similar texture for your appetizer and dessert.
• When planning any menu, bear in mind the foods which are in season and likely to be at their best. It is usually easiest to select the main course and from there choose the other dishes to give the necessary contrast in ingredients, flavor, color and texture.
• Keep a watchful eye on the budget. You don't have to choose the most expensive cuts of meat to produce a good meal. The less expensive cuts can be turned into delicious dishes.
• Do not choose dishes all of which require last minute attention. It's possible to select an appetizer and a dessert which can be prepared in advance, leaving you free to concentrate on the main course.
• Bear in mind the facilities you have. Don't invite 20 people to a formal meal unless you have adequate seating space, tableware, china, glasses, etc.
• It does help to plan your shopping list and order of work. This way you can be sure that nothing is forgotten.
• Wash up and keep the kitchen tidy as you go along. If you have a freezer use it to its fullest advantage when entertaining.
• Start your preparation well in advance to avoid any last minute panic.
• Serve hot food on warm plates.
• Make sure that your tableware and glasses are shiny.

Buffets

If you plan to invite a large number of people, a buffet meal is usually the best way of coping. Certain extra points have to be borne in mind when planning a buffet:

• Choose food which your guests will be able to eat with a fork.
• Arrange the food on the table in such a way that your guests can help themselves easily.
• Be sure to have sufficient serving utensils, tableware, dishes and napkins.
• Make sure there are enough chairs and small tables for your guests to put their plates and glasses.
• When your guests have served themselves, put the contents of half-empty bowls together so that the buffet looks appetizing for seconds.
• Avoid having candles on a buffet table as they can be easily knocked over. Instead, have a low arrangement of flowers.
• Keep hot food on a hotplate.

Successful Parties

Parties can be the liveliest and most spontaneous kind of entertainment, providing that the hostess plans the event beforehand. There are many types of parties, but whatever type you plan to give the following guide lines will help yours to be a success:

• Bear in mind the size of the room. Do not invite more people than can be comfortably accommodated in the space you have available.
• Plan to have somewhere for everyone to sit, and provide sufficient small tables and ashtrays.
• Choose your guests carefully. Avoid inviting people known to dislike each other. Do not invite either too many men, or too many women.
• Invite your guests well in advance – at least a week – and ask them to let you know whether they can come.
• Don't keep secret the reason for your party if you are celebrating a birthday, anniversary or other happy event.
• Give your guests a hint about what clothes to wear. No

one likes to arrive formally dressed for an informal party, for example.

• Give your guests a specific time to arrive to avoid your party getting off to a slow start.

• As soon as your guests arrive offer them a drink.

• When catering for large numbers you may need to hire tableware, china and glasses. Alternatively, for an informal buffet, you could use paper plates.

• Keeping drinks cold can be a problem. If you have a freezer make plenty of ice cubes in advance.

• If you are not inviting your neighbors, it is fair to tell them that you are planning to hold a party.

• If at the end of the party some of your guests may have had a little too much to drink, order a taxi to take them home.

Advice on Drinks and Wines

What drinks and wines you serve does of course depend on your pocket, menu and on the likes and dislikes of your guests. Remember you may have some guests who prefer non-alcoholic drinks, so their needs must be catered for too.

As a cocktail before a meal or to welcome your guests you can offer champagne, sherry, Campari, Pernod, whisky, bourbon, vodka or gin. Cocktails may be served with whatever mixers are preferred – tonic, soda, ginger ale, etc. Pernod is served with iced water. With the pre-dinner cocktails offer your guests a selection of tit-bits – nuts, potato chips, small savory crackers etc.

Wines Fine wines deserve more attention than any other drinks and much has been written about them. It is said that good wine pleases three of our senses: the color pleases the eye, the bouquet pleases the nose and the taste pleases the palate. To achieve these three pleasures wine must be treated with the respect it deserves. Choose the correct glass – it must not be too small as a wine glass should not be more than half-filled in order to allow the bouquet to gather in the glass. The glass should be slightly bulbous in shape, narrowing at the top, so that the bouquet remains in the glass, and finally it should be made of clear, colorless glass so that you can see the true color of the wine.

Wine only gives off its best aroma if stored and served at the correct temperature. White wines should certainly be served chilled, but not straight from the refrigerator. Red wines are normally served at room temperature.

If you are anxious to serve (and drink) wines at the correct temperature – which does take practice – you can buy a wine thermometer which is placed in a glass of wine to determine the exact temperature. Achieving the correct temperature is a matter of putting the bottle in the correct temperature a few hours before consumption.

Always serve lighter wines before the fuller, heavier ones; chilled wines before warmed ones and dry white wines before red. Give your guests a glass of water to sip and bread to nibble between wines to clear their palates. Here are a few hints on what wines to serve:

• A dry white wine with shellfish. With oysters, a Chablis, champagne or Muscadet.

• It is not necessary to serve a wine with soup, but if the soup contains wine you can serve the same wine to accompany it.

• With fish dishes, a white Burgundy; for delicately flavored dishes serve a Moselle or Loire wine. A white Burgundy is excellent with salmon.

• With lightly seasoned pork and veal dishes a dry white wine is pleasant.

• With lamb and beef dishes, red wines are best – Bordeaux or Burgundy. These wines also go well with ham dishes.

• Full-bodied, dark red wines go well with game dishes.

• With poultry dishes – and in particular chicken dishes – which are delicate in flavor, serve a white Burgundy or a light red wine. With duck and goose serve a Rhine wine or red, such as Châteauneuf du Pape.

• With desserts, serve Madeira, port, Muscatel, Tokay or a Sauternes.

A Guide to Cooking Terms

Here is a list of some cooking terms with which you may be unfamiliar.

Al dente Refers to pasta when sufficiently cooked – firm to the bite.
Au gratin Cooked food, coated with a sauce and sprinkled with grated cheese and breadcrumbs. The dish is browned under the broiler before serving.

Bain marie A pan containing hot water; a dish containing the food to be cooked is placed in the pan of water so that the food cooks slowly and evenly.
Bake blind To partly bake a pastry case without any filling. This prevents the filling making the pastry soggy.
Barding Covering cuts of lean meat, game birds and poultry with pieces of bacon to keep the flesh moist during roasting.
Basting Spooning the cooking juices over meat and poultry during roasting.
Beurre manié Twice as much butter as flour kneaded together to form a paste. The mixture is beaten into a sauce or casserole, bit by bit, at the end of the cooking time, to thicken it.

Canapé A small hors d'oeuvre with a toast, bread or cracker base topped with a savory mixture.
Cocotte Small ovenproof dishes used for baking and serving egg dishes, mousses and soufflés.

Dice To cut food (usually raw vegetables) into small cubes.
Dough A basic mixture which is kneaded or rolled into the required shape.
Dredging Sprinkling food with flour or sugar.
Dressing A cold sauce based on vinegar and oil which is served with salads.
Drippings The fat which drips out of a meat cut, poultry or game during roasting. This can be stored and re-used.
Dumpling A savory mixture formed into balls and simmered in liquid. Served with soups and stews.

En croûte Food encased and cooked in a pastry case.

Fines herbes A mixture of finely chopped fresh herbs – parsley, chervil, tarragon and chives.
Flake To separate food into smaller pieces.
Flambé Cooking in a pan to which brandy (or other spirit) is added and set alight.

Garnish To enhance a savory dish with an edible decoration e.g. parsley.
Gelatin A powder made from animal bones which melts in hot water and is used to set or stiffen dishes.
Giblets The edible internal organs from poultry and game.
Glaze A glossy finish given to food by brushing it with milk, beaten egg, or syrup before baking. A jelly glaze may be spooned over cooked and cooled dishes.
Gugelhupf (or Kugelhopf) A yeast cake baked in a fluted mold.

Hulling Removing the stalks from soft fruits.

Infusing Steeping ingredients in hot water or other liquid to extract their flavor.

Kebab Pieces of food threaded on a skewer and broiled or barbecued.

Larding Threading strips of bacon through a lean cut of meat to keep it moist, from within, during cooking.

Marinade A mixture of oil, wine, vinegar and seasoning used to flavor and tenderize pieces of meat, fish etc. prior to cooking.
Marinate To steep food in a marinade.
Meringue A mixture of egg whites and sugar. Either spooned on top of desserts or piped into shapes and baked in a very cool oven.
Moussaka An eastern dish containing ground meat (usually lamb), eggplants, onions and tomatoes, topped

with a cheese sauce, savory custard or plain yogurt.
Mousse A light-textured sweet or savory dish.

Niçoise A dish containing tomatoes, onions, garlic and olives.

Paella A traditional Spanish dish containing rice, saffron, chicken and shellfish.
Pasta A food made from flour and water, sometimes with the addition of eggs and spinach, and formed into various shapes.
Pastry A dough made from flour, fat and water – sometimes enriched with egg yolks.
Pâté A savory meat mixture served cold.
Pipe To form a mixture, placed into a bag fitted with a nozzle, into various shapes.
Piquant Pleasantly sharp in flavor.
Pith The white layer beneath the skin of citrus fruits.
Pizza A savory mixture on a yeast or biscuit/bread base.
Purée Raw or cooked food pressed through a strainer or blended.

Quiche A savory tart.

Ragoût A meat and vegetable stew.
Ratatouille A vegetable dish made from eggplants, tomatoes, onions, garlic, peppers and zucchini.
Reduce To concentrate the flavor of a liquid by rapid boiling.
Rice paper An edible paper used to line baking sheets for a macaroon mixture.

Sauté To cook food quickly in hot fat, sometimes prior to the main cooking.
Savarin A yeast cake baked in a ring mold and soaked in a sugar syrup flavored with a liqueur.
Score To cut grooves into the surface of food.
Seasoned flour A mixture of flour, salt and pepper which is used to coat food prior to cooking.

Sifting Passing foods through a sifter or strainer to remove lumps.
Simmering Cooking food in a liquid which is kept at just below boiling point.
Skewer Metal or wooden utensil used to secure food during cooking.
Sousing Preserving food in brine or vinegar.
Spit (Rotisserie) A revolving metal skewer on to which meat and poultry is secured and cooked in front of the direct heat.
Strudel Thin pieces of pastry filled with a sweet or savory filling, formed into rolls and baked.
Stuffing A savory mixture, based on breadcrumbs, used to fill poultry, meat or fish.

Trussing Tying a bird or cut of meat into a neat shape prior to cooking.

Vanilla sugar Sugar stored in a container with a vanilla bean to give flavor to the sugar. Vanilla sugar is used in baking.
Variety meats The edible internal organs from an animal.

Zest The oily outer skins of citrus fruits, grated and used to flavor food.

Index

330

331

333